NEW ENGLANDERS
IN THE 1600S

NEW ENGLANDERS
IN THE 1600s

A Guide to Genealogical Research
Published Between 1980 and 2005

by

MARTIN E. HOLLICK

NEW ENGLAND HISTORIC GENEALOGICAL SOCIETY
Boston, Massachusetts
2006

International Standard Book Number: 0-88082-197-3
Library of Congress Control Number: 2006928884

Interior layout by Nathaniel Taylor
Cover design by Carolyn Oakley
Cover photo: "Vermont Fall Color" by Linda Lewis Taylor, www.tayimages.com
Printed by Quebecor World, Leominster, Massachusetts
Reprinted October 2006

Published by
New England Historic Genealogical Society
101 Newbury Street
Boston, MA 02116-3007
www.NewEnglandAncestors.org

Dedicated to
Marshall Kenneth Kirk, 1957-2005
Scholar and Friend

CONTENTS

INTRODUCTION

In 1997 in an article for *The American Genealogist*, I wrote, "And therein lies a large problem in accessing the recent scholarship in genealogy: the lack of a comprehensive, regularly-updated index of scholarly material in periodicals or multi-family works."[1] A year before Gary Boyd Roberts of the New England Historic Genealogical Society wrote, "A subject-index to such material [multi-ancestors studies] is more needed now than ever."[2] This index is designed to fill such a void.

Herein indexed are all articles, multi-family genealogies, many single-family genealogies, and other scholarly compendia that have dealt with New England immigrants born before the year 1700. The date range of publication of these materials is the twenty-five years from 1980 to 2005. This time period has seen several revolutions in genealogy and was not chosen at random.

The Mayflower Five Generation Project was largely conducted during this time period. These all-descendants-in-every-line works are a model of scholarship and research. The Great Migration Study Project began and has published eight volumes thus far on those immigrants who came to New England between 1620 and 1635. The late Dean Crawford Smith, with Melinde Lutz Sanborn, published (thus far) six volumes of Smith's ancestry, all of which have been models for the multi-ancestor work. And certainly not the least of the influences on genealogy has been the advent of the personal computer and the Internet during this same period.

Scholarly journals now regularly use numbered footnotes to primary sources, as do many compiled genealogies. The statewide journals of New England have either been resurrected or greatly improved in their standards.

---

[1] Martin E. Hollick, "Accessing the Genealogical Literature: Problems Facing Historians and Genealogists" *The American Genealogist* 72 (1997):387-98.

[2] Gary Boyd Roberts, "Recent Progress in Seventeenth Century New England Genealogy: A Bibliographical Essay," *The New England Historical and Genealogical Register* 150 (1996):451-72 at 469.

In fact, the print world of genealogy for New England has never been better. Add to these trends the journal *The Genealogist,* which began publication during this time period, and one can see how rich the landscape is for genealogical research.

There is no lack of solid research now being done and published. The next step is to ensure proper access to such information. I hope this index will be such a tool.

SCOPE AND CONTENTS

- Seventeenth-century immigrants to New England were included if they (a) were born prior to 1700; (b) left descendants; and (c) if they left no descendants, but appeared in more than one work. In some cases immigrants whose specific birth year was not known, but which was ca. 1700, were also included. Some works indexed herein included non-New England families and those families are NOT indexed herein.

- Multi-ancestor works were taken from Gary Boyd Roberts's list in his aforementioned essay and his updated list from his most recent work, *The Best Genealogical Sources in Print* (pp. 375-79).

- Single-family genealogies were included if they won the Donald Lines Jacobus Award[3] or if they were reviewed favorably in any of the journals herein indexed.

- The Mayflower Five Generation Project was indexed for both the *Mayflower* passenger and for all female descendants down to the third or fourth generation who married an immigrant to New England or the son of an immigrant.

- The Great Migration Study Project was indexed only for those immigrants who had descendants.

- Publications were chosen based on Henry Hoff's wonderful index for New England articles that appears in the July issues of NEHGR.

- Second, third, and sometimes fourth generation descendants are included under their immigrant ancestor if that person was born before 1700.

- Finally, any work indexed was chosen for its scholarly content, the rating of which was in my sole discretion. Many multi-family genealogies

---

[3] A full list of winners can be viewed at: http://www.fasg.org/jacobus_award.html

are just compilations of other works and do not offer any new or better information than the works from which they spring. These works were not included.

- All works that were reviewed in the journals indexed here have those review citations indexed with their bibliographic entry for the reader to better understand those works.

- No Internet websites are included. Most websites are poorly footnoted— if they are footnoted at all. Those few websites that do properly cite their information are citing either directly or indirectly the works herein indexed. To paraphrase Elaine Stritch, the Broadway actress, "If there is someone putting original scholarly work on New England families on the web, will they please call me."

Other Indexes

In addition to this index, there are other tools available to the researcher when beginning work on a New England family. Donald Lines Jacobus published such an index in 1953, called "My Own Index," as volume three in his *Index to Genealogical Periodicals*. This index covers families in 57 works published before that date. His work is available in several incarnations: (i) the original; (ii) the 1964 reprint by the Genealogical Publishing Co.; and (iii) the 1983 revised edition by Carl Boyer 3rd.

Another work is Meredith Colket's *Founders of Early American Families*, which covers immigrants from 1607 to 1657 and does not confine itself to New England. There are over 4400 entries from single-, multi-family, and periodical articles in this index. Originally published in 1975, it was revised and reissued in 1985.

Mr. Colket's work notwithstanding, there is a gap in the multi-family indexing now between Jacobus (1953) and this work (1980). A list of those genealogies is given by Gary Boyd Roberts at NEHGR 135 (1981):196-98; it is just a list of titles, but worthy of consideration.

Many of the major journals have subject indexes for some or all of their runs which will cover the time period of 1953 to 1980. NEHGR, TAG, NYGBR (in CD-ROM format), NGSQ (also in CD-ROM format), and CN are among those journals with such indexes.

The Genealogical Dictionary of Maine and New Hampshire, first published in 1939 and reprinted several times since (most recently in 1988), is still the best source for 17th century families from those two states. However, as so much has been published in the intervening sixty plus years, the researcher should be aware of this and use my book in conjunction with GDMNH.

Lastly, Savage's *Genealogical Dictionary of the First Settlers of New England Before 1692* is available online, at:

http://www.usgennet.org/usa/topic/newengland/savage

Readers can send corrections and/or additions to me care of the New England Historic Genealogical Society, 101 Newbury Street, Boston, MA 02116.

Martin E. Hollick
West Roxbury, Massachusetts
April 2006

ACKNOWLEDGMENTS

The first and biggest acknowledgement goes to the many authors whose works are herein indexed. Without their tireless research and perseverance, there would be nothing to index. It is they who unlock the history of our ancestors.

Gary Boyd Roberts, retired Senior Research Fellow of the New England Historic Genealogical Society, has been calling for such an index for more than 25 years. He is the dean of genealogical bibliography in this country and without his lists of solid genealogical works, this index could not have been started. This index is for you, Gary.

The staff at the NEHGS Library in Boston, who have been helping me for more than 20 years. If their collective brains could be downloaded to a computer or the page, this index would be superfluous. Thanks to Jerome E. Anderson, for his helpful advice and superb expertise. Thanks to the publications committee at NEHGS who shepherded this work to completion: Martha G. Bustin, Scott C. Steward, Michael J. Leclerc, and Penelope Stratton. Thanks to Nathaniel Taylor for encouragement and formatting the final version for publication.

To Betty Kohlenberg of San Francisco, who convinced me not to stay in my "don'ts."

My friend and research partner Scott Andrew Bartley, for his help and his insanely well-stocked genealogical library, located but four blocks from me, and Christopher Norris, Scott's partner (they are a team and you can't thank one and not the other).

My family, particularly, my parents. My late great-uncle Warren, who got me interested in genealogy in the first place. And Michael, who makes everything possible.

ABBREVIATIONS OF WORKS CITED

26Imm   John Brooks Threlfall, *Twenty-Six Great Migration Colonists to New England & Their Origins* (Madison, WI: the author, 1993).

31Imm   Dorothy C. and Gerald E. Knoff, *Thirty-One English Emigrants Who Came to New England by 1662* (Baltimore, MD: Gateway Press, 1989). Reviews: CN 23:513-14, NGSQ 80:219-20, MQ 56:157.

50Imm   John Brooks Threlfall, *Fifty Great Migration Colonists to New England & Their Origins* (Madison, WI: the author, 1990). Reviews: NHGR 8:135, MQ 57:183.

AK   Robert Walden Coggeshall, *Ancestors and Kin* (Spartanburg, SC, 1988).

AL   Carl Boyer, 3rd, *Ancestral Lines: 206 Families in England, Wales, the Netherlands, Germany, New England, New York, New Jersey and Pennsylvania with additional ancestral tables* (Santa Clarita, CA: the author, 1998, 3rd edition). Reviews: NEHGR 138:51-54, NYGBR 113:122, 130:69; TAG 74:155.

Angell   Dean Crawford Smith; Melinde Lutz Sanborn, editor, *The Ancestry of Emily Jane Angell 1844-1910* (Boston, MA: NEHGS, 1992) [winner of 1993 Donald Lines Jacobus Award]. Reviews: CN 27:418-19, TAG 68:121, NEHGR 148:368-69.

Bartlett   Robert S. Wakefield, *Robert Bartlett of the "Anne" and his Descendants of Four Generations* (Plymouth, MA: General Society of Mayflower Descendants, 2000).

Brewer   Dorothy Brewer Erikson, *Descendants of Thomas Brewer Connecticut to Maine 1682-1996 with Allied Families* (Boston, MA: NEHGS, 1996). Reviews: MG 19:177, CN 30:227-28, NEHGR 151:243-44.

Brewster   Barbara Lambert Merrick, *Mayflower Families in Progress: William Brewster of the Mayflower and His Descendants for Four Generations* (Plymouth, MA: General Society of Mayflower Descendants, 2000, 3rd edition). Reviews: TAG 69:251, CN 34:40.

Brewster2   Barbara Lambert Merrick, *Mayflower Families in Progress: William Brewster of the Mayflower and the Fifth Generation Descendants of his daughter Patience* (Plymouth, MA: General Society of Mayflower Descendants, 2001). Reviews: CN 35:76.

Brewster3   Barbara Lambert Merrick, *Mayflower Families in Progress: William Brewster of the Mayflower and the Fifth Generation Descendants of his son Jonathan* (Plymouth, MA: General Society of Mayflower Descendants, 1999).

Brewster4   Barbara Lambert Merrick, *Mayflower Families in Progress: William Brewster of the Mayflower and the Fifth Generation Descendants of his son Love* (Plymouth, MA: General Society of Mayflower Descendants, 2003).

CA   *Connecticut Ancestors* volume 23 (1980/1) to volume 47 no. 1 (September 2004).

Cameos   Roger Thompson, *Cambridge Cameos: Stories of Life in Seventeenth-Century New England* (Boston, 2005).

Chase   Alice Crane Williamson, *Chase-Wigglesworth Genealogy: the Ancestors and Descendants of Philip Putnam Chase and his wife Anna Cornelia Wigglesworth* (Baltimore, MD: Gateway Press, 1990). Reviews: NHGR 8:47-48, TAG 65:248, NEHGR 146:299-300.

Church   Robert S. Wakefield, *Mayflower Families in Progress: Richard Church and His Descendants for Four Generations* (Plymouth, MA: General Society of Mayflower Descendants, 1998).

CN   *The Connecticut Nutmegger* volume 13 (1980/1) to volume 37 (2004/5).

Colonial   Mary Naomi Foster and Edward H. Little, editors, *Colonial Ancestors: Four Lineal Genealogies of Eastern Connecticut Families descending from: William Andrews of Hartford, Robert Fuller of Salem and Rehoboth, Lazarus Manley of Coventry and Mansfield, John White of Hartford and Hadley* (Camden, ME: Penobscot Press, 1991). Reviews: CN 25:99, NEHGR 146:184-85.

Cooley   Harl Preslar Aldrich, Jr., *George Lathrop Cooley and Clara Eliza-beth Hall: Their Ancestors and Descendants in America* (Rock-port, ME: Penobscot Press, 2001). Reviews: NEHGR 156:395-96, CN 34:584, 35:228.

Croll   Robert Croll Stevens, *Ancestry of the Children of Robert Croll Ste-vens and Jane Eleanor (Knauss) Stevens, Volume II: The Genealogy of John Christian Croll 1707-1758* (Pittsford, NY: Tucker Print-ers, Inc. 1985); Volumes V and VI are errata and addendum volumes, and should be consulted with this volume. This work is unpaginated and denotes families by number.

Crosby   Paul W. Prindle, *Ancestors and Descendants of Timothy Crosby, Jr., 1957, With Supplement H, Ancestry of Mary Morey, Wife of Timo-thy Crosby, Sr.* (Orleans, MA: 1981). Reviews: TAG 58:186-87, NYGBR 113:246, NGSQ 71:135-36.

Dancing   Susan E. Keats, *There Will Be Dancing: The History of a Johnson Family* (Boston, MA: FMR Corp., 2000). Reviews: NEHGR 156:86-87.

Davis   Walter Goodwin Davis, *Massachusetts and Maine Families in the Ancestry of Walter Goodwin Davis* (Baltimore, MD: Genea-logical Publishing Co., 1996); available on CD-ROM (1998) [works are referenced to the 1996 edition with the bracketed names of the original works without page references]. Reviews: MG 18:138-40, NHGR 13:143, NYGBR 127:178, VG 1:135-6, TAG 71:122-23, MQ 62:134-35.

Delano   Muriel Curtis Cushing, *Philip Delano of the "Fortune" 1621 and His Descendants for Four Generations* (Plymouth, MA: General Society of Mayflower Descendants, 1999) and *Philip Delano of the "Fortune" 1621 and His Descendants in the Fifth and Sixth Generations, Part One* (Plymouth, MA: General Society of May-flower Descendants, 2004). Reviews: CN 33:581, TAG 75:79, CN 37:438.

Doctors   Ethel Farrington Smith, *Colonial American Doctresses: A Genea-logical and Biographical Account of Women who Practiced Medi-cine and Chirurgery in Colonial America* (Boston, MA: Newbury Street Press, 2003). Reviews: NEHGR 158:160-61.

EB   Edmund K. Swigart, Ph.D., *An Emerson-Benson Saga: The An-cestry of Charles F. Emerson and Bessie Benson and the Struggle to*

Settle the United States Including 194 Allied Lines (Baltimore, MD: Gateway Press, 1994). Reviews: CN 28:252-53, TAG 71:255, NEHGR 149:315-17.

Foundations *Foundations: Newsletter of the Foundation for Medieval Genealogy*, Volume 1, nos. 1 to 6 (2003-2005). Reviews: TAG 78:138-42.

Freeman Patty Barthell Myers, *Ancestors and Descendants of Lewis Ross Freeman, With Related Families, Based Partially on the Work of Freeman Worth Gardner and Willis Freeman* (Camden, ME: 1995). Reviews: NYGBR 127:120, TAG 71:56, NEHGR 150: 225-26.

Gateway Christy Hawes Bond and Alicia Crane Williams, *Gateway Families: Ancestors and Descendants of Richard Simrall Hawes, III, and Marie Christy Johnson* (Concord, MA: 1994). Reviews: NYGBR 126:283, TAG 70:186-87, NGSQ 84:56.

GMB Robert Charles Anderson, *The Great Migration Begins: Immigrants to New England 1620-1633* (Boston, MA: NEHGS, 1995); available on CD-ROM (2000); available online at http://www.newenglandancestors.org (subscription needed). Reviews: MG 18:91-93, NYGBR 128:71, TAG 71:252-54, NGSQ 85:72-73, NEQ 70:319-20.

GM2 Robert Charles Anderson, George F. Sanborn, Jr., and Melinde Lutz Sanborn, *The Great Migration: Immigrants to New England 1634-1635* (Boston, MA: NEHGS, 1999 [vol. 1], 2001 [vol. 2], 2003 [vol. 3], 2005 [vol. 4]; series not yet complete). Immigrants with surnames A to L. Reviews: MG 22:43-44; MG 23:141-42; MG 25:94-95; MD 49:91-92, 50:182, 52:157, NYGBR 131:233, 132:310, 134:236, TAG 75:75-76, TAG 76:154-55, 78:236-37, NEHGR 157:182-83, CN 453-55.

Goodman Harrison Black, *The Ancestry of Frances Maria Goodman 1829-1912, Wife of Learner Blackman Harrison* (Boston, MA: Newbury Street Press, 2001). Reviews: TAG 77:320-21, NEHGR 156:395-96, CN 35:449.

Howland1 Elizabeth Pearson White, *John Howland of the Mayflower, Volume 1: The First Five Generations; Documented Descendants Through His First Child Desire Howland and Her Husband Captain John Gorham* (Camden, ME: Picton Press, 1990). Reviews:

CA 35:145-46, CN 24:127, NYGBR 122:123, TAG 66:121-22, NEHGR 146:94, NGSQ 79:228, MQ 57:82-83.

Howland2 Elizabeth Pearson White, *John Howland of the Mayflower, Volume 2: The First Five Generations; Documented Descendants Through His Second Child John Howland and His Wife Mary Lee* (Camden, ME: Picton Press, 1993). Reviews: CN 26:575-76, NYGBR 124:248, TAG 68:188-89; NEHGR 147:279-80.

Jessup William Jessup Cleaver, *The Ancestry of Allen Grinnell Cleaver and Martha Irene Jessup: 172 Allied Families* (Baltimore, MD: Gateway Press, 1989).

JIC Neil D. Thompson and Robert Charles Anderson, editors, *A Tribute to John Insley Coddington on the Occasion of the Fortieth Anniversary of the American Society of Genealogists* (New York, NY: Association for the Promotion of Scholarship in Genealogy, Ltd., 1980). Reviews: NYGBR 113:53, NGSQ 69:301-2.

Johnson Willard Marshall Bollenbach, Jr., *The New England Ancestry of Alice Everett Johnson, 1899-1986, Memoirs and Bollenbach Genealogy* (Baltimore, MD: Gateway Press, 2003).

JPG Joan S. Guilford, *The Ancestry of Dr. J.P. Guilford, Volume I: Seventeenth-Century New England Colonials* (Orange, CA, 1990) and *Volume II: Seventeenth-Century New England Colonials and a Few Eighteenth-Century Immigrants* (Orange, CA, 2003). Volume II has an errata and addendum section to Volume I, pp. 553-704. Reviews: NHGR 20:181, VG1:137, 9:100, TAG 68:58-60, TAG 79:320-21, CN 37:271.

Kempton Dean Crawford Smith; Melinde Lutz Sanborn, editor, *The Ancestry of Eva Belle Kempton 1878-1908, Part I: The Ancestry of Warren Francis Kempton 1817-1879* (Boston, MA: NEHGS, 1996). Reviews: MG 19:42-43, CN 30:226-27, NYGBR 128:73, VG 1:189, TAG 73:157, NEHGR 152:373-74, NGSQ 85:142-43.

Kempton3 Dean Crawford Smith; Melinde Lutz Sanborn, editor, *The Ancestry of Eva Belle Kempton 1878-1908, Part III: The Ancestry of Henry Clay Bartlett 1832-1892* (Boston, MA: NEHGS, 2004). Reviews: NYGBR 136:151, TAG 80:155, NEHGR 159:161, NGSQ 93:66.

Kempton4 Dean Crawford Smith; Melinde Lutz Sanborn, editor, *The Ancestry of Eva Belle Kempton 1878-1908, Part IV: The Ancestry of Linda Anna Powers 1839-1879* (Boston, MA: NEHGS, 2000). Reviews: VG 7:42, TAG 77:78-79, NGSQ 90:146-47.

LENE Daniel Allen Hearn, *Legal Executions in New England: A Comprehensive Reference 1623-1960* (Jefferson, NC: McFarland & Co., Inc., 1999). Reviews: NEHGR 154:245-46.

Lyon Patty Barthell Myers, *Ancestors and Descendants of Thomas Rice Lyon and his Wife Harriet Wade Rice with Related Families* (San Antonio, TX: 2003).

Makepeace Zelinda Makepeace Douhan, ed., *The Ancestry of Russell Makepeace of Marion, Massachusetts, 1904-1986, A Descendant of Thomas Makepeace of Dorchester, Massachusetts* (Boston, MA: Newbury Street Press, 2005). Reviews: MD 54:182, TAG 80:315.

MBT John Brooks Threlfall, *The Ancestry of Margaret Brooks Threlfall* (Madison, WI: 1985). Unpaginated, this work is indexed by ancestor number.

MCA Douglas Richardson, Kimball G. Everingham, editor, *Magna Carta Ancestry: A Study in Colonial and Medieval Families* (Baltimore, MD: Genealogical Publishing Co., 2005). Reviews: MD 54:184, VG 10:229-30.

MD *The Mayflower Descendant* 1985-2005, Volumes 35-55. Note there was no volume for 1999, so vol. 48 (1998) continues in vol. 49 (2000). Reviews: NEHGR 139:260-61; MQ 66:336-37.

MF4 Bruce Campbell MacGunningle, *Mayflower Families Through Five Generations: Volume Four: Edward Fuller* (Plymouth, MA: General Society of Mayflower Descendants, 1995, 2nd Edition). Reviews: TAG 66:123, NEHGR 147:285-86.

MF5 Ruth C. McGuyre and Robert S. Wakefield (Winslow) and Harriet W. Hodge (Billington), *Mayflower Families Through Five Generations: Volume Five: Edward Winslow and John Billington* (Plymouth, MA: General Society of Mayflower Descendants, 1997, 2nd Edition). Reviews: TAG 67:121, NEHGR 147:89-90.

MF6 John D. Austin, *Mayflower Families Through Five Generations: Volume Six: Stephen Hopkins* (Plymouth, MA: General Society of Mayflower Descendants, 2001, 3rd Edition). Reviews: TAG 68:254, CN 34:584.

MF7   Robert S. Wakefield, *Mayflower Families Through Five Generations: Volume Seven: Peter Brown* (Plymouth, MA: General Society of Mayflower Descendants, 2002). Reviews: TAG 68:254.

MF8   Robert S. Wakefield, editor, Mrs. Charles Delmar Townsend, Robert S. Wakefield, and Margaret Harris Stover, compilers, *Mayflower Families Through Five Generations: Volume Eight: Degory Priest* (Plymouth, MA: General Society of Mayflower Descendants, 1994). Reviews: TAG 70:128.

MF9   Lee Douglas Van Antwerp, compiler, Robert S. Wakefield, revisor, *Mayflower Families Through Five Generations: Volume Nine: Francis Eaton* (Plymouth, MA: General Society of Mayflower Descendants, 1996). Reviews: TAG 71:125-26, NEHGR 153:122.

MF10   Katherine Warner Radasch and Arthur Hitchcock Radasch, compilers, Margaret Harris Stover and Robert S. Wakefield, revisors, *Mayflower Families Through Five Generations: Volume Ten: Samuel Fuller* (Plymouth, MA: General Society of Mayflower Descendants, 1996).

MF11   Peter B. Hill, *Mayflower Families Through Five Generations: Volume Eleven: Edward Doty* (Plymouth, MA: General Society of Mayflower Descendants, 1996-2000) in three volumes. Reviews: TAG 73:235.

MF12   Ralph V. Wood, Jr., *Francis Cooke of the Mayflower: The First Five Generations* (Camden, ME: Picton Press, 1996). Reviews: TAG 73:75.

MF13   Ruth Wilder Sherman and Robert Moody Sherman, authors, Robert S. Wakefield, editor, *Mayflower Families Through Five Generations: Volume 13: William White* (Plymouth, MA: General Society of Mayflower Descendants, 2002, 2nd edition). Reviews: TAG 73:235, CN 36:54.

MF14   Robert S. Wakefield, editor, Russell L. Warner, compiler, *Mayflower Families Through Five Generations: Volume 14: Myles Standish* (Plymouth, MA: General Society of Mayflower Descendants, 1997).

MF15   Robert Moody Sherman and Verle Delano Vincent, compilers, Robert S. Wakefield, revisor (Chilton), and Robert Moody Sherman, Robert S. Wakefield, and Lydia Dow Finlay (More), *Mayflower Families Through Five Generations: Volume 15: Rich-*

ard More (Plymouth, MA: General Society of Mayflower Descendants, 1997). Reviews: TAG 73:235.

MF16 Esther Littleford Woodworth-Barnes, compiler, Alicia Crane Williams, editor, *Mayflower Families Through Five Generations: Volume 16: John Alden* (Plymouth, MA: General Society of Mayflower Descendants, 1999-2002), 3 vols. Reviews: TAG 74:235-36, NEHGR 153:501-2, CN 37:614.

MF17 Robert S. Wakefield and Margaret Harris Stover, *Mayflower Families Through Five Generations: Volume 17: Isaac Allerton* (Plymouth, MA: General Society of Mayflower Descendants, 1998). Reviews: TAG 74:320; NEHGR 153:502-3.

MF18 Robert S. Wakefield, compiler, Judith H. Swan, revisor, *Mayflower Families Through Five Generations: Volume 18: Richard Warren* (Plymouth, MA: General Society of Mayflower Descendants, 2004), 3 vols. Reviews: TAG 74:320, NEHGR 153:502-3, CN 34:589, 37:432.

MF19 Alice W.A. Westgate, compiler, Ann T. Reeves, revisor, *Mayflower Families Through Five Generations: Volume 19: Thomas Rogers* (Plymouth, MA: General Society of Mayflower Descendants, 2000).

MF20 Robert Moody Sherman and Ruth Wilder Sherman, compilers, Robert S. Wakefield, editor, *Mayflower Families Through Five Generations: Volume 20: Henry Samson* (Plymouth, MA: General Society of Mayflower Descendants, 2000-2005), 2 vols. Reviews: CN 35:77, TAG 80:320.

MF21 Harriet W. Hodge, compiler, Robert S. Wakefield, revisor, *Mayflower Families Through Five Generations: Volume 21: John Billington* (Plymouth, MA: General Society of Mayflower Descendants, 2001). Reviews: CN 35:76.

MF22 Ann Smith Lainhart and Robert S. Wakefield, *Mayflower Families Through Five Generations: Volume 22: William Bradford* (Plymouth, MA: General Society of Mayflower Descendants, 2004). Reviews: CN 37:432-33.

MG *The Maine Genealogist* 1991-2005; preceded by *The Maine Seine*, vols. 3-12 (1981-1990). Reviews: TAG 73:238.

MJ *Search for the Passengers of the Mary & John 1630*, volumes 1 (1985) to 27 (1999). Reviews: TAG 64:59, 65:121-23, 72:58,

NYGBR 117:243, 118:245, 120:123, 121:116, 122:249, NEHGR 150:502-3. For the most accurate list of actual passengers of the *Mary & John* see NEHGR 147:148-61. Volume 10 is an index to volumes 1 to 9; volume 23 is an index to all previous volumes (1-22); and volume 24 is excerpts from previous volumes. These three volumes were not indexed.

Morgan   David L. Mordy, Jean W. Perney and Betty L. Storey, *Ancestors and Descendants of Daniel Morgan and Polly Frost* (Indianapolis, IN: 1996). Reviews: NYGBR 128:135, TAG 72:59-60, NEHGR 151:485-86.

Mower   Lyman Mower, *The Ancestry of Calvin Robinson Mower (1840-1927)* (Durham, NH: 2004).

MQ   *The Mayflower Quarterly* 1980-2005, volumes 46 to 71.

NEA   *New England Ancestors* volumes 1-6 (2000-2005).

NECL   Carl Boyer, 3rd, *New England Colonial Families, Volume 1, Brown Families of Bristol Counties, Massachusetts and Rhode Island, from the Immigrants to the Early Nineteenth Century* (Newhall, CA: the author, 1981).

NEHGR   *The New England Historical and Genealogical Register* 1980-2005, volumes 134 to 159; searchable online to 1995 at http://www.newenglandancestors.org (subscription needed).

NEQ   *New England Quarterly*, 1980 to 2005, volumes 53 to 78.

NEXUS   *NEHGS NEXUS* volumes I to XVI (1983-1999).

NGSQ   *National Genealogical Society Quarterly*, 1980 to 2005 (volumes 68 to 93). Also available on CD-ROM (to volume 85).

NHGR   *The New Hampshire Genealogical Record*, volumes 7 no. 3 to 22 (1990-2005). Reviews: TAG 66:254.

Nichols   Clara Pierce Olson Overbo, *Ancestors and Descendants of Clark Proctor Nichols and Sarah (Sally) Stoughton in England and America 1620-2001* (Decorah, IA: Anundsen Publishing Company, 2002). Reviews: NEHGR 156:395-96.

NYGBR   *New York Genealogical and Biographical Record*, 1980-2005, volumes 111 to 136, also available in CD-ROM up to volume 70.

Ordway   Dean Crawford Smith, Melinde Lutz Sanborn, editor, *The Ancestry of Samuel Blanchard Ordway 1844-1916* (Boston, MA:

NEHGS, 1990), winner of 1993 Donald Lines Jacobus Award. Reviews: NHGR 7:191-92, CN 24:123-24, NYGBR 122:184, TAG 66:249, NEHGR 145:174-75, NGSQ 79:229-30.

PA   Douglas Richardson, Kimball G. Everingham, editor, *Plantagenet Ancestry: A Study in Colonial and Medieval Families* (Baltimore, MD: Genealogical Publishing Co., 2004). Reviews: MD 53:186, VG 10:128-29, TAG 80:58-67, CN 37:434, MQ 70:285.

PM   Robert Charles Anderson, *The Pilgrim Migration: Immigration to Plymouth Colony 1620-1633* (Boston, MA: New England Historic Genealogical Society, 2004). Reviews: NYGBR 136:225, MD 54:84, TAG 79:318-19, NEHGR 159:158.

Pond   Robert Croll Stevens, *Ancestry of the Children of Robert Croll Stevens and Jane Eleanor (Knauss) Stevens, Volume IV: The Genealogy of Robert Pond ?-1637* (Pittsford, NY: Tucker Printers, Inc. 1990); Volumes V and VI are errata and addendum volumes and should be consulted with this volume. This work is unpaginated and denotes families by number.

Puritans Alden T. Vaughan and Edward W. Clark, editors, *Puritans Among the Indians: Accounts of Captivity and Redemption 1676-1724* (Cambridge, MA: Belknap Press/Harvard University Press, 1981). Reviews: NEHGR 136:254-55, NEQ 55:123-25.

RD600   Gary Boyd Roberts, *The Royal Descents of 600 Immigrants to the American Colonies of the United States, Who Were Themselves Notable or Left Descendants Notable in American History* (Baltimore, MD: Genealogical Publishing Co., 2004). Reviews: NYGBR 136:73, VG 9:101-2, TAG 79:155-56, NEHGR 158:162, NGSQ 232-33, CN 37:84-85, MQ 70:285. A second updated edition of this work was published in early 2006.

RFI   Marston Watson, *Royal Families: Americans of Royal and Noble Ancestry, Volume One: Governor Thomas Dudley* (Baltimore, MD: Genealogical Publishing Co., 2004, 2nd edition). Reviews: NHGR 20:47-48, 22:47, MD 52:90-91, 54:88, VG 7:189-90, 10:133, TAG 77:238, CN 35:630; MQ 68:287.

RF2   Marston Watson, *Royal Families: Americans of Royal and Noble Ancestry, Volume Two: Rev. Francis Marbury* (Baltimore, MD: Genealogical Publishing Co., 2004). Reviews: NHGR 21:48,

VG 9:102-3. MD 53:85, TAG 79:322-23, NGSQ 92:231-32, CN 37:85-86.

RIR   *Rhode Island Roots* 1980-2005, volumes 6 to 31.

Sex   Roger Thompson, *Sex in Middlesex: Popular Mores in a Massa-chusetts County, 1649-1699* (Amherst, MA: University of Massachusetts Press, 1986). Reviews: NEQ 59:577-83.

Soule   John E. Soule, Milton E. Terry, compilers, Robert S. Wakefield and Louise Walsh Throop, revisers, *Mayflower Families in Progress: George Soule*, 4th edition (Plymouth, MA: General Society of Mayflower Descendants, 2002); one pamphlet for generations 1-4; four pamphlets for the fifth generation (2002-2005).

Spooner   Esther Littleford Woodworth-Barnes, *Spooner Saga: Judah Paddock Spooner and His Wife Deborah Douglas of Connecticut and Vermont and Their Descendants; Alden Spooner's Autobiography; Spooner, Douglas, and Jermain Ancestry* (Boston, MA: Newbury Street Press, 1997), Reviews: CN 31:239, NYGBR 129:136, TAG 73:233-34, NEHGR 152:116-17.

Stevens   Robert Croll Stevens, *Ancestry of the Children of Robert Croll Stevens and Jane Eleanor (Knauss) Stevens, Volume I: The Genealogy of Otho Stevens, 1702-1771, Together with Kent, Hills, Hastings, Smith, Proctor, Sproule and Associated Lines* (Pittsford, NY: Tucker Printers, Inc. 1982); Volumes V and VI are errata and addendum volumes and should be consulted with this volume. This work is unpaginated and denotes families by number.

Stone   Alicia Crane Williams, *Stone-Gregg Genealogy: The Ancestors and Descendants of Galen Luther Stone and His Wife Carrie Morton Gregg* (Baltimore, MD: Gateway Press, 1987). Reviews: TAG 63:189-90, NEHGR 141:262.

Stowers   Kay Haviland Freilich, Ann Carter Fleming, and Rudena Kramer Mallory, *Stowers and Glascock Families, An American Saga: Ancestry of James Evans Stowers, Jr. and Virginia Ann (Glascock) Stowers* (Baltimore, MD: Gateway Press, 2003).

TAG   *The American Genealogist* 1980-2005, Volumes 56 to 80. Reviews: MQ 64:351

TEG   *The Essex Genealogist* 1981-2005, Volumes 1 to 25.

TG   *The Genealogist* 1980-2005; Volumes 1-10 (1980-1989); publi-
            cations suspended and recommenced with Volume 11 in 1997
            through Volume 19 (2005). Reviews: MG 20:91-92, NYGBR
            129:138-39, TAG 77:317; NEHGR 152:252.

Thompson   Roger Thompson, *Divided We Stand: Watertown, Massachusetts
            1630-1680* (Amherst, MA: University of Massachusetts Press,
            2001). Reviews: TAG 76:319-20.

TW   John Anderson Brayton, *The [Complete] Ancestry of Tennessee
            Williams* (Winston-Salem, NC, 1993). Reviews: CN 28:250-
            51, TAG 70:57, NEHGR 149:437.

VG   *Vermont Genealogy* 1996-2005, volumes 1 to 10.

WRR   D. Brenton Simons, *Witches, Rakes, and Rogues: True Stories of
            Scam, Scandal, Murder, and Mayhem in Boston 1630-1775* (Bev-
            erly, MA: Commonwealth Editions, 2005).

INDEX OF NEW ENGLANDERS

ABBE, JOHN, b. ca. 1613, d. Salem, Mass., ca. 1689. JPG II:3-21.

ABBOTT, DANIEL, ca. 1610, d. Providence, R.I., 1647. GMB I:1-3.

ABBOTT, GEORGE, b. ca. 1617, d. Andover, Mass., 24 December 1681. TEG 20:19-23.

ABBOTT, GEORGE, b. ca. 1625, d. Norwalk, Conn., between 2 May 1690 and 11 March 1690/1. Johnson, pp. 5-8.

ABBOTT, GEORGE, b. ca. 1630, d. Andover, Mass., 22 March 1688/9. TEG 20:19-23.

ABBOTT, GEORGE, d. Rowley, Mass., before 28 September 1647. MBT #816.

ABBOTT, PETER, d. Hartford, Conn., 16 October 1667. LENE, p. 41.

ABBOTT, ROBERT, b. ca. 1605, d. Branford, Conn., 30/31 September 1658. GM2 I:1-6.

ABBOTT, WALTER, d. Portsmouth, N.H., between 16 May and 26 June 1667. TAG 70:85-95 (son Thomas[2]).

ABDY, MATTHEW, b. ca. 1620, d. Boston, Mass., after 5 April 1682. GM2 I:6-8.

ABELL, ROBERT, b. ca. 1605, d. Rehoboth, Mass., 20 June 1663. RD600, pp. 312-13; PA, p. 34; MCA p. 2; TG 5:158-71, 9:89; GMB I:3-6; Johnson, pp. 8-16; AL, pp. 1-8, including a ten generation ancestor table for Robert Abell; see also Carl Boyer, 3rd, *Medieval English Ancestors of Robert Abell Who Died in Rehoboth, Plymouth Colony 20 June 1663, with English Ancestral Lines of Other Colonial Americans* (Santa Clarita, CA: the author, 2001).

ABORN, SAMUEL, b. ca. 1610, d. Salem, Mass., before 20 November 1699. TEG 16:30-37, 88-94.

ACRES, HENRY, b. ca. 1652, d. after 1694 possibly Newbury, Mass. Stevens, 40.

ADAMS, HENRY, b. 1582/3, d. Braintree, Mass., 6 October 1646. Goodman, pp. 10-42, including English origins; Lyon, pp. 151-58; John[3] Joseph[2] at TAG 71:21-25; NEHGR 153:213-20 (notes on line John[6] Joseph[5] John[4-3-2]); MJ 17:3-9, 25:7, 27:1.

ADAMS, JAMES, b. Scotland before 1680, d. Londonderry, N.H., between 5 March 1742/3 and 25 May 1743. Angell, pp. 179-82.

ADAMS, JAMES, b. ca. 1670, d. Charlestown, R.I., before 30 December 1741. CN 17:160-69, 343-52, 517-26, 699-708, CN 18:152-62, a multi-generational article; CN 25:573-75 (possible parentage).

ADAMS, JEREMY, b. ca. 1611, d. Hartford, Conn., 11 August 1683. GMB I:6-11.

ADAMS, JOHN, d. Plymouth, Mass., between 1 July and 24 August 1633. GMB I:11-2; PM 1-2.

ADAMS, RICHARD, b. ca. 1606, d. Malden, Mass., 6 October 1674. GM2 I:8-11; MJ 19:1.

ADAMS, ROBERT, b. ca. 1601, d. Newbury, Mass., 12 October 1682. MBT #1646; NEHGR 151:308-312 (Joanna[3] Hannah[2]).

ADAMS, WILLIAM, b. 1594, d. Ipswich, Mass., 1661. Kenneth L. Bosworth, *William Adams, 1594-1661, of Ipswich, Massachusetts, and Some of His Descendants: A History of the Ancestral Adams Lineage of Madeline (Adams) Whitehead and Descendants of John Quincy Adams of Mound City, Kansas with Details of Related Families, Including: Dickinson, Knowlton, Leach, Locke, Burnap, Eliot, Wilson, Mapes, Cochran, Whitehead, and Eaton* (Bowie, Md.: Heritage Books, 1996). Reviews: CN 26:275.

ADDIS, WILLIAM, b. ca. 1600, d. New London, Conn., after 15 February 1661/2. TAG 57:181-83; wife's ancestry at TAG 58:209-16; TAG 64:33-43 (mother-in-law's Flower ancestry).

AGER, WILLIAM, b. ca. 1610, d. Salem, Mass., between 3 March 1653/4 and 30 June 1654. GMB I:14-15.

ALBEE, BENJAMIN, b. ca. 1620, d. Mendon, Mass., after 1675. Johnson, pp. 16-17.

ALBRO, JOHN, b. ca. 1620, d. Portsmouth, R.I., 1 December 1712. GM2 I:15-20.

ALCOCK, GEORGE, b. ca. 1605, d. Roxbury, Mass., December 1640. GMB I:15-18; Sarah[3] John[2] at Doctors, pp. 103-4; NGSQ 85:195-218.

ALCOCK, JOHN, d. York, Me., ca. 1674-5. EB, pp. 65-67.

ALCOCK, THOMAS, b. ca. 1614, d. Boston, Mass., 14 September 1657. GMB I:18-20; NGSQ 85:195-218.

ALDEN, HENRY, b. ca. 1663, d. Needham, Mass., 18 February 1729/30. MD 43:21-29, 133-38, 44:27-30, 181-84, a multi-generational study.

ALDEN, JOHN, *Mayflower* passenger, b. 1598, d. Duxbury, Mass., 12 September 1687. MF 16, five generations all lines; GMB I:21-26; PM 4-10; Spooner; Jessup, pp. 108-19; MD 39:111-22, 40:133-36 (theory on origins); MQ 65:125-41; MQ 69:226-29 (John[2]); Dorothy Wentworth, *The Alden Family in the Alden House* (Duxbury, Mass.: Duxbury Rural and Historical Society, 1980). Reviews: NEQ 54:431-32, MQ 48:142-43.

ALDERMAN, WILLIAM, b. ca. 1640, d. Farmington, Conn., 1 August 1697. Verne R. Spear, *The Descendants of William Alderman Who Settled First at Windsor, Connecticut and Later Simsbury, Connecticut 1671-2002* (2 vols., South Deerfield, Mass.: the author, 2002). Reviews: CN 35:629-30.

ALDIS, NATHAN, b. 1592, d. Dedham, Mass., 15 March 1675/6. Lyon, pp. 159-60; NEHGR 150:473-94 (corrected English ancestry).

ALDRICH, GEORGE, d. Mendon, Mass., 1 March 1683. Pond, 212.

ALFORD SEE ALSO ALVORD

ALFORD, WILLIAM, b. ca. 1605, d. Boston, Mass., January 1676/7. GM2 I: 23-26.

ALGER, ANDREW, b. ca. 1610, d. Scarborough, Me., ca. 10 October 1675. GMB I:27-29.

ALLANSON, RALPH, b. 1621, d. after 1676, Scarborough, ME. Davis I:1-5 [Sarah Miller], including English origins, wife Anne's Dixon ancestry given at Davis I:429-436 [Sarah Miller]; her Watt ancestry given at Davis III:588-595 [Sarah Miller].

ALLEN, ALEXANDER, b. ca. 1659, d. Windsor, Conn., 19 August 1708. CN 20:43, 26:35-39.

ALLEN, ANDREW, of Andover, Mass., LENE, pp. 87-89 (Martha[2]).

ALLEN, EDWARD, d. Boston, Mass., after 1698. Goodman, pp. 44-47.

ALLEN, GEORGE, b. ca. 1592, d. Sandwich, Mass., May 1648. GM2 I:27-35; son, William[2], MF7, four generations all lines; Jessup, pp. 119-30; Johnson, pp. 17-21; JPG I:1-14, II:22-31; AL, pp. 9-17; TAG 80:27-37 (George[2]); NEHGR 155:212-14 (note).

ALLEN, JAMES, b. 1632, d. Boston, Mass., 22 September 1710. 31Imm, pp. 1-5, including English origins.

ALLEN, JOHN, b. ca. 1625, of Barnstable, Mass., d. Newport, R.I., 30 October 1708. Wife Elizabeth (Bacon)'s origins at TAG 57:103-8.

ALLEN, JOHN, Dedham, Mass. Wife Katherine (Deighton) at RD600, pp. 259-262; PA, p. 263; MCA, p. 265.

ALLEN, MATTHEW, b. 1605, d. Windsor, Conn., 1 February 1670/1. Wife Margaret (Wyatt) at RD600, pp. 489-91; GMB I:40-44; son Thomas[2] at LENE, pp. 26-28; Nichols, pp. 173-74; CN 20:34-43, including English origins; grandson Samuel[3] (Thomas[2]) at CN 25:182-89; TAG 57:115-19 (English parish registers); MJ 17:9-12.

ALLEN, ROBERT, d. Norwich, Conn., 1683. JPG II:337-39.

ALLEN, SAMUEL, d. Windsor, Conn., April 1648. MJ 1:21, 4:1-8.

ALLEN, WALTER, b. ca. 1601, d. Charlestown, Mass., 8 July 1681. Nichols, pp. 46-47.

ALLEN, WILLIAM, b. 1640, d. West Barrington, R.I., 1685. Johnson, pp. 21-23.

ALLEN, WILLIAM, b. before 1648, d. Medfield, Mass., 26 June 1738. Kempton3, pp. 33-38.

ALLEN, WILLIAM, b. ca. 1602, d. Manchester, Mass., 30 January 1678/9. GMB I:31-35; Stevens, 59.

ALLEN, WILLIAM, d. Salisbury, Mass., 18 June 1686. Davis I:6-12 [Abel Lunt].

ALLERTON, ISAAC, *Mayflower* passenger, b. ca. 1586, d. New Haven, Conn., between 1 and 12 February 1658/9. MF17, five generations all lines; GMB I:35-39; PM 10-15; Lyon, pp. 160-63; son Bartholomew[2] at MD 40:7-10; notes on third wife at MD 42:124; MQ 47:14-18; MQ 48:170-71; MQ 50:109-12; MQ 69:230-45.

ALLEY, HUGH, b. ca. 1609, d. Lynn, Mass., 25 January 1673/4. GM2 I:40-42; Chase, pp. 49-54, TEG 18:17-27.

ALLIN SEE ALLEN

ALLING, ABRAHAM, b. ca. 1645, of Marblehead, Mass., d. Oyster Bay, N.Y. after 1 July 1711. NYGBR 129:76-80, 183-88.

ALLYN SEE ALLEN

ALMY, WILLIAM, b. ca. 1602, d. Portsmouth, R.I., between 28 February 1676/7 and 23 April 1677. GM2 I:42-47; Johnson, pp. 23-24.

ALSOP, JOSEPH, b. ca. 1621, d. New Haven, Conn., 8 November 1698. GM2 I:47-51.

ALVORD, BENEDICT, d. Windsor, Conn., 23 April 1683. TAG 65:13-16 (identification of his wife); MJ 18:3-6.

AMBROSE, HENRY, b. 1613, d. Boston, Mass., before 19 November 1658. English origins at NHGR 9:49-56.

AMERIDITH, JOHN, b. ca. 1615, d. Dartmouth, Mass., 16 January 1691. MJ 19:1-2.

AMES, WILLIAM, b. 1605, d. Braintree, Mass., 1 January 1653/4. Kempton3, pp. 41-45, including possible English origins; EB, pp. 67-69; MJ 19:2-6; Ann Theopold Chaplin, *Descendants of William Ames of Braintree, Massachusetts* (Boston, MA: Newbury Street Press, 2004), a multi-generational study of this family, including English origins. Reviews: NHGR 22:48, MD 54:85-86, NEHGR 159:160-61, NGSQ 93:225, MQ 71:426.

AMIDON, ROGER, d. Rehoboth, Mass., November 1673. JPG I:15-26.

AMOS, HUGH, d. Norwich, Conn., 4 December 1707. EB, pp. 69-71.

AMSDEN, ISAAC, d. Cambridge, Mass., 7 April 1659. Son Isaac[2] at Sex, pp. 73-74.

ANDERSON, JAMES, b. Ireland ca. 1700, d. North Yarmouth, Me., 8 January 1758. Brewer, pp. 320-27.

ANDREW, WILLIAM, b. ca. 1600, d. Cambridge, Mass., between September 1651 and April 1652. TAG 71:26-27 (William[3] Samuel[2]'s wife identified); NEHGR 150:190-97 (wife of Samuel[2]'s English ancestry); Craig Partridge, *The Descendants of William Andrew of Cambridge, Massachusetts* (Camden, ME: Penobscot Press, 1995). Reviews: CN 29:232-33, TAG 70:190-91.

ANDREWS, FRANCIS, b. ca. 1620, d. Fairfield, Conn., ca. 1663. Johnson, pp. 24-26.

ANDREWS, HENRY, b. ca. 1605, d. Taunton, Mass., between 13 March 1651/2 and 10 February 1652/3. AL, pp. 33-34.

ANDREWS, JOHN, b. ca. 1600, d. Kittery, Me., ca. 1671. Jessup, pp. 130-31.

ANDREWS, JOHN, b. ca. 1620, d. Ipswich, Mass., 20 April 1708. 50Imm, pp. 1-8.

ANDREWS, RALPH, b. ca. 1640, d. Gloucester, Mass., 25 February 1718. TG 17:109-15.

ANDREWS, ROBERT, b. ca. 1593, d. Ipswich, Mass., between 1 March 1643/4 and 26 March 1644. GM2 I:52-6; Goodman, pp. 49-51; Davis I:13-16 [Annis Spear]; EB, pp. 71-72.

ANDREWS, SAMUEL, b. ca. 1598, d. Saco, Me., before 1 August 1638. GM2 I:56-59.

ANDREWS, THOMAS, b. ca. 1572, d. Hingham, Mass., 21 August 1643. GM2 I:61-62; Chase, pp. 55-62.

ANDREWS, THOMAS, b. ca. 1611, d. Dorchester, Mass., 20 May 1673. GM2 I:59-60.

ANDREWS, WILLIAM, b. ca. 1607, d. Hartford, Conn., between 1 April and 8 August 1659. GM2 I:63-67; Colonial, pp. 1-47; CN 29:570-74.

ANGELL, THOMAS, b. before 1619, d. Providence, R.I., between August 1688 and 18 September 1694. Angell, pp. 1-177, including extensive English research into his origins. Wife Alice Ashton's English origins given at Angell, pp. 185-93; TAG 66:129-32.

ANGIER, EDMUND, b. 1610, d. Cambridge, Mass., 4 March 1691/2. Davis I:17-26 [Abel Lunt], including English origins.

ANNABLE, ANTHONY, b. ca. 1595, d. Barnstable, Mass., between 23 April and 4 June 1674. GMB I:47-50; PM 16-20.

ANNABLE, JOHN, b. ca. 1623, d. Ipswich, Mass., before 7 November 1664. Jessup, pp. 131-32.

ANNIS, CURMAC, b. ca. 1638, d. Newbury, Mass., 19 December 1717. Ordway, pp. 119-37; Davis I:27-34 [Annis Spear]; Stevens, 42; TAG 70:239 (note).

ANTHONY, JOHN, b. ca. 1607, d. Portsmouth, R.I., 28 July 1675. Johnson, pp. 26-27; AL, pp. 34-40, with English ancestry.

ANTROBUS, JOAN (ARNOLD), b. ca. 1567, d. Ipswich, Mass., after 1635. GM2 I:67-69; Jessup, pp. 133-36; see also Lawrence and Tuttle.

ANTRUM, THOMAS, b. 1601, d. Salem, Mass., between 24 January and 17 February 1662/3. GM2 I:69-71.

APPLEGATE, THOMAS, b. ca. 1598, of Weymouth, Mass., and Newport, R.I., d. Gravesend, N.Y. between 18 January 1656 and 1657. GM2 I:72-75.

APPLETON, SAMUEL, b. 1586, d. Rowley, Mass., June 1670. Davis I:37-53 [Phoebe Tilton], including English origins; RD600, pp. 487-88. Wife Judith (Everard) at RD600, pp. 565-67; NEHGR 147:3-10 (royal line corrected).

ARCHER, HENRY, b. 1604/5, d. Ipswich, Mass., after 1671. NEHGR 158:117-23 (English origins); NEHGR 158:341-46 (additional English ancestry).

ARCHER, JOHN, of Portsmouth, R.I., d. Fall River, Mass., 25 June 1675. NEHGR 157:101-15.

ARCHER, SAMUEL, b. ca. 1608, d. Salem, Mass., before 26 November 1667. GMB I:50-53.

ARMITAGE, GODFREY, b. ca. 1618, d. Boston, Mass., before 11 February 1674/5. TEG 18:233-34.

ARMITAGE, JOSEPH, b. ca. 1600, d. Lynn, Mass., 27 June 1680. TEG 18:229-33.

ARMITAGE, THOMAS, b. ca. 1601, of Plymouth, Sandwich, Mass., Stamford, Conn., d. Oyster Bay, N.Y. before 1667. GM2 I:76-81.

ARNOLD, JOHN, b. ca. 1603, d. Hartford, Conn., between 22 August and 26 December 1664. GM2 I:81-83.

ARNOLD, SAMUEL, b. ca. 1622, d. Marshfield, Mass., 1 September 1693. Son Seth[2] at MF15, for two generations. Son Samuel[2]'s wife's identity at NEHGR 145:374.

ARNOLD, WILLIAM, b. 1587, d. Providence, R.I., between mid-1675 and 3 November 1677. GM2 I:84-91; AK, pp. 142-44; RIR 9:54; MJ 18:7-10, 25:8.

ARRINGTON SEE ERRINGTON

ASHLEY, ROBERT, d. West Springfield, Mass., 29 November 1682. Nichols, p. 175.

ASPINWALL, WILLIAM, b. ca. 1605, Charlestown, Boston, and Portsmouth, R.I., d. Chester, England after 13 April 1662. NEA 1:4:37-39; GMB I:55-60.

ASTWOOD, JOHN, b. ca. 1609, of Roxbury, Mass., and Milford, Conn., d. England between 27 June and 31 August 1654. GM2 I:92-95.

ATHERTON, HUMPHREY, b. ca. 1609/10, d. Dorchester, Mass., 16 September 1661. Pond, 244.

ATHERTON, MARY, fl. Worcester, Mass., 1690s. Sex, pp. 148-49, et al.

ATKINS, THOMAS, d. Phippsburg, Me., before 10 November 1686. EB, pp. 72-74.

ATKINSON, LUKE, d. Middletown, Conn., ca. 1665. JPG I:27-29.

ATKINSON, THEODORE, b. ca. 1614, d. Boston, Mass., August 1701. GM2, I:95-103; WRR, pp. 46-53.

ATWELL, BENJAMIN, of New London, Conn., 1660s, d. there ca. 1683. TG 14:131-58.

ATWELL, JOHN, b. ca. 1650, d. Lynn, Mass., after 1685. TEG 22:43-54.

ATWOOD, HENRY, b. ca. 1615, d. Middleborough, Mass., before 30 September 1670. MD 48:13-20, 135-40, 49:55-61, 119-24.

ATWOOD, JOHN, b. 1614, d. Plymouth, Mass., between 22 November 1675 and 7 March 1675/6. Nichols, pp. 77-78; MD 44:137-42, 45:9-12, 127-30, 46:15-20, a multi-generational article; NEHGR 144:23-28; MQ 48:127-30 (Mary, wife of Nathaniel[2]).

ATWOOD, PHILIP, b. ca. 1620, d. Bradford, Mass., 1 February 1700/1. GM2 I:104-6.

ATWOOD, STEPHEN, b. ca. 1620, d. Eastham, Mass., February 1693/4. MD 46:131-36, 47:33-40, 123-30, a multi-generational article.

ATWOOD, THOMAS, d. Wethersfield, Conn., 1682. TAG 63:214.

AUSTIN, JONAS, b. 1598, d. Taunton, Mass., 30 July 1683. GM2 I:106-9; 31Imm, pp. 6-12, including English origins.

AUSTIN, MATTHEW, b. ca. 1620, d. York, Me., before 1 March 1685/6. EB, pp. 74-76.

AUSTIN, RICHARD, b. 1598, d. Charlestown, Mass., 1638. Goodman, pp. 53-62; Jim and Liz Austin Carlin, *Some Descendants of Richard Austin of Charlestown, Massachusetts 1638* (Baltimore, MD: Gateway Press, 1998). Reviews: CN 32:240-41, NGSQ 88:62-64.

AUSTIN, ROBERT, b. ca. 1634, d. Kingstown, R.I., before 1687. Johnson, pp. 27-29.

AVERILL, WILLIAM, b. 1595, d. Ipswich, Mass., between 3 June 1652 and 29 March 1653. Davis I:54-64 [Dudley Wildes], including English origins; daughter Sarah[2] at LENE, pp. 80-83.

AVERY, CHRISTOPHER, b. ca. 1590, d. New London, Conn., March 1679. Maureen A. Taylor, *The Avery Family: The Ancestors and Descendants of Christopher Avery* (Boston, MA: Newbury Street Press, 2004). Reviews: NEHGR 158:393-94.

AVERY, JOSEPH, b. ca. 1600, of Newbury, Mass., d. at sea 15 August 1635. GM2 I:109-113.

AVERY, WILLIAM, b. ca. 1622, d. Boston, Mass., 18 March 1686. AL, pp. 42-43.

AXTELL, THOMAS, b. 1618/9, d. Sudbury, Mass., 8 March 1645/6. Kempton3, pp. 47-53, including English origins; CN 31:390-92 (possible identification of wife).

AYER, JOHN, b. ca. 1590, d. Haverhill, Mass., 31 March 1657. Freeman, pp. 421-76, including English origins; Scott C. Steward, *The Sarsaparilla Kings: A Biography of Dr. James Cook Ayer and Frederick Ayer, with a Record of Their Family* (Cambridge, MA: the author, 1993), pp. 52-55, 59-62. Reviews: TAG 68:253.

AYERS, HENRY, b. ca. 1600, d. Portsmouth, R.I., after 1655. Johnson, pp. 29-30.

AYERS, JOHN, d. Brookfield, Mass., 2 August 1675. Thomas D. Ayres, *Ayres Genealogy: Some of the Descendants of Captain John Ayres of Brookfield, Massachusetts* (Simsbury, Conn.: the author, 1995, 5th ed.). Reviews: NYGBR 118:53.

AYRES, WILLIAM, b. ca. 1625, d. North Kingstown, R.I., after May 1671. TAG 75:197-205, 301-9.

BABB, PHILIP, d. Isle of Shoals, N.H., before 4 July 1671. Jean A. Sargent and Ina Babb Mansur, *Babb Families of New England and Beyond* (Laurel, MD: the authors, 1987). Reviews: CN 20:702-3.

BABCOCK, JAMES, b. ca. 1612, d. Stonington, Conn., 12 June 1679. AL, pp. 44-66.

BABSON, ISABEL [WIDOW OF THOMAS], b. ca. 1577, d. Gloucester, Mass., 6 April 1661. Chase, pp. 63-70; MJ 26:9-10; Ann Theopold Chaplin, *The*

Babson Genealogy 1606-1997: Descendants of Thomas and Isabel Babson who first arrived in Salem, Massachusetts in 1637 (Baltimore, MD: Gateway Press, 1997). Reviews: TAG 74:76-77, NEHGR 152:245-46.

BACHELOR, JOHN, b. ca. 1610, d. Reading, Mass., 3 May 1676. GM2 I:117-122; Stevens, 57.

BACHELOR, WILLIAM, b. ca. 1596, d. Charlestown, Mass., 22 February 1669/70. GM2 I:122-26; Goodman, pp. 65-68; TAG 80:23-24 (marriage).

BACHILER, STEVEN, b. 1561, d. England October 1659, NHGR 8:14-17; GMB I:61-69.

BACKUS, WILLIAM, b. ca. 1606, d. Norwich, Conn., 1 June 1664. Johnson, pp. 30-33; NEHGR 142:253-54 (English origins); NEHGR 143:24 (wife's identification); NEHGR 153:499 (note).

BACON, GEORGE, b. ca. 1592, d. Hingham, Mass., May 1642. GM2 I:127-29; Lyon, pp. 166-67.

BACON, MICHAEL, b. 1579, d. Dedham, Mass., 18 April 1648. JPG I:30-40, including English ancestry.

BACON, NATHANIEL, b. ca. 1621, of Plymouth and Barnstable, Mass. TAG 57:103-8 (English origins).

BACON, WILLIAM, d. Salem, Mass., before 26 September 1653. TAG 73:23-32 (wife Rebecca's English origins); TAG 79:309-315 (additional Fenn ancestry).

BADCOCK, ROBERT, d. Milton, Mass., 12 November 1694. Lyon, pp. 167-69.

BADGER, GILES, b. ca. 1610, d. Newbury, Mass., 17 July 1647. TAG 58:1-11, 91-98 (English origins).

BADLAM, WILLIAM, b. ca. 1660, of Boston and Weymouth, Mass., d. at sea between 1701 and 1718. NEHGR 141:3-18, 135-50 (six generation study).

BAILEY, JOHN, b. 1585, d. Newbury, Mass., 2 November 1651. Davis I:65-67 [Phoebe Tilton]; EB, pp. 93-98; TAG 77:241-47 (English origins).

BAILEY, RICHARD, b. ca. 1619, d. Rowley, Mass., February 1647/8. Stevens, 19.

BAILEY, THOMAS, b. ca. 1602, d. Weymouth, Mass., between May and October 1681. Louis G. Bailey and Billie Cooke Bailey, *Bailey Genealogy: Descendants of Thomas Bayley/Bailey of Weymouth, Massachusetts* (Dallas, TX: the authors, 1999). Reviews: NEHGR 154:379.

BAILEY, WILLIAM, d. Newport, R.I., before 1676. AL, pp. 66-67.

BAKER, ALEXANDER, b. ca. 1607, d. Boston, Mass., between 18 February 1684/5 and 11 May 1685. GM2 I:130-32.

BAKER, EDWARD, b. ca. 1610, d. Lynn, Mass., 16 March 1687. EB, pp. 76-77; TEG 18:147-153; Ruth[3] (Joseph[2]) at TAG 80:265-277.

BAKER, FRANCIS, b. ca. 1611, d. Yarmouth, Mass., 23 July 1696. EB, pp. 77-79.

BAKER, JOHN, b. ca. 1589, d. Ipswich, Mass., in the 1680s. Croll, 164.

BAKER, JOHN, b. ca. 1620, d. Boston, Mass., between 26 March 1665/6 and 3 July 1666. TW, pp. 158-79.

BAKER, JOHN, b. ca. 1633, of Cambridge and Woburn, Mass. He and wife Susannah (Martin) at Cameos, pp. 61-65.

BAKER, JOHN, d. poss. Boston, Mass., after 1641. GMB I:72-78.

BAKER, NATHANIEL, b. ca. 1614, d. Hingham, Mass., 3 June 1682. GM2 I:133-39.

BAKER, NICHOLAS, b. ca. 1610, d. Scituate, Mass., 22 or 29 August 1678. GM2 I:139-45; Lyon, pp. 169-70; NEHGR 142:121-25.

BAKER, RICHARD, b. ca. 1614, d. Dorchester, Mass., 25 October 1689. TW, pp. 158-62.

BAKER, THOMAS, b. ca. 1620, d. Boston, Mass., 3 January 1697. TW, pp. 151-58.

BAKER, WILLIAM, b. ca. 1613, d. Charlestown, Mass., 8 November 1658. GMB I:80-83.

BALCH, JOHN, b. ca. 1605, d. Salem, Mass., between 15 May and 28 June 1648. GMB I:84-86.

BALDWIN, JOHN, b. ca. 1632, d. Norwich, Conn., before 1681. Johnson, pp. 33-34.

BALDWIN, JOHN, d. Billerica, Mass., 25 September 1687. Stone, pp. 47-51.

BALDWIN, JOSEPH, d. Hadley, Mass., 8 December 1676. NEHGR 156:103-11 (Joseph[2]).

BALDWIN, RICHARD, b. 1622, d. Milford, Conn., 23 July 1665. Wife Elizabeth (Alsop) at RD600, pp. 342-43; PA, p. 37; MCA, p. 6.

BALDWIN, SYLVESTER, b. ca. 1597, d. at sea June 1638, widow lived at Milford, Conn. English origins at TG 11:111-15.

BALE, BENJAMIN, b. ca. 1634, d. Boston, Mass., 1680. MJ 18:10-11, 25:9-10, 98-101.

BALL, JOHN, b. ca. 1585, d. Concord, Mass., 1 November 1655. Stone, pp. 53-58; Thompson, pp. 108-9, et al.

BALLARD, JOHN, d. Portsmouth, N.H., before 1700. EB, pp. 79-80.

BALLARD, WILLIAM, b. ca. 1603, d. Lynn, Mass., between 13 March 1638/9 and 6 June 1639. GM2 I:146-51; AL, pp. 68-69; TAG 72:135-36 (note); NEHGR 146:107-29 (three generation study of descendants of Sherebiah[3] (John[2])); TEG 16:71-77.

BALLARD, WILLIAM, b. ca. 1617, d. Andover, Mass., 10 July 1689. MBT #820.

BANBRIDGE, GUY, b. ca. 1595, d. Cambridge, Mass., April 1645. GM2 I: 151-53.

BANCROFT, THOMAS, b. ca. 1625, d. Lynn, Mass., 19 August 1691. TEG 19:211-18, 20:34-43.

BANE, LEWIS, d. York, Me., 7 April 1677. EB, pp. 80-83.

BANGS, EDWARD, b. ca. 1591, d. Eastham, Mass., between 19 October 1677 and 5 March 1677/8. GMB I:86-91; PM, pp. 23-29; Croll, 132; Brewer, pp. 329-30.

BANISTER, CHRISTOPHER, b. ca. 1636, d. Marlborough, Mass., 30 March 1678. Lyon, pp. 171-78; Sex, pp. 99-100, et al.

BANKS, JOHN, b. ca. 1631, d. Chelmsford, Mass., July 1683. Kempton4, pp. 61-63.

BANNING, JOHN, b. ca. 1640s, d. Lyme, Conn., October 1717. CN 27:388-91; NEHGR 153:323-39.

BARBER, MOSES, b. ca. 1652, d. So. Kingstown, R.I., between 15 April 1728 and 13 December 1733. His children by second wife Susanna (West) continued in Soule for three generations; Samuel[2]'s wife's identity discussed at RIR 17:43-45; Lois J. (Barber) Schroeder, *Moses Barber of South Kingstown, R.I., and Many Descendants 1642-1984* (Decorah, IA: Anundsen Publishing, Co., 1984). Reviews: RIR 10:79-80, TAG 60:127-28.

BARBER, THOMAS, b. 1612, d. Windsor, Conn., 11 September 1662. GM2 I:154-57; AL, pp. 69-70; TAG 71:111-12 (English origins); Donald S.

Barber, *The Connecticut Barbers: A Genealogy of the Descendants of Thomas Barber of Windsor, Connecticut* (Utica, KY: McDowell Publications, 2001, 2nd edition). Reviews: CN 25:449-450.

BARDEN, JAMES, b. 1686, d. Walpole, Mass., 23 December 1745. Kempton4, pp. 67-85, including English origins.

BAREFOOT, WALTER, d. Newcastle, N.H., between 3 and 8 October 1688. NEA 6:1:48-49.

BARKER, FRANCIS, d. Concord, Mass., before 24 October 1655. Kempton3, pp. 57-72.

BARKER, RICHARD, d. Andover, Mass., shortly after 27 April 1688. TEG 20:164-68.

BARKER, ROBERT, b. ca. 1616, d. Duxbury, Mass., between 18 February 1689 and 14 March 1691/2. GMB I:92-7; PM, pp. 29-34.

BARLOW, JOHN, b. ca.1600, d. Fairfield, Conn., before 9 June 1674. CN 25:549-51.

BARNABY, JAMES, d. Plymouth, Mass., before 30 October 1677. MF18, three generations all lines; Bartlett.

BARNARD, JOHN, b. ca. 1607, d. Watertown, Mass., June 1646. GM2 I:161-66.

BARNARD, THOMAS, b. ca. 1612, d. Amesbury, Mass., before October 1677. Stone, pp. 59-64; EB, pp. 83-85; NEXUS 6:146-48; TEG 8:29-38.

BARNES, JOHN, b. ca. 1608, d. Plymouth, Mass., between 6 March 1667/8 and 30 August 1671. GMB I:97-103; PM, pp. 35-42; Jonathan[3-2] and William[3] (Jonathan[2]) at Brewster4, pp. 19-21 and 24-28.

BARNES, MARY, d. Hartford, Conn., ca. January 1663. LENE, pp. 33-41; CN 13:4-10.

BARNES, THOMAS, b. ca. 1602, d. Hingham, Mass., 29 November 1672. Angell, pp. 195-208; Johnson, pp. 34-36.

BARNES, THOMAS, b. ca. 1613, d. Middletown, Conn., 1693. Jessup, pp. 156-58.

BARNES, THOMAS, b. ca. 1615, d. Farmington, Conn., 9 June 1688. Frederic Wayne and Edna Cleo (Bauer) Barnes, *Thomas Barnes Hartford, Connecticut: 14 Generations* (Baltimore, MD: Gateway Press, 2001). Reviews: CN 28:407, 35:447, MQ 62:134.

BARNES, WILLIAM, b. ca. 1610, d. Amesbury, Mass., 14 March 1697/8. 50Imm, pp. 9-12; Stevens, 31; MBT #942.

BARNEY, JACOB, b. ca. 1601, d. Salem, Mass., 28 April 1673. GMB I:104-8; 31Imm, pp. 19-25, including English origins; Eugene Dimon Preston, *Genealogy of the Barney Family in America* (Springfield, VA: Barney Family Historical Association, 1990). Reviews: NYGBR 122:183.

BARRON, ELLIS, b. ca. 1610, d. Watertown, Mass., 30 October 1676. Kempton, pp. 119-31; Freeman, pp. 477-527; Lyon, pp. 178-81.

BARROW, JOHN, b. ca. 1609, d. Plymouth, Mass., 14 February 1691/2. EB, pp. 85-91; TAG 80:53-55 (daughter Deborah).

BARROW, ROBERT, d. Plymouth, Mass., between 9 and 19 December 1707. EB, pp. 85-91 with possible parentage.

BARSHAM, WILLIAM, b. ca. 1610, d. Watertown, Mass., 3 or 13 July 1684. GMB I:108-11.

BARSTOW, GEORGE, b. ca. 1614, d. Cambridge, Mass., 18 March 1652/3. GM2 I:167-70.

BARSTOW, MICHAEL, b. ca. 1600, d. Watertown, Mass., between 30 October 1674 and 13 May 1676. GM2 I:171-74; Thompson, pp. 44-50, et al.; NYGBR 120:1-9, 98-101, 142-47, 229-36, 121:96-101 (notes on English origins); NEHGR 146:230-34 (wives' identities).

BARSTOW, WILLIAM, b. ca. 1612, d. Dedham, Mass., 1 January 1668/9. GM2 I:174-180; Lyon, pp. 182-85.

BARTHOLOMEW, WILLIAM, b. ca. 1603, d. Charlestown, Mass., 18 January 1680/1. GM2 I:180-6.

BARTLETT, HENRY, b. ca. 1654, d. Marlborough, Mass., after 1718. Kempton3, pp. 1-31.

BARTLETT, RICHARD, b. ca. 1575, d. Newbury, Mass., 1647. CN 18:738-41.

BARTLETT, ROBERT, b. ca. 1604, d. Plymouth, Mass., between 19 September and 29 October 1676. MF18, four generations all lines; Bartlett; GMB I:112-17; PM, pp. 42-48; Crosby II:342-350; MJ 18:11-13.

BARTLETT, ROBERT, b. ca. 1612, d. Northampton, Mass., 14 March 1675/6. GMB I:117-20.

BARTLETT, THOMAS, b. ca. 1605, d. Watertown, Mass., 26 April 1654. GMB I:120-22.

Bartoll, John, b. 1601, d. Marblehead, Mass., before 1 October 1664. MJ 18:13-16.

Barton, Rufus, b. ca. 1615, d. Warwick, R.I., 1648. Johnson, pp. 36-37.

Bartram, William, d. Swansea, Mass., between 10 April 1688 and 19 November 1690. NEHGR 149:230-43 (daughter Elizabeth); TEG 6:178-85.

Bascom, Thomas, b. ca. 1605, d. Northampton, Mass., 9 May 1682. GM2 I:186-88; JPG I:41-47, including English and French ancestry; CN 28:186-88; MJ 1:21-22, 3:1-4, 4:9-23, 19:6-8.

Basford, Jacob, Hampton, N.H., d. ca. 1735. Davis I:68-72 [Nicholas Davis].

Bass, Samuel, b. ca. 1600, d. Braintree, Mass., 30 December 1694. GMB I:122-27; son John[2] in MF16, four generations all lines; JPG II:340-46.

Bassett, John, d. New Haven, Conn., 1652. NEA 5:2:44-45, 53 (DNA Study).

Bassett, Thomas, b. ca. 1598, d. Fairfield, Conn., before 14 January 1669/70. GM2 I:188-90; NEA 5:2:44-45, 53 (DNA Study).

Bassett, William, b. 1624, d. Lynn, Mass., 31 March 1703. GM2 I:190-95; NEA 5:2:44-45, 53 (DNA Study); English ancestry of his parents at TAG 79:181-83. Daughter Elizabeth[2] married John Proctor for whom see LENE, pp. 83-84; Johnson, pp. 37-39; TEG 18:28-39.

Bassett, William, b. ca. 1600, d. Bridgewater, Mass., between 3 April and 12 May 1667. GMB I:127-30; PM, pp. 48-52; NEA 5:2:44-45, 53 (DNA Study); Johnson, pp. 39-40; AL, pp. 70-72.

Bassett, William, d. New Haven, Conn., 1684. NEA 5:2:44-45, 53 (DNA Study).

Batchelder see also Bachelor or Bachiler

Batchelder, John, b. ca. 1610, d. Salem, Mass., 13 November 1675. Chase, pp. 71-81, including English origins.

Bate, Clement, b. 1594/5, d. Hingham, Mass., 17 September 1671. GM2 I:195-98.

Bate, James, b. 1582, d. Dorchester, Mass., between 26 November 1655 and 8 January 1655/6. GM2 I:198-200; Pond, 234-37.

Bateman, William, b. 1582, d. Fairfield, Conn., 1658. Lyon, pp. 185-86.

BATES, EDWARD, b. 1606, d. Weymouth, Mass., 25 March 1686. EB, pp. 92-93; TAG 65:33-43, 89-96 (English origins).

BATES, EDWARD, b. ca. 1616, d. Boston, Mass., between 28 April 1644 and 7 November 1645. GMB I:131-32.

BATT, CHRISTOPHER, b. 1601, d. Boston, Mass., 10 August 1661. Additions to English ancestry at TG 17:86-95; Davis I:73-86 [Abel Lunt], including English origins. Wife Anne (Baynton)'s ancestry given at Davis I:89-135 [Abel Lunt]. Their St. Barbe ancestry given at Davis III:369-76 [Abel Lunt]. Wife Anne's Weare alias Browne ancestry given at Davis III:596-600 [Abel Lunt]. His royal line at PA, p. 62; RD600, p. 407; MCA, p. 49. Anne's royal line at RD600, pp. 270-72; PA, p. 70; MCA, p. 53; TAG 79:85-99 (new royal line).

BATT, NICHOLAS, b. ca. 1608, d. Newbury, Mass., 6 December 1677. GM2 I:200-4.

BATTER, EDMUND, b. ca. 1609, d. Salem, Mass., 29 July 1685. GM2 I:204-13.

BATTLES, EDWARD, b. ca. 1685, d. Hingham, Mass., between 22 April 1758 and 13 April 1759. Kempton, pp. 133-142.

BAUDOUIN SEE BOWDOIN

BAULSTON, WILLIAM, b. ca. 1605, d. Portsmouth, R.I., after 11 March 1677/8. GMB I:133-37; AL, pp. 75-76; MJ 19:8-11.

BAXTER, GREGORY, b. ca. 1607, d. Braintree, Mass., 21 June 1659. GMB I:137-39.

BAXTER, NICHOLAS, d. Boston, Mass., ca. 1680. EB, pp. 98-99.

BAXTER, THOMAS, b. ca. 1653, d. Yarmouth, Mass., 22 June 1713. Howland1, four generations all lines; NGSQ 75:51-54.

BEAL, JOHN, d. Hingham, Mass., 1 April 1688. Stone, pp. 65-70, including clues to English origins.

BEALE, THOMAS, b. 1599, d. Cambridge, Mass., 7 September 1661. GM2 I:214-17; Cameos, pp. 195-98.

BEALE, WILLIAM, b. ca. 1629, d. Marblehead, Mass., after 4 January 1693/4. Sex, pp. 61-70, et al.

BEAMON, GAMALIEL, b. ca. 1623, d. Dorchester, Mass., 23 March 1678/9. GM2 I:217-19.

BEAMON, JOHN, b. ca. 1612, d. Salem, Mass., before July 1647. GM2 I: 219-20.

BEAMON, WILLIAM, b. ca. 1608, d. Saybrook, Conn., 4 February 1698/9. GM2 I:220-22.

BEAMSLEY, WILLIAM, b. ca. 1607, d. Boston, Mass., 29 September 1658. GMB I:139-42; 50Imm, pp. 13-16; MBT #390.

BEARDSLEY, WILLIAM, b. ca. 1605, d. Stratford, Conn., between 28 September 1660 and 6 July 1661. GM2 I:222-27; Johnson, pp. 40-42.

BEARSE, AUSTIN (AUGUSTINE), b. ca. 1618, d. Barnstable, Mass., between 1686 and 1697. Croll, 154.

BECK, ALEXANDER, b. ca. 1613, d. Boston, Mass., between 31 March 1668 and 26 October 1674. GMB I:143-45.

BECK, HENRY, b. ca. 1617, d. Portsmouth, N.H., after 13 March 1693/4. GM2 I:228-30.

BECKLEY, DANIEL, Cambridge, Mass., fl. 1660s. Sex, pp. 120-23.

BECKWITH, MATTHEW, b. ca. 1612, d. New London, Conn., 21 October 1680. Angell, pp. 223-41.

BEECHER, JOHN, b. ca. 1590, of New Haven, Conn., d. New England 1637/8. TAG 79:28-33 (English origins).

BEERE, HENRY, b. ca. 1638, d. Providence, R.I., 11 June 1691. RF2, four generations all lines; TAG 65:193-99 (Henry[2]); NEHGR 152:56-68.

BEERS, RICHARD, of Watertown, Mass., d. Squakeag, Mass., 4 September 1675. Thompson, pp. 44-50, 151-52, et al.

BELCHER, EDWARD, b. ca. 1600, d. Boston, Mass., between 17 October 1670 and 17 March 1672/3. GMB I:149-51.

BELCHER, GREGORY, b. 1606, d. Braintree, Mass., 25 November 1674. Spooner.

BELCHER, JEREMY, b. ca. 1614, d. Ipswich, Mass., between 28 July 1674 and 30 September 1690. GM2 I:231-37.

BELDEN, RICHARD, b. ca. 1594, d.Wethersfield, Conn., August 1655. Lyon, pp. 187-91; TAG 76:20-28, 122-28 (English origins).

BELDEN, WILLIAM, b. 1609, d. Wethersfield, Conn., ca. 27 March 1655. TAG 76:20-28, 122-28 (possible English origins).

BELKNAP, ABRAHAM, b. 1589/90, d. Lynn, Mass., September 1643. Chase, pp. 83-90, including English origins; EB, pp. 99-102; 50Imm, pp. 17-36; MBT #1900.

BELL, JAMES, b. ca. 1633, d. Taunton, Mass., May 1676. Kempton4, pp. 88-94.

BELL, THOMAS, b. ca. 1606, of Roxbury, Mass., d. London, England, 30 April 1672. GM2 I:237-43.

BELL, THOMAS, b. ca. 1610, d. Boston, Mass., 7 June 1655. TAG 74:281-91.

BELLINGHAM, RICHARD, b. ca. 1592, d. Boston, Mass., 7 December 1672. GM2 I:243-50; WRR, pp. 191-93.

BELLOWS, JOHN, b. ca. 1624, d. Marlborough, Mass., 10 January 1683. GM2 I:250-53; EB, pp. 102-4.

BEMIS, JAMES, d. New London, Conn., 1665. Jessup, pp. 170-72.

BEMIS, JOSEPH, b. ca. 1619, d. Watertown, Mass., before 7 Ocotber 1684. Thompson, pp. 184-85, et al.

BENCHLEY, WILLIAM, b. 1685, d. Providence, R.I., after 9 July 1757. NEHGR 142:3-15, 177-95, 281-97, 371-85, 143:52-69, 152-65, 143:361 (origins and five generation study).

BENDALL, EDWARD, b. 1607, of Boston, Mass., d. London, England between March 1657 and 26 January 1660/1. GMB I:151-56.

BENEDICT, THOMAS, b. 1617, d. Wilton, Conn., early 1690. Johnson, pp. 42-44; CA 40:55-63 (single line to Eli[5] and his descendants).

BENHAM, JOHN, b. ca. 1605, d. New Haven, Conn., before 3 January 1661/2. GMB I:156-60; JPG II:32-44; son Joseph[2] at CN 28:556-62.

BENJAMIN, JOHN, b. ca. 1595, d. Watertown, Mass., 14 June 1645. GMB I:160-64; Pond, 278-79; Dancing, pp. 255-84; son Samuel[2] at Thompson, pp. 127-28, 191-92, et al.

BENJAMIN, RICHARD, b. ca. 1616, of Cambridge and Watertown, d. Southold, Long Island after 28 March 1678. GMB I:164-66.

BENNETT, JOHN, b. ca. 1612, d. Marblehead, Mass., before 29 June 1663. GMB I:167-68; MJ 25:80.

BENNETT, SAMUEL, b. ca. 1610, d. Boston or Lynn, Mass., after 18 January 1682/3 and possibly on 28 March 1691. GM2 I:255-60; TEG 17:87-95.

BENNETT, WILLIAM, b. ca. 1604, d. Manchester, Mass., 20 November 1682. Ordway, pp. 139-42; GMB I:168-71; PM, pp. 52-56; Stevens, 66; NEHGR 153:221 (wife's identity established); MJ 25:80-81.

BENSON, HENRY, b. ca. 1670, d. Kittery, Me., after 7 March 1742/3. Richard H. Benson, *The Benson Family of Colonial Massachusetts* (Boston, MA: Newbury Street Press, 2003), pp. 369-404. Reviews: NEHGR 158:393-94.

BENSON, JOHN, b. ca. 1607, d. Hull, Mass., 13 January 1678/9. EB, pp. 47-64; JPG II:347-53; NEHGR 142:269-72, 143:361; Richard H. Benson, *The Benson Family of Colonial Massachusetts* (Boston, MA: Newbury Street Press, 2003). Reviews: NEHGR 158:393-94.

BENT, JOHN, b. ca. 1603, d. Sudbury, Mass., 27 September 1672. Son Joseph[2] at Sex, pp. 58-59, 68-69, et al.

BENTLEY, WILLIAM, b. 1640, d. Kingstown, R.I., 1720. Johnson, p. 45.

BERNON, GABRIEL, b. 1644, d. Providence, R.I., 1 February 1735/6. RIR 11:69-70; Scott Campbell Steward and Newbold Le Roy, 3rd, *The Le Roy Family in America 1753-2003* (Boston, MA, and Laconia, NH: the authors, 2003), pp. 6-8. Reviews: NYGBR 135:153.

BERRY, JOHN, b. ca. 1660, d. Middleton, Mass., between 15 March 1734/5 and July 1738. Chase, pp. 91-93.

BERRY, THADDEUS (TEAGUE), b. ca. 1635, d. Boston, Mass., 1718. NEHGR 148:331-41; Mower, pp. 49-51; TEG 8:17-28, 86-95, 132-40, 9:47-48.

BERRY, THOMAS, d. Ipswich, Mass., 1693. Davis I:169 [Bethia Harris].

BESBEECH, THOMAS, b. 1589/90, d. Sudbury, Mass., 9 March 1673/4. GM2 I:263-66.

BESSEY, ANTHONY, b. ca. 1609, d. Sandwich, Mass., between 10 February 1656/7 and 21 May 1657. GM2 I:266-70; EB, pp. 104-10.

BETSCOMBE, RICHARD, b. 1601, of Hingham, Mass., d. England after 1647. GM2 I:271-72; MJ 17:16-18, 26:86-90.

BETTS, JOHN, b. ca. 1594, d. Cambridge, Mass., 21 February 1662/3. GM2 I:273-77; Cameos, pp. 47-54.

BETTS, THOMAS, b. 1615, d. Norwalk, Conn., between 10 May and 4 December 1688. Johnson, pp. 45-48.

BETTS, WILLIAM, b. ca. 1614, of Scituate, Barnstable and Dorchester, Mass., d. Westchester, N.Y. between 12 February 1673/4 and 2 January 1675/6. GM2 I:278-81; TAG 78:37-41.

BIBBLE, JOHN, d. Malden, Mass., July 1653. NEHGR 142:273-74; MJ 19:151-53 (wife); MJ 26:10-12.

BICKNELL, ZACHARY, b. ca. 1590, d. Weymouth, Mass., before 9 March 1636/7. GM2 I:282-83; MJ 18:16-18, 27:1-10.

BIDWELL, RICHARD, b. ca. 1587, d. Windsor, Conn., 25 December 1647. Joan J. Bidwell, *Bidwell Family History 1587-1982* (Baltimore, MD: Gateway Press, 1984). Reviews: CN 16:699.

BIGELOW, JOHN, b. 1617/8, d. Watertown, Mass., 14 July 1703. Mower, pp. 55-66; MBT #402.

BIGG, RACHEL, b. 1565, d. Dorchester, Mass., between 17 November 1646 and 30 June 1647. GM2 I:284-89; 50Imm, pp. 37-62; MBT #2162.

BILL, JAMES, b. ca. 1590, d. Boston, Mass., ca. 1638. TAG 60:193-201 (English origins).

BILLINGS, JOHN, b. ca. 1616, d. Kittery, Me., before 6 July 1646. GM2 I: 290-92.

BILLINGS, ROGER, b. 1618, d. Dorchester, Mass., 15 November 1683. AK, pp. 133-34; TAG 74:15-30 (English origins disproved); MJ 19:12-13, 25:12.

BILLINGS, WILLIAM, b. ca. 1629, d. Stonington, Conn., 16 March 1712/3. TAG 74:15-30 (English origins disproved).

BILLINGTON, JOHN, *Mayflower* passenger, b. ca. 1580, d. Plymouth, Mass., 30 September 1630. MF5, five generations, all lines; MF21, five generations all lines; LENE, pp. 5-6; GMB I:173-74; PM, pp. 56-58; son Francis[2] at TG 3:228-48; MQ 68:65-68, 71:157-60.

BINGHAM, THOMAS, b. 1642, d. Windham, Conn., 16 January 1730. Donna Bingham Munger, *The Bingham Family in the United States: The Descendants of Thomas Bingham of Connecticut* (New York, NY: The Bingham Association, 1996). Reviews: NYGBR 128:74.

BIRCHARD, THOMAS, b. 1595, d. Norwich, Conn., between 9 May 1683 and 16 September 1684. GM2 I:293-98; Johnson, pp. 48-50.

BIRD, THOMAS, d. Farmington, Conn., before 10 August 1662. Lyon, pp. 191-93.

BIRDSALL, HENRY, b. ca. 1585, d. Salem, Mass., before 17 November 1651. GM2 I:301-2; EB, pp. 110-12.

BISCOE, NATHANIEL, of Watertown, Mass., returned to England in 1651. Thompson, pp. 60-61, 68-71, et al.

BISHOP, EDWARD, d. Salem, Mass., after 21 January 1694/5. Wife Bridget, a Salem witch victim. See TAG 57:129-38, 58:163; LENE, pp. 64-69; TAG 64:207 (her origins).

BISHOP, JOHN, b. 1610, d. Stamford, Conn., between 16 November and 31 December 1694. CA 23:169-70 (English origins).

BISHOP, JOHN, b. ca. 1604, d. Guilford, Conn., February 1661, Goodman, pp. 71-74, Pond, 233.

BISHOP, NATHANIEL, b. ca. 1607, d. Boston, Mass., between 10 and 15 June 1687. GM2 I:302-6.

BISHOP, RICHARD, b. ca. 1603, d. Salem, Mass., 30 December 1674. GM2 I:307-10.

BISHOP, RICHARD, d. Plymouth, Mass., before 1640/1. Wife Alice, d. there on 4 October 1648. LENE, pp. 16-17.

BISSELL, JOHN, b. ca. 1591, d. Windsor, Conn., 3 October 1677. Lyon, pp. 193-96.

BISSON, JOSHUA, b. 1652, d. Beverly, Mass., 28 September 1750. TEG 14:112-14.

BITFIELD, SAMUEL, b. 1601/2, d. Boston, Mass., 1 September 1660. TAG 67:236-42 (English origins).

BIXBY, JOSEPH, b. 1621, d. Boxford, Mass., 17 April 1701. 26Imm, pp. 1-33; MBT #324; NEHGR 141:228-43 (English origins).

BLACK, DANIEL, of Topsfield, Mass., NEA 5:2:54-55.

BLACK, JOHN, b. ca. 1591, d. Beverly, Mass., 16 March 1674/5. GMB I:175-77.

BLACK, JOHN, d. Beverly, Mass., 16 March 1675. TEG 14:110-11.

BLACKLEACH, JOHN, b. ca. 1605, d. Wethersfield, Conn., 23 August 1683. GM2 I:313-18; NEHGR 148:7-44, 189 (four generation study).

BLACKLEACH, RICHARD, b. ca. 1654, d. Stratford, Conn., 4 September 1731. NEHGR 148:38-44.

BLACKMAN, ADAM, d. Stratford, Conn., 1666. TAG 74:128-30 (Deliverance[2]); TAG 78:181-85 (English origins).

BLACKSTONE, WILLIAM, b. ca. 1595, d. Boston, Mass., 26 May 1675. GMB I:177-81; RIR 8:51.

BLAISDELL, RALPH, b. ca. 1607, d. Salisbury, Mass., before 24 June 1651. GM2 I:319-323; Davis I:178-185 [Nicholas Davis]; Stowers, pp. 63-66; TAG 66:74 (note).

BLAKE, JASPER, b. ca. 1623, d. Hampton, N.H., 1673. NEHGR 154:259-89 (English origins); Aaron[3] (Timothy[2]) at NHGR 20:57-59; Carlton E. Blake, *Descendants of Jasper Blake Emigrant from England to Hampton, N.H., ca. 1643, 1649-1979* (Baltimore, MD: Gateway Press, 1980). Reviews: NGSQ 71:221.

BLAKE, WILLIAM, b. 1594, d. Dorchester, Mass., 25 October 1663. 31Imm, pp. 26-27, including English origins; TAG 74:15-30 (English origins disproved); NEHGR 158:110-11 (John[3] James[2]); MJ 12:72-80, 13:79-81, 17:19-22, 25:12-13, 26:12-13.

BLAKEMAN SEE BLACKMAN

BLANCHARD, THOMAS, d. Charlestown, Mass., 21 May 1654. Goodman, pp. 81-85, including English origins; EB, pp. 112-16; son Thomas[2]'s wife at NEHGR 140:312-16.

BLAND ALIAS SMITH, JOHN, b. ca. 1585, d. Edgartown, Mass., before 6 January 1668. Wife Joanna at Doctors, pp. 9-10; TAG 61:18-31.

BLANEY, JOHN, b. ca. 1630, d. Lynn or Salem, Mass., ca. 1714. TEG 16:23-29, 78-87.

BLATCHLEY, THOMAS, b. ca. 1615, d. Boston, Mass., before 30 January 1674. Shirley Hathaway Stebbings, *Blatchley Physicians and Pioneers: A Family History of Descendants of Thomas Blatchley 1635-1929* (Baltimore, MD: Gateway Press, 1983). Reviews: CN 16:512.

BLESSING SEE VERMAYES

BLINMAN, RICHARD, b. ca. 1615, of Marshfield, Mass., and New London, Conn., d. Bristol, England between 13 April and 26 July 1687. TG 4:173-186.

BLINN, PETER, b. ca. 1641, d. Wethersfield, Conn., 7 March 1724/5. NEHGR 143:303-24 (three generation study).

BLISS, GEORGE, b. ca. 1591, d. Newport, R.I., 31 August 1667. Aaron Tyler Bliss, *Genealogy of the Bliss Family in America* (Midland, MI: the author, 1982). Reviews: CN 16:157-58, TAG 59:25-27, NGSQ 71:221-22.

BLISS, THOMAS, b. ca. 1588, d. Rehoboth, Mass., between 7 and 21 October 1647. NEHGR 151:31-37 (Jonathan[2]); Aaron Tyler Bliss, *Genealogy of the Bliss Family in America* (Midland, MI: the author, 1982). Reviews: CN 16:157-58, TAG 59:25-27, NGSQ 71:221-22.

BLISS, THOMAS, b. ca. 1590, d. Hartford, Conn., ca. 1650-1. Pond, 239-40; Jessup, pp. 173-79; Johnson, pp. 50-54; AL, pp. 91-95; TAG 60:202 (marriage); Aaron Tyler Bliss, *Genealogy of the Bliss Family in America* (Midland, MI: the author, 1982). Reviews: CN 16:157-58, TAG 59:25-27, NGSQ 71:221-22.

BLIVEN, EDWARD, b. 1674, d. Westerly, R.I., 1718. Earl P. Crandall, *Five Families of Charlestown, R.I.* (Salem, MA: Higginson Book Co., 1993). Reviews: RIR 19:100-1.

BLODGETT, THOMAS, b. ca. 1605, d. Cambridge, Mass., between 10 August 1641 and 10 December 1642. GM2 I:324-26.

BLOIS, EDMUND, b. ca. 1588, d. Watertown, Mass., between 18 November 1679 and 1 March 1680/1. GM2 I:326-29; EB, pp. 116-19.

BLOOMFIELD, THOMAS, d. Newbury, Mass., 1639. Freeman, pp. 529-576.

BLOOMFIELD, WILLIAM, b. ca. 1605, d. Newtown, Conn., between 1 March 1666/7 and 26 February 1667/8. GM2 I:329-33.

BLOSSOM, THOMAS, b. ca. 1580, d. Plymouth, Mass., before 25 March 1633. GMB I:182-84; PM, p. 58-60; TAG 63:65-77, 238-46, 64:23-31 (a five generation study with English origins); TAG 64:113-18; MQ 59:10-15.

BLOTT, ROBERT, b. ca. 1584, d. Boston, Mass., between 27 March and 22 August 1665. GM2 I:334-38; 31Imm, pp. 38-43; EB, pp. 119-21; Nichols, p. 176; Johnson, pp. 54-55; JPG I:48-52; Lyon, pp. 196-99; TAG 67:65-68 (English origins).

BLOWER, THOMAS, b. 1587, d. Boston, Mass., before 9 September 1639. GM2 I:338-40; MBT #1514; children's baptisms at TAG 56:99-100; TAG 65:241-47 (Strutt ancestry of wife).

BOADEN, AMBROSE, b. ca. 1589, d. Scarborough, Me., October 1675. MJ 19:13-14.

BOLLES, JOSEPH, b. 1608, d. Wells, Me., 1678. RD600, pp. 267-69; PA, p. 125; MCA, p. 107. NEXUS 11:104-8 (notable descendants).

BOLSTER, ISAAC, b. ca. 1690, d. Uxbridge, Mass., 28 April 1753. Kempton, pp. 163-67.

BOND, JOHN, d. Beverly Mass., before 23 June 1691. NEHGR 137:18-33.

BOND, JOHN, d. Haverhill, Mass., 3 December 1674. Stevens, 10.

BONHAM, NICHOLAS, b. ca. 1630, d. Piscataway, N.J., 20 July 1684. MF4, three generations all lines.

BONNEY, THOMAS, b. ca. 1614, d. Duxbury, Mass., between 2 January 1688/9 and 1 May 1693. GM2 I:340-43; Richard Whiting Bonney, *The Thomas Bonney Genealogy: The Descendants of Thomas Bonney Who Came from Sandwich, England, to Duxbury, Mass., in the "Hercules" in 1634* (n.p., the author, 1984). Reviews: CN 18:542, NEHGR 142:305.

BONUM, GEORGE, b. ca. 1618, d. Plymouth, Mass., 28 November 1704. EB, pp. 121-22.

BONYTHON, RICHARD, b. 1580, d. Saco, Me., before 29 June 1654. GM2 I:343-47; MJ 19:14-15.

BOOMER, MATTHEW, d. Freetown, R.I., between 17 October 1688 and 25 June 1690. TAG 60:77-79.

BOONE, NICHOLAS, b. ca. 1645, d. Boston, Mass., between 1679 and 1697. Johnson, pp. 55-57.

BOOSEY, JAMES, b. ca. 1604, d. Wethersfield, Conn., 22 June 1649. GM2 I:347-350.

BOOTEMAN SEE BUTMAN

BOOTH, JOHN, b. ca. 1634, of Scituate, Mass., d. Duxbury, Mass., between 2 August 1704 and 21 October 1709. EB, pp. 122-25; TAG 74:175-82 (Benjamin[2]); NEHGR 159:220-34.

BOOTH, RICHARD, b. ca. 1607/8, d. Stratford, Conn., after 1688. Pond, 249; CN 37:362-75 (Johanna[3] Ephraim[2]).

BORDEN, JOHN, b. 1606/7, d. Watertown, Mass., ca. 1635-6. GM2 I: 350-51.

BORDEN, RICHARD, b. 1595/6, d. Portsmouth, R.I., 25 May 1671. Jessup, pp. 180-201, including English origins; Johnson, pp. 57-59; AL, pp. 95-

99, including English ancestry; ancestry of wife Joan (Fowle) at AL, pp. 256-58.

BOREMAN, THOMAS, b. 1601, d. Ipswich, Mass., between 3 May and 19 June 1673. GM2 I:352-55.

BOSWORTH, EDWARD, b. ca. 1586, d. Boston Harbor, Mass., 1634. GM2 I:356-57; AL, pp. 101-3; sons Benjamin[2] and Nathaniel[2] at NEHGR 142:274-79, 394.

BOSWORTH, JONATHAN, b. ca. 1613, d. Rehoboth, Mass., 3 January 1687/8. GMB I:187-91, son of Edward 1586-1634, above.

BOSWORTH, ZACCHEUS, b. ca. 1612, d. Boston, Mass., 28 July 1655. GMB I:191-93.

BOTFISH, ROBERT, b. ca. 1614, d. Sandwich, Mass., 19 November 165?. GM2 I:357-58.

BOTSFORD, HENRY, b. 1608, of Conn. Samuel[3] (Elnathan[2]) at TAG 59:193-200; NEHGR 141:358 (identification of wife).

BOUDE, GRIMSTONE, b. ca. 1660/1, of Marblehead, Mass., d. Philadelphia, Penn., before April 1716. TG 2:74-114, 6:232-43.

BOUGHTON SEE ALSO BOUTON

BOUGHTON, JOHN, d. Norwalk, Conn., before 1647. Matthew[3] (John[2]) at TAG 65:97-106; TAG 73:33-43, 146-55 (John[4-3-2]).

BOUNDS, THOMAS, b. ca. 1685, d. Rehoboth, Mass., after 1720. TAG 57:205-7.

BOURNE, JARED, b. ca. 1614, d. Swansea, Mass., after 9 February 1673/4. GM2 I:360-63.

BOURNE, NEHEMIAH, of Boston, Mass. NEHGR 159:235-36 (marriage).

BOURNE, RICHARD, d. Sandwich, Mass., before 18 September 1682. Crosby II:351-56; MJ 19:16.

BOURNE, THOMAS, b. ca. 1581, d. Marshfield, Mass., May 1664. Spooner; EB, pp. 125-26; Johnson, pp. 60-61.

BOUTON SEE ALSO BOUGHTON

BOUTON, JOHN, d. Danbury, Conn., 1689. Nichols, p. 85.

BOWDEN, ABRAHAM, b. ca. 1680, d. York, Me., between 10 July and 7 August 1751. MG 9:18-22.

BOWDEN, RICHARD, Boston, Mass., d. before 1684. Davis I:200-1 [Nicholas Davis].

BOWDITCH, WILLIAM, b. 1639, d. Salem, Mass., before 12 October 1681. Chase, pp. 95-105, including English origins; NGSQ 69:278-79.

BOWDOIN, PIERRE, d. Boston, Mass., 1704. Russell E. Train, *The Bowdoin Family: Including Some Account of the Belgrave, Grinnell, Hamilton, Howland, Irving, Kingsford, Ligon, Means, Morris, and Sullivan Families* (Washington, DC: the author, 2000). Reviews: MG 22:183.

BOWEN, GRIFFITH, of Boston, Mass., d. London, England, ca. 1675. RD600, pp. 485-86. CN 19:588-96; wife Margaret (Fleming), RD600, pp. 485-86; CN 19:335-41; TAG 76:263-78.

BOWEN, RICHARD, b. ca. 1590, d. Rehoboth, Mass., February 1674/5. Mower, pp. 69-83; AL, pp. 103-118; TAG 76:263-78 (English origins).

BOWER, GEORGE, b. ca. 1590, d. Cambridge, Mass., between 8 November and 30 December 1656. Croll, 102; son Benanuel at Cameos, pp. 173-81.

BOWERMAN, THOMAS, d. Barnstable, Mass., between 9 May and 4 June 1663. Makepeace, pp. 87-95; TAG 77:302-12 (daughter Hannah).

BOWERS, GEORGE, d. Cambridge, Mass., between 8 November and 30 December 1656. Makepeace, pp. 97-111.

BOWMAN, NATHANIEL, b. ca. 1605, d. Cambridge, Mass., 26 January 1681/2. GMB I:193-96.

BOWNE, WILLIAM, b. ca. 1600, of Salem, Mass., d. Middletown, N.J., before 21 January 1677/8. GM2 I:363-66.

BOYCE, JOSEPH, b. ca. 1609, d. Salem, Mass., between 4 November 1684 and 18 February 1694/5. Chase, pp. 107-13; TAG 73:23-32; TAG 79:309-15 (additional Fenn ancestry).

BOYDEN, THOMAS, b. ca. 1613, d. Medfield, Mass., after 15 April 1678. GM2 I:366-68; Lyon, pp. 249-52; son Thomas[2] at Sex, pp. 123-25.

BOYES, JAMES, b. before 1670, d. Londonderry, N.H., 8 April 1724. Angell, pp. 250-57.

BOYES, JOSEPH, b. before 1704, d. Londonderry, N.H., between 11 November 1779 and 29 March 1780. Angell, pp. 243-48.

BOYLSTON, THOMAS, b. 1614/5, d. Watertown, Mass., between 26 July 1652 and 12 March 1654/5. GM2 I:368-72; Goodman, pp. 87-93, including English origins.

BRACKENBURY, RICHARD, b. ca. 1600, d. Beverly, Mass., between 20 March 1683/4 and 1 April 1684. GMB I:196-99.

BRACKENBURY, WILLIAM, b. ca. 1602, d. Malden, Mass., August 1668. GMB I:199-202.

BRACKETT, PETER, b. ca. 1608, d. Boston, Mass., ca. July 1688. NEHGR 155:279-94 (English origins, children, and a focus on Sarah[2]).

BRACKETT, RICHARD, b. 1610, d. Braintree, Mass., 3 March 1690. GMB I:203-6; granddaughter Hannah[3] (John[2]) at Cameos, pp. 285-88; 50Imm, pp. 63-116; MBT #756; NEHGR 157:199-208 (Josiah[2]).

BRACY SEE BRESSEY

BRADBURY, THOMAS, b. 1610/1, d. Salisbury, Mass., 16 March 1694/5. GM2 I:375-81; RD600, pp. 560-61; EB, pp. 127-29; 50Imm, pp. 117-20; MBT #922; TAG 56:13-23 (Abbott ancestry); TAG 57:35-44, 55-56 (Cotton ancestry); TAG 57:97-99 (additions to ancestry); TAG 58:168-80 (Heigham ancestry); further clues to English ancestry at NEHGR 153:259-77; full ancestry at John Brooks Threlfall, *The Ancestry of Thomas Bradbury (1611-1695) and His Wife Mary (Perkins) Bradbury (1615-1700) of Salisbury, Massachusetts* (Madison, WI: the author, 1995, 2nd edition). Reviews: TAG 64:58-59, NEHGR 144:268-69.

BRADFORD, ROBERT b. ca. 1626, d. Beverly, Mass., 13 January 1706/7. Davis I:212-16 [Bethia Harris].

BRADFORD, ROBERT, d. Boston, Mass., before 28 December 1680. MF22, Appendix, MD 53:1-18, 97-115.

BRADFORD, WILLIAM, *Mayflower* passenger, b. 1589/90, d. Plymouth, Mass., 9 May 1657. MF22, five generations all lines; NEA 2:4:24-26; GMB I:207-9; PM, pp. 62-66. Hannah[3] (William[2]) at Doctors, pp. 73; NEHGR 155:245-50 (William[2]'s wife); NEQ 65:389-421; MQ 57:140-43, 244-47; MQ 61:110-18 (wife Dorothy May's origins); MQ 62:6-19; MQ 65:277; Douglas Anderson, *William Bradford's Books: "Of Plimmoth Plantation" and the Printed Word* (Baltimore, MD: Johns Hopkins University Press, 2003). Reviews: NEQ 77:500-3.

BRADISH, ROBERT, b. ca. 1607, d. Boston, Mass., between 12 May 1657 and 8 September 1659. GM2 I:381-84; Nichols, pp. 48-49; Cameos, pp. 155-

59; TAG 75:47-50, TAG 78:96-102 (James[2]); Juanita Bradish Curley, *A Genealogy & History of Robert Bradish in America* (Northville, MI: Unicorn Press, 2000), includes possible English origins. Reviews: NYGBR 132:311, NGSQ 90:74-75.

BRADLEY, DANIEL, b. ca. 1615, d. Haverhill, Mass., 13 August 1689. Stevens, 35.

BRADLEY, PETER, d. New London, Conn., 3 April 1662. Brewster, two generations all lines; Brewster3, three generations all lines.

BRADSTREET, HUMPHREY, b. ca. 1594, d. Ipswich, Mass., between 21 July and 6 September 1655. GM2 I:384-88.

BRADSTREET, SIMON, b. 1603/4, d. Salem, Mass., 28 March 1696/7. RF1, four generations in all lines; GBM I:209-15; Dudley[2]'s wife's identity at NEHGR 139:139-142; NEQ 71:517-42 (wife Anne).

BRAGG, EDWARD, d. Ipswich, Mass., before 6 September 1708. Wife Sarah at NEHGR 141:19-21.

BRANCH, JOHN, b. ca. 1627, d. Marshfield, Mass., 7 May 1711. Jessup, pp. 207-12, including English origins.

BRANKER, JOHN, b. ca. 1601, d. Windsor, Conn., 27 May 1662. GMB I:215-17; JIC, pp. 59-69 (English origins of him and his wife); MJ 26:13-15.

BRATTLE, THOMAS, b. ca. 1624, d. Boston, Mass., before 12 April 1683. NEQ 63:584-600 (Thomas[2]).

BRAWNE, JOHN, b. ca. 1605, d. York, Me., after 26 October 1668. English origins at NHGR 18:1-6.

BRAWNE, MICHAEL, b. ca. 1609, d. N.H., after 1666. English origins at NHGR 18:1-6.

BRAYTON, FRANCIS, b. ca. 1612, d. Little Compton, R.I., before 5 September 1692. EB, pp. 129-31.

BRECK, EDWARD, b. ca. 1595, d. Dorchester, Mass., 2 November 1662. Mower, pp. 85-97.

BREED, ALLEN, b. ca. 1599, d. Lynn, Mass., 17 March 1690/1. TEG 11:196-203, 12:30-37, 100-7, 157-67, 211-20, 13:19, 40-50, 97-104, 166, 229-30.

BREED, ALLEN, b. ca. 1600, d. Lynn, Mass., 17 March 1690/1. Chase, pp. 115-24, including possible English origins.

BRENTON, WILLIAM, b. ca. 1610, d. Taunton, Mass., between 25 September and 13 November 1674. GMB I:218-24; RIR 15:33; TAG 59:84-89.

BRESSEY, THOMAS, b. 1601, d. New Haven, Conn., before 1649. GM2 I:372-75; Davis I:202-11 [Sarah Stone]. Wife Phebe Bisby's ancestry given at Davis I:170-77 [Sarah Stone]. His royal line at RD600, pp. 403-4; PA, p. 154; MCA, p. 133; TG 7/8:132-36.

BREWER, CRISPUS, b. ca. 1625, d. Lynn, Mass., between 10 December 1706 and 23 January 1707. TEG 19:77-80.

BREWER, DANIEL, b. ca. 1600, d. Roxbury, Mass., 28 March 1646. GMB I:225-27.

BREWER, JOHN, b. ca. 1620, d. Sudbury, Mass., 1684. Johnson, pp. 61-62.

BREWER, THOMAS, b. ca. 1655, d. Glastonbury, Conn., between 27 December 1742 and March 1743. Brewer, pp. 1-294.

BREWSTER, NATHANIEL, b. 1620, d. Brookhaven, Long Island, 18 December 1690. First wife (surnamed Reymes) at RD600, pp. 344-45. Second wife Sarah Ludlow, daughter of Roger (see Ludlow); MJ 19:17-19.

BREWSTER, WILLIAM, *Mayflower* passenger, b. ca. 1566/7, d. Plymouth, Mass., 10 April 1644. Brewster, four generations all lines; fifth generation in Brewster2 and Brewster3; GMB I:227-30; PM, pp. 66-70; NEA 1:3:36-41; NEA 4:2:55-56, 59; Croll, 106; Spooner; Lucretia (Oldham), wife of Jonathan² at Doctors, pp. 21-23; MQ 51:161-67, 52:6-16, 57-63 (Jonathan²); MQ 56:218-21, 324-26, 57:24-28; Mary B. Sherwood, *Pilgrim: A Biography of William Brewster* (Falls Church, VA: Great Oak Press, 1982).

BRIANT, CORNELIUS, b. before 1717, d. Smithfield, R.I., after 14 September 1738. Angell, pp. 261-63.

BRIAR, RICHARD, fl. 1670s in Newbury and Ipswich, Mass. Brewer, p. 331.

BRIDGE, JOHN, b. ca. 1593, d. Cambridge, Mass., 15 April 1665. GM2 I:393-97.

BRIDGEN, THOMAS, b. ca. 1604, d. Charlestown, Mass., 20 June 1668. GM2 I:397-400.

BRIDGES, EDMUND, b. ca. 1612, d. Ipswich, Mass., 13 January 1684/5. GM2 I:389-92; son Obadiah² at Sex, pp. 60-61, 69.

BRIDGES, WILLIAM, b. ca. 1615, d. Charlestown, Mass., before 6 February 1648/9. GMB I:231-34; PM, pp. 70-75.

BRIDGMAN, JAMES, d. Northampton, Mass., 17 March 1676. JPG I:53-67.

BRIGGS, CLEMENT, b. ca. 1600, d. Weymouth, Mass., before 23 February 1648/9. GMB I:234-37; PM, pp. 76-79.

BRIGGS, JOHN, b. ca. 1615, d. Sandwich, Mass., before 1 June 1641. EB, pp. 131-34; TAG 59:175-79 (English origins).

BRIGGS, RUTH NEE PINION, d. ca. June 1668. LENE, pp. 41-44.

BRIGGS, WILLIAM, b. ca. 1605, d. Lyme, Conn., after 5 February 1680/1. NEHGR 151:87-101.

BRIGHAM, THOMAS, b. ca. 1603, d. Cambridge, Mass., 8 December 1653. GM2 I:401-4.

BRIGHT, HENRY, b. 1602, d. Watertown, Mass., 9 October 1686. Goodman, pp. 95-106, including English origins; GMB I:239-43; Thompson, pp. 110-11, et al.

BRINSDON, ROBERT, b. ca. 1638, d. Boston, Mass., 22 November 1701. TEG 13:110-11.

BRINSMADE, JOHN, b. ca. 1614, d. Roxbury, Mass., 1673. MJ 18:18-20, 25:13-21.

BRITTON, JAMES, b. ca. 1614, d. Boston, Mass., 21 March 1644. LENE, pp. 10-11.

BROCK, HENRY, b. ca. 1590, d. Dedham, Mass., between 22 April 1646 and 19 October 1652. NEHGR 144:124-137 (wife's English origins).

BROCK, PETER, of Newport, R.I., d. St. Iago, West Indies, 15 November 1707. TAG 65:193-99; NEHGR 152:56-68.

BROCKWAY, WOLSTONE, b. ca. 1638, d. Lyme, Conn., before 11 November 1717. NEHGR 151:87-101; Angell, pp. 515-17; TAG 68:160-75; TAG 70:233-38 (daughter Elizabeth).

BROMFIELD, EDWARD, b. 1648/9, d. Boston, Mass., June 1734. RD600, pp. 287-88.

BRONSDON SEE BRINSDON

BRONSON, JOHN, b. 1602, d. Farmington, Conn., November 1680. Goodman, pp. 109-15, including English origins; Pond, 276, including English origins; TAG 71:206-14 (Isaac[2]).

BROOKS, GILBERT, b. ca. 1621, d. Rehoboth, Mass., 13 June 1695. GM2 I:407-11.

BROOKS, THOMAS, d. Concord, Mass., 21 May 1667. MBT #512.

BROOKS, WILLIAM, b. ca. 1615, d. Scituate, Mass., between 7 July 1680 and 24 January 1682/3. GM2 I:412-15.

BROOKS, WILLIAM, d. Deerfield, Mass., 30 December 1688. JPG I:68-71.

BROUGHTON, THOMAS, b. ca. 1613 d. Boston, Mass., 12 November 1700. RD600, pp. 466-68.

BROWN, ABRAHAM, b. 1588, d. Watertown, Mass., between 26 March 1645 and December 1648. Kempton, pp. 169-96, including English origins for him and his wife; GMB I:244-46; TAG 56:24 (a correction on their English origins).

BROWN, ANDREW, b. 1619, Scarborough, ME, d. Boston, Mass., after 1696. Davis I:225-43 [Joseph Waterhouse, Sarah Miller].

BROWN, CHAD, b. ca. 1600, d. Providence, R.I., ca. 1665. NECL, pp. 65-73; CN 13:701-10; TAG 62:193-201.

BROWN, FRANCIS, b. ca. 1610, d. New Haven, Conn., 1668. Nichols, p. 86.

BROWN, FRANCIS, b. ca. 1628, of Stamford, Conn., d. Rye, N.Y., after 1707. CA 36:53-65.

BROWN, GEORGE d. England between 22 August and 8 November 1633. Widow Christian and three sons, Henry, William, and George, all migrate to Salisbury, Mass. Davis I:217-20 [Lydia Harmon]; Stevens, 15.

BROWN, JAMES, b. ca. 1604, d. Salem, Mass., 3 November 1676. GMB I:249-54.

BROWN, JAMES, b. ca. 1615, d. Boston, Mass., between 9 May and 7 August 1651. GMB I:248-49.

BROWN, JAMES, b. ca. 1650, d. Hatfield, Mass., 8 July 1711 or Colchester, Conn., 9 May 1704. JPG I:72-95.

BROWN, JOHN, b. ca. 1591, d. Rehoboth, Mass., 10 April 1662. GM2, I:420-29; NECL, pp. 9-65; AL, pp. 169-72; MQ 49:109-14, 161-67, 50:5-9, 57-61; MQ 57:318-22, 58:16-20, 126-30 (English origins).

BROWN, JOHN, b. ca. 1600, d. Watertown, Mass., June 1636. GMB I:255-57.

BROWN, JOHN, b. ca. 1610, d. Duxbury, Mass., before 4 June 1684. GMB I:257-59; PM, pp. 80-82; NEHGR 140:331-32 (note).

BROWN, JOHN, d. Hampton, N.H., 28 February 1687. Davis I:221 [Sarah Stone].

BROWN, JOHN, d. Ipswich, Mass., 13 September 1677. Davis I:222-24 [Phoebe Tilton].

BROWN, NATHANIEL, b. ca. 1622, d. Middletown, Conn., before 26 August 1658. GM2 I:429-31; RD600, pp. 422-23; PA, p. 653; MCA, p. 750; TAG 60:91.

BROWN, NICHOLAS, d. Portsmouth, R.I., between 16 November and 27 December 1694. NECL, pp. 74-85.

BROWN, NICHOLAS, d. Reading, Mass., ca. 1673. NECL, pp. 85-94, including English origins; TEG 8:178-88.

BROWN, PETER, *Mayflower* Passenger, d. Plymouth, Mass., between 25 March and 28 October 1633. MF7, five generations, all lines; GMB I:259-61; PM, pp. 82-85; TAG 79:161-78 (English origins).

BROWN, RICHARD, b. ca. 1576, d. Charlestown, Mass., between 16 August 1659 and 6 October 1660. GMB I:262-66; Thompson, pp. 42-43, 65-66, et al.

BROWN, RICHARD, b. ca. 1613, d. Newbury, Mass., 26 April 1661. GM2 I:432-35.

BROWN, THOMAS, b. ca. 1606, d. Newbury, Mass., 8 January 1686/7. GM2 I:435-38; EB, pp. 134-35; NEHGR 152:347-52.

BROWN, THOMAS, b. ca. 1628, d. Lynn, Mass., 28 August 1693. TEG 18:222-28.

BROWN, THOMAS, of Sudbury, Concord, Mass., d. Cambridge, Mass., between 23 November 1690 and January 1690/1. Son Boaz[2] at NEHGR 140:317-20.

BROWN, WILLIAM, b. 1586, of Saybrook, Conn., d. Hempstead, N.Y., ca. 1650. EB, pp. 135-37.

BROWN, WILLIAM, b. ca. 1609, d. Salem, Mass., 20 January 1687/8. GM2 I:439-45.

BROWN, WILLIAM, b. ca. 1640, d. Charlestown, Mass., 1678. Sex, pp. 145-48, et al.

BROWN, WILLIAM, b. ca. 1669, d. Uxbridge, Mass., after 1 April 1740. Kempton4, pp. 97-113; Carol Willits Brown, *William Brown: English Immi-*

grant of Hatfield and Leicester, Massachusetts and His Descendants ca. 1669 to 1994 (Baltimore, MD: Gateway Press, 1994). Reviews: CN 28:251, NYGBR 126:217.

BROWN, WILLIAM, d. Eastham, Mass., ca. 1694. Croll, 107.

BROWNE SEE BROWN

BROWNELL, THOMAS, b. 1608, d. Portsmouth, R.I., 24 September 1664. AL, pp. 178-82; William[2] at RIR 21:100.

BROWNING, NATHANIEL, b. 1626, d. Conn., after 1680. RD600, pp. 455-56; PA, p. 163; MCA, p. 146; AL, pp. 182-83.

BROWNING, THOMAS, b. ca. 1587, d. Salem, Mass., between 16 February 1670 and 28 June 1671. Davis I:244-47 [Amos Towne].

BRUCE, THOMAS, d. Marlborough, Mass., between 1714 and 1721. NEHGR 136:294-306.

BRUFF, EDMUND, d. Boston soon after 1658. MF15, three generations all lines.

BRUNDISH, JOHN, b. ca. 1604, d. Wethersfield, Conn., between 20 May and 27 October 1639. GM2 I:445-48.

BRYANT, ABRAHAM, b. ca. 1635, d. Reading, Mass., 6 July 1720. NEHGR 137:235-59, 317-39, a multi-generational study.

BRYANT, JOHN, b. ca. 1640, d. Plymouth, Mass., 26 January 1730/1 [son-in-law of Stephen Bryant below]. NEHGR 153:413-34, 154:41-60, 227-43, 370-74, 477-94, 155:189-211 (four generation study).

BRYANT, STEPHEN, b. ca. 1620, d. Plymouth, Mass., after 26 October 1698. NEHGR 153:413-34, 154:41-60, 227-43, 370-74, 477-94, 155:189-211 (five generation study); NEHGR 155:416 (correction).

BUCK, HENRY, b. ca. 1626, d. Wethersfield, Conn., July 1712. NEHGR 158:126-38 (line through William[5] John[4] Samuel[3-2])

BUCK, ISAAC, b. ca. 1602, d. Scituate, Mass., 1695. Lyon, pp. 252-55.

BUCK, WILLIAM, b. ca. 1585, d. Cambridge, Mass., 24 January 1657/8. GM2 I:448-50.

BUCKINGHAM, THOMAS, d. Milford, Conn., between 19 September 1657 and 23 May 1659. Jessup, pp. 231-37.

BUCKLAND, THOMAS, b. ca. 1613, d. Windsor, Conn., 28 May 1662. GM2 I:450-53; MJ 19:19-21.

BUCKLAND, WILLIAM, b. ca. 1609, d. Rehoboth, Mass., August–September 1638. GM2 I:454-56.

BUCKLEY, WILLIAM, d. Salem, Mass., 2 January 1702/3. TAG 79:274-77.

BUCKMAN, JOHN, d. Boston, Mass., between 20 April and 13 May 1681. Ann Theopold Chaplin, *A Bucknam-Buckman Genealogy: Some Descendants of William Bucknam of Charlestown and Malden and John Buckman of Boston* (Baltimore, MD: Gateway Press, 1988). Reviews: NEHGR 143:76, TAG 65:60.

BUCKNAM, WILLIAM, b. ca. 1602, d. Malden, Mass., 28 March 1679. Sex, pp. 132-33, 177-180, 237-38, et al.; Ann Theopold Chaplin, *A Bucknam-Buckman Genealogy: Some Descendants of William Bucknam of Charlestown and Malden and John Buckman of Boston* (Baltimore, MD: Gateway Press, 1988). Reviews: NEHGR 143:76.

BUELL, WILLIAM, b. ca. 1610, d. Windsor, Conn., 16 or 23 November 1681. EB, pp. 137-41.

BUFFAM, ROBERT, d. Salem, Mass., before 2 December 1669. Davis III:405-8 (wife Thomasine's Ward ancestry); RD600, pp. 450-51; NEQ 74:355-84 (Joshua[2]).

BUFFINGTON, THOMAS, d. Salem, Mass., between 18 September 1725 and 28 August 1729. Benjamin[2] at TAG 62:182-84. Thomas's will at TAG 62:184.

BUGBY, EDWARD, b. ca. 1594, d. Roxbury, Mass., 27 January 1668/9. GM2 I:456-59; TAG 67:8-10 (Edward[3] Joseph[2]).

BULKELEY, PETER, b. 1582/3, d. Concord, Mass., 9 March 1658/9. GM2 I:459-65; Goodman, pp. 117-130, including English origins; EB, pp. 141-45; second wife Grace (Chetwode)'s royal line at RD600, pp. 336; PA, p. 205; MCA, p. 189. His royal line at PA, p. 165; RD600, pp. 442-44; MCA, p. 147-48. First wife Jane (Allen)'s royal line at RD600, pp. 417-21; MCA, p. 3; see Cameos, pp. 135-38 for son Edward[2]. Dorothy[3] (Gershom[2]) at Doctors, pp. 93-95.

BULL, HENRY, b. ca. 1610, d. Newport, R.I., 22 January 1693/4. GM2 I:465-69; RIR 8:25; will at RIR 10:32-35; TAG 77:282-89 (notes on his wife's identity); TAG 78:291-92 (note).

BULL, JOHN, d. Saybrook, Conn., 19 April 1703. TAG 63:78-81; TAG 69:140-41.

BULL, ROBERT, b. ca. 1620, d. Saybrook, Conn., after 1679. John[2] at TAG 63:78-81; wife's identity at TAG 63:184; TAG 69:140-41.

BULL, THOMAS, b. ca. 1610, d. Hartford, Conn., between 20 April and 24 October 1684. GM2 I:469-76; possible English origins at TAG 63:78-81; NEHGR 135:135-37 (note); Mary Louise B. Todd, *Thomas and Susannah Bull of Hartford, Connecticut and Some of Their Descendants* (Lake Forest, IL: Heitman Printers, 1981). Reviews: CN 14:700-1, TAG 58:121, NYGBR 115:120.

BULL, WILLIAM, b. ca. 1618, d. Cambridge, Mass., between 21 May and 12 October 1687. Son Elisha at Cameos, pp. 309-11.

BULLARD, GEORGE, b. ca. 1602, d. Watertown, Mass., 14 January 1688/9. NEHGR 154:172-88 (more on English ancestry).

BULLARD, JOHN, b. ca. 1596, d. Medfield, Mass., 27 October 1678. Kempton, pp. 199-214, including English origins; NEHGR 146:279-80 (wife's English origins); NEHGR 154:172-88 (more on English ancestry).

BULLARD, ROBERT, b. ca. 1598, d. Watertown, Mass., 24 April 1639. Lyon, pp. 255-57; Kempton, pp. 199-214, including English origins; Morgan; son Jacob[2] at Thompson, pp. 90-91, et al.; NEHGR 146:279-80 (wife's English origins); NEHGR 154:172-88 (more on English ancestry).

BULLARD, WILLIAM, b. ca. 1594, d. Dedham, Mass., 23 December 1686. Pond, 220; NEHGR 154:172-88 (more on English ancestry).

BULLEN, SAMUEL, d. Medfield, Mass., 16 January 1691/2. Lyon, pp. 257-58.

BULLOCK, HENRY, b. ca. 1595, d. Salem, Mass., 27 December 1663. GM2 I:477-80; TEG 5:90-91 (John[3] Henry[2]).

BULLOCK, RICHARD, b. ca. 1622, d. Rehoboth, Mass., before 22 Oct. 1667. His children by second wife Elizabeth (Billington) at MF5 and MF21, for three generations, all lines; Mower, pp. 99-103; AL, pp. 184-88.

BULMAN, ALEXANDER, d. Boston after 1695. Spooner.

BUMPAS, EDWARD, b. ca. 1605, d. Marshfield, Mass., between 4 July 1679 and 5 March 1683/4. GMB I:273-76; PM, pp. 85-88. Son Philip[2] in MF9 for three generations all lines; TAG 67:155 (daughter Elizabeth).

BUMSTEAD, THOMAS, d. Boston, Mass., between 25 May and 4 August 1677. Son Jeremiah[2] at NEHGR 140:312-16.

BUNCE, THOMAS, b. ca. 1612, d. Hartford, Conn., ca. 1683. EB, pp. 145-47.

BUNDY, JOHN, b. ca. 1617, d. Taunton, Mass., between April and 29 October 1681. GM2 I:480-83; MF15, three generations all lines.

BUNKER, GEORGE, b. ca. 1599, d. Charlestown, Mass., between 12 March 1663/4 and 4 October 1664. GM2 I:483-87; Lyon, pp. 259-61.

BUNKER, JAMES, b. ca. 1634, d. Kittery, Me., between 14 October 1697 and 24 June 1698. MJ 27:10.

BUNN, EDWARD, b. ca. 1612, d. Hull, Mass., 1673. NEHGR 142:279-80.

BUNN, MATTHEW, of Boston, Mass., d. Woodbridge, N.J., before 1680. Pond, 283.

BUNNELL, WILLIAM, of New Haven, Conn., d. after 1652, possibly at Barbados on 5 August 1678. Ruth Cost Duncan, *William Bunnell and His Descendants* (Decorah, IA: Anundsen Publishing, Co., 1986). Reviews: CN 20:317.

BURCHSTED, JOHN HENRY, b. ca. 1657, d. Lynn, Mass., 20 September 1721. TEG 15:139-44, 195-204.

BURDEN, GEORGE, b. ca. 1611, d. Boston, Mass., between 14 October 1652 and 30 April 1657. GM2 I:487-91; NEHGR 155:91-102 (wife Anne).

BURDEN, ROBERT, fl. Charlestown, Mass., 1650s. Sex, pp. 177-80, et al.

BURDETT, GEORGE, b. ca. 1602, of Salem, Mass., Dover, N.H., and York and Pemaquid, Me., d. Ireland 1671. GM2 I:491-97.

BURGESS, JOHN, d. Weymouth, Mass., 22 October 1678. MJ 18:20-23.

BURGESS, THOMAS, d. Sandwich, Mass., between 4 October 1684 and 2 March 1684/5. NEA 6:5/6:45-46 (DNA Study); MJ 18:23-25; TAG 80:304-7 (note).

BURLINGAME, ROGER, b. 1620, d. Cranston, R.I., 1 September 1718. JPG I:96-108, including English ancestry.

BURNAP, ROBERT, b. ca. 1595, d. Reading, Mass., 27 September 1689. NEHGR 155:353-56 (Thomas[2] distinguished with his wife).

BURNHAM, THOMAS, b. ca. 1617, d. Podunk, Conn., 28 June 1688. TAG 67:32-46; TAG 68:83 (note on daughter Rebecca); TAG 74:33-37.

BURNHAM, THOMAS, d. Ipswich, Mass., 19 May 1694. Wife Mary (Lawrence) at GM2 IV:258-59; Job[3] (Thomas[2]) at MG 17:71-80.

Burr, Jehu, b. ca. 1605, d. Fairfield, Conn., by 1654. GMB I:278-80.

Burrell, George, b. 1588/9, d. Lynn, Mass., between 18 October 1653 and 21 June 1654. Chase, pp. 125-33, including English origins; Ruth Burell-Brown, *The Burrell/Burill Genealogy* (Baltimore, MD: Gateway Press, 1990). Reviews: NHGR 8:144, VG 2:187, NEHGR 144:362, NYGBR 121:184, MQ 57:292-93.

Burrell, John, d. Weymouth, Mass., after October 1675. Ruth Burell-Brown, *The Burrell/Burill Genealogy* (Baltimore, MD: Gateway Press, 1990). Reviews: NHGR 8:144, VG 2:187, NEHGR 144:362, NYGBR 121:184, MQ 57:292-93.

Burrill, John, b. ca. 1609, d. Roxbury, Mass., between 3 August 1654 and 15 February 1656/7. GM2 I:499-500.

Burrough(s), Nathaniel, resident of Roxbury, Mass., and Calvert Co., Md., d. England early 1682. PA, p. 176; MCA, p. 160; RD600, pp. 276-77. Son George[2] at LENE, pp. 85-86; NEXUS 9:108-11; TAG 56:43-45 (identity of George[2]'s third wife); TAG 60:140-42; TAG 76:17-19 (identity of Hannah Fisher, George[2]'s first wife).

Burroughs, James, b.c 1650, d. Bristol, Mass., after 10 October 1699. TAG 58:85-90, 150-58 (five generation study); MF18, three generations for children of his first wife, Sarah (Church); Church.

Bursley, John, b. ca. 1600, d. Barnstable, Mass., before 21 August 1660. GMB I:280-83; PM, pp. 89-92.

Burt, Henry, b. ca. 1596, d. Springfield, Mass., 30 April 1662. JPG I:109-18, including English ancestry; MJ 17:22-25.

Burt, Hugh, b. 1590, d. Lynn, Mass., 2 November 1661. GM2 I:501-4; second wife's ancestry at TAG 79:181-83; she also at Doctors, pp. 25-26; Johnson, p. 63.

Burt, James, d. Taunton, Mass., between 17 October 1679 and 10 October 1680. TAG 75:109-16, 206, 319.

Burt, Richard, d. Sudbury, Mass. Son John[2] at NEXUS 13:114-17.

Burton, Edward, d. Hingham, Mass., before 21 October 1670. GMB I:283-85.

Burton, Stephen, d. Bristol, R.I., 22 July 1693. TAG 59:84-89

Burwell, John, b. 1602, d. Milford, Conn., 17 August 1649. Johnson, pp. 63-65.

BUSBY, NICHOLAS, b. ca. 1582, d. Boston, Mass., 28 August 1657. Crosby, pp. I:5-12, including English origins.

BUSECOT, PETER, b. ca. 1605, d. Warwick, R.I., after 1692. TAG 58:230 (English origins).

BUSH, JOHN, b. ca. 1626, d. Cambridge, Mass., 1 January 1662/3. Kempton3, pp. 75-81; Cameos, pp. 111-15; Thompson, pp. 191-92.

BUSH, REYNOLD, b. ca. 1610, d. Cambridge, Mass., ca. 1684. Johnson, p. 66.

BUSHNELL, EDMUND, b. 1606, d. Boston, Mass., 28 March 1636. GM2 I:507-9.

BUSHNELL, FRANCIS, b. ca. 1580, d. Guilford, Conn., ca. 1646. Pond, 231; Jessup, pp. 237-44, including English origins; son Francis[2] at GM2 I:510-12.

BUSHNELL, JOHN, b. 1615, d. Boston, Mass., 5 August 1667. GM2 I:512-14.

BUSWELL, ISAAC, b. ca. 1592, d. Salisbury, Mass., 8 July 1683. NEHGR 158:33-39 (English origins).

BUTLER, NICHOLAS, b. ca. 1590, d. Edgartown, Mass., 13 August 1671. Goodman, pp. 133-36.

BUTLER, RICHARD, b. ca. 1610, d. Hartford, Conn., 6 August 1684. GMB I:285-88; JPG I:119-27; Samuel[2] at TAG 60:27-32.

BUTLER, THOMAS, of Lynn, Sandwich and Duxbury, Mass., d. after 12 March 1689. Croll, 96; Jessup, pp. 244-51.

BUTMAN, JEREMIAH, b. 1633/4, d. Beverly, Mass., 6 February 1693/4. MG 19:147-59, including English origins.

BUTTERFIELD, BENJAMIN, d. Chelmsford, Mass., 2 March 1687/8. Nichols, pp. 87-88.

BUTTERWORTH, HENRY, b. ca. 1598, d. Weymouth, Mass., 18 January 1640/1. Mower, pp. 105-7; TAG 77:302-12 (John[2]).

BUTTOLPH, THOMAS, b. ca. 1603, d. Boston, Mass., between 25 May and 18 June 1667. GM2 I:517-22; EB, pp. 147-49; TAG 58:129-40, 231-42 (four generation study).

BUTTON, MATTHIAS, b. ca. 1610, d. Haverhill, Mass., 13 August 1672. GMB I:292-98.

BUTTRICK, WILLIAM, b. ca. 1616, d. Concord, Mass., 3 June 1698. GM2 I:522-26.

BUTTRY, NICHOLAS, b. ca. 1602, d. Cambridge, Mass., before 8 September 1636. GM2 I:526.

BUXTON, ANTHONY, b. ca. 1610, d. Salem, Mass., between 8 March 1683/4 and 29 July 1684. Davis I:248-56 [Sarah Johnson]; MJ 18:25-27, 26:15-21.

BUXTON, CLEMENT, d. Stamford, Conn., before 3 September 1657. CA 32:112-39; CA 35:176-78.

BYRAM, NICHOLAS, b. ca. 1610, d. East Bridgewater, Mass., 13 April 1688. MBT #574; John Arnold Byram, *Byrams in America* (Baltimore, MD: Gateway Press, 1996, 2nd ed.). Reviews: NYGBR 120:56, TAG 72:143, MQ 55:158-59, 62:273.

CABLE, JOHN, b. ca. 1615, d. Fairfield, Conn., between 4 April and 21 September 1682. GMB I: 299-301.

CABOT, GEORGE, b. 1677/8, d. Boston, Mass., before 5 November 1717. John G.L. Cabot, *The George Cabots: Descendants of George Cabot (1678-1717) of Salem and Boston* (Manchester, MA: NEHGS, 1997). Reviews: NEHGR 151:490-91.

CADE, JAMES, b. 1611, d. Hingham, Mass., MJ 18:27-29.

CADMAN, WILLIAM, d. Portsmouth, R.I., after 11 January 1684. AL, pp. 191-92.

CADY, NICHOLAS, b. ca. 1610, d. Watertown, Mass., between 1685 and 1712. Morgan.

CAHOONE, WILLIAM, d. Swansea, Mass., 24 June 1675. AK, pp. 146-48.

CAKEBREAD, THOMAS, b. ca. 1595, d. Sudbury, Mass., 4 January 1642/3, GMB I:301-3.

CALEF, ROBERT, b. 1648, d. Boston, Mass., 1719. TAG 66:135-45 (Kerrington ancestry).

CALKINS, HUGH, b. ca. 1600, d. Norwich, Conn., 1690. Kenneth W. Calkins, *Calkins Family in America* (Golden, CO: Calkins Family Association, 2000). Reviews: CN 34:229.

CALL, PHILIP, d. Ipswich, Mass., between 6 May and 30 September 1662. TEG 14:172-73 (Philip$^{3-2}$).

CALL, THOMAS, b. ca. 1597, d. Malden, Mass., May 1676. Goodman, pp. 139-45.

CALLENDER, ELLIS, b. ca. 1639, d. Boston, Mass., 18 May 1728. NEHGR 144:195-210, 319-30, 145:31-43 (five generation study); NEHGR 145:373 (correction).

CALLUM, JOHN, d. Haverhill, Mass., 25 February 1693/4. TAG 70:1-8, 104-11.

CALLUM, MACKUM, d. Lynn, Mass., after 26 February 1677. TAG 70:1-8, 104-11.

CAMP, EDWARD, b. ca. 1603, d. New Haven, Conn., before 22 September 1659. CA 32:140-44.

CANE, CHRISTOPHER, b. ca. 1613, d. Cambridge, Mass., 9 December 1653. GM2 II:2-6; son Jonathan[2] at Sex, pp. 87-88.

CANEDY, ALEXANDER, d. Plymouth, Mass., after 1688. Jessup, pp. 251-53.

CANNEY, THOMAS, b. ca. 1600, d. Dover, N.H., after June 1681. NHGR 19:1-7; Jessup, pp. 253-57.

CAPEN, BERNARD, b. ca. 1562, d. Dorchester, Mass., 8 November 1638. GMB I:309-11; NEHGR 158:110-11 (Hannah[3] John[2]); MJ 17:25-27.

CARD, JOHN, b. ca. 1620, d. York, Me., 25 Janaury 1691/2. Probable English origins at MG 19:22-30.

CARD, RICHARD, d. Jamestown, R.I., before 1 July 1674. John[2] at TAG 58:40-42.

CARDER, RICHARD, b. ca. 1615, d. Newport or Warwick, R.I., not long after 29 November 1675. GM2 II:6-10; Johnson, pp. 66-68; TAG 79:100-8 (Richard[3] John[2]).

CARGILL SEE GREGG

CARLETON, EDWARD, b. 1610, of Rowley, d. before 27 November 1678, possibly in England. RD600, p. 220; PA, p. 189-90; MCA, p. 173. Wife Ellen (Newton) at PA, p. 547; RD600, pp. 395-96; MCA, p. 624.

CARLISLE, JOSEPH, b. ca. 1663, d. York, Me., 17 March 1717/8. Donald Bradford Macurda, *Joseph Carlile of York, Me. (York and Lincoln County Descendants) and the Antiquity of the Carlyle Name* (n.p., the author, 1986). Reviews: CN 20:141-42.

CARMAN, JOHN, b. ca. 1608, of Roxbury, Mass., d. Hempstead, N.Y., before 29 May 1654. GMB I:311-13.

CARNES, JOHN, b. ca. 1675, d. Boston, Mass., 1698. TW, pp. 211-20.

CARPENTER, ALEXANDER, of Wrington, Somerset, England. His daughters all migrated to New England (Juliana, Alice, Agnes, Mary and Priscilla). MJ 18:29-31, 27:10-12.

CARPENTER, WILLIAM, b. 1605, d. Rehoboth, Mass., 7 February 1658/9. Johnson, pp. 68-72; AL, pp. 200-3; TAG 70:193-204 (English origins); NEHGR 159:43-54, 361-62 (John^5 Benjamin^4 Joseph^3 William^2 and John^5 Oliver^4 Abiah^3 William^2); NEHGR 159:54-68, 362-64 (Abiah^3 William^2).

CARPENTER, WILLIAM, b. ca. 1610, d. Providence, R.I., 7 September 1685. RIR 13:75; NEHGR 159:43-54, 361-62 (John^4 Joseph^3 William^2); NEHGR 159:54-68, 362-64 (Joseph^2).

CARR, CALEB, b. ca. 1624, d. Newport, R.I., 17 December 1695. GM2 II:11-16; TAG 63:223-30 (descendant Peleg^4 Caleb^3).

CARR, GEORGE, b. ca. 1613, d. Salisbury, Mass., 4 April 1682. GM2 II:17-22.

CARR, ROBERT, b. ca. 1614, d. Newport, R.I., between 20 April and 4 October 1681. GM2 II:24-27; AL, pp. 203-5.

CARRELL, NATHANIEL, b. ca. 1637, d. Salem, Mass., after 1692. TAG 70:205-8 (wife's identity).

CARRINGTON, EDWARD, b. ca. 1615, d. Charlestown, Mass., 15 September 1684. GMB I:315-18.

CARRINGTON, JOHN, b. ca. 1602, d. Hartford, Conn., 1 April 1651. Wife died same day. LENE, p. 19-20; Johnson, p. 72.

CARTER, JOHN, b. ca. 1600, d. Woburn, Mass. Sex, pp. 119-20; son Joseph^2 at Sex, pp. 107-8, et al.

CARTER, JOSHUA, b. ca. 1613, d. Windsor, Conn., 1647. GMB I:318-20.

CARTER, THOMAS, b. ca. 1610, d. Salisbury, Mass., between 30 October and 14 November 1676. GM2 II:27-30.

CARTER, THOMAS, d. Woburn, Mass., 5 September 1684. Johnson, pp. 72-74.

CARTHRICK, MICHAEL, b. ca. 1610, d. Salisbury, Mass., between 16 and 25 January 1646/7. GM2 II:31-32.

CARVER, RICHARD, b. ca. 1577, d. Watertown, Mass., between 18 December 1638 and 9 September 1641. NEHGR 146:230-34 (wives' identities).

CARWITHEN, DAVID, of Salem, Mass., d. Southold, N.Y., after 30 August 1665. JPG I:128-34.

CARY, JAMES, b. ca. 1600, d. Charlestown, Mass., 2 November 1681. MJ 19:21-26.

CARY, JOHN, d. Bridgewater, Mass., 31 October 1681. Son Francis[2] at TAG 61:129-32; TAG 78:187-95 (John[2]); MJ 19:26-27.

CARY, JOHN, d. Bristol, R.I., between 1700 and 1706. TAG 78:187-95.

CARY, MATTHEW, fl. Boston, Mass., ca. 1692-8, d. there December 1706. WRR, pp. 214-19; NEHGR 159:5-11.

CASE, JOHN, d. Simsbury, Conn., 21 February 1703/4. Lyon, pp. 261-65.

CASWELL, THOMAS, d. Taunton, Mass., between 15 March 1696/7 and 14 September 1697. Jessup, pp. 258-63; JPG I:135-43, II:354-63; MD 35:111-20, 36:1-10, 125-34, 37:11-22, 189-94, 38:69-80, 125-32, 39:5-13, 187-94, 40:71-79, 145-54, 42:63-66 (a multi-generational article).

CATLIN, JOHN, d. Wethersfield, Conn., before 17 July 1655. Pond, 273.

CATLIN, JOHN, of Hartford, Conn., and Deerfield, Mass. Daughter Elizabeth at TAG 80:265-77.

CAULKINS, HUGH, b. ca. 1600, d. Norwich, Conn., 1690. JPG II:364-66.

CAZNEAU, PAIX, d. Boston, Mass., 21 July 1720. NEHGR 142:126-48 (four generation study).

CENTER, JOHN, b. ca. 1626, d. Chelsea, Mass., before 15 July 1667. Johnson, pp. 75-76.

CHADBOURNE, WILLIAM, b. 1582, d. Kittery, Me., after 16 November 1652. GM2 II:33-36; English origins at NHGR 10:101-14, 167; TAG 68:106-12 (William[4] Humphrey[3-2]); Elaine Chadbourne Bacon, *The Chadbourne Family in America: A Genealogy* (Camden, ME: Penobscot Press, 1994), Reviews: MG20:141-42, 2000 edition reviewed at MG 23:46-47, NEHGR 155:227-28.

CHADWICK, THOMAS, b. ca. 1648, d. Lyme, Conn., 3 April 1731. MBT #426.

CHAFFE, THOMAS, b. ca. 1613, d. Swansea or Rehoboth, Mass., between 25 July 1680 and 6 March 1683. NEHGR 142:350-51; AL, pp. 205-7.

CHALKER, ALEXANDER, b. ca. 1620, d. Saybrook, Conn., February 1672/3. TAG 68:225-31; TAG 69:171-73.

CHALLIS, PHILIP, b. ca. 1617, d. Amesbury prior to 1680. Ordway, pp. 145-63; TAG 79:57-61 (English origins).

CHAMBERLAIN, HENRY, b. ca. 1592, d. Hull, Mass., 15 July 1674. NEHGR 139:126-38; NEHGR 142:351-56; NEHGR 152:56-68 (Sarah[3] William[2]).

CHAMBERLAIN, HENRY, b. ca. 1598, of Hingham, Mass., returned to England, d. there between 28 July 1649 and 3 March 1649/50. NEHGR 139:126-38.

CHAMPNEY, JOHN, b. ca. 1610, d. Cambridge, Mass., before 1643. GM2 II:37-39.

CHAMPNEY, RICHARD, b. ca. 1604, d. Cambridge, Mass., 26 November 1669. GM2 II:39-46; son Samuel[2] at Cameos, pp. 149-54.

CHANDLER, EDMUND, b. ca. 1587, d. Duxbury, Mass., between 3 May and 2 June 1662. GMB I:326-30; PM, pp. 97-101.

CHANDLER, ROGER, d. Duxbury, Mass., between 1658 and 3 October 1665. MF15, four generations all lines; GMB I:330-32; PM, pp. 101-3; Nichols, p. 50.

CHANDLER, WILLIAM, b. 1595, d. Roxbury, Mass., 1641/2. TAG 73:50-57 (new Information on English ancestry); TAG 80:27-37 (daughter Sarah).

CHANTRELL, JOHN, b. ca. 1640, d. Boston, Mass., after 30 December 1694. Kempton, pp. 217-22.

CHAPIN, SAMUEL, b. 1598, d. Springfield, Mass., 11 November 1675. 31Imm, pp. 44-51, including English origins; Johnson, pp. 76-78; MJ 17:27-28.

CHAPMAN, EDWARD, b. 1612, d. Ipswich, Mass., 18 April 1678. Johnson, pp. 78-84.

CHAPMAN, JOHN, b. ca. 1613, d. Stamford, Conn., before 17 December 1657. GMB I:332-35.

CHAPMAN, RALPH, b. ca.1615, d. Marshfield, Mass., between 28 November 1671 and 5 March 1671/2. GM2 II:51-55; 31Imm, pp. 52-56, including English origins.

CHAPMAN, ROBERT, b. ca. 1616, d. Saybrook, Conn., 13 October 1687. Pond, 238; Jessup, pp. 268-79; TAG 66:30-32 (origins disproved); NEHGR 159:316 (autobiographical letter of Robert).

CHAPMAN, WILLIAM, of New London, Conn. Son Joseph[2] at CN 25:41-53; NEHGR 135:299-300 (note).

CHAPPELL, GEORGE, b. ca. 1615, d. New London, Conn., before 8 June 1682. GM2 II:55-59; NEHGR 150:48-73, 214-15 (three generation study); NEHGR 157:394 (correction).

CHARLES, JOHN, b. 1606, d. Branford, Conn., 1673. Johnson, pp. 84-85.

CHASE, AQUILA, b. ca. 1618, d. Newbury, Mass., 27 December 1670. Ordway, pp. 165-205; Davis I:257-58 [Annis Spear]; Chase, pp. 1-36; Stevens, 8; John Carroll Chase and George Walter Chamberlain, *Seven Generations of the Descendants of Aquila and Thomas Chase* (Camden, ME: Picton Press, 1983, 1993). Reviews: CN 27:587-88, NGSQ 73:59.

CHASE, THOMAS, b. ca. 1616, d. Hampton, N.H., before 5 October 1652. Chase, pp. 1-36; John Carroll Chase and George Walter Chamberlain, *Seven Generations of the Descendants of Aquila and Thomas Chase* (Camden, ME: Picton Press, 1983, 1993). Reviews: CN 27:587-88, NGSQ 73:59.

CHASE, WILLIAM, b. ca. 1605, d. Yarmouth, Mass., between 4 and 13 May 1659. GMB I:336-39; AL, pp. 209-12.

CHATER, JOHN, d. Newbury, Mass., before 19 September 1671. Davis I:259-61 [Sarah Miller].

CHAUNCY, CHARLES, of Cambridge, Mass., president of Harvard College. English ancestry additions at TG 16:183-88; RD600, pp. 483-84; MCA, p. 180; NEHGR 148:161-66 (note).

CHECKLEY, SAMUEL, b. 1653, d. Boston, Mass., 27 December 1738. NEXUS 9:25-29, 57-60.

CHEESEBOROUGH, WILLIAM, b. ca. 1595, d. Stonington, Conn., 9 June 1667. GMB I:339-45.

CHEEVER, EZEKIEL, b. 1614, d. Boston, Mass., 21 August 1708. TEG 19:36-42, 98-104.

CHENEY, JOHN, b. ca. 1600, d. Newbury, Mass., 28 July 1666. GM2 II:60-63; Davis I:262-65 [Phoebe Tilton]; TAG 76:245-47 (English origins).

CHENEY, WILLIAM, b. ca. 1605, d. Roxbury, Mass., 30 June 1667. Kempton, pp. 225-39; son William[2] d. Boston, Mass., 22 September 1681; LENE, p. 54; JPG I:144-54.

CHESHOLM, THOMAS, b. ca. 1604, d. Cambridge, Mass., 18 August 1671. GM2 II:63-67; Cameos, pp. 55-60.

CHESTER, LEONARD, b. ca. 1610, d. Wethersfield, Conn., 1648. GMB I:345-49; his mother Dorothy (Hooker) Chester at GM2 II:67-68.

CHICKERING, FRANCIS, b. ca. 1600, d. Dedham, Mass., 10 October 1658. AL, pp. 213-14; ancestry of wife Anne Fiske, at AL, pp. 252-54.

CHILD, EPHRAIM, b. ca. 1599, d. Watertown, Mass., 13 February 1662/3. GMB I:349-53; Thompson, pp. 43-50, et al.; TAG 62:28-29 (marriage); TAG 63:17-28 (English origins).

CHILD, RICHARD, d. Marshfield, Mass., 1691. JPG II:45-49.

CHILTON, JAMES, *Mayflower* passenger, b. ca. 1556, d. on board the *Mayflower* 18 December 1620. MF15, five generations, all lines; GMB I:353-55; PM, pp. 103-5; Pond, 270; Nichols, p. 51-53; NEHGR 153:407-12.

CHIPMAN, JOHN, b. ca. 1614, d. Sandwich, Mass., 7 April 1708. Makepeace, pp. 113-27; Mower, pp. 109-27; Joseph[3] Samuel[2] at MD 50:105-16; James[3] John[2] at MD 52:19-38, 111-18; TAG 61:2-6; MJ 17:28-30.

CHITTENDEN, THOMAS, b. ca. 1584, d. Scituate, Mass., between 7 October and 9 November 1668. GM2 II:70-72.

CHITTENDEN, WILLIAM, b. 1594, d. Guilford, Conn., February 1660/1. EB, pp. 148-53.

CHRISTOPHERS, CHRISTOPHER, b. ca. 1631, d. New London, Conn., 23 July 1687. Brewster, two generations all lines; Brewster3, three generations all lines; TAG 68:182-83, TAG 70:240-49.

CHUBB, THOMAS, b. ca. 1609, d. Beverly, Mass., 27 November 1679. GMB I:355-58.

CHUBBOCK, THOMAS, b. ca. 1606, d. Hingham, Mass., 9 December 1676. GM2 II:73-75.

CHURCH, GARRETT, b. ca. 1611, d. Watertown, between 20 July 1685 and 3 February 1685/6. GMB I:358-60.

CHURCH, RICHARD, b. ca. 1600, d. Hadley, Mass., 16 December 1667. Gateway, #3584.

CHURCH, RICHARD, b. ca. 1608, d. Dedham, Mass., 27 December 1668. MF18, four generations all lines; Church; GMB I:360-64; PM, pp. 105-9; Pond, 257; Lyon, pp. 265-68; TAG 60:129-39.

CHURCHILL, JOHN, d. Plymouth, Mass., 1 January 1662/3. EB, pp. 153-56.

CHURCHILL, JOSIAH, d. Wethersfield, Conn., between 17 November 1683 and 5 January 1687. Pond, 224; Gateway, #3586.

CLAPP, EDWARD, b. ca. 1609, d. Dorchester, Mass., 8 January 1664/5. GM2 II:76-81; Mower, pp. 129-36.

CLAPP, ROGER, b. 1609, d. Boston, Mass., 2 February 1690/1. GMB I:364-70; EB, pp. 156-60; MJ 1:23-24, 4:51-69, 11:73-74, 17:30-34.

CLAPP, THOMAS, b. ca. 1608, d. Scituate, Mass., 20 April 1684. Kempton4, pp. 115-195, including extensive English research and origins; Davis I:270-76 [Joseph Neal], including English origins; Lyon, pp. 268-72; MJ 17:34-36.

CLARK, DANIEL, d. Topsfield, Mass., between 10 January 1688/9 and 28 March 1690. Davis I: 277-82 [Dudley Wildes]. Wife Mary (Beane)'s ancestry at Davis I:136-39 [Dudley Wildes]; TAG 80:123-27 (wife's English origins).

CLARK, GEORGE, b. ca. 1615, d. Milford, Conn., August 1690. Nichols, pp. 89-90; TAG 74:72-73 (English origins).

CLARK, JAMES, b. ca. 1610, d. Muddy River, Mass., 1673. MJ 19:31-32.

CLARK, JAMES, b. ca. 1615, d. Roxbury, Mass., 18 December 1674. Johnson, pp. 86-87.

CLARK, JEREMIAH, b. 1605, d. Newport, R.I., January 1651/2. RD600, pp. 270-72, PA, p. 211; MCA, p. 205. Son Walter[2] in RF2, four generations all lines. Wife Frances (Latham) at TG 4:187-202, see also Dungan; notable descendants at NEXUS 11:140-45; RIR 9:78; additional royal line at RIR 15:41-43.

CLARK, JOHN, b. 1609, d. Newport, R.I., 20 April 1676. Sydney V. James, *John Clarke and His Legacies: Religion and Law in Colonial R.I., 1638-1750* (University Park, PA: Pennsylvania State University Press, 1999). Reviews: NEQ 73:300-3.

CLARK, JOHN, b. ca. 1600, d. Milford, Conn., 5 February 1673/4. EB, pp. 160-62; Jessup, pp. 279-83; Morgan.

Clark, John, b. ca. 1637, d. New Haven, Conn., 22 March 1718. Nichols, pp. 91-92.

Clark, Jonas, b. ca. 1619, d. Cambridge, Mass., 11 January 1698/9. Goodman, pp. 147-54; NEHGR 146:377-82 (Samuel[2]'s wife).

Clark, Joseph, b. 1613, d. Medfield, Mass., 6 January 1683/4. Lyon, p. 273; NEHGR 152:3-23 (English origins); NEHGR 153:180-82.

Clark, Joseph, b. ca. 1611, d. Windsor, Conn., 1641. GM2 II:82-85.

Clark, Nicholas, b. ca. 1613, d. Hartford, Conn., 2 July 1680. GMB I:373-75.

Clark, Thaddeus, d. Falmouth, Me., 16 May 1690. MBT #268.

Clark, Thomas, b. ca. 1599, d. Plymouth, Mass., 24 March 1697. GMB I:375-80; PM, pp. 109-15; CN 13:348-52.

Clark, Thomas, b. ca. 1613, d. Ipswich, Mass., 9 January 1689/90. GM2 II:86-98; Mower, pp. 139-47.

Clark, Thomas, d. Boston, Mass., between 15 August 1679 and 22 March 1682/3. TW, pp. 222-24.

Clark, Thomas, d. Boston, Mass., shortly after 4 May 1678. TW, pp. 221-22.

Clark, Thurston, b. ca. 1590, d. Duxbury, Mass., 6 December 1661. GM2 II:99-101; Jessup, pp. 283-84.

Clark, William, b. ca. 1595, d. Woburn, Mass., 15 March 1664. Nichols, p. 20.

Clark, William, b. ca. 1620, d. Haddam, Conn., 22 July 1681. Johnson, pp. 87-88; CN 30:188-90.

Clark, William, d. Yarmouth, Mass., 7 December 1668. Pond, 280.

Clarke see Clark

Clary, John, b. ca. 1612, d. Watertown, Mass. Son John[2] at Thompson, pp. 123-24, et al.

Cleaves, William, d. Beverly, Mass., 27 January 1714/5. NEHGR 155: 225-26 (wife's identity); TEG 17:112-13.

Cleaves, William, d. Sudbury, Mass., 21 April 1676. TAG 80:27-37.

CLEEVE, GEORGE, b. ca. 1586, d. Wells, Me., after 13 November 1666. Wife Joan(na) (Price) at RD600, p. 499; GMB I:383-89; 26Imm, pp. 35-62; MBT #1078; NEHGR 140:180-81 (note).

CLEMENTS, AUGUSTINE, b. ca. 1603, d. Dorchester, Mass., 1 October 1674. GM2 II:101-6; wife Elizabeth (Bullock) at RD600, 2nd printing (2006), pp. 835-37.

CLEMENTS, ROBERT, b. 1595, d. Haverhill, Mass., 29 September 1658. MBT #862.

CLEMENTS, THOMAS, b. ca. 1625, d. Providence, R.I., before 16 May 1688. RIR 6:9-14, with a focus on the descendants of Richard[3-2]; TAG 69:109 (Richard[3-2]); NEHGR 155:131-66, 416-17 (four generation study).

CLEMENTS, WILLIAM, d. Cambridge, Mass., before 15 March 1669/70. Sex, pp. 115-17.

CLIFFORD, JOHN, b. ca. 1614, d. Hampton, N.H., 17 October 1694. Davis I: 283-89 [Nicholas Davis].

CLOICE, JOHN, b. ca. 1610, d. Falmouth, Me., 1676. Stone, pp. 71-74.

CLOUGH, JOHN, b. ca. 1614, d. Salisbury, Mass., 26 July 1691. GM2 II:107-14; NEA 4:1:50-51 (DNA Study); Stevens, 14; MBT #946.

COAS, WILLIAM, b. ca. 1700, d. Gloucester, Mass., 2 January 1764. TAG 78:22-29, 120-29 (a five generation study).

COATES, ROBERT, b. ca. 1626, d. Lynn, Mass., between 1691 and 1708. TEG 19:162-64.

COATES, THOMAS, b. ca. 1630, d. Lynn, Mass., after June 1681. TEG 19:154-61.

COBB, AUGUSTINE, fl. Taunton, Mass., 1670-9. AL, pp. 216-17.

COBB, HENRY, b. ca. 1607, d. Barnstable, Mass., between 22 February 1678/9 and 3 June 1679. GMB I:392-95; PM, pp. 118-22; NEA 6:1:43-44 (DNA Study); Brewer, pp. 333-34; Mower, pp. 149-55; grandson Joseph[3] Jonathan[2] at MD 50:26-39.

COBB, JOHN, b. ca. 1605, d. Taunton, Mass., between 25 November 1690 and 18 November 1691. 31Imm, pp. 57-63, including English origins; TAG 56:106-7.

COBBETT, JOSIAH, b. ca. 1614, d. Boston, Mass., between 21 March 1691/2 and 2 October 1705. GM2 II:114-21.

COBHAM SEE COBBETT

COCHRAN, PETER, b. ca. 1626, d. Londonderry, N.H., 25 December 1722. Angell, pp. 279-311, includes Irish origins.

COCKERILL, WILLIAM, b. ca. 1601, d. Salem, Mass., before 6 December 1661. GM2 II:121-22; Mower, pp. 157-59.

COCKERUM, WILLIAM, b. ca. 1609, of Hingham, Mass., d. England, between 2 February 1657/8 and 11 February 1660/1. GM2 II:122-25.

CODDINGTON, STOCKDALE, b. 1569/70, d. Hampton, N.H., before 7 April 1650. TAG 79:179-80 (English origins).

CODDINGTON, WILLIAM, b. ca. 1601, d. Newport, R.I., November 1678. GMB I:395-401; RIR 7:24; wife of William[3] Nathaniel[2] in Scott Campbell Steward and Newbold Le Roy, 3rd, *The Le Roy Family in America 1753-2003* (Boston, MA, and Laconia, NH: the authors, 2003), pp. 7-8.

COE, JOHN, of Stamford, Greenwich, Conn., d. Rye, N.Y., after 1685. TAG 78:37-41.

COE, ROBERT, b. 1596, of Watertown, Mass., and Wethersfield and Stamford, Conn., d. Hempstead, N.Y., between 30 June 1687 and 28 June 1690. GM2 II:125-32; TAG 78:37-41.

COFFIN, TRISTRAM, b. 1609/10, d. Nantucket, Mass., 2 October 1681. Wife's brother's will at TAG 61:77-78; MJ 17:36-39.

COGGAN, HENRY, b. 1607, of Dorchester, Scituate and Barnstable, Mass., d. England 16 June 1649. GM2 II:132-36; JPG II:50-54; MJ 18:31-33, 27:12-15.

COGGAN, JOHN, b. ca. 1590/1, d. Boston, Mass., 27 April 1658. GMB I:401-5; EB, pp. 162-65; JPG II:50-54; MJ 17:39-41.

COGGESHALL, JOHN, b. 1601, d. Newport, R.I., November 1647. GMB I:405-9; AK, pp. 13-79; Johnson, pp. 88-90; AL, pp. 217-24, including English ancestry; RIR 8:71; TAG 67:156-60 (Joshua[4-3-2]); NEHGR 149:361-73 (John's divorce).

COGSWELL, JOHN, b. 1592, d. Ipswich, Mass., 29 November 1669. GM2 II:137-40; EB, pp. 165-67; Stevens, 51.

COIT, JOHN, d. Marblehead, Mass., 15 April 1675. (Grand)daughter Mary at Doctors, pp. 45-46.

Coker, Robert, b. ca. 1606, d. Newbury, Mass., between 20 September 1678 and 29 March 1681. GM2 II:142-44; Davis I:290-93 [Abel Lunt].

Colbron, William, b. ca. 1593, d. Boston, Mass., 1 August 1662, GMB I:409-13.

Colburn, Edward, b. ca. 1618, d. Chelmsford, Mass., 17 February 1700/1. GM2 II:144-49; granddaughter Susannah[3] Edward[2] at Sex, pp. 48-53, et al.

Colburn, Nathaniel, b. ca. 1615, d. Dedham, Mass., 14 May 1691. NEHGR 153:180-82 (English origins); Lyon, pp. 277-80.

Colby, Anthony, b. 1605, d. Salisbury, Mass., 11 February 1660/1. Stone, pp. 75-79; GMB I:413-16; 50Imm, pp. 121-48; Stevens, 27; MBT #1792.

Colcord, Edward, b. ca. 1615, d. Hampton, N.H., 10 February 1681/2. NEHGR 141:114-21 (wife's identity and ancestry).

Coldham, Thomas, b. ca. 1602, d. Lynn, Mass., 8 April 1675. GMB I:417-20.

Cole, Daniel, Yarmouth, Mass., by 1643, d. there 20 December 1694. Son John[2], MF6, three generations all lines; son William[2], MF6, two generations all lines; son Daniel[2] MF10, three generations all lines; Brewer, pp. 335-40; TAG 75:124-29 (Daniel[2]).

Cole, Isaac, b. ca. 1607, d. Woburn, Mass., 10 June 1674. GM2 II:153-56.

Cole, James, b. ca. 1600, d. Plymouth, Mass., after October 1678. GMB I:420-24; PM, pp. 122-26; Mower, pp. 161-66; Hugh[2] at TAG 64:139-41; TAG 67:243-45 (James[2]'s family).

Cole, Job, b. ca. 1609, d. Eastham, Mass., between 1683 and 29 December 1698. GMB I:424-26; PM, pp. 126-28; TAG 71:198-99 (Samuel[2]); TAG 75:124-29 (Daniel[2]).

Cole, John, b. ca. 1629, d. North Kingstown, R.I., 1707. RF2, four generations all lines.

Cole, Peter, fl. Charlestown, Mass., 1676. Sex, pp. 237-38.

Cole, Rice, b. ca. 1590, d. Charlestown, Mass., 15 May 1646. GMB I:426-29; TAG 78:181-85 (English origins).

Cole, Samuel, b. ca. 1597, d. Boston, Mass., between 21 December 1666 and 13 February 1666/7. GMB I:430-35; Johnson, pp. 91-92.

COLE, THOMAS, d. Salem, Mass., between 25 December 1678 and 27 June 1679. TEG 21:89-97.

COLEMAN, THOMAS, b. ca. 1602, d. Nantucket, Mass., before 1 August 1682. GM2 II:157-62.

COLEMAN, THOMAS, b. ca. 1610, d. Hadley, Mass., between 20 and 30 September 1674. NEHGR 146:28-34 (wife's English ancestry).

COLES, ROBERT, b. ca. 1605, d. Warwick, R.I., between 27 April and 25 October 1655. GMB I:435-39.

COLLAMORE, ANTHONY, d. Scituate, Mass., 16 December 1693. RD600, pp. 548-550; MJ 19:33-35.

COLLER, JOHN, b. ca. 1633, d. Sudbury, Mass., after 23 October 1702. Kempton, pp. 249-55.

COLLICOTT, RICHARD, b. ca. 1604, d. Boston, Mass., 7 July 1686. GMB I:439-46; MJ 19:35-36.

COLLIER, THOMAS, b. ca. 1597, d. Hingham, Mass., 6 April 1647. GM2 II:162-64; NEHGR 142:356-59.

COLLIER, WILLIAM, b. ca. 1585, d. Duxbury, Mass., between 29 May 1670 and 5 July 1671. GMB I:446-50; PM, pp. 128-33; Spooner.

COLLINS, HENRY, b. ca. 1606, d. Lynn, February 1686/7. GM2 II:164-69.

COLLINS, HENRY, b. ca. 1606, d. Lynn, Mass., February 1687. TEG 10:145-52, 198-207, 11:17-26, 90-95, 151-65, 12:225-28.

COLLINS, JOSEPH, b. ca. 1645, d. Eastham, Mass., 18 February 1723/4. Brewer, pp. 341-42; NEHGR 151:3-30, 442 (three generation study); NEHGR 155:415 (correction).

COLT, JOHN, of Hartford, Conn. TAG 74:97-100 (wife identified); TAG 80:81-93.

COLTMAN, JOHN, b. 1613, d. Wethersfield, Conn., before 1 September 1691. TAG 77:248-57.

COLVER SEE CULVER

COLVIN, JOHN, d. Providence, R.I., 28 November 1729. JPG I:155-171.

COMINS SEE CUMMINGS

COMPTON, JOHN, b. ca. 1607, d. Boston, Mass., between 30 January 1651/2 and 12 November 1664. GM2 II:170-71.

CONANT, ROGER, b. 1592, d. Beverly, Mass., 19 November 1679. GMB I:451-59; PM, pp. 134-43; Chase, pp. 135-46, including English origins; Pond, 261; NEHGR 147:234-39 (English ancestry of wife's father); NEHGR 148:107-29 (more on English ancestry and connections); MJ 17:44-46, 26:21-22.

CONKLIN, JOHN, b. ca. 1600, of Salem, Mass., d. Huntington, N.Y., 23 February 1684. CA 24:59.

CONVERSE, ALLEN, d. Woburn, Mass., 19 April 1679. TAG 75:329-30 (maternal ancestry).

CONVERSE, EDWARD, b. 1588/9, d. Woburn, Mass., 10 August 1663. GMB I:459-63; NEHGR 146:130-32 (notes on English origins); NEHGR 153:81-96 (English origins of his wife); Marion Edwards Lee, *The Lees of New England and Some Allied Families* (Ponca City, OK: the author, 1981). Reviews: CN 15:159-60.

COOKE ALIAS BUTCHER, THOMAS, b. 1600, d. Portsmouth, R.I., 6 February 1677. Johnson, pp. 92-95; TAG 56:93-94 (English data); MJ 17:46-48; Jane Fletcher Fiske, *Thomas Cooke of R.I.* (Boxford, MA: the author, 1987). Reviews: RIR 14:68, TAG 62:187, NEHGR 141:263, NYGBR 119:57, NGSQ 76:157.

COOKE, AARON, b. 1613/4, d. Northampton, Mass., 5 September 1690. Goodman, pp. 157-70, including English origins; GMB I:464-67; MJ 18:37-39.

COOKE, FRANCIS, *Mayflower* passenger, b. ca. 1582, d. Plymouth, Mass., 7 April 1663. MF12, five generations all lines; GMB I:467-71; PM, pp. 144-48; Spooner; Jessup, pp. 312-19; Lyon, pp. 280-82; AL, pp. 224-27.

COOKE, GEORGE, b. 1610, of Cambridge, Mass., d. Ireland ca. 1652. GM2 II:171-77; Davis I:295-302 [Bethia Harris].

COOKE, HENRY, b. ca. 1615, d. Salem, Mass., 25 December 1661. EB, pp. 167-68.

COOKE, JOSEPH, b. 1608, of Cambridge, Mass., returned to England. GM2 II:178-83; Davis I:295-302. Wife Elizabeth (Haynes) at RD600, p. 339; PA, p. 393; MCA, p. 426; NEHGR 148:240-58 (daughter Mary and ancestry of wife Elizabeth).

COOKE, JOSIAS, b. ca. 1610, d. Eastham, Mass., 17 October 1673. GMB I:472-75; PM, pp. 149-53; son Josiah[2], MF6, three generation all lines; Croll, 109.

COOKE, NATHANIEL, b. ca. 1620, d. Windsor, Conn., 19 May 1688. MJ 19: 36-37.

COOKE, RICHARD, b. ca. 1610, d. Boston, Mass., between 1 and 25 December 1673. GM2 II:185-191.

COOKE, RICHARD, d. Norwich, Conn., ca. 1695. Pond, 282.

COOKE, ROBERT, of Boston, Mass., NEHGR 155:391-96 (account book of Robert[2]).

COOLEY, BENJAMIN, b. ca. 1617, d. Springfield, Mass., 17 August 1684. Cooley, pp. 5-77.

COOLIDGE, JOHN, b. 1604, d. Watertown, Mass., 7 May 1691. GM2 II:191-98; Kempton3, pp. 83-116, including English origins; Chase, pp. 147-54, including English origins; wife of Obadiah[3] Simon[2] at TAG 59:47-48; wife Mary (Ravens)'s origins at TAG 62:65-77, 161-70; TAG 64:44 (additional note on wife).

COOMBS, JOHN, b. ca. 1610, d. Plymouth, Mass., before 15 October 1646. MF8, four generations all lines; GMB I:476-79; PM, pp. 153-56, with clues to English origins; TAG 71:247-50 (probable English origins).

COOMES, ROBERT, b. ca. 1636, d. Hull, Mass., 14 December 1696. NEHGR 142:359-60.

COOPER, ANTHONY, b. ca. 1584, d. Hingham, Mass., before 26 February 1635/6. GM2 II:198-99.

COOPER, JOHN, b. ca. 1594, of Lynn, Mass., d. Southampton, N.Y., after 6 May 1662. GM2 II:202-4.

COOPER, JOHN, b. ca. 1610, d. East Haven, Conn., 23 November 1689. Johnson, pp. 95-97.

COOPER, THOMAS, b. 1603, d. Rehoboth, Mass., 17 March 1690. 31Imm, pp. 65-71, including English origins; AL, pp. 227-29.

COOPER, THOMAS, b. ca. 1617, d. Springfield, Mass., 5 October 1675. GM2 II:205-12.

COOPER, TIMOTHY, b. ca. 1615, d. Lynn, Mass., before 29 March 1659. TEG 11:212-16, 12:38-47.

COOS(E) SEE COAS

COREY, GILES, b. ca. 1619, d. Salem, Mass., 19 September 1692. LENE, pp. 89-97 (he, his wife, and daughter Mary); TEG 5:11-14.

COREY, JOHN, b. ca. 1680, d. Roxbury, Mass., ca. 1730. JPG II:55-88.

COREY, WILLIAM, b. ca. 1635, d. Portsmouth, R.I., 8 February 1681/2. Clue to English origins at NEHGR 145:122-24; son John[2] at RIR 18:100-6, 19:62-63; NEHGR 147:162-63 (further notes on English ancestry).

CORLISS, GEORGE, b. ca. 1617, d. Haverhill, Mass., 19 October 1686. Ordway, pp. 207-20; Johnson, pp. 97-100; Lyon, pp. 283-84.

CORNELL, THOMAS, d. Newport, R.I., 23 May 1673. LENE, pp. 46-47; TAG 58:77-83 (single line of descent through Thomas[2]). Elaine Forman Crane, *Killed Strangely: the Death of Rebecca Cornell* (Ithaca, NY: Cornell University Press, 2002), Reviews: NYGBR 135:156, TAG 77:318-19.

CORNISH, RICHARD, of Weymouth, Mass., d. York, Me., 1644. Wife Katherine d. there December 1644. LENE, p. 11-12.

CORNWALL, WILLIAM, b. 1609, d. Middletown, Conn., 21 February 1677/8. GMB I:481-84.

CORWIN SEE CURWEN

COTTA, ROBERT, b. ca. 1611, d. Salem, Mass., after 15 November 1664. GM2 II:215-17.

COTTON, JOHN, 1584, d. Boston, Mass., 23 December 1652. GMB I:484-87; son Seaborn[2] in RF1, three generations all lines. English ancestry at NHGR 16:145-70; NEQ 56:78-102; NEQ 76:73-107; Sargent Bush, Jr., ed., *The Correspondence of John Cotton* (Chapel Hill, NC: University of North Carolina Press, 2001). Reviews: NEQ 75:323-25.

COTTON, WILLIAM, fl. Boston, Mass., 1640s-1660s. JPG I:172-77.

COTYMORE, THOMAS, b. ca. 1611, of Charlestown, Mass., d. at sea 27 December 1644. JIC, pp. 136-49; NEHGR 138:39-41 (note).

COURSER, WILLIAM, b. ca. 1608, d. Boston, Mass., between 15 April and 26 July 1673. GM2 II:218-21.

COUSINS, ISAAC, b. ca. 1613, d. Boston, Mass., 23 July 1702. Davis I:303-9 [Lydia Harmon].

COWES, GILES, b. 1642, d. Ipswich, Mass., 14 August 1696. Davis I:310-14 [Bethia Harris], including English origins.

CRACKBONE, GILBERT, b. ca. 1596, d. Cambridge, Mass., 2 January 1671/2. GM2 II:223-26; son Benjamin[2] at Cameos, pp. 161-65.

CRAFTS, GRIFFIN, b. ca. 1603, d. Roxbury, Mass., 4 October 1689. GMB I:489-91; Johnson, pp. 100-3; JPG I:178-84.

CRAGGEN, JOHN, d. Woburn, Mass., 27 October 1708. TAG 69:81-85.

CRAM, JOHN, b. 1596/7, d. Hampton, N.H., 5 March 1681/2. GM2 II:227-30; Davis I:315-17 [Phoebe Tilton], including English origins.

CRAMPTON, JOHN, d. Norwalk, Conn., before 26 December 1709. CN 37:542-64 (Joseph[2]).

CRANDALL, JOHN, b. ca. 1612, d. Newport, R.I., before 29 November 1676. EB, pp. 168-70; Johnson, pp. 103-4.

CRANE, HENRY, b. ca. 1624, d. Milton, Mass., 21 March 1710. Stone, pp. 81-86.

CRANSTON, JOHN, b. ca. 1626, d. 1680. RD600, pp. 114-15; notable descendants at NEXUS 11:140-45.

CRAPO, PETER, b. ca. 1670, possibly France, d. Rochester, Mass., between 20 February and 1 May 1756. MF13, two generations.

CRAWFORD, JOHN, d. Watertown, Mass., 12 August 1634. Goodman, p. 173; GM2 II:230-31 (which notes that his first name is unknown).

CRISP, BENJAMIN, b. ca. 1610, d. Watertown, Mass., between 5 November and 21 December 1683. Davis I:318-21 [Sarah Hildreth]; GMB I:493-95; MBT #1110; TAG 62:25-27.

CROCKER, WILLIAM, b. ca. 1608, d. Barnstable, Mass., 1692. Makepeace pp. 129-47.

CROCKETT, THOMAS, b. ca. 1615, d. Kittery, Me., before 20 March 1678/9. GMB I:495-98; MJ 19:37-38, 25:31.

CROMWELL, THOMAS, b. ca. 1617, d. Boston, Mass., ca. 1649. NEXUS 2:157-58.

CROSBY, SIMON, b. ca. 1609, d. Cambridge, Mass., September 1639. GM2 II:232-36.

CROSBY, THOMAS, b. ca. 1575, d. Rowley, Mass., May 1661. Dancing, pp. 285-312; Crosby, pp. I:13-36, including English origins; wife of Simon[2], Anne (Brigham)'s ancestry at Crosby I:1-4; descendants of Timothy[7] at Crosby I:75-205, II:206-340.

CROSS, JOHN, b.c 1584, d. Ipswich, Mass., between 18 December 1650 and 25 March 1651. GM2 II:237-40.

CROSS, ROBERT, b. ca. 1613, d. Ipswich, Mass., between 30 April 1697 and 31 March 1702. GM2 II:240-45; Ordway, pp. 223-46; Davis I:322-32 [Phoebe Tilton]; JPG I:185-98; MJ 27:15-19.

CROSWELL, THOMAS, b. ca.1633, d. Charlestown, Mass., 30 August 1708. Morgan; Sex, pp. 159-74.

CROUCH, SARAH, fl. Charlestown, Mass., 1668-1670s. Sex, pp. 41-53, et al.

CROW, JOHN, b. ca. 1590, d. Yarmouth, Mass., after 2 March 1651/2. GM2 II:245-48; JPG II:89-100.

CROW, JOHN, b. ca. 1606, d. Hartford, Conn., 16 January 1686. Nichols, pp. 158-59; Johnson, pp. 105-6.

CROW/CROWE/CROWELL, CHRISTOPHER, b. ca. 1629, d. Boston, Mass., before 7 November 1668. Ordway, pp. 249-69.

CROWELL SEE CROW

CROWNE, WILLIAM, b. ca. 1617, d. Boston, Mass., before 28 February 1682/3. Wife Agnes (Mackworth) at RD600, pp. 163-66; PA, p. 485; MCA, p. 547.

CUDWORTH, JAMES, b. 1612, of Scituate and Barnstable, Mass., d. London, England, late 1681. GM2 II:249-58; RD600, p. 337; Lyon, pp. 285-90; MJ 18:39-43.

CULVER, EDWARD, b. ca. 1610, d. Mystic or New London, Conn., 1685. Johnson, pp. 106-10; Valerie Dyer Giorgi, *Colver-Culver Family Genealogy as Descended from Edward Colver of Groton, Connecticut to the Thirteen Generations in America* (Santa Maria, CA: the author, 1984). Reviews: TAG 64:56-57, NYGBR 120:181, NGSQ 74:150.

CUMMINGS, ISAAC, b. 1601, d. Topsfield, Mass., between 8 and 22 May 1677. NEA 4:3:49-53 (DNA Study); NEHGR 145:239-40; NEHGR 158:228-30 (Abraham[4-3] John[2]); TEG 20:174-75.

CUMMINGS, JOHN, b. ca. 1668, d. Oxford, Mass., 10 April 1751. NEHGR 153: 52-72; NEA 4:3:49-53 (DNA Study); Abbott Lowell Cummings, *Descendants of John Comins: (ca. 1668-1751) and his wife Mary of Woburn and Oxford, Massachusetts, and Windham County, Connecticut* (Boston, MA: Newbury Street Press, 2001), winner of the Donald Lines Jacobus Award for 2003. Reviews: MG 24:96, VG 7:138-39, TAG 77:76, NEHGR 157:89, NGSQ 91:228-29, CN 35:451-52.

CURRIER, JEFFREY, b. ca. 1635, d. Isle of Shoals, N.H., after 15 July 1690. Philip Joseph Currier, *Currier Family Records of U.S.A. and Canada, Vol-*

ume II (Henniker, NH: the author, 1984). Reviews: NEHGR 140:344-46, NYGBR 116:184, NGSQ 74:69.

CURRIER, RICHARD, b. ca. 1617, d. Amesbury, Mass., 22 February 1686/7. Stone, pp. 87-94; Philip Joseph Currier, *Currier Family Records of U.S.A. and Canada, Volume I: Descendants of Richard Currier (1616-1686/7) of Salisbury and Amesbury, Massachusetts* (Henniker, NH: the author, 1984). Reviews: NEHGR 140:344-46, 157:89-90, NYGBR 116:184, NGSQ 74:69.

CURRIER, SAMUEL, b. ca. 1636, d. Haverhill, Mass., 14 March 1712/3. Philip Joseph Currier, *Currier Family Records of U.S.A. and Canada, Volume II* (Henniker, NH: the author, 1984). Reviews: NEHGR 140:344-46, NYGBR 116:184, NGSQ 74:69.

CURTIS, FRANCIS, b. ca. 1650, d. Plympton, Mass., 24 April 1717. Son John[2] at TAG 67:2-7.

CURTIS, HENRY, b. ca. 1618, d. Sudbury, Mass., before 27 September 1678. Son Ephraim[2] at Thompson, pp. 60-61, et al.

CURTIS, RICHARD, b. ca. 1625, d. Scituate, Mass., 15 October 1693. Stone, pp. 95-97, including English origins.

CURTIS, THOMAS, b. ca. 1598, d. Wethersfield, Conn., 13 November 1681. CN 25:192-98; TAG 71:220-24 (Samuel[2]); Rose Mary Goodwin, *A Family Named Curtis: Descendants of Thomas Curtis of Wethersfield, Conn., 1598-1982* (Sunland, CA: the author, 1983). Reviews: CN 16:695-96.

CURTIS, THOMAS, b.1619, d. York, Me., between 19 April 1680 and 1 October 1706. JPG I:199-205, including English origins.

CURTIS, WILLIAM, b. 1592, d. Roxbury, Mass., 9 December 1672. GMB I:499-501.

CURTIS, WILLIAM, b. ca. 1665, d. Danvers, Mass., after 15 April 1752. JIC, pp. 31-46.

CURTIS, WILLIAM, of Salem, Mass. William[2] at TAG 59:71-76.

CURTIS, ZACHEUS, b. ca. 1619, d. Rowley, Mass., before November 1682. GM2 II:261-64; Davis I:333-56 [Amos Towne, Sarah Stone]; JPG I:206-25.

CURWEN, GEORGE, b. 1610, d. Salem, Mass., 3 January 1684/5. MF5, four generations all lines for children of second wife Elizabeth (Winslow). RD600, pp. 517-18; NEHGR 150:190-97 (first wife's English origins).

Curwen, Matthias, b. ca. 1602, of Ipswich, Mass., d. Southold, N.Y., ca. 1658. GM2 II:264-67; NEHGR 150:180-89 (wife's identity proven).

Cushing, Matthew, b. 1589, d. Hingham, Mass., 30 September 1660. Chase, pp. 155-60, including English origins.

Cushman, Thomas, b. 1607/8, d. Plymouth, Mass., 10/11 December 1691. MF17, four generations all lines; GMB I:502-4 and PM, pp. 158-60 (father Robert Cushman, who returned to England); Brewer, pp. 343-47; Lyon, pp. 291-95; Robert E. Cushman and Franklin P. Cole, *Robert Cushman of Kent (1577-1625): Chief Agent of the Plymouth Pilgrims (1617-1625)* (Plymouth, MA: General Society of Mayflower Descendants, 2005, 2nd edition).

Cutler, James, b. ca. 1606, d. Lexington, Mass., 17 July 1694. GM2 II:267-72; EB, pp. 170-73; Thompson, pp. 193-95, et al.

Cutter, Richard, b. ca. 1620, d. Cambridge, Mass., 1693. Cameos, pp. 105-9. 299-301; Mower, pp. 171-82; TAG 74:292-98 (hypothesis on wife Elizabeth's identity).

Cutting, John, b. ca. 1593 d. Newbury, Mass., 20 November 1659. Davis I:357-63 [Abel Lunt].

Cutting, Richard, b. 1621/2, d. Watertown, Mass., 21 March 1695/6. GM2 II:272-75; Kempton, pp. 257-85, including English origins. Paternal grandmother's Finch ancestry at Kempton pp. 305-9. Mother's Stone and Church ancestry given at Kempton, pp. 445-49, and 241-46, respectively; TAG 68:205-6 (James[2]'s sons).

Dady, William, b. ca. 1605, d. Charlestown, Mass., 10 April 1682. GMB I:505-8.

Dake see Deake

Dalton, Philemon, b. ca.1590, d. Hampton, N.H., 4 June 1662. GM2 II:277-80; clue to English origins at NHGR 9:109, 10:81; NEHGR 153:180-82; NEHGR 154:259-89 (English origins).

Dalton, Timothy, b. ca. 1577, d. Hampton, N.H., 28 December 1661. NEHGR 154:259-89 (English origins).

Damon, John, b. 1621, d. Scituate, Mass., before 3 October 1676. Richard A. Damon, Jr. and D. Bradford Damon, *Damon Family of Scituate, Mass., Genealogy, 2000: One of 3 Separate Colonial Massachusetts Damon Families* (Amherst, MA: the authors, 2002). Reviews: CN 35:633-34.

DAMON, JOHN, b. 1621/2, d. Reading, Mass., 8 April 1708. Goodman, pp. 175-79; Mower, pp. 185-87; Richard A. Damon, Jr., *The Damon Family of Reading, Massachusetts* (Camden, ME: Penobscot Press, 1999), includes English origins.

DAMON, THOMAS, b. 1627, d. Reading, Mass., 7 December 1683. Richard A. Damon, Jr., *The Damon Family of Wayland, Massachusetts* (Camden, ME: Penobscot Press, 1997). Reviews: CN 32:238.

DANA, RICHARD, b. 1617, d. 1690. Chase, pp. 161-73, including possible English origins; Morgan.

DANE, JOHN, b. ca. 1587, d. Roxbury, Mass., 14 September 1658. Stevens, 49; MBT #1700.

DANE, THOMAS, d. Concord, Mass., 6 February 1675. GM2 II:281 (a note about the possibility of there being two Thomas Danes); Sex, pp. 135-40.

DANFORTH, NICHOLAS, b. 1589/90, d. Cambridge, Mass., April 1638. GM2 II, pp. 281-85; 31Imm, pp. 72-78, including English origins; son Thomas[2] at Cameos, various pages and specifically at pp. 145-48, 173-81, 235-38, 249-65, 289-94; Thomas[2] also at various pages in Sex, specifically, pp. 41-42; son Jonathan[2]'s wife's ancestry at NEHGR 141:215-27.

DANIEL, ROBERT, b. ca. 1592, d. Cambridge, Mass., 6 July 1655. EB, pp. 173-76.

DARLING, DENNIS, b. ca. 1640, d. Mendon, Mass., 25 January 1717/8. Kempton, pp. 287-303.

DARLING, GEORGE, b. ca. 1620, d. Salem, Mass., before 9 October 1693. Lou Ella J. Martin and William A. Martin, *George Darling of Lynn and Marblehead and Some of His Descendants 1650 to 1920* (Placentia, CA: Creative Continuum, 2001). Reviews: NGSQ 89:301-2.

DARWIN, EPHRAIM, b. ca. 1650, d. Guilford, Conn., before 27 October 1725. TAG 71:28-35; TAG 73:194-95.

DAVENPORT, JOHN, b. 1597, d. Boston, Mass., 15 March 1669/70. RD600, pp. 422-23; wife Elizabeth at Doctors, p. 31-33; NEQ 70:265-84 (wife Elizabeth); Robert Ralsey Davenport, *Davenport Genealogy* (the author, 1982). Reviews: CN 15:705-6, TAG 59:54, NEHGR 137:168-69, NGSQ 72:297-98.

DAVENPORT, RICHARD, b. ca. 1606, d. Boston, Mass., 15 July 1665. GMB I: 509-14; NEA 5:1:18-19; NEHGR 158:5-22 (Mary[4] Walker, Rebecca[3] Eleazar[2]).

DAVENPORT, THOMAS, b. ca. 1620, d. Dorchester, Mass., 9 November 1685. Johnson, pp. 110-13; Mower, pp. 189-201; Lyon, pp. 296-98; NEHGR 158:5-22 (James[3] Ebenezer[2]).

DAVIE, HUMPHREY, b. 1625, d. Hartford, Conn., 18 Feb. 1688/9. PA, pp. 259; RD600, pp. 149-53; MCA, p. 261-22.

DAVIS, BARNABAS, b. ca. 1599, d. Charlestown, Mass., 27 November 1685. GM2 II:286-92.

DAVIS, DOLOR, b. ca. 1599, d. Barnstable, Mass., between 13 September 1672 and 19 June 1673. GM2 II:292-97; Jessup, pp. 332-45; possible son Nicholas at TAG 64:113-18.

DAVIS, ISAAC, d.ca. 1687, Kennebec, ME. TEG 23:159-66, 179.

DAVIS, JAMES, b. ca. 1583, d. Haverhill, Mass., 29 January 1678/9. Wife Cecily (Thayer)'s English origins at TAG 73:81-90, 209-19. Elisha[3] James[2]'s wife identified at TG 9:98-133; Joseph[3] John[2] at NHGR 20:4-6; Croll, 201; Stevens, 17; CN 26:198-209.

DAVIS, JAMES, b. ca. 1606, d. Boston, Mass., 17 October 1661. GM2 II:298-300.

DAVIS, JOHN, b. ca. 1660, d. Newbury, Mass., between 1708 and 1710. Davis I:364-417 [Nicholas Davis]; son John[2] at MG 26:147-57.

DAVIS, JOHN, d. Watertown, Mass., before 19 June 1656. Daughter and wife, both Marys, at Thompson, pp. 109-13, et al.; Sex, pp. 77-78, et al.

DAVIS, MARGARET, b. ca. 1603, d. Braintree, Mass., 13 September 1669. GM2 II:303-4.

DAVIS, NICHOLAS, b. ca. 1595, d. York, Me., between 27 April 1667 and 12 March 1669/70. GM2 II:304-9; EB, pp. 176-78.

DAVIS, ROBERT, b. ca. 1667, d. Warwick, R.I., 17 December 1718. RIR 23:97-102.

DAVIS, ROBERT, d. Barnstable, Mass., between 14 April 1688 and 29 June 1693. Croll, 126.

DAVIS, SAMUEL, d. Watertown, Mass., between 2 May and 4 July 1672. JPG II:101-5.

DAVIS, THOMAS, b. ca. 1603, d. Haverhill, Mass., 27 July 1683. GM2 II:310-16; Johnson, p. 114; Lyon, pp. 298-99.

DAVIS, WILLIAM, b. ca. 1597, d. Boston, Mass., before 7 March 1643/4. GM2 II:316-20.

DAVIS, WILLIAM, b. ca. 1617, d. Roxbury, Mass., 9 December 1683. Chase, pp. 175-79.

DAWES, WILLIAM, b. ca. 1619, d. Boston, Mass., 24 March 1703/4. GM2 II:320-25.

DAY, ROBERT, b. ca. 1604, d. Hartford, Conn., between 20 May and 14 October 1648. GM2 II:325-29.

DAY, ROBERT, b. ca. 1605, d. Ipswich, Mass., between 11 August and 25 September 1683. GM2 II:329-33; EB, pp. 178-79.

DE LA FOREST, JOHN ARMUNG, d. Plymouth, Mass., 1 August 1690. LENE, pp. 60-61.

DEACON, RICHARD, fl. Worcester, Mass., 1689. Sex, pp. 148-53.

DEAKE, RICHARD, b. ca. 1687, d. Westerly, R.I., between 11 November 1753 and 25 February 1754. RIR 25:1-15.

DEANE, JOHN, b. ca. 1600, d. Taunton, Mass., between 25 April and 7 June 1660. Jessup, pp. 345-49, including English origins; MBT #564; NEHGR 139:324-25 (note on English ancestry); MJ 26:22-25, 27:87-99.

DEANE, RACHEL, b. ca. 1604, d. Marshfield, Mass., after 17 April 1671. GM2 II:335-36.

DEANE, STEPHEN, b. ca. 1605, d. Plymouth, Mass., between 10 March 1633/4 and 2 October 1634. GMB I:515-17; PM, pp. 162-63.

DEANE, WALTER, b. 1613, d. Taunton, Mass., after 25 November 1693. JPG I:226-43, including English ancestry; Lyon, pp. 299-312; TAG 59:224-30; NEHGR 147:240-54 (thoughts on wife's identity); MJ 17:48-49, 26:22-25, 27:87-99.

DEERING, SAMUEL, d. Braintree, Mass., 23 October 1671. Davis I:418-19 [Annis Spear].

DELANO, PHILIP, b. 1602, d. Plymouth, Mass., between 22 August 1681 and 4 March 1681/2. Delano, five generations all lines; GMB I:517-21; PM, pp. 164-68; son Philip[2] at NEA 5:1:22; MQ 46:57-59 (Deborah[3] Thomas[2]); MQ 66:39 (Thomas[2]).

DEMING, JOHN, d. Wethersfield, Conn., ca. 1694. Pond, 228; TAG 62:140-42.

DENISON, WILLIAM, b. 1571, d. Roxbury, Mass., 25 January 1653/4. GMB I:521-24; EB, pp. 179-82; son Daniel[2] in RF1, four generations all lines; TAG 50-57 (wife's Chandler ancestry); NEHGR 158:361-63 (addition to English ancestry).

DENNING, WILLIAM, b. ca. 1616, d. Boston, Mass., 20 February 1653/4. GMB I:525-26.

DENNISON, GEORGE, b. ca. 1695, d. Gloucester, Mass., 14 March 1747/8. Stone, pp. 99-104.

DENSLOW, HENRY, b. ca. 1610, d. Windsor, Conn., 4 April 1676. MJ 19:38-40.

DENSLOW, NICHOLAS, b. ca. 1585, d. Windsor, Conn., 8 March 1666/7. GMB I:526-29; MJ 1:24, 3:8, 4:71-74, 17:50-51, 19:42-44 (wife Elizabeth), 27:19-22.

DERBY, JOHN, b. ca. 1610, d. Yarmouth, Mass., between 4 October 1655 and 22 February 1655/6. Crosby, pp. I:37-43, including English origins; MJ 17:51-68.

DERBY, RICHARD, b. 1613, d. after 1640. MJ 17:51-70.

DESBOROUGH, ISAAC, b. 1615, of Lynn, Mass., d. England ca. 1658. GM2 II:338-42.

DESBOROUGH, WALTER, b. ca. 1584, of Roxbury, Mass., d. England ca. 1641. GM2 II:342-44; TAG 80:261-63 (English origins of his wife Phebe).

DEVEREUX, JOHN, b. ca. 1614, d. Marblehead, Mass., between 24 December 1694 and 20 May 1695. GMB I:530-37.

DEWEY, THOMAS, b. ca. 1613, d. Windsor, Conn., 27 April 1648. GMB I:537-39; Johnson, pp. 114-15.

DEXTER, RICHARD, b. ca. 1598, d. Charlestown, Mass., after 27 August 1666. He, wife, and daughter at Sex, pp. 60-69, 132-33.

DEXTER, THOMAS, b. ca. 1594, d. Boston, Mass., after 26 October 1676. GMB I:540-45; TAG 78:181-85 (English origins).

DIAMOND, JOHN, d. Kittery, Me., before 9 July 1667. Jessup, pp. 350-51.

DIBBLE, ROBERT, b. ca. 1586, d. Dorchester, Mass., after 7 February 1641/2. GM2 II:345-47; NEHGR 155:273-78 (Samuel[3] Thomas[2]); CN 36:204-8 (Samuel[3] Thomas[2]); MJ 25:31.

DICKERMAN, THOMAS, b. ca. 1602, d. Dorchester, Mass., 11 September 1657. Johnson, pp. 115-18.

DICKINSON, NATHANIEL, b. 1601, d. Hadley, Mass., 16 June 1676. NEHGR 152:159-78 (correct English origins).

DIGGINS, JEREMIAH, b. ca. 1650, d. East Windsor, Conn., 23 November 1736. TAG 70:18-26.

DIKE, ANTHONY, b. ca. 1610, of Salem, Mass., d. at sea 15 December 1638. GMB I:545-47; PM, pp. 169-71.

DILL, DANIEL, b. ca. 1628, d. York, Me., before 1721. Brewer, pp. 349-51.

DILL, PETER, b. ca. 1645, d. Chelmsford, Mass., 13 August 1692. JPG I:244-46.

DILLINGHAM, JOHN, b. 1606, d. Ipswich, Mass., between December 1634 and July 1636. GMB I:547-50.

DIMMOCK, THOMAS, b. ca. 1610, d. Barnstable, Mass., before 4 June 1658. GM2 II:347-51; JPG I:247-52; CN 21:169-74, 359-64, 550-54, 742-46, a multi-generational article; MJ 27:22-23.

DIMON, THOMAS, d. Fairfield, Conn., autumn 1658. John McKay Sheftall, *The Dimons of Fairfield, Connecticut: A Family History* (Roswell, GA: W.H. Wolfe Associates, 1983). Reviews: NEHGR 139:326-29, NYGBR 116:56.

DINELY, WILLIAM, b. ca. 1606, d. Boston, Mass., 15 December 1638. GM2 II:351-55.

DINGLEY, JOHN, d. Marshfield, Mass., before 18 March 1689/90. JPG II:367-69; TAG 56:207-10 (discussion of English origins); TAG 61:234-40.

DIVAN, JOHN, b. ca. 1621, d. Lynn, Mass., 4 October 1684. TEG 18:114-16.

DIX, EDWARD, b. ca. 1610, d. Watertown, Mass., 9 July 1660. GMB I:551-53.

DIX, LEONARD, d. Wethersfield, Conn., 7 December 1697. TAG 68:115-18 (John[2]).

DIXEY, WILLIAM, b. ca. 1607, d. Beverly, Mass., between 11 August 1688 and 24 June 1690. Davis I:420-27 [Sarah Stone]; GMB I:553-57.

DIXWELL, JOHN, b. ca. 1607, d. New Haven, Conn., 18 March 1688/9. Chase, pp. 181-88, including English ancestry; RD600, pp. 466-68.

DOANE, JOHN, b. ca. 1590, d. Eastham, Mass., 21 February 1685/6. GMB I:558-63; PM, pp. 171-77; EB, pp. 182-86; Brewer, pp. 353-58.

DODGE, RICHARD, b. ca. 1602, d. Salem, Mass., 15 June 1672. MJ 18:43-45, 26:25-29.

DODGE, TRISTRAM, b. ca. 1607, d. Block Island, R.I., before 6 December 1683. AL, pp. 232-37.

DODGE, WILLIAM, b. ca. 1604, d. Beverly, Mass., after 12 May 1685. GMB I:563-68; Lyon, pp. 312-15; TAG 79:278-82 (John[2]); MJ 18:43-45.

DOGGETT, JOHN, b. ca. 1600, d. Martha's Vineyard, Mass., between 13 and 26 May 1673. GMB I:568-70; 31Imm, pp. 80-87, including English origins; TAG 72:89-100 (wife's identity and English ancestry).

DOLE, RICHARD, b. 1621, d. Newbury, Mass., before 26 July 1705. TAG 74:53-57 (English origins).

DOLLIBER, JOSEPH, b. ca. 1602, d. Marblehead, Mass., 1688. Brewer, pp. 359-61; TEG 2:22-26; MJ 19:40-42.

DOLLIBER, SAMUEL, b. 1608/9, d. Marblehead, Mass., 22 July 1683. MJ 19:40-42.

DOLLIVER SEE DOLLIBER

DORCHESTER, ANTHONY, b. ca. 1620, d. Springfield, Mass., 28 August 1683. Janice P. Dorchester, *Anthony Dorchester and His Descendants* (Vineyard Haven, MA: the author, 1998). Reviews: CN 32:236.

DORMAN, THOMAS, b. ca. 1600, d. Topsfield, Mass., 25 April 1670. GM2 II:357-60; Davis I:437-43 [Dudley Wildes]; Franklin Abbott Dorman, *Thomas Dorman of Topsfield, Massachusetts (1600-1670): Twelve Generations of Descendants* (Bowie, MD: Heritage Books, 1994). Reviews: MG 17:94, TAG 70:123-24, NEHGR 149:433-34.

DOTY, EDWARD, *Mayflower* passenger, d. Plymouth, Mass., 23 August 1655. MF11 five generations all lines; GMB I:573-77; PM, pp. 177-82; Jessup, pp. 351-63; TAG 63:215; TAG 71:114-20 (Thomas[2]).

DOUD, HENRY, of Guilford, Conn. TAG 76:296-99 (identification of wife of John[2]).

DOUGLAS, WILLIAM, b. ca. 1610, d. New London, Conn., 26 July 1682. Spooner; JPG II:370-77; TAG 74:275-80 (English origins of wife).

Dow, Henry, b. ca. 1608, d. Hampton, NH, 21 April 1659. Joseph[3-2] at NHGR 7:97-107, 174-86, 8:33-43, 114-16, 183-92, 9:130-35, 10:82-93, 186-203; Thomas[2] at TAG 60:75-76; NEHGR 142:255-58 (English origins).

Dow, Thomas, b. 1600, d. Haverhill, Mass., 31 May 1654. Johnson, pp. 118-19; Lyon, pp. 315-18.

Downam, John, d. Braintree, Mass., after 1673. EB, pp. 186-87.

Downer, Moses, d. Hampton, N.H., 24 October 1699. Jessup, pp. 363-64.

Downing see also Dunning

Downing, Emanuel, b. 1585, of Salem, Mass., d. after 6 September 1658, possibly in Scotland. JPG I:253-58, including English ancestry; TAG 74:161-74, 299-308 (English ancestry); TAG 76:137 (addendum).

Downing, Mary, b. ca. 1615, d. Boston, Mass., 16 June 1647. GMB I:579-80. Married Anthony Stoddard.

Downs, William, d. Bristol, Mass., before 26 February 1706/7. Howland1, three generations all lines.

Drake, John, b. ca. 1585, d. Windsor, Conn., 17 August 1659. TAG 63:193-206, TAG 65:87-88; MJ 1:25, 66, 3:9-11, 4:75-98, 25:82-83.

Drinker, Philip, b. 1595, d. Charlestown, Mass., 23 June 1647. GM2 II:362-65.

Drinkwater, Thomas, b. ca. 1660, d. Taunton or Dighton, Mass., before 25 June 1715. Soule, three generations all lines.

Driver, Robert, b. ca. 1592, d. Lynn, Mass., 3 April 1680. GM2 II:365-68.

Driver, Robert, d. Boston, Mass., 18 March 1675. GM2, II:368; LENE, p. 48.

Drury, Hugh, b. ca. 1617, d. Boston, Mass., July 1689. Lyon, pp. 318-22; MBT #528.

Dudley, Thomas, b. 1576, d. Roxbury, Mass., 31 July 1653. GMB I:581-88; English ancestry addition at TG 19:112-28; RD600, pp. 214-16; PA, pp. 280-81; MCA, p. 291. Second wife Katherine (Deighton) at RD600, pp. 259-62; PA, p. 263; MCA, p. 265; NEA 1:2:38-41. RF1, five generations in all lines. Son Samuel[2] at NEXUS 11:104-8 (notable descendants); daughter Sarah

(Dudley) (Keayne) Pacy at WRR, pp. 198-207; TAG 62:43-46 (maternal ancestry addition); NEHGR 139:60 (parents' marriage); NEHGR 139:283-87 (additions to maternal English ancestry); NEHGR 140:219-29 (more maternal ancestry); NEHGR 142:227-44 (more maternal ancestry); TAG 71:200-5 (maternal ancestry); TAG 77:57-65 (corrections and additions to ancestry).

Dumaresq, Philip, d. Boston, Mass., ca. 1744. RD600, pp. 310-11.

Dumbleton, John, b. ca. 1619, d. Springfield, Mass., 1702. TAG 67:11-14.

Dummer, Richard, b. ca. 1598, d. Newbury, Mass., 14 December 1679. GMB I:588-95; Thompson, pp. 157-58, et al.

Dummer, Stephen, b. ca. 1599, of Newbury, Mass., d. England September 1670. EB, pp. 187-89.

Dunbar, Robert, b. ca. 1630, d. Hingham, Mass., 19 September 1693. Pond, 255; Ann Theopold Chaplin, *The Descendants of Robert Dunbar of Hingham, Massachusetts 1630-1693* (Deborah, IA: Anundsen Publishing Co., 1992). Reviews: NHGR 9:143-44, CN 26:82, TAG 68:63, NEHGR 147:281.

Duncan, Nathaniel, b. 1586, d. Boston, Mass., before 26 January 1668/9. GMB I:595-99; MJ 1:25, 67, 3:12-13, 4:99-104, 18:45-46.

Dungan, William, b. ca. 1600, d. England September 1636. His wife Frances (Latham) immigrated to New England with her Dungan children. TG 4:187-202, 9:167-94.

Dunham, John, b. ca. 1589, d. Plymouth, Mass., 2 March 1668/9. GMB I:599-603; PM, pp. 182-86; son Jonathan[2] in Delano, four generations all lines for children from his first wife Mary (Delano); Jessup, pp. 364-69; multiple Nathaniels at TAG 62:5-18, 19-20; TAG 71:130-33 (English origins); TAG 71:250 (note); TAG 73:101-4 (English origins disproved); MQ 54:201-3.

Dunkin, Samuel, b. ca. 1619, d. Roxbury, Mass., after 24 March 1680/1. GM2 II:369-71.

Dunlop, Archibald, b. 1672, d. Stratford, Conn., 24 September 1713. NEHGR 152:186-96; NEHGR 154:321-24 (royal line); RD600, p. 100; PA, p. 662.

Dunning, Theophilus, of Salem, Mass., d. after 25 March 1644. Son Benjamin[2] at CA 40:107-16.

DUNSTER, HENRY, b. 1610, d. Scituate, Mass., 27 February 1659. First president of Harvard College. Cameos, pp. 67-73.

DURAND, JOHN, b. 1664, d. Derby, Conn., 29 March 1727. Alvy Ray Smith, *Dr. John Durand (1664-1727) of Derby, Connecticut and His Family Through Four Generations Featuring the Branch of His Youngest Son Ebenezer Durand Through Ten Generations to 2003* (Boston, MA: Newbury Street Press, 2003). Reviews: NYGBR 135:153-54, TAG 78:316, NEHGR 158:393-94, CN 37:88, 261-62.

DURFEE, THOMAS, b. ca. 1643, d. Portsmouth, R.I., summer 1712. AL, pp. 237-39.

DURHAM, EPHRAIM, d. Guilford, Conn., before 27 October 1725. JPG II:106-135; Azuba Ruth Ward, *The Descendants of Ephraim Durham of Guilford, Connecticut* (n.p., the author, 2000). Reviews: VG 5:142.

DURKEE, WILLIAM, of Ipswich, Mass. Son John[2] at CN 19:425-27, CN 21:401.

DURRANT, JOHN, fl. Billerica, Mass., 1680. Sex, pp. 140-153.

DURRELL, PHILIP, b. ca. 1660, d. Arundel, Me., between 1743/4 and 1749. NEHGR 132:115-22, 264-77, 133:40-48, 118-24, 216-19, 280-85, 134:65-69, 148-55, 220-27, 276-81, 135:16-21 (five generation study).

DUTCH, OSMUND, b. ca. 1603, d. Gloucester, Mass., November 1684. Davis I:444-74 [Charity Haley, Phoebe Tilton, Nicholas Davis]; son Samuel[2] in MF15, four generations all lines; Brewer, pp. 363-67; MJ 19:44-47; David Earle Dutch, *The Dutch Family: Pioneers of New England Descendants of Osmund Dutch of Gloucester, Massachusetts* (Portsmouth, NH: Peter E. Randall Publisher, 2004). Reviews: NEHGR 159:302.

DUTTON, THOMAS, b. ca. 1619, d. Woburn, Mass. Sex, pp. 119-27, et al.

DWIGHT, JOHN, b. ca. 1601, d. Dedham, Mass., 24 January 1660/1. GM2 II:371-78.

DYER, GEORGE, b. ca. 1590, d. Dorchester, Mass., 18 June 1672. GMB I: 603-6; EB, pp. 189-90; MJ 1:26, 2:97, 4:105-12.

DYER, WILLIAM, b. 1609, d. Newport, R.I., before 24 October 1677. GM2 II:379-85; RIR 9:3; wife Mary (Barrett) Dyer, the Quaker martyr, d. Boston, Mass., 1 June 1660, LENE, pp. 29-32; NEHGR 145:22-28 (daughter Mary); NEHGR 146:294-95 (daughter Elizabeth's marriage identified); NEHGR 158:27-28 (clue to Mary's ancestry).

EAMES, ANTHONY, b. ca. 1592, d. Marshfield, Mass., after 28 June 1670. GM2 II:387-92; EB, pp. 190-91; JPG II:378-81; Lyon, pp. 322-23; AL, pp. 239-41; MJ 17:70-72, 27:23.

EAMES, ROBERT, d. Woburn, Mass., 30 July 1712. Lyon, pp. 324-28.

EAMES, THOMAS, b. 1618, d. Sherborn, Mass., 25 January 1679/80. Goodman, pp. 181-83; Lyon, pp. 324-28.

EARLE, RALPH, b. 1606/7, d. Portsmouth, R.I., 1678. Jessup, pp. 369-74.

EASTMAN, ROGER, b. 1610, d. Salisbury, Mass., 16 December 1694. EB, pp. 191-96.

EASTON, JOSEPH, b. ca. 1614, d. Hartford, Conn., 14 August 1688. GM2 II:392-96.

EASTON, NICHOLAS, b. ca. 1593, d. Newport, R.I., 15 August 1675. GM2 II:396-403; RIR 12:41; RIR 17:69-75, 101-8, 18:9-19, 45-53, 19:101; NEHGR 154:159-71 (English origins).

EATON, FRANCIS, *Mayflower* passenger, d. Plymouth, Mass., before 8 November 1633. MF9, five generations all lines; GMB I:608-10; PM, pp. 187-89; Brewer, pp. 369-72; TAG 72:301-4 (English origins); TAG 72:305-9 (notes).

EATON, JOHN, b. 1590, d. Haverhill, Mass., 29 October 1668. 26Imm, pp. 63-82; Stevens, 18; MBT #394; TAG 68:48-54 (English origins).

EATON, JOHN, b. ca. 1605, d. Dedham, Mass., 17 November 1658. GM2 II:403-7.

ECCLES, RICHARD, b. ca. 1619, d. Cambridge, Mass., before 1697. Cameos, pp. 183-88, 303-8.

EDDY, JOHN, b. 1597, d. Watertown, Mass., 12 October 1584. GMB I:610-14; PM, pp. 189-94; Pond, 279.

EDDY, SAMUEL, b. 1608, d. Swansea, Mass., 12 November 1688. GMB I:614-18; PM, pp. 194-98, Pond, 279.

EDENDEN, EDMUND, b. 1599, d. Boston, Mass., after 1669. Goodman, pp. 185-89, including English origins; 26Imm, pp. 83-88.

EDGE, ROBERT, d. York, Me., after September 1672. Davis I:475-76 [Annis Spear].

EDGECOMB, JOHN, b. ca. 1654, d. New London, Conn., 11 April 1721. TAG 61:146-58 (John[2]).

EDGECOMB, NICHOLAS, b. ca. 1593, d. Casco, Me., ca. 1681. Davis I:477-503 [Charity Haley, Nicholas Davis]; MJ 19:47-50.

EDGERLY, THOMAS, d. Durham, N.H., after 1717. NHGR 13:49-64, 129-42, 14:25-34, 145-54, 15:22-32.

EDMONDS, WILLIAM, b. ca. 1610, d. Lynn, Mass., between 15 June 1681 and 8 September 1693. GM2 II:407-11; TEG 16:202-11, 17:25-31.

EDMUNDS, WALTER, b. ca. 1595, d. Charlestown, Mass., 13 July 1667. 26Imm, pp. 89-106; MBT #518.

EDSON, SAMUEL, b. 1613, d. Bridgewater, Mass., 19 July 1692. 26Imm, pp. 107-22; MBT #572.

EDWARDS, ALEXANDER, d. Northampton, Mass., 4 September 1690. 31Imm, pp. 13-18, including English origins of his wife Sarah (Baldwin); JPG I:259-68.

EDWARDS, JOHN, b. ca. 1600, d. Wethersfield, Conn., 27 December 1664. NEHGR 145:317-41, NEHGR 150:215-16 (correction); TAG 71:235-41 (Joseph[2]); NEHGR 149:41-45 (daughter Hannah).

EDWARDS, MARY, b. ca. 1642, of Charlestown, Mass., in the 1660s. Sex, pp. 180-82.

EDWARDS, RICE, d. Beverly, Mass., after 15 June 1683. NEHGR 155:225-26 (daughter Martha); TEG 22:100-8.

EDWARDS, ROBERT, b. ca. 1613, d. Concord, Mass., before 8 December 1646. GM2 II:411-12.

EDWARDS, WILLIAM, b. 1618, d. Hartford, Conn., after 1680. Wife Agnes (Harris) at RD600, pp. 548-50; MCA, p. 416; her origins at TAG 63:33-45; NEHGR 146:35-56 (the daughters of Timothy[3] Richard[2]).

EELES, JOHN, b. ca. 1600, of Dorchester, Mass., and Windsor, Conn., d. England after 1641. GMB I:618-20; son Samuel[2]'s wife Ann Lenthall's ancestry at TG 19:222-30.

EGGLESTON, BIGOD, b. 1586/7, d. Windsor, Conn., 1 September 1674. GMB I:620-24; CN 22:616-21; TAG 69:193-201 (identity of his mother); MJ 1:26-27, 67, 2:86, 97, 3:14, 4:113-30, 11:67-69, 15:53-57, 25:83-85.

EGGLESTON, JANE, widow, d. Woburn, Mass., 10 March 1687. MBT #718.

ELIOT, FRANCIS, d. Braintree, Mass., before 29 October 1677. Daughter Rachel at Doctors, pp. 105-7.

ELIOT, JACOB, b. 1606, d. Boston, Mass., 6 May 1651. GMB I:626-30; NEHGR 146:377-82 (Asaph[2]'s wife).

ELIOT, JOHN, b. 1604, d. Roxbury, Mass., 21 May 1690. GMB I:630-32; grandson John at Cameos, pp. 285-88; wife Ann (Mountford) at Doctors, pp. 41-44; NEQ 62:346-68; NEQ 66:416-33; NEQ 69:3-32; Richard W. Cogley, *John Eliot's Mission to the Indians before King Philip's War* (Cambridge, MA: Harvard University Press, 1999). Reviews: NEQ 73:518-21; Michael P. Clark, ed., *The Eliot Tracts: With Letters from John Eliot to Thomas Thorowgood and Richard Baxter* (Westport, CT: Praeger Publishers, 2003). Reviews: NEQ 78:127-30.

ELIOT, PHILIP, b. 1602, d. Roxbury, Mass., 22 October 1657. GM2 II:413-16; TAG 80:102-16, 201-16 (wife's English origins).

ELKINS, HENRY, b. ca. 1613, d. Hampton, N.H., 19 November 1688. GM2 II:417-19; NHGR 10:133-46.

ELLENWOOD SEE ELLINGWOOD

ELLERY, WILLIAM, b. ca. 1643, d. Gloucester, Mass., 9 December 1696. Stevens, 72.

ELLET, JOHN, b. ca. 1608, d. Stamford, Conn., after 30 November 1658. GMB I:632-34.

ELLINGWOOD, RALPH, b. ca. 1608, d. Beverly, Mass., between 7 and 30 January 1673/4. GM2 II:420-24; son Ralph[2] at MG 17:59-68.

ELLIS, JOHN, b. ca. 1620, d. Sandwich, Mass., before 23 March 1676/7. EB, pp. 196-202; Jessup, pp. 376-82.

ELLSWORTH, JOSIAH, b. ca. 1629, d. East Windsor, Conn., 20 August 1689. Nichols, pp. 156-57.

ELMER, EDWARD, b. ca. 1613, d. Hartford, Conn., before 6 June 1676. GMB I:634-38.

ELMES, RHODOLPHUS, b. ca. 1620, d. Scituate, Mass., 19 March 1711/2. GM2 II:424-26.

ELWELL, ROBERT, b. ca. 1609, d. Gloucester, Mass., 18 May 1683. GM2 II:426-31; Davis I:504-20 [Charity Haley, Nicholas Davis]; Chase, pp. 189-95.

ELWOOD SEE ELLINGWOOD

ELY, NATHANIEL, b. ca. 1609, d. Springfield, Mass., 25 December 1675. GM2 II:432-39; Marion Edwards Lee, *The Lees of New England and Some Allied Families* (Ponca City, OK: the author, 1981). Reviews: CN 15:159-60.

ELY, RICHARD, b. ca. 1620, d. Lyme, Conn., 24 November 1684. Johnson, pp. 119-20.

ELY, WILLIAM, b. 1647, d. New London, Conn., 1717. Spooner.

EMERSON, MICHAEL, b. 1627, d. Salem, Mass., between 18 July 1709 and 1715. 31Imm, pp. 90-97, including English origins; daughter Hannah (Emerson) Dustan at Puritans, pp. 161-64; LENE, pp. 102-3 (daughter Elizabeth).

EMERSON, THOMAS, b. 1584, d. Ipswich, Mass., 1 May 1666. Stone, pp. 105-11, including English origins; EB, pp. 1-46; JPG I:269-83; Stowers, pp. 355-60.

EMERY, ANTHONY, b. 1601, d. Portsmouth, R.I., between 9 March 1680/1 and 10 May 1700. GM2 II:441-46.

EMERY, JOHN, b. 1599, d. Newbury, Mass., 3 November 1683. GM2 II:446-52; Davis I:521-31 [Sarah Miller, Phoebe Tilton], including English origins; 31Imm, pp. 99-105, including English origins; EB, pp. 202-5; Jessup, pp. 382-88; MBT #932; TAG 65:211-13 (identification of wife Alice Grantham).

ENDICOTT, JOHN, b. ca. 1600, d. Boston, Mass., 15 March 1664/5. GMB I:639-46; MJ 17:42-44 (wife Elizabeth Cogan); MJ 17:72-73.

ENO, JAMES, b. 1625, d. Windsor, Conn., 11 June 1682. Lyon, pp. 329-34.

ENSIGN, JAMES, b. 1606, d. Hartford, Conn., between 23 November and 23 December 1670. GM2 II:452-58; TAG 56:219-20, 60:97-100, 75:1-15, 130-44, 229-40 (English origins, including a chart of relationships).

ENSIGN, THOMAS, b. 1599, d. Scituate, Mass., between 16 July 1663 and 17 February 1663/4. Lyon, pp. 335-37; TAG 56:219-20, 60:97-100, 73:241-55, 75:1-15, 130-44, 229-40 (English origins, including a chart of relationships).

ERRINGTON, ABRAHAM, b. ca. 1620, d. Cambridge, Mass., 9 May 1677. Sex, pp. 88-90.

ESTES, MATTHEW, b. 1645, d. Lynn, Mass., between 4 June and 18 July 1723. TEG 18:90-98.

Estow, William, b. ca. 1600, d. Hampton, N.H., 23 November 1655. Davis I:532-34 [Sarah Stone], including English origins; NEHGR 142:258-60 (English origins).

Evans, Jane, fl. Billerica, Mass., 1654. Sex, pp. 158-64.

Eveleth, Silvester, b. 1603/4, d. Gloucester, Mass., 4 January 1689. Stevens, 71; NEHGR 134:299-309, 135:23-35, 98-108 (a multi-generational study); NEHGR 155:414-15 (correction); MJ 18:46-47.

Everard, Richard, b. 1597, d. Dedham, Mass., 3 July 1682. NEHGR 154:259-89 (English origins).

Everett, Richard, b. 1597, d. Dedham, Mass., 3 July 1682. Kempton4, pp. 197-216, including English origins; EB, pp. 205-7.

Everill, James, b. ca. 1603, d. Boston, Mass., between 11 and 29 December 1682. GM2 II:469-76.

Ewell, Henry, b. ca. 1613, d. Scituate, Mass., between 21 May 1683 and 13 March 1688/9. GM2 II:476-79.

Ewer, Thomas, b. 1592/3, d. Charlestown, Mass., between 5 June and 20 August 1638. GM2 II:479-83.

Eyre, Simon, b. 1588, d. Boston, Mass., 10 November 1658. GM2 II:483-89; Thompson, pp. 42-43, et al.; TAG 65:17-23.

Fairbanks, Jonathan, b. ca. 1594, d. Dedham, Mass., 5 December 1668. Kempton3, pp. 119-58, including English origins; EB, pp. 207-10.

Fairbanks, Richard, b. ca. 1608, d. Boston, Mass., between 29 January 1654/5 and 15 April 1667. GMB I:647-50.

Fairchild, Thomas, b. ca. 1610, d. Stratford, Conn., 14 December 1670. TAG 69:224-30 (Thomas[2]); Jean Fairchild Gilmore, *Early Fairchilds in America and Their Descendants* (Baltimore, MD: Gateway Press, 1991). Reviews: CN 25:96-97, NYGBR 125:125.

Fairweather, Thomas, b. ca. 1613, d. Boston, Mass., 8 January 1638/9. GMB I:650-51; NEHGR 144:3-21, 151-68, 225-44, 331-49, 145:57-75, 141-58, 241-57, 146:59-76, 143-60, 287-93 (a seven generation study); NEHGR 146:377-82 (Thomas[3] John[2]'s wife); NEHGR 146:383-87 (corrections).

Fallowell, Gabriel, b. ca. 1584, d. Plymouth, Mass., 28 December 1667. NEHGR 148:315-27 (wife's English origins).

FARLEY, GEORGE, b. ca. 1615, d. Billerica, Mass., 27 December 1693. NEHGR 136:43-62, 133-47.

FARMER, EDWARD, b. ca. 1640, d. Billerica, Mass., 21 May 1727. Stone, pp. 113-16, including English origins.

FARNHAM, HENRY, d. Killingworth, Conn., 13 January 1699/1700. TAG 62:33-40.

FARNHAM, RALPH, b. ca. 1603, d. Ipswich, Mass., before 1648. GM2 II:493-94; 50Imm, pp. 149-50; MBT #818; TAG 69:32-36 (English origins); Russell Clare Farnham, *The New England Descendants of the Immigrant Ralph Farnum of Rochester, Kent County, England and Ipswich, Massachusetts* (Portsmouth, NH: Peter E. Randall, 1999). Reviews: MG 21:93-94, CN 32:414, 33:235.

FARR, GEORGE, b. ca. 1594, d. Lynn, Mass., 24 October 1662. GMB III:2077-79; TEG 19:25-29; MJ 18:47-48.

FARRAR, JOHN, b. ca. 1617, d. Lynn, Mass., 23 February 1693/4. TEG 17:171-73.

FARRAR, THOMAS, b. 1614/5, d. Lynn, Mass., 23 February 1693/4. Mower, pp. 203-7.

FARRINGTON, EDMUND, b. ca. 1588, d. Lynn, Mass., 20 January 1670/1. GM2 II:494-98; TAG 65-69 (English origins); TAG 66:9 (wife's identity confirmed); TAG 73:119-22; TEG 17:142-53.

FARRINGTON, JOHN, d. Dedham, Mass., 27 April 1676. Pond, 219.

FARROW, JOHN, b. ca. 1608, d. Hingham, Mass., 7 July 1687. GM2 II:498-501.

FARWELL, HENRY, b. ca. 1605, d. Chelmsford, Mass., 1 August 1670. Wife Olive (Welby) at RD600, p. 338; PA, p. 757-58; MCA, p. 874.

FAUNCE, JOHN, b. ca. 1608, d. Plymouth, Mass., 29 November 1653. GMB I:651-54; PM, pp. 201-3; EB, pp. 210-12.

FAWER, BARNABAS, b. ca. 1614, d. Boston, Mass., 13 December 1654. GM2 II:501-5.

FAWNE, JOHN, b. ca. 1596, d. Haverhill, Mass., between 10 October 1650 and 11 February 1665/6. GM2 II:505-7; TAG 77:28-31 (English origins).

FAXON, THOMAS, b. ca. 1601, d. Braintree, Mass., 23 November 1680. Dancing, pp. 325-56; Lyon, pp. 337-38; TAG 74:41-49 (English origins).

FEAKE, HENRY, b. ca. 1590, of Lynn, Sandwich, Mass., d. Newtown, Long Island, between 24 September 1657 and 2 April 1658. GMB I:654-56.

FEAKE, ROBERT, b. ca. 1602, d. Watertown, Mass., 1 February 1660/1. GMB I:656-60; Thompson, pp. 42-43, 187-89, et al.

FEAVOUR, NICHOLAS, d. Boston, Mass., 18 March 1675. LENE, p. 48.

FELLOWS, RICHARD, d. Hadley, Mass., 1663. NEHGR 138:17-23 (note on origins).

FELLOWS, SAMUEL, d. Salisbury, Mass., 6 March 1697/8. NEHGR 138:17-23 (note on origins).

FELLOWS, WILLIAM, b. ca. 1610, d. Ipswich, Mass., between 29 November and 21 December 1676. GM2 II:507-12; NEHGR 138:17-23 (note on origins).

FELT, GEORGE, b. ca. 1614, d. Malden, Mass., after 1692. GMB I:660-64.

FELTON, BENJAMIN, b. 1604, d. Salem, Mass., before 25 March 1689. GM2 II:512-16.

FENN, BENJAMIN, of Milford, Conn. CN 35:21 (wife of John[4] Joseph[3] Benjamin[2]).

FENNER, JOHN, b. 1631, d. Saybrook, Conn., 1709. Johnson, pp. 120-21; CN 27:410-12.

FENWICK, GEORGE, b. 1603, d. Saybrook, Conn., 1656/7. RD600, pp. 186-88. Wife Catherine (Haselrige) at RD600, pp. 169-70. Wife Alice Apsley at RD600, pp. 397-98.

FERNALD, RENALD, d. Portsmouth, N.H., before October 1656. Davis I:535-55 [Joseph Waterhouse].

FERRIS, JEFFREY, b. ca. 1604, d. Greenwich, Conn., 31 May 1666. GM2 II:517-21.

FESSENDEN, NICHOLAS, b. ca. 1651, d. Cambridge, Mass., 24 February 1718/9. Chase, pp. 197-200.

FIELD, ZACHARIAH, b. 1596, d. Hatfield, Mass., 30 June 1666. Pond, 274, including English origins.

FIFIELD, WILLIAM, b. ca. 1614, d. Hampton, N.H., 18 December 1700. GM2 II:522-26; clues to wife's identity at NHGR 10:32-34. Clues to English origins at NHGR 20:60-63. Son William[2] at NHGR 22:8-14.

FILER, WALTER, b. ca. 1613, d. Windsor, Conn., 12 December 1683. GMB I:665-67; MJ 1:28-29, 4:151-52, 8:139-40; 19:55-58.

FINCH, DANIEL, b. ca. 1585, d. Fairfield, Conn., between 5 and 11 March 1666/7. GMB I:667-69.

FINCH, JOHN, b. ca. 1595, d. Stamford, Conn., 5 September 1657. GMB I:669-71; CN 22:315, 419, 560.

FINNEY SEE PHINNEY

FIRMAGE SEE VERMAYES

FIRMIN, GILES, b. ca. 1590, d. Boston, Mass., between 1 September and 6 October 1634. GMB I:673-75.

FIRMIN, JOHN, b. ca. 1588, d. Watertown, Mass., before 10 May 1642. GMB I:675-78.

FISH, JOHN, d. Sandwich, Mass., before 3 May 1664. Nathan[3] Nathaniel[2]'s wife's identification at TAG 80:53-55, NEHGR 138:130-33.

FISH, THOMAS, b. 1619, d. Portsmouth, R.I., 1687. Johnson, pp. 121-23; AL, pp. 249-52, including English ancestry.

FISHCOCK, EDWARD, b. ca. 1595, of Richmond Island, d. New Amsterdam, N.Y., before 12 March 1645. GM2 II:526-28.

FISHER, ANTHONY, b. 1591, d. Dorchester, Mass., 18 April 1671. Kempton4, pp. 219-71, including English origins; EB, pp. 212-16; Lyon, pp. 343-46; NEHGR 151:171-91 (English origins); NEHGR 151:291-99 (Crispe ancestry); NEHGR 151:300-7 (Godbold ancestry); NEHGR 154:495-96 (addition to Godbold ancestry).

FISHER, EDWARD, d. Portsmouth, R.I., 10 September 1677. TAG 67:193-200 (wife's identity and ancestry).

FISHER, JOSHUA, b. 1587/8, d. Medfield, Mass., 18 October 1674. Kempton4, pp. 219-71, including English origins; Lyon, pp. 339-42; TAG 66:133-34; NEHGR 151:171-91 (English origins); NEHGR 151:291-99 (Crispe ancestry); NEHGR 151:300-7 (Godbold ancestry); NEHGR 154:495-96 (addition to Godbold ancestry); NEHGR 158:25-34 (Abigail[2]).

FISHER, THOMAS, b. ca. 1604, d. Dedham, Mass., 10 August 1638. GM2 II:528-32; Pond, 221; TAG 67:29 (marriage).

FISKE, JOHN, d. Chelmsford, Mass., 14 January 1676. Sex, pp. 86-87.

FISKE, WILLIAM, d. Wenham, Mass., before 16 September 1654. NEHGR 149:230-43 (Joseph[2]).

FITCH, JAMES, b. 1622, d. Lebanon, Conn., 18 November 1702. Son James[2] in MF22, three generations; NEXUS 10:156-58; John T. Fitch, *Descendants of the Reverend James Fitch 1622-1702* (Rockport, ME: Picton Press, 1996, 2003). Reviews: MG 13:50, CN30:225-26, NYGBR 128:255, TAG 72:139, NEHGR 151:371, NGSQ 85:319, MQ 63:154; John T. Fitch, *Puritan in the Wilderness: A Biography of Reverend James Fitch 1622-1702* (Camden, ME: Picton Press, 1993). Reviews: NEHGR 149:313-14, NGSQ 82:302-3; John T. Fitch, *A Fitch Family History: English Ancestors of the Fitches of Colonial Connecticut* (Camden, ME: Picton Press, 1990). Reviews: CN 23:513, NYGBR 122:55, TAG 66:185, NEHGR 144:363, NGSQ 79:146, MQ 58:84.

FITCH, JAMES, b. ca. 1605, d. Boston, Mass., before 16 February 1645/6. GM2 II:532-33.

FITCH, JOSEPH, b. 1630, d. East Windsor, Conn., between 17 November 1719 and 3 October 1727. Nichols, pp. 146-48; TAG 68:1-10, 95-105 (English origins and family); TAG 73:272 (identity of wife of Joseph[2]).

FITCH, THOMAS, Norwalk, Conn. Wife's Stacie English origins at TG 11:163-75; TG 12:91-98; TG 18:59-73.

FITZRANDOLPH, EDWARD, b. 1607, d. Piscataway, N.J., ca. 1684/5. Resided in Scituate and Barnstable, Mass. RD600, pp. 431-32, MCA, p. 343.

FLACK, COTTON, b. 1577, d. Boston, Mass., between 30 April 1656 and 31 July 1658. GMB I:679-80.

FLAGG, THOMAS, b. ca. 1615, d. Watertown, Mass., 6 February 1697/8. Mower, pp. 209-11.

FLEMING, JOHN, b. ca. 1597, d. Watertown, Mass., 4 June 1657. Thompson, pp. 183-84, et al.; Sex, pp. 176-77.

FLETCHER, JOHN, b. ca. 1602, d. Milford, Conn., ca. 1662. EB, pp. 217-18.

FLETCHER, MOSES, *Mayflower* passenger, b. ca. 1565, d. Plymouth early 1621. GMB I:681-82; PM, pp. 204-5; NEHGR 153:407-12.

FLETCHER, ROBERT, b. ca. 1593, d. Concord, Mass., 3 April 1677. Kempton4, pp. 273-83; Nichols, pp. 93-95; JPG I:284-94; MBT #520; family members Joshua and Grizell at Sex, pp. 86-87.

FLINT, HENRY, b. ca. 1615, d. Braintree, Mass., 27 April 1668. GM2 II:534-37.

FLINT, THOMAS, b. ca. 1630, d. Salem, Mass., 15 April 1663. Mower, pp. 213-17.

FLOOD, JOSEPH, b. ca. 1590, of Dorchester and Lynn, Mass., d. after 4 August 1646. GM2 II:537-39.

FLOOD, PHILIP, d. Newbury, Mass., 14 November 1717. Stevens, 39.

FLOUNDERS, THOMAS, d. Wickford, R.I., 2 November 1670. LENE, p. 45.

FLOWER, LAMROCK, b. 1658, d. Hartford, Conn., 19 June 1716. JPG I:295-307.

FLYE, JOHN, of Isle of Shoals and Falmouth, Me., d. Devon, England, 23 June 1696. Lyon, p. 346.

FOBES, JOHN, b. ca. 1600, d. Sandwich, Mass., 1660. Johnson, pp. 123-25.

FOGG, RALPH, b. ca. 1600, of Salem, Mass., d. Plymouth, England ca. 15 March 1673/4. GMB I:682-86; PM, pp. 206-10.

FOLSOM, JOHN, b. ca. 1615, d. Exeter, N.H., 1681. Davis I:556-64 [Abel Lunt], including English origins.

FOOTE, JOSHUA, d. Providence, R.I., 1655. TAG 58:165-67 (addition to English ancestry); TAG 71:149-50; TAG 72:49-55 (including a chart of Foote family connections).

FOOTE, NATHANIEL, b. ca. 1592, d. Wethersfield, Conn., between 1 August and 20 November 1644. GM2 II:540-44; 31Imm, pp. 107-11, including English origins; Pond, 225-26; Gateway #7174; Johnson, pp. 126-31; TAG 58:165-67 (addition to English ancestry); TAG 71:149-50; TAG 72:49-55 (including a chart of Foote family connections).

FORBES SEE ALSO FOBES

FORBES, JAMES, b. ca. 1635, d. Hartford, Conn., 27 November 1692. Karen L. Forbes, *Descendants of James Forbes of Hartford, Connecticut (ca. 1635–1692)* (Baltimore, MD: Gateway Press, 1997). Reviews: CN 31:232-33, NYGBR 129:295, NGSQ 88:65-66.

FORBUSH, DANIEL, d. Marlborough, Mass., October 1687. Dancing, pp. 357-84.

FORD, MARTHA, WIDOW, d. Plymouth ca. 1630. GMB I:686-87; PM, pp. 211-12; TAG 56:32-35.

FORD, MATTHEW/MARTIN, b. ca. 1661, d. Haverhill, Mass., between 1 November 1694 and 23 September 1697. EB, pp. 218-21.

FORD, THOMAS, b. ca. 1591, d. Northampton, Mass., 28 November 1676. GMB I:688-90; 31Imm, pp. 112-17, including English origins; EB, pp. 222-25; MJ 1:26-27, 2:91, 4:131-50, 11:83, 12:67-71, 15:32, 18:48-53.

FORD, WILLIAM, b. ca. 1604, d. Marshfield, Mass., ca. September 1676. Davis I: 565-68 [Joseph Neal].

FORREST, WILLIAM, b. before 1703, d. Canterbury, N.H., after 10 August 1773. Ordway, pp. 271-74.

FOSDICK, STEPHEN, b. ca. 1584, d. Charlestown, Mass., 21 May 1664. GM2 II:545-51; Sex, pp. 175-76.

FOSKETT, JOHN, d. Charlestown, Mass., 11 July 1689. CN 27:219-20 (identification of his wife).

FOSTER, BARTHOLOMEW, b. ca. 1640, d. Gloucester, Mass., 5 December 1689. TG 17:96-108, 234-48, 18:74-96.

FOSTER, CHRISTOPHER, b. ca. 1603, of Lynn, Mass., d. Southampton, N.Y., between 6 August 1684 and 18 October 1687. GM2 II:551-54.

FOSTER, EDWARD, b. ca. 1610, d. Scituate, Mass., between 24 November 1643 and February 1643/4. GMB I:690-92; PM, pp. 212-14; Johnson, pp. 131-33.

FOSTER, HOPESTILL, SEE HIS MOTHER, FOSTER, PATIENCE

FOSTER, PATIENCE, b. 1588, d. Dorchester, Mass., between 18 March 1637/8 and 17 November 1646. GM2 II:554-55; TAG 80:26 (marriage and English origins).

FOSTER, RENALD, b. ca. 1595, d. Ipswich, Mass., between April 1680 and 9 June 1981. Davis I:569-75 [Dudley Wildes]; EB, pp. 225-27.

FOSTER, RICHARD, d. Plymouth, Mass., between 1657 and 27 June 1659. MF18, three generations all lines; Bartlett.

FOSTER, THOMAS, d. Billerica, Mass., 20 April 1682. JPG II:382-88; TAG 68:14-22 (note on English origins).

FOWLE, GEORGE, b. 1610/11, d. Charlestown, Mass., 19 September 1682. Goodman, pp. 191-97; Eugene Chalmers Fowle, compiler, Gary Boyd Roberts and Neil D. Thompson, editors, *Descendants of George Fowle (1610/11?-1682) of Charlestown, Massachusetts* (Boston, MA: NEHGS,

1990). Reviews: NHGR 9:148, CN 24:124-25, NYGBR 122:184, TAG 66:252-53, NGSQ 79:302.

Fowler, Philip, b. ca. 1591, d. Ipswich, Mass., 24 June 1679. GM2 II:560-64; Jessup, pp. 400-4.

Foxwell, Richard, b. ca. 1604, d. Scarborough, Me., before 6 November 1677. GMB I:693-98.

Foxwell, Richard, b. ca. 1610, d. Barnstable, Mass., between 19 and 30 May 1668. GM2 II:565-68; Mower, pp. 219-23.

Fraile, George, b. ca. 1615, d. Lynn, Mass., 9 December 1663. TEG 17:17-24.

Franklin, William, b. ca. 1608, of Ipswich and Boston, Mass., d. London, England, before 28 July 1658. GM2 II:568-73.

Franklin, William, d. Boston, Mass., June 1644. LENE, p. 11.

Frary, John, b. ca. 1600, d. Medfield, Mass., 14 June 1675. Margaret Murphy Frary and Anne Frary Lepak, *The Frary Family in America 1637-1980* (Hampton, NH: Peter E. Randall, 1981). Reviews: CN 15:696-97, NEHGR 137:168-69.

Freame, Thomas, b. ca. 1650, d. Amesbury, Mass., after 1708. 50Imm, pp. 151-54; MBT #450.

Freeborn, William, b. ca. 1594, d. Portsmouth, R.I., 28 April 1670. GM2 II:573-75; Johnson, pp. 133-34; AL, pp. 258-60.

Freeman, Edmund, b. 1596, d. Sandwich, Mass., before November 1682. GM2 II:576-82; Croll, 103, 104; EB, pp. 227-32; sons John[2] and Edmund[2] at Brewster, two generations all lines; both at Brewster3, three generations all lines; Jessup, pp. 410-20.

Freeman, John, b. ca. 1600, d. Sudbury, Mass., 15 September 1648. EB, pp. 232-36; Johnson, pp. 134-35; JPG II:389-91.

Freeman, Samuel, b. ca. 1600, d. Watertown, Mass., between 1644 and 15 October 1646. GMB I:698-700; TAG 75:169-77, 293-99 (five generations from Robert[2]).

Freethy, William, b. ca. 1617, d. York, Me., after 25 April 1688. GM2 II:583-87.

French, John, b. ca. 1612, d. Braintree, Mass., 6 August 1692. Stone, pp. 117-27.

FRENCH, JOHN, b. ca. 1622, d. Northampton, Mass., 1 February 1697. Pond, 271.

FRENCH, RICHARD, of Cambridge, and Billerica, Mass., Sex, pp. 158-64.

FRENCH, STEPHEN, b. ca. 1600, d. Weymouth, Mass., between 18 March 1678/9 and 29 July 1679. GMB I:700-3; MJ 19:50-53, 25:31-33.

FRENCH, THOMAS, b. 1608, d. Ipswich, Mass., 8 August 1680. GMB I:703-6; Davis I:576-84 [Dudley Wildes, Amos Towne]; Croll, 165; 50Imm, pp. 155-64; Johnson, pp. 135-38; MBT #642; NEHGR 142:250-52, 393, 143:363-64 (English origins).

FRENCH, WILLIAM, b. ca. 1604, d. Billerica, Mass., 20 November 1681. GM2 II:588-93; Lyon, pp. 347-49; MBT #758.

FRIEND, JOHN, b. ca. 1605, d. Manchester, Mass., between 4 November 1655 and 27 January 1656. TEG 16:138-45, 212-20, 17:32-39, 102-11, 161-70, 180.

FRISBIE, EDWARD, d. Branford, Conn., 10 May 1690. Nora G. Frisbie, *Edward Frisbie of Branford and His Descendants* (Baltimore, MD: Gateway Press, 1984). Reviews: CN 18:736-37.

FROST, EDMOND, b. ca. 1609, d. Cambridge, Mass., 12 July 1672. GM2 II:593-97; Morgan; son or grandson Samuel at Sex, pp. 21-39; sons Thomas and Ephraim at Sex, p. 100; NEHGR 153:278-90 (English origins of wife).

FROST, NICHOLAS, b. ca. 1595, d. Kittery, Me., between 7 July and 24 September 1663. GMB I:706-8; MJ 18:53-54.

FROST, WILLIAM, d. Fairfield, Conn., 1645. TAG 64:161-67, 208-13.

FROTHINGHAM, WILLIAM, b. ca. 1605, d. Charlestown, Mass., 10 October 1651. GMB I:708-11.

FRY(E), ANTHONY, b. ca. 1645, d. Bristol, R.I., before 3 May 1695. TAG 77:302-12.

FRY(E), GEORGE, b. ca. 1616, d. Weymouth, Mass., 1676. AL, pp. 265-66; MJ 17:73-74, 25:33-35, 26:32-35.

FRY(E), JOHN, b. ca. 1606, d. Andover, Mass., 9 November 1693. AK, pp. 429-30.

FRY(E), THOMAS, b. 1632, d. Newport, R.I., 11 June 1704. Johnson, pp. 138-43.

FRY(E), WILLIAM, b. ca. 1614, d. Weymouth, Mass., October 1642. MJ 19:53-55.

FULLER, EDWARD, *Mayflower* passenger, b. 1575, d. Plymouth, Mass., ca. January 1620/1. MF4, five generations all lines; GMB I:712-13; PM, pp. 215-17; son Matthew[2] at TAG 61:194-99; MQ 66:275-76.

FULLER, JOHN, b. 1611, d. Cambridge, Mass., 1698. Cameos, pp. 199-204.

FULLER, JOHN, b. ca. 1617, d. Ipswich, Mass., 4 June 1666. GM2 II:598-602; TAG 77:267-70 (English origins).

FULLER, JOHN, d. Lynn, Mass., 6 April 1695. TAG 65:65-69 (English origins); TEG 17:154-60.

FULLER, ROBERT, b. ca. 1615, d. Rehoboth, Mass., 10 May 1706. Colonial, pp. 49-116; TAG 76:263-78.

FULLER, SAMUEL, *Mayflower* passenger, b. 1580, d. Plymouth, Mass., between 9 August and 26 September 1633. MF10, five generations all lines; GMB I:713-17; PM, pp. 217-21; MQ 54:102-6; MQ 66:276-78.

FULLER, WILLIAM, b. 1609/10, d. Hampton, N.H., 26 May 1693. TAG 77:267-70 (English origins).

FURBER, WILLIAM, b. ca. 1614, d. Dover, N.H., between 23 June 1687 and 2 September 1689. GM2 II:606-12.

GAGE, JOHN, b. ca. 1605, d. Bradford, Mass., 24 March 1672/3. GMB II:719-22.

GAGER, WILLIAM, b. 1592, d. Boston, Mass., 20 September 1630. GMB II:722-24; Johnson, pp. 143-46; Edmund R. Gager, *The Gager Family: The Descendants of Dr. William Gager of Suffolk County, England and Charlestown, Mass., through His Only Surviving Son, John Gager, Who Later Settled in Norwich, Connecticut* (Baltimore, MD: Gateway Press, 1985). Reviews: NYGBR 118:56.

GAINES, HENRY, d. Lynn, Mass., before 14 January 1644/5. TAG 65:65-69 (English origins); further clues to English origins NHGR 9:180-81.

GALE, RICHARD, d. Watertown, Mass., 22 March 1679. Thompson, pp. 196-97, et al.

GALLEY, JOHN, b. ca. 1605, d. Beverly, Mass., between 22 May and 9 November 1683. GM2 III:1-4.

GALLOP, JOHN, b. ca. 1593, d. Boston, Mass., January 1649/50. GMB II:725-28; EB, pp. 236-43; TAG 68:11-13 (English origins); MJ 1:29-30, 67, 3:15, 5:1-16, 11:84-85.

GAMLIN, ROBERT, b. ca. 1585, d. Concord, Mass., September 1642. GMB II:728-29.

GANNETT, MATTHEW, b. 1617/8, d. Scituate, Mass. NEHGR 158:57-60 (English origins); MJ 18:54-56.

GANNETT, THOMAS, b. 1611, d. Bridgewater, Mass., between 19 June and 7 August 1655. NEHGR 158:57-80 (English origins).

GARDE, ROGER, b. ca. 1587, d. York, Me., before 28 July 1645. MJ 18:56-57.

GARDINER, LYON, b. ca. 1599, of Boston, Mass., and Saybrook, Conn., d. East Hampton, N.Y., between 14 January 1662/3 and 12 April 1664. GM2 III:6-12.

GARDNER, JAMES, d. Gloucester, Mass., 8 December 1684. Davis II:1-4 [Charity Haley, Nicholas Davis].

GARDNER, PETER, b. ca. 1617, d. Roxbury, Mass., 4 November 1698. GM2 III:12-16; JPG I:308-13; NEHGR 159:40-42 (English origins of wife).

GARDNER, RICHARD, b. ca. 1619, d. Charlestown, Mass., 29 May 1698. Appears with daughter Anna at Sex, pp. 78-87.

GARDNER, SAMUEL, d. Swansea, Mass., 8 December 1696. AL, pp. 267-68.

GARDNER, THOMAS, b. ca. 1592, d. Salem, Mass., 29 December 1674. Chase, pp. 201-10; GMB II:731-37; Jessup, pp. 422-32; NEHGR 150:190-97 (wife of Samuel[2]'s English ancestry).

GARDNER, THOMAS, d. Roxbury, Mass., November 1638. JPG I:308-13.

GARFIELD, EDWARD, b. 1583, d. Watertown, Mass., 14 June 1672. GM2 III:16-23; Nichols, p. 30; NEHGR 156:327-32 (English origins).

GARFORD, JARVIS, b. ca. 1590, d. Salem, Mass., after 30 June 1657. GM2 III:23-25.

GARNET, JOHN, d. Hingham, Mass., 24 November 1668. Stone, pp. 129-32.

GARRETT, DANIEL, b. ca. 1612, d. Hartford, Conn., after 11 March 1683/4. Jessup, pp. 432-34; TAG 71:93-104.

Garrett, Richard, b. ca. 1595, of Charlestown, Mass., d. at sea 28 December 1630. GMB II:737-39.

Garrett, Richard, b. ca. 1615, d. Boston, Mass., 29 March 1662. Lyon, pp. 349-51.

Gatchell, John, b. ca. 1615, d. Marblehead, Mass., between 9 September 1686 and 6 August 1694. GM2 III:27-33; EB, pp. 243-44; son Jeremiah[2] at TG 2:74-114, 6:232-43; MJ 19:58-59, 27:25-29.

Gatchell, Samuel, b. ca. 1617, d. Salisbury, Mass., between 14 May 1686 and 6 October 1697. GM2 III:33-35; MJ 19:58-59, 27:25-29.

Gates, George, b. ca. 1634, d. East Haddam, Conn., 12 November 1724. Robert Cady Gates, *George Gates of East Haddam, Connecticut and Some of His Descendants* (Hudson, FL: the author, 2002). Reviews: CN 35:452, 36:233-34.

Gates, Stephen, b. ca. 1599, d. Cambridge, Mass., between 9 June and 7 October 1662. Davis II:5-10 [Sarah Miller]; Johnson, pp. 146-51; JPG II:392-402; NEHGR 137:146 (note).

Gaunt, Peter, of Lynn, Mass., d. Sandwich, Mass., ca. 1692. Croll, 95.

Gavitt, Philip, b. ca. 1651, d. Westerly, R.I., after 1714. Richard Edward Gavitt, *The Gavitts of Westerly, R.I.: A Genealogy* (Bristol, CT: the author, 1992). Reviews: RIR 12:19, NYGBR 117:177.

Gay, John, b. ca. 1613, d. Dedham, Mass., 4 March 1688/9. GM2 III:36-42; Samuel[3-2]'s wife's identity at TG 1:72-79.

Gaylord, William, b. ca. 1590, d. Windsor, Conn., 20 July 1673. GMB II:739-43; Johnson, pp. 151-52; TAG 58:218-23 (English origins); TAG 60:213-14; TAG 61:95-96; TAG 71:49-50 (Benjamin[3] Walter[2]'s wife); MJ 1:30-31, 5:17-34, 18:57-59, 26:35-39, 27:29-31.

Geary, William, d. Wenham, Mass., 13 November 1672. TEG 5:27-33.

Gee, John, b. ca. 1636, d. at sea before 27 December 1669. Brewer, pp. 373-74.

Geer, George, b. ca. 1621, d. Preston, Conn., January 1726/7. Stowers, pp. 363-66; NEHGR 142:39-50 (Daniel[2]); TAG 67:231-35, TAG 68:182-83, TAG 70:240-49 (Daniel[2]'s wife); TAG 71:220-24 (Joseph[2]).

Geere, Dennis, b. ca. 1605, d. Lynn, Mass., after 10 December 1635. GM2 III:43-45; NYGBR 120:211-13 (notes on origins).

GEORGE, JAMES, b. ca. 1633, d. Amesbury, Mass., ca. 1707. Keith H. George, *George Genealogy* (Kingman, AZ: H&H Printers, 1991). Reviews: NHGR 10:211-12.

GEORGE, JOHN, b. 1673, d. Haverhill, Mass., 28 February 1715/6. Ordway, pp. 277-79. Wife Ann Swaddock's English origins given at Ordway, pp. 393-95; Keith H. George, *George Genealogy* (Kingman, AZ: H&H Printers, 1991). Reviews: NHGR 10:211-12.

GEORGE, NICHOLAS, b.c 1600, d. Dorchester, Mass., February 1675/6. Keith H. George, *George Genealogy* (Kingman, AZ: H&H Printers, 1991). Reviews: NHGR 10:211-12.

GEORGE, PETER, b. ca. 1610, d. Block Island, R.I., 19 January 1693/4. AL, pp. 268-69.

GERRISH, WILLIAM, d. Salem, Mass., 9 August 1687. MJ 19:59-60.

GIBBARD, WILLIAM, d. New Haven, Conn., 9 August 1662. Nichols, p. 96.

GIBBONS, AMBROSE, b. ca. 1592, d. Dover, N.H., between 11 July 1656 and 9 May 1657. Davis II:17-22 [Nicholas Davis, Joseph Waterhouse]; GMB II:745-49.

GIBBONS, EDWARD, b. ca. 1606, d. Boston, Mass., 9 December 1654. GMB II:749-55.

GIBBONS, JAMES, b. ca. 1614, d. Kittery, Mass., after 17 July 1690. GM2 III:45-48; Davis II:11-16.

GIBBS, GILES, b. ca. 1600, d. Windsor, Conn., May 1641. GMB II:756-58; TAG 61:32-43, 97-109; MJ 1:31-32, 2:95, 5:35-47, 11:86-89, 26:39-41.

GIBBS, MATTHEW, d. Sudbury, Mass., before 1697. Nichols, pp. 56-57.

GIBBS, ROBERT, b.c 1636, d. Boston, Mass., 7 December 1673. RD600, pp. 534-37.

GIBSON, JOHN, b. ca. 1601, d. Cambridge, Mass., ca. 1688. GM2 III:49-52; Cameos, pp. 87-97.

GIDDINGS, GEORGE, b. 1609, d. Ipswich, Mass., 1 June 1676. GM2 III:52-56; Stone, pp. 133-37, including English origins; NEHGR 135:274-86 (English origins).

GIFFORD, JOHN, of Lynn, Mass. Wife Margaret at Doctors, pp. 47-49.

GIFFORD, WILLIAM, b. ca. 1626, d. Sandwich, Mass., 9 April 1687. AL, pp. 272-73.

GILBERT, JOHN, b. 1580, d. Taunton, Mass., between 5 April 1656 and 3 June 1657. GM2 III:56-60; MJ 17:74-76.

GILBERT, JONATHAN, b. 1617, d. Hartford, Conn., 19 December 1682. NEHGR 146:28-34 (wife's ancestry).

GILBERT, LYDIA, d. Hartford, Conn., ca. December 1654. LENE, pp. 26-28.

GILBERT, THOMAS, b. 1589, d. Wethersfield, Conn., before 5 September 1659. Spooner; TAG 67:161-66 (English origins).

GILES, EDWARD, b. ca. 1610, d. Salem, Mass., between 17 December 1649 and 10 December 1656. GMB II:764-66.

GILES, THOMAS, d. Pemaquid, Me., 2 August 1689. Son John[2] at Puritans, pp. 93-131.

GILL, ARTHUR, b. 1608, of Richmond Island, d. England before 16 January 1654/5. TAG 73:223-27 (clues to English origins).

GILL, JOHN, b. ca. 1660s, d. Needham, Mass., 20 September 1735. Kempton4, pp. 285-90.

GILL, THOMAS, b. ca. 1589, d. Hingham, Mass., 1678. Lyon, pp. 351-52.

GILLAM, BENJAMIN, b. ca. 1608, d. Boston, Mass., before 24 March 1669/70. GM2 III:60-65.

GILLETT, JEREMIAH, d. Simsbury, Conn., 24 March 1707/8. MJ 13:58-71, 18:59-65, 25:35-36.

GILLETT, JONATHAN, b. ca. 1609, d. Windsor, Conn., 23 August 1677. GMB II:766-70; Cornelius[3-2] and Joseph[3-2] at TAG 56:73-79; John[3] Joseph[2] at TAG 62:78-81; TAG 64:157-59 (further information on John[3]); MJ 1:32-33, 2:84-88, 97, 3:16-19, 5:49-81, 18:59-65, 25:35-36.

GILLETT, NATHAN, b. ca. 1613, d. Windsor, Conn., 15 September 1689. GMB II:770-72; TAG 56:129-40 (descendants to the fourth generation); MJ 1:33-34, 2:84-88, 97, 3:16-19, 5:83-90, 18:59-65, 25:35-36.

GILMAN, EDWARD, b. ca. 1587, d. Exeter, N.H., 1655. Davis II:23-30 [Abel Lunt], including English origins.

GIRLING, RICHARD, b. ca. 1599, d. Cambridge, Mass., 14 May 1636. GM2 III:66-69.

GLADDING, JOHN, b. ca. 1641, d. Bristol, R.I., 27 April 1726. TAG 64:143-47, 77:208-19, 271-78, 313.

GLASS, JAMES, d. at sea before 3 September 1652. MJ 18:66-67, 27:31-33.

GLASS, ROGER, b. 1623, d. Duxbury, Mass., 27 August 1692. MJ 18:66-67, 27:31-33.

GLEASON, THOMAS, b. ca. 1607, d. Cambridge, Mass., 1686. Nichols, pp. 58-59; Cameos, pp. 105-9.

GLINES, WILLIAM, b. ca. 1680, d. Durham, N.H., after 20 September 1725. Son John[2] at NHGR 8:117-25, 9:137-40.

GLOVER, ANN, d. Boston, Mass., 16 November 1688. LENE, pp. 57-59; WRR, pp. 20-26.

GLOVER, JOHN, b. 1600, d. Boston, Mass., between 26 January and 6 February 1653/4. GM2 III:72-76; Cameos, pp. 67-73.

GOARD, RICHARD, b. ca. 1618, d. Roxbury, Mass., 27 September 1683. GM2 III:78-81; Benjamin[2] d. Boston, Mass., 2 April 1674. LENE, p. 47.

GOBLE, THOMAS, b. ca. 1604, d. Concord, Mass., between 30 November and 11 December 1657. GM2 III:81-83; grandson Daniel d. Boston, Mass., d. 26 September 1676, LENE, p. 52; grandson Stephen d. Boston, Mass., 21 September 1676, LENE, p. 52.

GODBERTSON, GODBERT, b. ca. 1592, d. Plymouth, Mass., between 1 July and 24 October 1633. GMB II:776-78; PM, pp. 226-28.

GODDARD, DANIEL, d. Hartford, Conn., after 1646. Winfred R. Goddard, Jr., *The Goddards of Granby, Connecticut* (San Diego, CA: Goddard Enterprises, 1985). Reviews: CN 18:728-29.

GODDARD, JOHN, b. ca. 1608, d. Dover, N.H., 12 November 1666. GM2 III:84-88.

GODDARD, WILLIAM, b. 1627, d. Watertown, Mass., 6 October 1691. Stone, pp. 139-45, including English origins; Chase, pp. 211-22, including English origins; RD600, pp. 310-11; PA, p. 353; MCA, p. 371; TAG 63:17-28; NEHGR 156:131-44, 391 (correction on English ancestry and royal line).

GODFREY, EDWARD, 1584, of York, Me., d. London, England, 28 February 1663/4. GMB II:778-83.

GODFREY, RICHARD, b. 1631, d. Taunton, Mass., 16 October 1691. Johnson, p. 153.

GOFFE, EDWARD, b. ca. 1604, d. Cambridge, Mass., 26 December 1658. GM2 III:92-98; Cameos, pp. 99-103; son Samuel[2] at Cameos, pp. 229-33; Mower, pp. 225-36; NEHGR 158:101-4 (new information on English ancestry).

GOFFE, JOHN, d. Newbury, Mass., 4 December 1641. TAG 77:282-89.

GOFFE, PHILIP, d. Wethersfield, Conn., before 2 June 1674. TAG 68:115-18 (daughter Rebecca).

GOLDSTONE, HENRY, b. 1591, d. Watertown, Mass., July 1638. GM2 III:99-101; Goodman, pp. 203-5, including English origins; Johnson, pp. 153-54.

GOLDTHWAIT, THOMAS, b. ca. 1613, d. Salem, Mass., between 1 March 1682/3 and 29 March 1683. GMB II:783-86.

GOOCH, JOHN, b. ca. 1600, d. Wells, Me., between 7 May and 12 July 1667. Lyon, pp. 352-55; MBT #1062.

GOODALE, RICHARD, b. 1594, d. Salisbury, Mass., 16 September 1666. Davis II:31-37 [Abel Lunt], including English origins; Brewer, pp. 375-81.

GOODALE, ROBERT, b. ca. 1604, d. Newbury, Mass., between 12 October 1682 and 27 June 1683. GM2 III:101-8; Davis II:38-49 [Lydia Harmon]; George E. Williams, *A Genealogy of the Descendants of Robert Goodale/Goodell of Salem, Mass.,* (West Hartford, CT: the author, 1984). Reviews: CN 18:143.

GOODENOW, EDMUND, b. ca. 1611, d. Sudbury, Mass., 5/6 April 1688. Kempton3, pp. 161-85, including English origins; son John[2] at Sex, pp. 100-2, 171-72, et al.; TAG 61:65-69; Theodore James Fleming Banvard, *Goodenows Who Originated in Sudbury, Massachusetts 1638 A.D.: They Came from Wilts. and Dorset, England Across America They Roamed and Multiplied* (Baltimore, MD: Gateway Press, 1994). Reviews: CN 28:404, NYGBR 126:151.

GOODENOW, JOHN, b. ca. 1596, d. Sudbury, Mass., 28 March 1654. TAG 61:65-69; Theodore James Fleming Banvard, *Goodenows Who Originated in Sudbury, Massachusetts 1638 A.D.: They Came from Wilts. and Dorset, England Across America They Roamed and Multiplied* (Baltimore, MD: Gateway Press, 1994). Reviews: CN 28:404, NYGBR 126:151.

GOODENOW, THOMAS, b. ca. 1608, d. Marlborough, Mass., 1666. Lyon, pp. 355-56; daughters Mary and Jane at Sex, pp. 99-106; TAG 61:65-69; Theodore James Fleming Banvard, *Goodenows Who Originated in Sudbury, Massachusetts 1638 A.D.: They Came from Wilts. and Dorset, England Across America They Roamed and Multiplied* (Baltimore, MD: Gateway Press, 1994). Reviews: CN 28:404, NYGBR 126:151.

GOODHUE, WILLIAM, b. ca. 1612, d. Ipswich, Mass., after 31 July 1694. GM2 III:108-14; Stevens, 48.

GOODMAN, RICHARD, b. 1609, d. Hadley, Mass., 3 April 1676. GMB II:786-90; Goodman, pp. 207-38, including clues to English ancestry.

GOODRICH, RICHARD, d. Guilford, Conn., 7 May 1676. JPG II:185-88.

GOODRIDGE, WILLIAM, d. Watertown, Mass., before 3 April 1647. NEHGR 152:197-214, 465-84 (four generation study of Josiah[3] Benjamin[2]).

GOODSELL, THOMAS, d. East Haven, Conn., before 29 May 1713. Percy Hamilton Goodsell, Jr., *The Goodsell Family of Connecticut* (n.p., the author, 1986). Reviews: CN 19:142-43.

GOODWILL, THOMAS, b. ca. 1687, d. Boston, Mass., 21 December 1749. Thomas J. Goodwill, *Three Hundred Years in America: A History of the Goodwill Family* (Jamestown, NY: the author, 1985). Reviews: CN 19:331.

GOODWIN, CHRISTOPHER, b. ca. 1651, of Charlestown, Mass., Sex, pp. 160-62.

GOODWIN, EDWARD, d. Salisbury, Mass., after 3 March 1670/1. Jessup, pp. 444-46.

GOODWIN, WILLIAM, b. ca. 1591, d. Farmington, Conn., 11 March 1673. GMB II:790-94; Nichols, pp. 160-61; Johnson, pp. 154-55.

GOODYEAR, STEPHEN, b. 1598, of New Haven, Conn., d. London, England, before 20 October 1658. Johnson, pp. 155-56; TAG 57:1-11, 100-2 (English origins).

GOOKIN, DANIEL, b. 1612, d. Cambridge, Mass., 19 March 1686/7. Cameos, various pages, and specifically 139-44, 149-54, 285-88; Sex, various pages, specifically 38-42; son Samuel[2] at Cameos, pp. 229-33.

GORDON, ALEXANDER, b. ca. 1630, d. Exeter, N.H., 1697. Marian Otis, *Alexander Gordon and His Descendants: A Genealogy of the Gordon Family*

(Camden, ME: Penobscot Press, 1999). Reviews: CA 42:183, NEHGR 155:426-27.

GORE, JOHN, b. ca. 1606, d. Roxbury, Mass., 4 June 1657. GM2 III:114-20; NEHGR 148:61-65 (information on English ancestry).

GORHAM, JOHN, b. 1619/20, d. Swansea, Mass., 5 February 1675/6. Howland1, five generations all lines.

GORTON, SAMUEL, b. 1592/3, d. Warwick, R.I., between 27 November and 10 December 1677. Johnson, pp. 156-59; RIR 9:29-30; Thomas Arthur Gorton, Ph.D., *Samuel Gorton of R.I., and His Descendants* (Baltimore, MD: Gateway Press, 1985), a multi-generational work on this family with English origins. Reviews: CN 18:727; RIR 11:64; TAG 58:192; TAG 61:59; NEHGR 141:69-70.

GOSS, RICHARD, b. ca. 1662, d. Ipswich, Mass., 24 January 1714/5. TEG 13:23-28.

GOSS, RICHARD, d. Portsmouth, N.H., between October 1691 and 1694. TEG 13:92-96.

GOSSE, JOHN, b. ca. 1600, d. Watertown, Mass., February 1643/4. GMB II:795-98; TAG 63:184 (daughter Phebe).

GOTT, CHARLES, b. ca. 1600, d. Wenham, Mass., 15 January 1667/8. GMB II:798-800; TEG 3:22-28.

GOULD, EDWARD, b. ca. 1607, d. Hingham, Mass., 16 February 1684/5. GM2 III:121-23.

GOULD, JARVIS, b. ca. 1605, d. Boston, Mass., 27 May 1656. GM2 III:123-24.

GOULD, ROBERT, b. ca. 1645, d. Hull, Mass., between 11 June 1718 and 28 February 1718/9. NEHGR 143:40-50.

GOULD, ZACHEUS, b. ca. 1589, d. Topsfield, Mass., 1668. Davis II:50-57 [Dudley Wildes], including English origins; Croll, 163.

GOVE, JOHN, d. Charlestown, Mass., between 22 and 25 January 1647/8. English origins of wife Mary (Shard) at NHGR 11:174-79, 12:96. Son John at Cameos, pp. 303-8.

GOWING, ROBERT, b. ca. 1618, d. Lynn, Mass., 7 June 1698. TEG 8:39-42, 141-46, 198-207, 9:33-42, 14:116.

GOZZARD SEE GODDARD

GRANT, CHRISTOPHER, b. ca. 1610, d. Watertown, Mass., 4 or 6 September 1685. GM2 III:126-32; Thompson, pp. 60-61, et al.; son Christopher[2] at Sex, pp. 42-53, et al.

GRANT, MATTHEW, b. 1601, d. Windsor, Conn., 16 December 1681. GMB II:801-4; MJ 1:34-35, 2:97, 5:91-124.

GRANT, SETH, b. ca. 1610, d. Hartford, Conn., before 4 March 1646/7. GMB II:804-5.

GRAUNGER, THOMAS, b. ca. 1625, d. Plymouth, Mass., 8 September 1642. LENE, pp. 9-10.

GRAVES, JOHN, b. ca. 1599, d. Roxbury, Mass., 4 November 1644. GM2 III:133-36.

GRAVES, MARK, b. ca. 1620, d. Haverhill, Mass., 19 July 168?. TEG 20:214-22.

GRAVES, RICHARD, b. ca. 1612, d. Boston, Mass., before 15 June 1669. GM2 III:136-40; grandson Richard[3] Joseph[2] at Sex, pp. 49-53, et al.

GRAVES, SAMUEL, b. ca. 1622, d. Ipswich, Mass., 22 November 1679. TEG 20:223-27.

GRAVES, THOMAS, b. 1605, d. Charlestown, Mass., 31 July 1653. NEHGR 138:39-41.

GRAVES, THOMAS, b. ca. 1620, d. Lynn, Mass., 24 January 1695/6. TEG 20:204-13.

GRAY, EDWARD, b. ca. 1629, d. Plymouth, Mass., 30 June 1681. MF15 three generations all lines for his children by his first wife Mary (Winslow).

GRAY, HENRY, d. Fairfield, Conn., before October 1658. TAG 64:161-67, 208-13.

GRAY, JOHN, of Lynn, Mass., and Fairfield, Conn., d. Newtown, N.Y., before 25 February 1663. TAG 64:161-67, 208-13.

GRAY, PARNEL, b. 1602, d. Charlestown, Mass., 25 March 1687. NEHGR 138:39-41.

GRAY, ROBERT, b. ca. 1675, d. Lynn, Mass., 28 September 1731. TEG 20:102-5.

GREEN(E), BARTHOLOMEW, b. ca. 1590, d. Cambridge, Mass., before 8 February 1635/6. GMB II:809-10: Cameos, pp. 123-28 (son Samuel[2] and daughter Phebe[2]); several family member at Sex, various pages, specifically, pp. 120-23, 136-37.

GREEN(E), HENRY, d. Hartford, Conn., 1 June 1675. LENE, p. 48.

GREEN(E), JAMES, b. ca. 1610, d. Malden, Mass., 29 March 1687. Mower, pp. 239-42.

GREEN(E), JOHN, b. ca. 1593, d. Charlestown, Mass., 22 April 1658. GMB II:811-13.

GREEN(E), JOHN, b. ca. 1594, d. Warwick, R.I., between 28 December 1658 and 7 January 1658/9. GM2 III:141-48; Johnson, pp. 160-68; RIR 7:52; MJ 17:76-77.

GREEN(E), PERCIVAL, b. ca. 1603, d. Cambridge, Mass., 25 December 1639. GM2 III:148-50; JPG I:314-16.

GREEN(E), THOMAS, b. 1599/1600, d. Malden, Mass., 19 December 1667. Kempton4, pp. 293-310, including English origins.

GREENHILL, SAMUEL, b. ca. 1603, d. Hartford, Conn., before 1637. GM2 III:151-53.

GREENLEAF, EDMUND, b. ca. 1590, d. Boston, Mass., 24 March 1670/1. Mower, pp. 245-49; TW, pp. 255-60; TAG 56:107 (marriage record).

GREENSLADE, THOMAS, d. Salem, Mass., July 1674. LENE, pp. 99-100 (wife Ann).

GREENSMITH, NATHANIEL and wife Mary, d. Hartford, Conn., 24 January 1663. LENE, pp. 33-41; CN 13:4-10.

GREENWAY, JOHN, b. ca. 1576, d. Dorchester, Mass., between 5 February 1650/1 and 6 May 1652. GMB II:814-18; TAG 74:193-95 (English baptisms); MJ 1:35-36, 5:125-36, 27:99.

GREET, JOHN, b. ca. 1640, of Boston and Westfield, Mass., d. Southold, N.Y., before February 1687/8. TAG 72:42-48.

GREGG, DAVID, b. ca. 1684, d. Windham, N.H., 1758. Stone, pp. 37-44, including Irish origins.

GREGG, JAMES, b. ca. 1674, Scotland, d. Londonderry, N.H., 10 March 1758. Angell, pp. 313-43; wife Janet Cargill's ancestry given at Angell, pp. 275-77.

GRIDLEY, RICHARD, b. ca. 1602, d. Boston, Mass., between 19 and 28 October 1674. GMB II:818-23.

GRIDLEY, THOMAS, b. 1612, d. Hartford, Conn., before 12 June 1655. CN 26:210-21; CN 28:33-45 (English origins).

GRIFFIN(G), JASPER, b. ca. 1646, d. Southhold, Long Island, N.Y., 17 April 1718. TG 11:41-53, 194-217, 12:43-59, 232-49.

GRIFFIN, HUGH, d. Sudbury, Mass., 21 June 1656. Brewer, pp. 383-85.

GRIFFIN, HUMPHREY, b. ca. 1605, d. Ipswich, Mass., before 19 November 1661. Davis II:58-61 [Annis Spear]; EB, pp. 245-47.

GRIFFIN, ROBERT, b. ca. 1620, d. Newport, R.I., after 1659. Johnson, pp. 168-69.

GRIGGS, GEORGE, b. ca. 1593, d. Boston, Mass., 23 June 1660. GM2 III:154-59; NYGBR 136:243-52, an article to be continued in 2006 (John[2]).

GRIGGS, THOMAS, b. ca. 1585, d. Roxbury, Mass., 23 May 1646. JPG I:317-20, II:189-97; MBT #1082.

GRINNELL, MATTHEW, d. Newport, R.I., before 10 November 1643. Daniel[3-2] at TG 7/8: 144-277, three full generations of descendants; Jessup, pp. 456-86; NEHGR 147:71-72.

GRISWOLD, EDWARD, b. ca. 1607, d. Killingworth, Conn., ca. 1691. EB, pp. 247-49; Jessup, pp. 486-95; Lyon, pp. 357-60; CN 25:190-91; NEHGR 155:245-50 (wife of Francis[2]); Esther Griswold French and Robert Lewis French, *The Griswold Family: The First Five Generations in America* (Wethersfield, CT: The Griswold Family Association, 1990), pp. 5-184. Reviews: NYGBR 122:121.

GRISWOLD, FRANCIS, b. 1605/6, d. Charlestown, Mass., 2 October 1652. Esther Griswold French and Robert Lewis French, *The Griswold Family: The First Five Generations in America* (Wethersfield, CT: The Griswold Family Association, 1990), pp.1-5. Reviews: NYGBR 122:121.

GRISWOLD, MATTHEW, b. ca. 1620, d. Saybrook, Conn., 27 September 1698. Esther Griswold French and Robert Lewis French, *The Griswold Family: The First Five Generations in America* (Wethersfield, CT: The Griswold Family Association, 1990), pp. 185-228. Reviews: NYGBR 122:121.

GRISWOLD, MICHAEL, d. Wethersfield, Conn., 26 September 1684. CN 25:190-91; Esther Griswold French and Robert Lewis French, *The Griswold Family: The First Five Generations in America* (Wethersfield, CT: The Griswold Family Association, 1990), pp. 229-390. Reviews: NYGBR 122:121.

GROSS, ISAAC, b. ca. 1588, d. Boston, Mass., between 29 May and 5 June 1649. GM2 III:159-63; NEHGR 146:296 (Susannah[3] Edmund[2]); NEHGR 154:33-34 (English origins).

GROSS, SIMON, b. ca. 1650, d. Hingham, Mass., 26 April 1696. NEHGR 154:35-40.

GROVER, EDMUND, b. ca. 1600, d. Beverly, Mass., 11 June 1682. GMB II:824-26.

GROVES SEE LAGROVES

GRUBB, THOMAS, b. ca. 1598, d. Boston, Mass., between 2 May 1670 and 6 March 1673/4. GMB II:826-29.

GUILE, SAMUEL, d. Amesbury, Mass., 16 October 1675. LENE, p. 49.

GUILFORD, JOHN, b. ca. 1625, d. Hingham, Mass., ca. September 1660. JPG I:321-67.

GULL, WILLIAM, b. 1620/1, d. Hatfield, Mass., between 12 April and 18 December 1701. NEHGR 152:159-78 (correct English origins).

GUNN, JASPER, b. ca. 1606, d. Milford, Conn., 2 January 1670/1. GM2 III:164-69.

GUNN, THOMAS, b. ca. 1605, d. Westfield, Conn., 26 February 1680/1. GM2 III:170-73.

GUNNISON, HUGH, b. ca. 1612, d. Kittery, Me., between 15 September 1659 and 31 March 1660. GM2 III:173-80.

GUTCH, ROBERT, b. 1617, d. Kennebec, Me., 1666. MJ 18:68-69, 25:36-38.

HACKBURNE, SAMUEL, d. Roxbury, Mass., December 1642. Wife Katherine (Deighton) at RD600, pp. 259-62; PA, p. 263; MCA, p. 265.

HACKETT, JABEZ, b. ca. 1623, d. Taunton, Mass., 4 November 1686. TEG 18:79-82.

HACKETT, WILLIAM, b. ca. 1622, d. Boston, Mass., 30 December 1641. LENE, p. 9.

HACKETT, WILLIAM, d. Dover, N.H., after 1687. TEG 16:17-22.

HACKETT, WILLIAM, d. Salisbury, Mass., 6 March 1713/4. TEG 16:17-22.

HADDON, GARRETT, b. ca. 1605, d. Amesbury, Mass., between 20 January 1686/7 and 20 March 1689/90. GMB II:831-33.

HAFFIELD, RICHARD, b. ca. 1581, d. Ipswich, Mass., 1639. GM2 III:183-87.

HAFFORD, JOHN, d. Braintree, Mass., before 1710. EB, pp. 251-54.

HAGBORNE SEE HACKBURNE

HAGGETT, HENRY, b. ca. 1594, d. Wenham, Mass., 24 January 1677/8. 50Imm, pp. 165-68; MBT #398.

HAILE, RICHARD, b. ca. 1640, d. Swansea, Mass., 29 September 1720. Mower, pp. 251-77.

HAILSTONE, WILLIAM, b. ca. 1611, d. poss. Taunton, Mass., after 1675. Kempton4, pp. 313-17.

HAINES, SAMUEL, b. ca. 1603, d. Portsmouth, N.H., after 1684. GM2 III:187-92.

HAINES, WALTER, b. ca. 1583, d. Sudbury, Mass., 14 February 1664/5. EB, pp. 266-72; Mower, pp. 299-313; TAG 61:65-69.

HALE, MARY, fl. Boston, Mass., ca. 1677. WRR, pp. 16-19; possible daughter Winifred at CN 28:556-62.

HALE, ROBERT, b. ca. 1607, d. Charlestown, Mass., 16 July 1659. GMB II:834-38; Nichols, p. 60; Mower, pp. 279-89; Lyon, pp. 360-61.

HALE, THOMAS, b. 1606, d. Newbury, Mass., 21 December 1682. Davis II:62-69 [Phoebe Tilton], including English origins. Wife's Kirby ancestry given at Davis II:394-95 [Phoebe Tilton]; 50Imm, pp. 169-98; MBT #844; NEHGR 141:128-34 (wife's ancestry); TAG 68:77-83 (Mary^3 Thomas^2); TAG 69:212-18 (Mary^2).

HALE, THOMAS, b. ca. 1613, d. Norwalk, Conn., before 19 February 1678/9. GMB II:838-40; wife Jane (Lord) at GM2 IV:324-25.

HALEY, THOMAS, of Saco Me., d. between 1683 and 1724. Davis II:70-131 [Charity Haley, Thomas Haley].

HALL, EDWARD, d. Rehoboth, Mass., before 27 November 1670. EB, pp. 254-57; NGSQ 81:19-23 (Samuel^2).

HALL, GEORGE, b. ca. 1610, d. Taunton, Mass., 30 October 1669. Kempton4, pp. 319-55; Cooley, pp. 81-123; Jessup, pp. 502-5.

HALL, HUGH, d. Boston, Mass., 20 September 1732. NEXUS 9:25-29, 57-60.

HALL, JOHN, b. ca. 1605, d. Wallingford, Conn., before 3 May 1676. Johnson, pp. 172-73.

HALL, JOHN, b. ca. 1610, d. Newport, R.I., after 1655. EB, pp. 258-260.

HALL, JOHN, b. ca. 1611, d. Yarmouth, Mass., 23 July 1696. GMB II:840-44; Croll, 153.

HALL, JOHN, b. ca. 1676, d. Marshfield, Mass., 30 January 1770. Davis II:132-39 [Joseph Neal].

HALL, JOHN, d. Cambridge, Mass., before 1662. JPG I:368-79.

HALL, RICHARD, of Bradford, Mass. Son Richard[2] at NEXUS 8:139-42.

HALL, SAMUEL, of Taunton, Mass., NGSQ 81:19-23 (Samuel[2]).

HALL, THOMAS, d. Cambridge, Mass., before 5 October 1691. He, his brother Edward, and sons-in-law at Cameos, pp. 213-19.

HALL, WILLIAM, b. ca. 1613, d. Portsmouth, R.I., 1675. Johnson, pp. 174-76.

HALLETT, ANDREW, Jr., b. 1607, d. Yarmouth, Mass., between 14 March 1681/2 and 19 May 1684. Probable son of Andrew, Sr. below, but see GM2 III:195-200; MJ 19:60-68, 25:86-88.

HALLETT, ANDREW, Sr., d. Yarmouth. Son Joseph[2] in Howland1, four generations all lines; Crosby II:357-63.

HALLOWELL, JOSEPH, b. ca. 1646, d. Lynn, Mass., 29 November 1692. TEG 11:217-25.

HALLOWELL, SAMUEL, b. ca. 1695, d. Lynn, Mass., 15 December 1755. Chase, pp. 223-28.

HALSTEAD, NATHANIEL, b. ca. 1595, d. Dedham, Mass., 3 February 1643. Stevens, 20.

HAM, WILLIAM, d. Portsmouth, NH, between 21 December 1672 and 17 July 1673. English origins of him and his wife at NHGR 10:131-32; MJ 19:70-71.

HAMMOND, BENJAMIN, b. ca. 1621, d. Rochester, Mass., 27 April 1703. Spooner.

HAMMOND, WILLIAM, b. 1575, d. Watertown, Mass., 8 October 1662. GMB II:850-54; son John[2] at Thompson, ppp. 179-83, et al.; daughter Sarah at NYGBR 121:19-22.

HAMMOND, WILLIAM, b. ca. 1648, d. Swansea, Mass., 28 June 1675. NEHGR 149:211-29; NEHGR 149:230-43 (wife's identity); NEHGR 150:214, 216-20 (corrections).

HANCHETT, THOMAS, b. ca. 1620, d. Suffield, Conn., 11 June 1686. Lyon, pp. 361-63; Keith M. Seymour, *The Descendants of Thomas Hanchett* (San Francisco, CA: the author, 1985). Reviews: CN 19:147-48, NEHGR 141:70, NYGBR 118:54.

HANCOCK, NATHANIEL, b. ca. 1609, d. Cambridge, Mass., in late 1648. GM2 III:203-5; son Nathaniel[2] at Cameos, pp. 303-8.

HANFORD, EGLIN, NÉE HATHERLY, b. 1586, d. Scituate, Mass., after 17 January 1653/4. GM2 III:205-7; Johnson, pp. 176-77; JPG I:380-88; MJ 18:69-72, 74-75.

HANMER, JOHN, b. ca. 1614, d. Scituate, Mass., between 4 December 1676 and 2 March 1676/7. GM2 III:207-10.

HANNUM, WILLIAM, b. ca. 1612, d. Northampton, Mass., 1 June 1677. GM2 III:210-13; MJ1:36-37, 2:97, 6:1-14.

HANSCOM, THOMAS, b. 1631/2, d. Kittery, Me., between 1695 and 1697. TEG 7:85-91.

HANSETT, JOHN, b. ca. 1614, d. Roxbury, Mass., February 1683/4. GM2 III:213-16.

HANSON, THOMAS, d. Dover, N.H., before 27 June 1666. NHGR 17:97-119, 151-167.

HAPGOOD, SHADRACH, b. ca. 1642, d. Brookfield, Mass., 2 August 1675. Kempton, pp. 311-35, including English origins. His mother's Scullard ancestry given at Kempton, pp. 407-22, and her Blake ancestry at Kempton, pp. 145-61; NEHGR 150:141-56 (English origins).

HARDING, MARTHA, b. ca. 1612, d. Plymouth, Mass., between 25 March and 28 October 1633. GMB II:854-55; PM, pp. 232-33; Croll, 108; TAG 72:109-10 (Nathaniel[4] Joseph[3-2]).

HARDING, RICHARD, b. ca. 1583, d. Braintree, Mass., 1657. EB, pp. 260-62.

HARDING, ROBERT, b. ca. 1610, of Boston, Mass., d. England between 1654 and 1 March 1657/8. GMB II:855-58.

HARDY, JOHN, b. ca. 1591, d. Salem, Mass., between 30 March and 8 June 1652. GM2 III:218-21; MJ 19:71-74.

HARDY, SAMUEL, b. 1645, d. Beverly, Mass., 10 February 1699/1700. RF1, three generations all lines.

HARDY, THOMAS, b. ca. 1606, d. Bradford, Mass., 4 January 1677. GMB II:858-61; Ordway, pp. 281-309.

HARKER, ANTHONY, b. ca. 1608, Boston, Mass., between 2 March 1674/5 and 2 April 1675. GMB II:861-63.

HARLAKENDEN, ROGER, b. 1611, d. Cambridge, Mass., October 1638. GM2 III:221-25. Second wife Elizabeth (Bosvile) at RD600, p. 178-79; PA, p. 133; MCA, p. 114.

HARLOW, WILLIAM, b. ca. 1624, d. Plymouth, Mass., 25 August 1691. MF18, three generations all lines for children from first wife Rebecca (Bartlett); Bartlett; Alicia Crane Williams, *Harlow Family: Descendants of Sgt. William Harlow [1624/5 – 1691] of Plymouth, Massachusetts* (Baltimore, MD: Gateway Press, 1997). Reviews: CN 31:234-35, VG 3:39-40, TAG 75:80, NGSQ 87:63-64.

HARMON, JOHN, b. ca. 1639, d. York, Me., before 1695/6. Davis II:140-160 [Lydia Harmon], including possible origins.

HARNED SEE HARNETT

HARNETT, EDWARD, d. Salem, Mass., between 1658 and 1661. Freeman, pp. 627-47.

HARPER, ANDREW, b. ca. 1699, d. Harvard, Mass., 4 May 1755. NHGR 14:1-17, 49-63, 105-15.

HARPER, RICHARD, b. ca. 1630, d. Falmouth, Mass., after August 1704. AL, pp. 283-84.

HARRADEN, EDWARD, b. before 1627, d. Gloucester, Mass., 17 May 1683. Stone, pp. 147-51.

HARRIMAN, JOHN, b. ca. 1623, d. New Haven, Conn., 21 November 1683. NEHGR 150:29-47 (English origins).

HARRIMAN, LEONARD, b. ca. 1621, d. Rowley, Mass., between 12 May and 5 June 1691. NEHGR 150:29-47 (English origins); TEG 10:17-24, 100-105.

HARRIS SEE ALSO HERRIS

HARRIS, ARTHUR, b. ca. 1620, d. Boston, Mass., between 31 March and 7 July 1674. Pond, 267; NEHGR 159:261-73, 349-59 (four generation study).

HARRIS, JAMES, b. ca. 1642, d. New London, Conn., 9 June 1714. NEHGR 154:3-32.

HARRIS, JOHN, b. ca. 1630, d. Boston, Mass., before September 1664. TAG 72:333-43 (John[2]); TAG 78:47-54 (Philip[3] John[2]); NEHGR 152:344.

HARRIS, JOHN, b. ca. 1640s, of Boston, Mass., d. at sea 1679. NEHGR 152:313-46.

HARRIS, JOHN, d. Ipswich, Mass., 3 December 1738. Davis II:194-96 [Bethia Harris].

HARRIS, JOHN, of Boston, Mass., may have died Wethersfield or Lyme, Conn., before 26 January 1674/5. NEHGR 152:345; NEHGR 151:87-91.

HARRIS, JOHN, of Charlestown, Mass., d. North Yarmouth, Me., after 1684. NEHGR 152:344.

HARRIS, JOHN, of Lancaster, Mass., d. after April 1721. NEHGR 152:345-46.

HARRIS, RICHARD, b. ca. 1651, d. Boston, Mass., 10 March 1713/4. NEHGR 152:313-46.

HARRIS, RICHARD, d. Boston, Mass., 12 April 1697. NEHGR 148:28-29.

HARRIS, ROBERT, of Roxbury, d. Brookline, Mass., after 1659. NEHGR 152:344 (John[2]); NEHGR 159:327-32 (English origins of wife).

HARRIS (ALIAS WILLIAMS), THOMAS d. Charlestown, Mass., before September 1634. Davis II:161-93 [Bethia Harris], and 588, including English origins; GMB II:864-66; Johnson, pp. 177-79; Thomas[4] Ebenezer[3] Thomas[2] at TAG 63:154-60; Daniel[4-3-2] at NYGBR 119:9-15, 99-105, 151-57, 220-26; NEHGR 152:343-44 (John[2]).

HARRIS, THOMAS, b. ca. 1630, d. Hartford, Conn., between 1682 and May 1688. NGSQ 78:182-203; NYGBR 130:183-96, 269-82 (son Robert[2]).

HARRIS, THOMAS, b. ca. 1655, d. Killingworth, Conn., before 11 June 1697. NYGBR 128:11-24 (origins).

HARRIS, WALTER, b. ca. 1590, d. New London, Conn., 6 November 1654. NEHGR 156:145-58, 262-79, 357-72, 392 (four generation study); NYGBR 133:3-18 (Peter[3] Gabriel[2]); MJ 19:74-76.

Harris, Walter, b. ca. 1652, d. Wethersfield, Conn., 1 December 1715. NEHGR 142:323-49 (four generation study); NEHGR 143:303-24; NEHGR 150:214 (correction); NYGBR 122:12-17, 96-101, 152-58, 223-28, 123:40-47 (multi-generational study of Daniel[2]).

Harris, William, b. ca. 1640s, d. at sea or Boston, Mass., before 1 May 1691. NEHGR 152:313-46.

Harris, William, b. ca. 1644, d. Boston, Mass., 17 May 1684. NEHGR 152:313-46.

Harris, William, of Block Island, R.I. NYGBR 133:3-18 (Thomas[2]); TAG 70:233-39 (William[2]).

Harrison, Isaac, d. Hadley, Mass., 19 May 1676. Gateway, #1794.

Hart, Edmund, b. ca. 1610, d. Westfield, Mass., ca. 23 September 1672. GMB II:866-69; TAG 72:42-48.

Hart, Edward, of Providence, R.I., d. Flushing, N.Y., after 1661. Son Thomas[2] at Kay Kirlin Moore and Dorothy Higson White, *Descendants of Roger Williams, Book II: The Hart Line Through His Daughter Freeborn Williams* (East Greenwich, RI: The Roger Williams Family Association, 1998).

Hart, Isaac, b. ca. 1614, d. Lynn, Mass., 10 February 1699. TEG 18:40-46.

Hart, John b. ca. 1595, d. Marblehead, Mass., before 14 March 1655/6. GM2 III:227-30; Davis II:197-204 [Sarah Stone].

Hart, Samuel, b. ca. 1622, d. Lynn, Mass., 25 June 1683. TEG 18:46-50.

Hart, Stephen, b. ca. 1599, d. Farmington, Conn., between 16 March 1682/3 and 31 March 1683. GMB II:869-73.

Hartshorn, Thomas, b. ca. 1614, d. Reading, Mass., 18 May 1683. Derick S. Hartshorn, III, *The Hartshorn Families in America: A Genealogical Study of the Line of Thomas Hartshorn, the Immigrant, of Reading, Massachusetts, and Other Known Families Bearing the Hartshorn/e Surname That Arrived in America in Succeeding Years* (Baltimore, MD: Gateway Press, 1997). Reviews: NEHGR 152:376-78, NGSQ 86:230-31.

Hartwell, William, b. ca. 1608, d. Concord, Mass., between 26 October 1681 and 18 May 1683. TAG 76:39-40 (John[3] Samuel[2]).

Harvey, Richard, b. 1612, d. Stratford, Conn., between 15 July 1686 and 4 November 1689. GM2 III:231-33.

HARVEY, THOMAS, b. ca. 1617, d. Taunton, Mass., 1651. MJ 18:72-74.

HARVEY, WILLIAM, b. ca. 1614, d. Taunton, Mass., ca. 1691. 31Imm, pp. 118-23, including English origins; MJ 18:72-74.

HARWOOD, HENRY, b. ca. 1605, d. Charlestown, Mass., before 5 December 1637. GMB II:873-74.

HARWOOD, NATHANIEL, b. ca. 1640, d. Concord, Mass., 7 February 1715/6. Kempton3, pp. 188-95.

HARWOOD, ROBERT, b. ca. 1644, d. Boston, Mass., before 20 June 1678. Kempton3, p. 191.

HARWOOD, SARAH, b. ca. 1635, d. Boston, Mass., after 13 November 1684. Married first Thomas Scottow, second John Tucker. Her ancestry at Kempton3, p. 190.

HARWOOD, THOMAS, b. ca. 1627, d. Boston, Mass., 5 January 1707/8. Kempton3, pp. 189-90.

HASELTINE, ROBERT, b. 1609/10, d. Bradford, Mass., 27 August 1674. NGSQ 68:10-11 (clues to English origins); Earl D. Campbell and Frederick W. Richardson, *The Haseltine Genealogy: The Descendants of Robert Haseltine* (n.p., the authors, 1997). Reviews: VG 3:91-92.

HASKELL, MARK, b. 1621, d. 1668. MJ 17:81-83.

HASKELL, ROGER, b. 1613/4, d. Salem, Mass., 1667. Son John[2], Soule, four generations all lines; TAG 57:77-81 (initial corrections on John[2]'s descendants); NEGHR 138:223-27 (notes on English ancestry); TEG 6:25-33; MJ 17:81-83.

HASKELL, WILLIAM, b. 1618, d. Gloucester, Mass., 20 August 1693. MJ 17:81-83.

HASSELL, JOHN, b. ca. 1603, d. Ipswich, Mass., before 3 April 1668. GM2 III:234-35.

HASSELL, RICHARD, b. ca. 1622, d. Woburn, Mass., after 1683. EB, pp. 262-63.

HASTINGS, JOHN, d. Cambridge, Mass., 2 December 1657. Son Walter[2] at Cameos, 149-54.

HASTINGS, ROBERT, d. Haverhill, Mass., 1721. Stevens, 16.

HASTINGS, THOMAS, b. ca. 1605, d. Watertown, Mass., between 12 March 1682/3 and 7 September 1685. GM2 III:235-40; Thompson, pp. 43-50, 189-90, et al.

HASTY, DANIEL, d. Scarborough, Me., August 1756. Davis II:205-7 [Lydia Harmon].

HATCH, PHILIP, b. 1616, d. York, Me., after 4 July 1671. Davis II:208-19 [Annis Spear], including English origins.

HATCH, THOMAS, b. ca. 1596, d. Barnstable, Mass., before 27 May 1661. GMB II:875-76; TAG 80:68-78 (Sarah^3 Thomas^2).

HATCH, WILLIAM, b. ca. 1598, d. Scituate, Mass., 6 November 1651. GM2 III:241-44; Davis II:220-31 [Joseph Neal], including English origins; 26Imm, pp. 123-32; Stowers, pp. 381-84.

HATHAWAY, ARTHUR, b. ca. 1625, d. Dartmouth, Mass., 11 December 1711. MF12, three generations all lines; Spooner; AL, pp. 288-89.

HATHAWAY, NICHOLAS, b. ca. 1588, d. Taunton, Mass., before 1643. AL, pp. 289-90.

HATHERLY SEE HANFORD

HATHORNE, JOHN, b. 1621, d. Lynn, Mass., 12 December 1676. TEG 12:85-93, 139-41, 14:116.

HATHORNE, WILLIAM, b. ca. 1606, d. Salem, Mass., between 17 February 1679/80 and 28 June 1681. Davis II:232-44 [Dudley Wildes], including English origins; GMB II:881-87; Mower, pp. 291-97.

HAUGH, ATHERTON, b. ca. 1593, d. Boston, Mass., 11 September 1650. GMB II:1005-10; wife Elizabeth (Bulkeley) at PA, p. 165; RD600, pp. 442-44; MCA, p. 147.

HAVEN, RICHARD, d. Lynn, Mass., between 21 May 1701 and 14 June 1703. Lyon, pp. 365-67; TEG 21:148-60.

HAWES, EDMUND, b. 1612, d. Yarmouth, Mass., 9 June 1693. GM2 III:247-50; RD600, pp. 422-23; PA, p. 392; MCA, p. 425; TG 7/8:132-36; only child John^2 in Howland1, four generations all lines; Raymond Gordon Hawes, *Edmond Hawes and His American Descendants* (Baltimore, MD: Gateway Press, 2000). Reviews: CN 34:231.

HAWES, EDWARD, b. ca. 1628, d. Dedham, Mass., 28 June 1687. Kempton3, pp. 197-204; Pond, 210.

HAWES, RICHARD, b. 1606, d. Dorchester, Mass., before 22 January 1656/7. GM2 III:250-53; Raymond Gordon Hawes, *The Richard Hawes Genealogy: Richard Hawes ca. 1606-1656/7 of Dorchester, Massachusetts and his wife Ann and Some of Their Descendants through Thirteen Generations* (Baltimore, MD: Gateway Press, 2003). Reviews: CN 37:86, 262-63.

HAWKES, ADAM, b. 1604/5, d. Lynn, Mass., 13 March 1671/2. GM2 III:253-57; Stevens, 53; Ethel Farrington Smith, *Adam Hawkes of Saugus, Mass., 1605-1672: The First Six Generations in America* (Baltimore, MD: Gateway Press, 1980). Reviews: NEHGR 138:51-54, NYGBR 112:185, MQ 49:145.

HAWKES, JOHN, b. ca. 1613, d. Hadley, Mass., June 1662. GM2 III:257-61; Imogene Hawks Lane, *John Hawks: A Founder of Hadley, Massachusetts after a Sojourn of Twenty-Four Years at Windsor, Connecticut: Thirteen Generations in America* (Baltimore, MD: Gateway Press, 1989). Reviews: NYGBR 121:185.

HAWKINS, JAMES, b. ca. 1603, d. Boston, Mass., 14 March 1669/70. GM2 III:261-66.

HAWKINS, JOB, b. ca. 1620, d. Portsmouth, R.I., after 6 March 1681/2. GM2 III:266-70.

HAWKINS, RICHARD, d. Portsmouth, R.I., before 25 August 1656. Wife Jane at Doctors, pp. 53-54.

HAWKINS, ROBERT, b. ca. 1610, d. Fairfield, Conn., before 1650 GM2 III:273-75; Susan H. and Bayard C. Carmiencke, *A Hawkins Genealogy Supplement, Volume II: Record of the Descendants of Robert Hawkins of Charlestown, Massachusetts* (Baltimore, MD: Gateway Press, 2001). Reviews: NYGBR 121:250, TAG 66:57-58, CN 34:583.

HAWKINS, THOMAS, b. ca. 1609, of Dorchester, Mass., d. at sea between 20 October 1647 and 7 November 1648. NEHGR 151:192-216 (three generation study).

HAWKINS, TIMOTHY, b. ca. 1612, d. Watertown, Mass., before 27 September 1651. GMB II:887-90; TAG 64:47-51 (Timothy[2]'s wife's second marriage).

HAWKSWORTH, THOMAS, b. ca. 1612, d. Salisbury, Mass., 8 November 1642. GM2 III:275-77.

HAWLEY, THOMAS, of Roxbury, Mass., d. Sudbury, Mass., 21 April 1676. JPG I:389-403.

HAYDEN, JAMES, b. ca. 1608, of Charlestown, Mass., d. Barbados before October 1665. GM2 III:277-80.

HAYDEN, JOHN, b. ca. 1609, d. Braintree, Mass., between 31 October 1678 and February 1681/2. GMB II:890-93; Kempton3, pp. 207-34; EB, pp. 263-66.

HAYDEN, WILLIAM, d. Killingworth, Conn., 27 September 1669. MJ 1:37-38, 6:15-28.

HAYES, NATHANIEL, b. ca. 1620, d. Norwalk, Conn., after 1694. Johnson, pp. 179-80.

HAYNES SEE ALSO HAINES

HAYNES, EDMUND, d. Springfield, Mass., ca. 1646. JPG I:404-6.

HAYNES, JOHN, b. 1594, d. Hartford, Conn., before 9 January 1653/4. GMB II:893-97; second wife Mabel Harlakenden at RD600, pp. 483-84; MCA, p. 412; NEHGR 148:240-58 (first wife Mary's ancestry).

HAYNES, WILLIAM, d. Salem, Mass., ca. 1650. MBT #380.

HAYWARD, GEORGE, of Concord, Mass. by 1638, d. 29 March 1671. Son John[2], MF13, three generations all lines; Mary[3] Joseph[2] at Doctors, pp. 99-101; John[2] at Sex, pp. 180-82.

HAYWARD, HENRY, b. ca. 1627, d. Hartford, Conn., between 12 and 24 March 1708/9. GM2 III:282-86.

HAYWARD, NICHOLAS, d. Beverly, Mass., 24 February 1682/3. Davis II:245-49 [Abel Lunt].

HAYWARD, THOMAS, b. ca. 1599, d. Bridgewater, Mass., between 29 June 1678 and 8 March 1680/1. GM2 III:288-94; Pond, 259; MBT #562 or 568.

HAYWARD, WILLIAM, b. ca. 1608, d. Braintree, Mass., 10 May 1659. Kempton3, pp. 237-55; Pond, 215; JPG II:403-6.

HAYWOOD, ANTHONY, b. ca. 1639, d. Boston, Mass., 16 October 1689. NEHGR 153:141-63.

HAZARD, THOMAS, b. ca. 1610, d. Portsmouth, R.I., after 6 August 1677. GM2 III:294-98; Johnson, pp. 181-82; AL, pp. 293-94; RIR 12:21.

HEALD, JOHN, b. 1611, d. Concord, Mass., 24 May 1662. 26Imm, p. 133-34; 50Imm, pp. 199-202; MBT #754; AL, pp. 279-81.

HEALEY, WILLIAM, b. ca. 1613, d. Cambridge, Mass., 1683. Cameos, pp. 123-28; Sex, pp. 120-27, et al.

HEATH, BARTHOLOMEW, b. ca. 1615, d. Haverhill, Mass., 15 January 1681. Ordway, pp. 311-28; Stevens, 32-33; Valerie Dyer Giorgi, *Bartholomew Heath of Haverhill, Massachusetts and Some of His Descendants* (Santa Maria, CA: the author, 1994). Reviews: CN 28:409-10, NYGBR 126:217, NEHGR 150:357-58.

HEATH, ISAAC, b. ca. 1585, d. Roxbury, Mass., 21 January 1660/1. GM2 III:299-302; Davis II:250-55 [Annis Spear]; NEHGR 146:261-78 (English origins); NEHGR 149:173-86 (addition to English ancestry).

HEATH, WILLIAM, b. ca. 1591, d. Roxbury, Mass., 29 May 1652. GMB II:901-4; EB, pp. 272-74; NEHGR 146:261-78 (English origins); NEHGR 149:173-86 (addition to English ancestry); Valerie Dyer Giorgi, *William Heath of Roxbury, Massachusetts and Some of His Descendants* (Santa Maria, CA: the author, 1993). Reviews: NYGBR 125:124, NEHGR 148:184.

HEATON, JAMES, b. 1632, d. New Haven, Conn., 16 October 1712. NEHGR 151:329-41, 152:430-52 (English origins).

HEATON, NATHANIEL, b. 1602, d. Boston, Mass., between June 1648 and 1650. GM2 III:303-5; Kempton4, pp. 357-92, including English origins. Wife's origins (Wight) given at Kempton4, pp. 577-80; EB, pp. 274-76; NEHGR 152:430-52 (English origins).

HEDGES, WILLIAM, b. ca. 1612, d. Yarmouth, Mass., between 30 June and 5 July 1670. GMB II:904-8.

HEFFERNAN, WILLIAM, of Newport and South Kingstown, R.I. NEHGR 146:296 (wife identified).

HELME, CHRISTOPHER, b. ca. 1615, d. Warwick, R.I., between 26 May 1649 and 19 December 1650. Donald Henry Strahle, *Some Descendants of Christopher Helme of R.I.* (Ontario, Canada: the author, 2002, 2nd edition). Reviews: RIR 25:136.

HEMINGWAY, RALPH, b. ca. 1609, d. Roxbury, Mass., June 1678. GMB II:908-10; EB, pp. 276-78; Johnson, pp. 182-83; NEXUS 5:99-100 (clues to origins).

HEMPSTEAD, ROBERT, b. ca. 1613, d. New London, Conn., between 30 September 1653 and 17 November 1654. Angell, pp. 345-50; Spooner.

HENCHMAN, DANIEL, d. Worcester, Mass., 15 October 1685. First wife Sarah at RD600, pp. 385-86.

HENDRICK, DANIEL, d. Haverhill, Mass., between 1700 and 27 February 1718/9. 50Imm, pp. 203-4; MBT #478.

HENSHAW, JOSHUA, b. ca. 1643, d. after 1701. RD600, p. 218.

HEPBURNE, GEORGE, b. ca. 1592, d. Charlestown, Mass., 9 February 1665/6. GM2 III:307-11.

HERBERT, JOHN, b. 1612, of Salem, Mass., d. Southold, N.Y., between 4 August and 16 September 1658. GM2 III:311-13; NEHGR 153:448-52, 156:389 (correction).

HERRICK, HENRY, b. ca. 1598, d. Salem, Mass., between 24 November 1670 and 28 March 1671. GMB II:910-14; Chase, pp. 229-36; JPG I: 407-19.

HERRINGTON, HEZEKIAH, b. ca. 1690, d. Marshfield, Mass., between 1716 and 1720. TG 11:131-62.

HERRIS, THOMAS, b. ca. 1620, of Boston, Mass., and Hartford, Conn., d. Philadelphia, Penn., before 14 September 1713. NGSQ 80:36-56.

HETT, THOMAS, b. 1611, d. Charlestown, Mass., 6 June 1668. GMB II: 915-18; Goodman, pp. 241-45, including English origins; NEHGR 143:50-51; NEHGR 155:357-58 (English origins); Maurice R. Hitt, Jr., *Descendants of Henry Hitt of Woodbury, Conn., Arriving in America 1665 to Include Thomas Hett of Massachusetts and Some Descendants of James Hitt of R.I.* (Interlaken, NY: Windswept Press, 1993), pp. 521-28. Reviews: NEHGR 150:103-4.

HEWES, JOHN, b. ca. 1608, d. Scituate, Mass., between 6 February 1671 and 22 February 1674. GMB II:918-21; PM, pp. 240-43.

HEWES, JOSHUA, b. ca. 1612, d. Boston, Mass., 25 January 1675/6. GMB II:921-24; Johnson, pp. 184-85.

HEYFORD SEE HAFFORD

HIBBARD, ROBERT, b. 1612, d. Beverly, Mass., 7 May 1684. Johnson, pp. 185-87; Stevens, 67.

HIBBINS, WILLIAM, d. Boston, Mass., 23 July 1654. Wife Anne d. Boston, Mass., 19 June 1656. LENE, pp. 28-29; WRR, pp. 7-15.

HICKS, ROBERT, b. ca. 1578, d. Plymouth, Mass., 24 May 1647. GMB II:924-28; PM, pp. 243-48; EB, pp. 278-82; AL, pp. 300-2.

HIDDEN, ANDREW, d. Rowley, Mass., ca. 1701. TEG 24:165-68.

HIGGINS, RICHARD, b. ca. 1609, of Plymouth and Eastham, Mass., d. Piscataway, N.J., between 20 November 1674 and 1 June 1675. GMB II:928-32; PM, pp. 249-53; Croll, 131; Brewer, pp. 395-96.

HIGGINSON, FRANCIS, b. 1586, d. Salem, Mass., 6 August 1630. GMB II: 933-37; MBT #1112.

HILDRETH, RICHARD, b. ca. 1605, d. Chelmsford, Mass., 23 February 1693. Davis II:263-83 [Sarah Hildreth]; Nichols, pp. 97-98; NEHGR 146:337-42 (Joanna[3] Isaac[2]).

HILL, CHARLES, d. New London, Conn., before October 1684. Brewster, two generations all lines; Brewster3, three generations all lines.

HILL, HENRY, b. 1656, d. Boston, Mass., 8 July 1726. Chase, pp. 237-42, including English origins.

HILL, JOHN, b. 1602, d. Dorchester, Mass., 31 May 1664. Lyon, pp. 367-70.

HILL, PETER, b. ca. 1610, d. Saco, Me., before 3 September 1667. GMB III:2080-81.

HILL, RALPH, d. Billerica, Mass., 29 April 1663. NGSQ 72:3-32, 77:141 (four generation study).

HILL, ROGER, b. ca. 1640s, d. Beverly, Mass., between 8 January 1708/9 and 28 December 1710. Ordway, pp. 331-38, including English origins.

HILL, VALENTINE, b. ca. 1603, d. Dover, N.H., between 20 December 1660 and 28 June 1661. GM2 III:318-28; Jean A. Sargent, *Valentine Hill: Sparkplug of Early New England* (Laurel, MD: the author, 1981). Reviews: CN 14:698-99.

HILL, WILLIAM, b. ca. 1594, d. Fairfield, Conn., between 9 and 24 September 1649. GMB II:937-41; MJ 1:38-39, 68, 2:93, 98, 3:20-24, 6:29-38, 18:75-84.

HILLARD, WILLIAM, b. ca. 1614, d. Hingham, Mass., after 25 February 1654/5. GM2 III:329-31 [which claims the following article has conflated two men of the same name]; MD 49:95-115, 50:117-41, 51:117-29, a multigenerational work on the Hingham man and his descendants.

HILLS, JOSEPH, b. 1601/2, d. Newbury, Mass., 5 February 1687/8. Kempton4, pp. 395-419, including English origins; Stevens, 5; son Joseph[2] at Sex, pp. 132-33, 178-79.

HILLS, WILLIAM, b. ca. 1607, d. Hartford, Conn., before July 1683. GMB II:941-6; Nichols, pp. 229-230; NEHGR 149:41-5 (Joseph[2]).

HILTON, EDWARD, b. 1596, d. Exeter, N.H., between October 1670 and 6 March 1670/1. GMB II:947-51.

HILTON, WILLIAM, b. ca. 1591, d. York, Me., between June 1655 and 30 June 1656. GMB II:951-57; PM, pp. 254-61.

HIMES, JOHN, b. ca. 1645, d. North Kingstown, R.I., after 1676. Johnson, pp. 187-88.

HINCKLEY, SAMUEL, b. 1589, d. Barnstable, Mass., 31 October 1662. GM2 III:331-35; Makepeace, pp. 149-61; Mower, pp. 315-21; MG 27:147-68 (a line through Samuel$^{4-3}$ Thomas^2).

HINDS, JAMES, b. ca. 1613, of Salem, Mass., d. Southold, N.Y., March 1653. Johnson, pp. 188-91; Lyon, pp. 371-73.

HINSDALE, ROBERT, d. Deerfield, Mass. TAG 68:159 (English origins).

HITCHCOCK, MATTHEW, b. ca. 1610, d. New Haven, Conn., November 1669. GM2 III:336-38.

HITCHCOCK, RICHARD, b. ca. 1608, d. Saco, Me., June 1671. GM2 III: 339-42.

HITCHINGS, DANIEL, b. ca. 1632, d. Lynn, Mass., 15 April 1731. TEG 11:204-11, 12:48-53.

HITCHINGS, JOSEPH, b. ca. 1637, d. Lynn, Mass., 31 July 1693. TEG 12:53.

HITT, HENRY, b. ca. 1648, d. Woodbury, Conn., ca. 1689. Maurice R. Hitt, Jr., *Descendants of Henry Hitt of Woodbury, Conn., Arriving in America 1665 to Include Thomas Hett of Massachusetts and Some Descendants of James Hitt of R.I.* (Interlaken, NY: Windswept Press, 1993). Reviews: NEHGR 150:103-4.

HITT, JAMES, b. ca. 1670, d. Warwick, R.I., after 1702. Maurice R. Hitt, Jr., *Descendants of Henry Hitt of Woodbury, Conn., Arriving in America 1665 to Include Thomas Hett of Massachusetts and Some Descendants of James Hitt of R.I.* (Interlaken, NY: Windswept Press, 1993), pp. 531-61. Reviews: NEHGR 150:103-4.

HOAG, JOHN, b. ca. 1643, d. Hampton, N.H., ca. 1728. Jessup, pp. 522-26.

HOAR, HEZEKIAH, b. 1608, d. Taunton, Mass., after 27 February 1692/3. GM2 III:342-46; EB, pp. 282-84; JPG I:420-31; NEHGR 141:22-33 (English origins); NEHGR 142:17-24 (single line of descent through Hezekiah^{3-2-1}); NEHGR 142:393 (correction); NEHGR 144:143-46 (English origins part II); MJ 17:84-85.

HOAR, LEONARD, b. ca. 1632, d. Boston, Mass., 28 November 1675. Cameos, pp. 155-59; wife Bridget (Lisle) at RD600, pp. 259-62.

HOBART, EDMUND, b. ca. 1575, d. Hingham, Mass., 8 March 1646/7. GMB II:958-60; Josiah[3] Peter[2] and Joshua[3] Peter[2] at NEA 1:5/6:23; TAG 67:28 (Peter[2]'s marriage).

HOBSON, JOHN, b. ca. 1611, d. Guilford, Conn., 3 July 1701. CA 27:2-8.

HODGES, GEORGE, d. Salem, Mass., before 2 July 1709. Chase, pp. 243-48.

HODGES, WILLIAM, d. Taunton, Mass., 2 April 1654. Makepeace, pp. 163-75; Mower, pp. 323-48.

HODGKINS, WILLIAM, b. ca. 1622, d. Ipswich, Mass., 26 December 1693. Brewer, pp. 397-440.

HODSMAN, EDWARD, fl. Reading, Mass., and R.I., 1670s. Sex, pp. 48-53, et al.

HOLBRIDGE, ARTHUR, b. ca. 1613, d. New Haven, Conn., before 22 May 1648. GM2 III:348-50.

HOLBROOK, JOHN, b. 1598, d. Weymouth, Mass., ca. 1644. Johnson, pp. 191-94; MJ 25:38, 26:41-42, 27:33-34.

HOLBROOK, THOMAS, b. ca. 1589, d. Weymouth, Mass., between 31 December 1668 and 24 April 1677. GM2 III:350-55; Stone, pp. 153-57, including English origins; Davis II:284-92 [Joseph Neal], including English origins; 31Imm, pp. 124-30, including English origins; EB, pp. 284-87; Lyon, pp. 374-79; AL, pp. 302-6, including English ancestry; MJ 17:85-90, 25:38, 26:41-42, 27:33-34.

HOLCOMBE, THOMAS, b. ca. 1609, d. Windsor, Conn., 7 September 1657. GMB II:964-67; Nichols, p. 162; Lyon, pp. 380-83; TAG 57:65-76, 160-69, 225-29 (five generation study); MJ 1:39-40, 2:98, 6:39-79.

HOLDEN, JUSTINIAN, b. 1611, d. Cambridge, Mass., between 12 August and 10 October 1691. GM2 III:355-62; Cameos, pp. 199-204; son Justinian[2] at Thompson, pp. 123-24.

HOLDEN, RANDALL, b. ca. 1612, d. Warwick, R.I., 23 August 1692. RIR 12:66.

HOLDEN, RICHARD, b. ca. 1609, d. Groton, Mass., between 23 March 1690/1 and 16 March 1693/4. GM2 III:363-68.

HOLDER, CHRISTOPHER, b. 1631, d. Portsmouth, R.I., 13 June 1688. RF2, four generations all lines.

HOLDRED, WILLIAM, b. ca. 1610, d. Exeter, N.H., after 5 June 1676. GM2 III:368-72; Stevens, 38.

HOLGRAVE, JOHN, b. ca. 1590, d. in Me. before 26 July 1666. GMB II: 967-70.

HOLLAND, JOHN, b. 1602, d. Dorchester, Mass., between 3 August and 10 September 1652. GM2 III:373-77; TAG 68:176-81 (English origins).

HOLLARD, ANGEL, b. 1614, d. Boston, Mass., 30 June 1670. GM2 III:377-80; MJ 19:82-84.

HOLLINGSWORTH, RICHARD, b. ca. 1595, d. Salem, Mass., between 29 June 1653 and 28 March 1654. GM2 III:380-84; TAG 78:241-44 (English origins).

HOLLISTER, JOHN, b. ca. 1612, d. Wethersfield, Conn., between 13 and 20 April 1665. Pond, 251.

HOLLOWAY, JOSEPH, d. Lynn, Mass., 29 November 1693. Chase, pp. 223-28.

HOLLOWAY, JOSEPH, d. Sandwich, Mass., November/December 1647. AL, pp. 306-7.

HOLLOWAY, WILLIAM, of Taunton, Mass. Wife Grace at NEA 5:1:20-21.

HOLMAN, JOHN, b. 1602/3, d. Dorchester, Mass., between 10 June 1652 and 18 March 1652/3. GMB II:973-76; MJ 1:40-41, 68, 3:25, 6:81-90, 17:90-93.

HOLMAN, WILLIAM, b. ca. 1595, d. Cambridge, Mass., 8 January 1652/3. GM2 III:389-91. Son Jeremiah[2] in MF8, three generations all lines; also at Cameos, pp. 277-80, 303-8; wife Winifred and daughter Mary at Cameos, pp. 87-97; son Abraham[2] at Cameos, pp. 249-55, 303-8.

HOLMES, JOHN, b. ca. 1611, d. Plymouth, Mass., after 7 October 1651. GMB II:977-78; PM, pp. 265-67; EB, pp. 287-91; NGSQ 74:83-110, 203-23 (four generation study); NGSQ 77:143-44.

HOLMES, JOHN, d. Duxbury, Mass., 24 December 1675. NEHGR 144: 23-28.

HOLMES, OBADIAH, b. 1609/10, d. Newport, R.I., 15 October 1682. AL, pp. 307-10, including English ancestry.

HOLMES, ROBERT, d. Cambridge, Mass., between 20 May and 13 June 1663. Daughter Elizabeth and wife Jane at Sex, pp. 85-86, 130-32, 227-28, et al.

HOLMES, ROBERT, of Stonington, Conn. Joshua[3-2] at NEHGR 142:165-76, 393.

HOLMES, SAMUEL, b. before 1651, d. Plymouth, Mass., before 7 March 1690/1. Ordway, pp. 341-55.

HOLMES, WILLIAM, b. ca. 1592, d. Marshfield, Mass., 8 November 1678. GM2 III:392-97; daughter Sarah identified as a wife of Samuel[2-1] Arnold at NEHGR 145:374.

HOLT, NICHOLAS, b. ca. 1608, d. Andover, Mass., 30 January 1685/6. GM2 III:397-401.

HOLTON, WILLIAM, b. 1610, d. Northampton, Mass., 12 August 1691. Makepeace, pp. 177-95; NEHGR 159:25-34 (John[2]).

HOLYOKE, EDWARD, b. 1585/6, d. Rumney Marsh [Chelsea], Mass., 4 May 1660. NEHGR 147:11-34 (English origins); NEHGR 147:164-73 (wife's English origins); NGSQ 69:11-12.

HOOD, JOHN, b. ca. 1600, d. Lynn, Mass., after February 1683. Chase, pp. 249-54, including English origins; TEG 18:51-57.

HOOKE, WILLIAM, b. 1612, of Salisbury, Mass., d. Bristol, England, July 1652. GM2 III:403-10.

HOOKER, THOMAS, b. 1586, d. Hartford, Conn., 7 July 1647. GMB II:982-85; NEXUS 10:13; CN 23:4-15, 196-207; CN 23:388-98, 626-35, TAG 75:225-28 (notes on wife's Gabrand ancestry); TAG 76:216 (baptism of daughter Sarah); NEQ 66:67-109; Sargent Bush, Jr., *The Writings of Thomas Hooker: Spiritual Adventure in Two Worlds* (Madison, WI: University of Wisconsin Press, 1980). Reviews: NEQ 54:585-85.

HOOMERY, JOHN, b. ca. 1652, d. Portsmouth, R.I., after 20 October 1675. TAG 77:302-12.

HOPKINS, JOHN, b. ca. 1606, d. Hartford, Conn., between 27 July 1653 and 14 April 1654. GM2 III:411-13; Goodman, pp. 247-53; TAG 77:25-27 (note on daughter Bethia).

HOPKINS, STEPHEN, *Mayflower* passenger, b. ca. 1580, d. Plymouth, Mass., between 6 June and 7 July 1644. MF6, five generations all lines; GMB II:986-89; PM, pp. 271-75; Croll, 144; EB, pp. 291-300; Lyon, pp. 383-86; TAG 73:161-71 (English origins); TAG 79:241-49 (probable parentage); MQ 51:5-9, 168-72; MQ 64:259-65, 350-51.

HOPKINS, THOMAS, b. 1616, of Providence, R.I., d. Oyster Bay, N.Y., 1684. MJ 18:85, 27:34.

HOPKINS, WILLIAM, d. Stratford, Conn., ca. 1643. EB, pp. 300-1.

HOPPIN, STEPHEN, b. ca. 1624, d. Roxbury, Mass., 1 November 1677. EB, pp. 301-2.

HOPSON SEE HOBSON

HORNE, JOHN, b. ca. 1602, d. Salem, Mass., between 4 and 25 November 1684. GMB II:990-94.

HORSINGTON, JOHN, b. ca. 1640, of Milton and Hadley, Mass., and Wethersfield, Conn., d. East Hampton, N.Y., 20 December 1703. NEHGR 141:38-55.

HORTON, THOMAS, d. Rehoboth, Mass., before 8 March 1715/6. Margaret R. Jenks and Frank C. Seymour, *Thomas Horton of Milton and Rehoboth, Massachusetts* (Kirkland, WA: the authors, 1984). Reviews: TAG 59:252-53, CN 17:339.

HOSFORD, WILLIAM, b. ca. 1595, of Dorchester, Mass., Windsor, Conn., and Springfield, Mass., d. England after 1655. GMB II:994-97; MJ 19:86-87; Norman F. and David H. Hosford, *A Hosford Genealogy: A History of the Descendants of William Hosford Sometime Resident of Beaminster, Dorsetshire; Dorchester, Massachusetts; Windsor, Connecticut; and Calverleigh, Devonshire* (West Kennebunk, ME: Phoenix Publishing, 1993). Reviews: CN 26:573, NYGBR 125:58, NEHGR 148:79.

HOSKINS, JOHN, b. ca. 1588, d. Windsor, Conn., between 1 May and 29 June 1648. GMB II:999-1002; MJ 1:41, 6:91-100, 13:47, 19:87-89.

HOSKINS, WILLIAM, b. ca. 1611, d. Plymouth, Mass., 7 September 1695. GM2 III:414-20; Brewer, pp. 445-48; JPG I:432-48; AL, pp. 284-87.

HOSLEY, JAMES, d. Dorchester, Mass., 9 July 1677. Stone, pp. 159-64.

HOSMER, JAMES, b. 1605, d. Concord, Mass., 7 February 1685/6. GM2 III:421-23.

HOSMER, THOMAS, b. 1602/3, d. Northampton, Mass., 12 April 1687. GMB II:1002-5; Jessup, pp. 538-42; Ronald Longaker Roberts, *The Hosmer Heritage: Ancestors and Descendants of the Emigrant Thomas Hosmer 1603-1687* (South Lake Tahoe, CA: the author, 1984). Reviews: NHGR 9:47-48, NYGBR 117:247, 119:185.

HOTCHKIN, JOHN, b. ca. 1633, d. Guilford, Conn., January 1681/2. Edgar E. Hotchkin, *Descendants of John Hotchkin of Guilford, Connecticut* (Baltimore, MD: Gateway Press, 1995). Reviews: CN 29:408.

HOTCHKISS, SAMUEL, b. ca. 1622, d. New Haven, Conn., 28 December 1663. Nellie Cowdell, *The Hotchkiss Family: First Six Generations, Descendants of Samuel Hotchkiss (ca. 1622-1663) of New Haven, Connecticut* (Baltimore, MD: Gateway Press, 1985). Reviews: CN 18:726-27, NYGBR 117:182.

HOUCHIN, JEREMIAH, b. ca. 1615, d. Boston, Mass., between 7 April and 31 May 1670. 31Imm, pp. 131-35; TAG 67:54.

HOUGH SEE ALSO HAUGH

HOUGH, WILLIAM, b. ca. 1618, d. New London, Conn., 10 August 1683. JPG II:407-9.

HOUSE, SAMUEL, b. 1610, d. Scituate, Mass., 12 September 1661. GM2 III:424-28.

HOVEY, DANIEL, b. 1617/8, d. Ipswich, Mass., 24 April 1692. Goodman, pp. 255-62.

HOWARD, JOHN, d. Bridgewater, Mass., d. 1700/1. MBT #280.

HOWARD, NATHANIEL, of Chelmsford, Mass., Nichols, p. 99.

HOWARD, WILLIAM, b. ca. 1634, d. Ipswich, Mass., 25 July 1709. TAG 66:111-18 (possible identification of his wife).

HOWE, ABRAHAM, b. 1635, d. Marlborough, Mass., 30 January 1694/5. Kempton3, pp. 257-88, with possible English origins.

HOWE, DANIEL, b. ca. 1608, of Lynn, Mass., d. England after 1656. GMB II:1011-13.

HOWE, EDWARD, b. 1587/8, d. Watertown, Mass., before 24 June 1644. GMB II:1013-16; Kempton, pp. 337-42, including English origins. He d.s.p. but see **TREADWAY.**

HOWE, EDWARD, b. ca. 1575, d. Lynn, Mass., April 1639. GM2 III:428-31; 26Imm, pp. 135-40; MBT #712.

HOWE, JAMES, b. ca. 1603, d. Ipswich, Mass., 17 May 1702. GM2 III: 431-35.

HOWE, JOHN, b. 1617, d. Marlborough, Mass., 28 May 1680. Kempton3, pp. 257-88, including possible English origins; Stone, pp. 165-71; Dancing, pp. 385-416; Nehemiah[3] Samuel[2] at NHGR 7:163-66.

HOWES, THOMAS, b. ca. 1590, d. Yarmouth, Mass., ca. October 1665. Croll, 117; Jessup, pp. 542-46.

HOWLAND, ARTHUR, b. ca. 1604, d. Marshfield, Mass., October 1675. Davis II: 293-97 [Annis Spear], including English origins; AL, pp. 312-16; NGSQ 71:84-93.

HOWLAND, HENRY, b. ca. 1603, d. Duxbury, Mass., 1 January 1670/1. GMB II:1016-19; PM, pp. 275-79; daughter Abigail[2] at NEXUS 15:28; NGSQ 75:105-16, 216-25, 278-88 (three generation study); Croll, 114; AL, pp. 312-18.

HOWLAND, JOHN, *Mayflower* passenger, b. ca. 1592, d. Plymouth, Mass., 23 February 1672/3. Descendants from first child Desire[2] in Howland1 for five generations all lines. Descendants from second child John[2] in Howland2 for five generations all lines; GMB II:1020-24; PM, pp. 279-84; Mower, pp. 351-63; MD 42:15-16 (Maine travels); AL, pp. 312-15; TEG 2:161-65 (wife Elizabeth); MQ 48:131-35.

HOWLETT, THOMAS, b. ca. 1605, d. Ipswich, Mass., between 44 November 1677 and 10 September 1678. GMB II: 1024-28; Davis II:298-304 [Dudley Wildes].

HOYT, JOHN, b. ca. 1610, d. Salisbury, Mass., 29 February 1687/8. Davis II:305-13 [Lydia Harmon]; Stevens, 28; MBT #1794.

HOYT, SIMON, b. ca. 1593, d. Stamford, Conn., 1 September 1657. GMB II:1028-32; Thomas[3] Walter[2] at TAG 66:217-18; MJ 18:85-86, 25:38-43, 27:34-35.

HUBBARD, BENJAMIN, b. ca. 1608, d. Charlestown, Mass., after 1638. GMB II:1032-35.

HUBBARD, WILLIAM, b. 1585, d. Boston, Mass., between 8 June and 19 August 1670. GM2 III:437-43; son Richard[2] in RF1, three generations all lines; wife Judith (Knapp) at RD600, 2nd printing (2006), pp. 842-43.

HUCKINS, THOMAS, b. ca. 1617, of Barnstable, Mass., d. at sea 9 November 1679. MQ 50:80-86 (Hope[3] John[2]).

HUDDLESTON, VALENTINE, b. ca. 1628, d. Dartmouth, Mass., 8 June 1727. TW, pp. 261-71.

HUDSON, DANIEL, b. 1620, d. Lancaster, Mass., 11 September 1697. TAG 56:25-28 (English origins); TAG 64:148-49 (further information on his grandfather).

HUDSON, JONATHAN, b. ca. 1616, d. Lynn, Mass., between 21 June 1698 and 3 December 1706. TEG 14:86-96.

HUDSON, RALPH, b. ca. 1593, d. Boston, Mass., between 24 September 1638 and 25 March 1639. GM2 III:445-48.

HUDSON, WILLIAM, b. ca. 1588, of Boston and Charlestown, Mass., d. England, after 17 February 1661/2. GMB II:1035-37.

HUESTIS, ROBERT, b. ca. 1595, d. Greenwich, Conn., between 8 July 1652 and 4 November 1654. GM2 III:448-50; NYGBR 129:1-12, 97-108, 191-206, 276-84, 130:54-60 (English origins of Robert[1] and a three generation study of Robert[2]); TAG 73:201-6 (Jonathan[3] Angell[2]); MJ 19: 89-90.

HUFF, FERDINANDO, b. ca. 1641, d. Portsmouth, N.H., after August 1702. Brewer, pp. 449-50.

HUIT, EPHRAIM, d. Windsor, Conn., 4 September 1644. JPG I:449-52.

HULBIRD, WILLIAM, b. ca. 1606, d. Northampton, Mass., 17 April 1694. GMB II:1038-40; MJ 1:41-42, 6:101-2, 13:9.

HULING, JAMES, b. ca. 1636, d. Newport, R.I., 6 March 1686. Esther Littleford Woodworth-Barnes, compiler, Jane Fletcher Fiske, editor, *Huling Genealogy: Descendants of James and Margaret Huling of Newport, R.I., and Lewes, Delaware* (Clemson, SC: the author, 1984), winner of the Donald Lines Jacobus Award for 1985. Reviews: RIR 11:15; TAG 60:190, NEHGR 139:326-29.

HULL, ANDREW, b. ca. 1606, d. New Haven, Conn., ca. 1641. GM2 III: 451-52.

HULL, GEORGE, b. ca. 1590, d. Fairfield, Conn., ca. August 1659. GMB II:1040-43; EB, pp. 303-6; MJ 1:42-43, 68-69, 2:94, 3:26-29, 6:103-28, 17:93-97, 19:103-4 (wife Thomasine), MJ 26:9; Robert E. Hull, *The Ancestors and Descendants of George Hull 1590-1659 and Thamzen Michell of Crewkerne, Somerset, England, Dorchester, Mass. . . .* (Baltimore, MD: Gateway Press, 1994). Reviews: CN 28:251-52; English ancestry of mother at Lindsay L. Brook, editor, *Studies in Genealogy and Family History in Tribute to Charles Evans on the Occasion of His Eightieth Birthday* (Salt Lake City, UT: Association for the Promotion of Scholarship in Genealogy, Ltd., 1989), pp. 44-51. Reviews: NYGBR 122:122, TAG 65:249, NGSQ 79:141-42.

HULL, JOSEPH, b. 1596, d. Isle of Shoals, N.H., 19 November 1665. GM2 III: 452-60; Jessup, pp. 548-66; AL, pp. 318-24; TAG 68:149 (note); TAG 68:232-38 (Patience[3] Samuel[2]); English ancestry of mother at Lindsay L. Brook, editor, *Studies in Genealogy and Family History in Tribute to*

Charles Evans on the Occasion of His Eightieth Birthday (Salt Lake City, UT: Association for the Promotion of Scholarship in Genealogy, Ltd., 1989), pp. 44-51. Reviews: NYGBR 122:122, TAG 65:249, NGSQ 79:141-42.

HULL, ROBERT, b. ca. 1599, d. Boston, Mass., 28 July 1666. GM2 III: 460-62.

HUMPHREVILLE SEE UMFREVILLE

HUMPHREY, JOHN, b. ca. 1597, of Lynn, Mass., d. England between 16 December 1651 and 20 April 1652. GM2 III:462-68; MJ 18:87-89.

HUMPHREY, JONAS, b. ca. 1587, d. Dorchester, Mass., 9 March 1661/2. Jessup, pp. 567-68; TAG 68:14-22 (English origins).

HUMPHREY, MICHAEL, b. 1620, d. Windsor, Conn. TAG 67:242 (note); MJ 13:11-12, 16:139-41 (English origins), MJ 18:89-91.

HUNKING, HERCULES, d. Portsmouth, N.H., before 6 September 1659. TAG 73:223-27 (clues to English origins).

HUNN, GEORGE, b. ca. 1601, d. Boston June 1640, GM2 III:468-69.

HUNT, EDMOND, b. ca. 1613, d. Duxbury, Mass., between 3 June 1656 and 24 October 1657. GM2 III:469-72; Stevens, 11.

HUNT, ENOCH, of Weymouth, Mass., d. England before 1647. Stone, pp. 173-78; Chase, pp. 255-70; Lyon, pp. 387-89; AL, p. 324-27.

HUNT, WILLIAM, b. 1604, d. Marlborough, Mass., October 1673. Stowers, pp. 393-98; Samuel[3-2]'s wife corrected at TEG 24:222.

HUNTER, WILLIAM, b. ca. 1624, d. Boston, Mass., before 9 September 1667. GM2 III:475-77.

HUNTING, JOHN, b. 1602, d. Dedham, Mass., 12 April 1689. NGSQ 74:3-6; NGSQ 78:85-97 (English origins).

HUNTINGTON, SIMON, b. ca. 1598, of Roxbury, Mass., d. at sea 1633. GMB II:1044-46.

HURIN SEE MAHURIN

HURLBUT, THOMAS, b. ca. 1610, d. Wethersfield, Conn., after 12 October 1671. Pond, 227.

HURRY, WILLIAM, b. ca. 1634, d. Charlestown, Mass., 10 January 1689/90. Goodman, pp. 265-66.

Hurst, James, b. ca. 1582, d. Plymouth, Mass., between 10 and 24 December 1657. GMB II:1046-48; PM, pp. 284-86.

Hussey, Christopher, b. 1598/9, d. Hampton, N.H., March 1685/6. GMB II:1048-52.

Husted see Huestis

Huston, William, b. ca. 1680, d. Falmouth, Me., after 28 April 1739. MG 25:147-63, 26:15-35.

Hutchins, David, d. Kittery, Me., 19 September 1708. Jessup, pp. 568-70.

Hutchins, Enoch, b. ca. 1640, d. Kittery, Me., 9 May 1698. Brewer, pp. 451-52.

Hutchins, John, d. Haverhill, Mass., 6 February 1685/6. TEG 21:46-49 (wife Frances).

Hutchinson, Edward, b. 1607, of Boston, Mass., and Portsmouth, R.I., d. England after 1669. GMB II:1052-54.

Hutchinson, Francis, b. ca. 1630, d. Reading, Mass., 12 November 1705. MF17, three generations all lines.

Hutchinson, George, b. ca. 1608, d. Charlestown, Mass., 11 December 1660. GMB II:1054-55.

Hutchinson, Richard, b. ca. 1602, d. Salem, Mass., between 19 January 1679/80 and 28 September 1682. Davis II:320-34 [Sarah Johnson]; MBT #846.

Hutchinson, Samuel, d. Andover, Mass., ca. 1696-97. Sex, pp. 116-23.

Hutchinson, William, b. 1586, d. Roxbury, Mass., ca. June 1641. GM2 III:477-84; wife Anne (Marbury) at TG13:189-98; RD600, pp. 278-81; PA, p. 493; MCA, p. 565. Son Edward[2] married Katherine Hamby for whose royal line see RD600, pp. 433-34; PA, p. 372; MCA, p. 401. RF2, five generations in all lines; NEHGR 145:99-121, 258-68 (English ancestry of Katherine Hamby); notable descendants at NEXUS 12:210-16; wife Anne at Doctors, pp. 55-57; RIR 8:9; NEHGR 138:317-20 (notes on Chamberlain ancestry); TAG 67:201-10 (Marbury ancestry); NEHGR 153:164-72 (more on English ancestry); wife Anne at NEQ 54:74-103 and NEQ 61:381-97.

Hutton, Richard, b. ca. 1621, d. Wenham, Mass., 21 June 1713. TEG 22:36-42.

HYDE, JONATHAN, b. ca. 1626, d. Newton, Mass., 5 October 1711. Lyon, pp. 389-93.

HYDE, SAMUEL, d. Cambridge, Mass., 14 September 1689. Son Job[2] at Cameos, pp. 239-42.

HYDE, WILLIAM, d. Norwich, Conn., 6 January 1681/2. Spooner.

HYLAND, THOMAS, b. 1604, d. Scituate, Mass., between 14 February 1682/3 and 3 May 1683. NEHGR 157:209-20, 379-91, 158:68-86, 391 (Richard[3] Thomas[2]).

IBROOK, RICHARD, b. ca. 1583, d. Hingham, Mass., 14 November 1651. GM2 IV:1-2; Davis II:335-36 [Annis Spear].

IDES, NICHOLAS, d. Rehoboth, Mass., October 1690. 31Imm, pp. 136-37.

INES, MATTHEW, b. ca. 1613, d. Boston, Mass., between 6 May 1657 and 16 April 1661. GMB II:1057-59.

INGALLS, EDMUND, b. 1586, d. Lynn, Mass., before 27 June 1649. Stevens, 50; MBT #392, with English ancestry; TEG 19:43-53, 105-9, 219-23; TEG 23:51-52, 59.

INGERSOLL, JOHN, b. 1626, d. Westfield, Mass., 2 September 1684. NEHGR 151:153-65 (English origins).

INGERSOLL, RICHARD, b. 1587, d. Salem, Mass., between 24 July and 4 October 1644. Davis II:337-42 [Abel Lunt], including English origins; Chase, pp. 271-80, including English ancestry; GMB II:1060-63; 26Imm, pp. 141-48; Johnson, pp. 194-97; Stevens, 69; MBT #762; TAG 79:274-77 (Richard[3] John[2]); TAG 79:278-82 (Richard[4-3] John[2]), TAG 80:78 (correction).

INGHAM, JOSEPH, b. ca. 1630, d. Saybrook, Conn., 28 December 1710. TAG 68:129-38, 242-48.

INGLES, MAUDIT, b. 1608, d. Boston, Mass., 27 December 1684. GM2 IV:2-4.

INGRAHAM, RICHARD, b. ca. 1595, d. Northampton, Mass., August 1683. AL, p. 330; Jeremiah[3] Jared[2] at NEXUS 14:22-25, 151.

INMAN, EDWARD, b. ca. 1620, d. Providence R.I., before 17 August 1706. Angell, pp. 365-75 including possible English origins; RIR 15:5-6.

IRELAND, SAMUEL, b. ca. 1603, d. Wethersfield, Conn., between 5 September 1639 and 2 April 1641. GM2 IV:5-6.

IRESON, EDWARD, b. ca. 1601, d. Lynn, Mass., December 1675. GMB II:1063-65.

IRESON, JOHN, b. ca. 1603, d. Lynn, Mass., December 1675. TEG 15:10-17.

IRISH, JOHN, b. ca. 1611, d. Duxbury, Mass., before 5 March 1677/8. GMB II:1065-68, PM, pp. 287-89; George E. Irish, *John Irish: His Life and Ancestors 1086-1677* (Baltimore, MD: Gateway Press, 1991). Reviews: CN 24:596-97, MQ 59:142.

IRONS, MATTHEWS, b. ca. 1615, d. Boston, Mass., 1661. RIR 26:1-130 (multi-generational study with other unconnected Irons families).

IVES, MILES, b. ca. 1608, d. Watertown, Mass., 26 August 1684. Sex, pp. 122, 151-52.

IVES, WILLIAM, b. ca. 1607, d. New Haven, Conn., before 6 June 1648. Johnson, pp. 197-99.

IVORY, WILLIAM, b. ca. 1600, d. Boston, Mass., 8 March 1652. TEG 10:33-41, 85-90, 153-54.

JACKLIN, EDMUND, b. ca. 1614, d. Boston, Mass., between 26 April 1680 and 24 September 1681. GM2 IV:9-13.

JACKSON, EDMUND, b. ca. 1611, d. Boston, Mass., 14 July 1675. GM2 IV:13-18.

JACKSON, EDWARD, b. ca. 1602, d. Cambridge, Mass., 17 June 1681. Cameos, pp. 205-11, 239-42.

JACKSON, HENRY, b. ca. 1606, d. Fairfield, Conn., between 11 November 1682 and 21 June 1686. GM2 IV:19-22; Johnson, pp. 199-201.

JACKSON, JOHN, b. 1608, d. Portsmouth, N.H., between 7 November and 6 December 1666. NEHGR 144:29-38 (English origins).

JACKSON, JOHN, b. 1624, of Kittery, Me., d. Dartmouth, England, after 1 February 1681/2. NEHGR 144:29-38 (English origins).

JACKSON, JOHN, b. ca. 1595, d. Salem, Mass., between 31 January and 10 March 1655/6. GM2 IV:23-25.

JACKSON, JOHN, b. ca. 1614, d. Ipswich, Mass., before 18 September 1648. GM2 IV:25-28.

JACKSON, RICHARD, b. ca. 1582, d. Cambridge, Mass., between 22 June and 10 October 1672. Cameos, pp. 145-48, 183-88.

JACKSON, THOMAS, d. Plymouth, Mass., 4 September 1638. LENE, p. 7.

JACKSON, WILLIAM, d. Rowley, Mass., April/May 1688. EB, pp. 306-7; LENE, pp. 78-80 (Elizabeth²).

JACOB, NICHOLAS, b. ca. 1604, d. Hingham, Mass., 5 June 1657. GMB II:1069-71.

JACOB, RICHARD, b. ca. 1614, d. Ipswich, Mass., between 6 September and 5 October 1672. GM2 IV:28-32; Davis II:343-49 [Phoebe Tilton].

JACOBS, GEORGE, b. 1608/9, d. 19 August 1692. TAG 58:65-76; LENE, pp. 86-87; TAG 79:3-12, 209-17, 253-59 (English origins).

JACQUES, HENRY, b. ca. 1619, d. Newbury, Mass., 24 February 1686/7. Davis II:350-54 [Phoebe Tilton].

JAKWAY, AARON, b. ca. 1652, d. South Kingston, R.I., before 7 April 1711. JPG II:198-210.

JAMES, FRANCIS, d. Hingham, Mass., 27 December 1647. NEHGR 151: 61-86.

JAMES, JOHN, b. ca. 1646, d. Scituate, Mass., before 5 March 1678/9. NEHGR 153:435-42.

JAMES, PHILIP, b. ca. 1600, d. Hingham, Mass., 1638. NEHGR 151:61-86 (three generation study).

JAMES, THOMAS, b. 1595, of Charlestown, Mass., Providence, R.I., and New Haven, Conn., d. in England between 5 February 1682/3 and 13 February 1683/4. GMB II:1072-76.

JAMES, WILLIAM, b. ca. 1620, d. Portsmouth, R.I., after 1655. Johnson, pp. 201-3.

JAMES, WILLIAM, b. ca. 1639, d. Newport, R.I., 19 October 1697. NEHGR 147:329-55 (four generation study); NEHGR 148:66 (correction).

JAMES, WILLIAM, b. ca. 1641, d. Newport, R.I., after 11 May 1722. NEHGR 155:36-68; NEHGR 157:209-20, 379-91, 158:68-86 (Elizabeth²); NEHGR 159:131-40, 274-81, 364 (additional information on William²).

JAMES, WILLIAM, b. ca. 1690, d. Newport, R.I., after 1730. NEHGR 149:122-40 (three generation study).

JANES, WILLIAM, d. Northampton, Mass., 20 September 1690. JPG I: 453-59.

JAQUA SEE JAKWAY

JAQUITH, ABRAHAM, d. Charlestown, Mass., 17 December 1676. George Oakes Jaquith and Georgetta Jaquith Walker, *The Jaquith Family in America* (Boston, MA: NEHGS, 1982). Reviews: NGSQ 71:307, MQ 50:43.

JEFFREYS, ROBERT, b. ca. 1605, d. Newport, R.I., after 11 November 1646. GM2 IV:33-36.

JEFFREYS, WILLIAM, b. ca. 1590, d. Newport, R.I., 2 January 1675. GMB II:1082-85.

JEFTS, HENRY, b. ca. 1606, d. Billerica, Mass., 24 May 1700. Daughter or granddaughter Mary at Sex, pp. 45-47.

JENKINS, EDWARD, b. ca. 1620, d. Scituate, Mass., between 2 March 1698/9 and 20 July 1699. GM2 IV:36-41.

JENKINS, JOEL, b. ca. 1626, d. Malden, Mass., before 2 November 1688. Kempton4, pp. 421-27; Mower, pp. 365-69.

JENKINS, JOHN, b. ca. 1609, d. Barnstable, Mass., between 25 September 1683 and 21 October 1685. GM2 IV:41-46; NEHGR 149:339-59, 150:74-90 (five generation study).

JENKINS, JOHN, of Sandwich, Mass. TAG 67:135.

JENKS, JOSEPH, b. 1599, d. Lynn, Mass., March 1683. AL, pp. 332-36, including English ancestry.

JENNER, SAMUEL, of Woodbury, Conn. TAG 78:37-41.

JENNER, THOMAS, b. ca. 1606, of Roxbury, Charlestown, and Weymouth, Mass., and Saco, Me., d. in England between 4 June 1672 and 26 May 1676. GM2 IV:46-50.

JENNINGS, NICHOLAS, b. ca. 1612, of Hartford and Saybrook, Conn., d. Newtown, N.Y., before 16 October 1673. GM2 IV:50-58.

JENNINGS, THOMAS, of Portsmouth, R.I. TAG 78:1-8 (wife's identification).

JENNISON, ROBERT, d. Watertown, Mass., 4 July 1690. Chase, pp. 281-85; EB, pp. 307-9; Thompson, pp. 190-92, et al.

JENNY, JOHN, b. ca. 1589, d. Plymouth, Mass., between 28 December 1643 and 25 May 1644. GMB II:1089-94; PM, pp. 291-96.

JEPSON, JOHN, b. 1608/9, d. Boston, Mass., before 29 March 1688. TAG 78:253-55 (English origins).

Jewell, Thomas, b. ca. 1608, d. Braintree, Mass., between 10 April and 21 July 1654. GM2 IV:59-62; MBT #742.

Johnson, Edmund, b. ca. 1612, d. Hampton, N.H., 10 March 1650/1. GM2 IV:62-65; EB, pp. 309-11.

Johnson, Edward, b. 1598, d. Woburn, Mass., 23 April 1672. 26Imm, pp. 149-74; MBT #808; NEHGR 139:60-61 (note on English ancestry); NEHGR 139:321-24 (note on English ancestry).

Johnson, Edward, b. ca. 1593, d. York, Me., after 9 January 1687/8. GMB II:1096-99.

Johnson, Elkanah, b. ca. 1673, d. Coventry, R.I., between 24 October and 31 December 1748. RIR 29:113-37, 169-81, 30:117-41; Bartholomew[2] at RIR 28:157-72; John[3-2] at RIR 31:101-27.

Johnson, Francis, b. ca. 1607, d. Boston, Mass., 3 February 1690/1. GMB II:1100-3.

Johnson, James, b. ca. 1612, d. Boston, Mass., 19 November 1684. GM2 IV:66-78; Dancing, pp. 417-51 (generations one to five; sixth generation descendant Samuel Johnson, pp. 1-254); TEG 7:187-93 (Samuel[2]).

Johnson, John, b. before 1593, d. Roxbury, Mass., 30 September 1659. GMB II:1105-10; Angell, pp. 377-91; Crosby II:364-65; NEHGR 146:261-78 (English origins); NEHGR 148:45-60 (English origins of the wife of Isaac[2]); NEHGR 149:173-86 (addition to English ancestry).

Johnson, John, b. ca. 1607, d. Andover, Mass., after 12 September 1683. GM2 IV:78-81.

Johnson, Marmaduke, of Cambridge, Mass. Sex, pp. 136-39, et al.

Johnson, Mary, d. Hartford, Conn., December 1648. LENE, p. 17.

Johnson, Richard, b. ca. 1612, d. Lynn, Mass., 26 August 1666. Chase, pp. 287-93; TEG 11:82-89, 140-150.

Johnson, Samuel, of Boston, Mass., d. there or at sea ca. 1656. NEHGR 156:213-21 (English origins of his wife Mary).

Johnson, Thomas, d. Falmouth, Mass., ca. 1683. Jessup, pp. 578-81.

Johnson, William, b. ca. 1605, d. Charlestown, Mass., 9 December 1677. GM2 IV:84-90; Johnson, pp. 215-18.

Johnson, William, b. ca. 1630, d. Wallingford, Conn., 1716. Johnson, pp. 203-15.

JOHNSTON, JAMES, d. Stroudwater, Me., ca. 1740. Davis II:355-68 [James Patten].

JOHNSTON, JOHN, of Lynn, Mass., d. Lyndeborough, N.H., 26 December 1784. Davis II:369-77 [Sarah Johnson].

JONES, EDWARD, b. ca. 1610, d. Charlestown, Mass., after 1644. GMB II:1111-12.

JONES, HUGH, b. ca. 1635, d. Salem, Mass., ca. 1688. Chase, pp. 295-301, including English origins.

JONES, JOHN, b. ca. 1594, d. Fairfield, Conn., between 17 January and 9 February 1664/5. GM2 IV:92-97; TAG 71:52-54.

JONES, JOHN, b. ca. 1614/5, d. Portsmouth, N.H., between 2 and 17 September 1667. NHGR 11:57-63.

JONES, JOHN, d. Charlestown, Mass. Makepeace, pp. 197-204.

JONES, LEWIS, b. ca. 1600, d. Watertown, Mass., 11 April 1684. Kempton, pp. 345-51; Lyon, pp. 394-96; Thompson, pp. 183-84, et al.

JONES, MARGARET, possible wife of Thomas of Charlestown, Mass., d. Boston, Mass., 14 June 1648. GM2 IV:97-98; LENE, pp. 14-16.

JONES, NATHANIEL, d. Ipswich, Mass., 3 March 1750. Davis II:378-82 [Bethia Harris].

JONES, RALPH, d. Barnstable, Mass., between 11 May 1691 and 20 May 1692. MF4, three generations all lines.

JONES, RICHARD, b. 1598, d. Dorchester, Mass., before 16 April 1641. GM2 IV:99-102; TAG 58:244-46 (English origins); MJ 25:43-46.

JONES, ROBERT, b. ca. 1596, d. Hingham, Mass., between 20 April 1688 and 27 January 1691/2. 50Imm, pp. 205-10; MBT #1902; NEHGR 143:121-24.

JONES, THOMAS, b. ca. 1594, d. Dorchester, Mass., 13 November 1667. GM2 IV:102-6.

JONES, THOMAS, b. ca. 1598, d. Gloucester, Mass., 26 August 1671. TEG 18:83-89.

JONES, THOMAS, b. ca. 1602, d. Manchester, Mass., before 9 March 1680/1. 31Imm, pp. 148-52; NEHGR 143:125-31.

JONES, THOMAS, b. ca. 1620, of Fairfield, Conn., d. Huntington, N.Y., February 1669/70. NYGBR 128:101-9, 167-76.

JONES, THOMAS, b. ca. 1644, of Watertown, Mass. Sex, pp. 42-53, et al.

JORDAN, FRANCIS, b. ca. 1610, d. Ipswich, Mass., 29 April 1678. GM2 IV:110-14.

JORDAN, JOHN, d. Guilford, Conn., ca. January 1649/50. Pond, 232.

JORDAN, JOHN, fl. Milton, Mass., 1670s. JPG II:410-13.

JORDAN, ROBERT, b. ca. 1612, d. Portsmouth, N.H., 1678. Lyon, pp. 396-402.

JORDAN, STEPHEN, b. ca. 1590, d. Newbury, Mass., 8 February 1669/70. GM2 IV:114-16; Davis II:383-84 [Phoebe Tilton]; JPG I:460-62; MBT #386.

JOSLIN, THOMAS, b. ca. 1592, d. Lancaster, Mass., 3 January 1660/1. GM2 IV:117-21; JPG II:414-29; TAG 56:153-54 (note on nonexistence of a Joseph[2]); NEHGR 158:330-40 (identification of wife Rebecca and her English origins).

JUDD, THOMAS, b. ca. 1608, d. Northampton, Mass., 12 November 1688. GM2 IV:121-26; Lyon, pp. 403-5.

KEAYNE, ROBERT, b. ca. 1594, d. Boston, Mass., 1656. GM2 IV:127-33; wife Anne (Mansfield) at PA, p. 298; MCA, p. 311; NEHGR 155:3-35; RD600, pp. 167-68. Son Benjamin[2] in RF1, four generations all lines; Benjamin[2] and his daughter Anna[3] at WRR, pp. 198-207.

KEECH, GEORGE, b. ca. 1635, d. R.I., after 1670. Johnson, p. 219.

KEELER, RALPH, b. ca. 1613, d. Norwalk, Conn., between 20 August and 5 November 1672. Notes on third wife at TAG 58:32-34; CN 36:362-69 (John[3-2]); TAG 80:177-87 (first wife); Wesley B. Keeler, *Keeler Family: Ralph Keeler of Norwalk, Conn., and Some of His Descendants* (Baltimore, MD: Gateway Press, 1985). Reviews: CN 13:524, CN 18:544-45, TAG 57:64, TAG 61:122, NYGBR 111:245.

KEEN, LAWRENCE, b. ca. 1690, d. Hanover, Mass., before 29 May 1738. JPG II:229-34.

KEENE, JOSIAH, d. Duxbury, Mass., before 15 September 1710. MF18, three generations for children of his first wife, Abigail (Little); JPG II:431-47.

KEENEY, ALEXANDER, b. ca. 1625, d. Wethersfield, Conn., before 15 October 1680. Brewer, pp. 453-54.

KELLOGG, DANIEL, b. 1630, d. Norwalk, Conn., 1688. Nichols, pp. 100-1; TAG 71:87-92 (maternal English ancestry).

KELLOGG, JOSEPH, b. 1626, d. Hadley, Mass., ca. 1707. Goodman, pp. 269-86, including English origins; 31Imm, pp. 153-63; Lyon, pp. 405-25; TAG 71:87-92 (maternal English ancestry).

KELLY SEE O'KILLEA

KELLY, JOHN, d. Newbury, Mass., 28 December 1644. MBT #928.

KELLY, ROGER, of Smuttynose Island, Me. NEA 5:3:48-49, 55.

KELSEY, WILLIAM, b. ca. 1609, d. Killingworth, Conn., between June 1675 and 21 September 1676. GMB II:1117-19; TAG 68:208-15; 69:218 (death record).

KEMP, WILLIAM, d. Duxbury, Mass., before 23 September 1641. JPG II: 235-37.

KEMPTON, EPHRAIM, b. 1591, d. Scituate, Mass., before 5 May 1645. Kempton, pp. 1-117, including English ancestry. His brother Manassas Kempton also immigrated but d.s.p.; TAG 67:132-35 (English origins); NEHGR 148:342-44 (Ephraim[2]).

KENDALL, ELIZABETH, d. Boston, Mass., 1650. LENE, pp. 17-18.

KENDALL, FRANCIS, b. ca. 1615, d. Woburn, Mass., 1708. Nichols, pp. 17-19; Johnson, pp. 219-21; Helen Schatvet Ullmann, *A Mills and Kendall Family History: American Ancestry and Descendants of Herbert Lee Mills and Bessie Delano Kendall* (Boston, MA: Newbury Street Press, 2002), pp. 103-47. Reviews: NYGBR 134:152, TAG 78:73, NEHGR 157:185-86, CN 36:57-58, 227-28.

KENDRICK, GEORGE, b. ca. 1609, d. Newport, R.I., after 1663. GM2 IV: 135-39.

KENDRICK, GEORGE, b. ca. 1625, d. Rehoboth, Mass., after 1691. AL, pp. 342-43.

KENT, JOSEPH, b. 1644, d. Swansea, Mass., 1704. AL, pp. 343-44.

KENT, RICHARD, JR., b. ca. 1605, d. Newbury, Mass., after 9 July 1685. GM2 IV:142-45.

KENT, RICHARD, SR., b. ca. 1597, d. Newbury, Mass., 15 June 1654. GM2 IV:140-42.

KENT, THOMAS, d. Gloucester, Mass., 1 May 1658. Stevens, 2.

KENYON, JAMES, d. Westerly, R.I., 1724. TAG 78:222-27, 79:207-8 (revision of English origins and early generation); TAG 78:306-8 (note on marriage).

KENYON, JOHN, b. ca. 1657, d. Westerly, R.I., 1732. TAG 78:222-27, 79:207-8 (revision of English origins and early generation).

KETTLE, EDWARD, b. ca. 1660, d. North Kingstown, R.I., after 1724. Johnson, pp. 221-22.

KETTLE, RICHARD, b. ca. 1614, d. Charlestown, Mass., 28 June 1680. GMB II:1124-28; Goodman, pp. 289-92.

KEYES, ROBERT, b. ca. 1606, d. Newbury, Mass., 16 July 1647. GMB II:1128-31; Croll, 166; Johnson, pp. 222-24; MBT #654; TAG 65:12 (note on origins).

KEYES, SOLOMON, d. Chelmsford, Mass., 28 March 1702. Stone, pp. 179-81.

KIDDER, JAMES, b. ca. 1626, d. Billerica, Mass., 16 April 1676. Lyon, pp. 426-28.

KILBORNE, GEORGE, d. Rowley, Mass., 14 October 1685. Davis II:385-90 [Sarah Stone].

KILBORNE, THOMAS, b. 1578, d. Wethersfield, Conn., before 3 September 1640. GM2 IV:148-51; Nichols, pp. 181-82; John Dwight Kilbourne, *The Ancestry of Thomas Kilbourn (1578 – ca. 1637) of Wood Ditton, Cambridgeshire, England and Wethersfield, Connecticut* (Decorah IA: Anundsen Publishing, Co., 1991). Reviews: CN 26:279.

KILLAM, AUSTIN, d. Wenham, Mass. TAG 67:53-54.

KIMBALL, HENRY, b. ca. 1590, d. Watertown, Mass., before 22 July 1648. GM2 IV:152-54.

KIMBALL, RICHARD, b. ca. 1595, d. Ipswich, Mass., 22 June 1675. GM2 IV:154-60; Davis II:391-93 [Phoebe Tilton]; MBT #832; Joseph^3 John^2 at RIR 11:23-26.

KIMBERLY, THOMAS, b. 1604, d. Stratford, Conn., between 11 January and 12 February 1672/3. GM2 IV:160-66; Johnson, pp. 224-25.

KING, DANIEL, b. 1599, d. Lynn, Mass., 27 May 1672. TEG 9:82-92, 136-41.

KING, JOHN, b. ca. 1650, d. Harwich, Mass., between 21 May and 14 October 1707. MF6, two generations, all lines.

KING, SAMUEL, b. ca. 1619, d. Plymouth, Mass., August 1705. JPG II:238-40; NEHGR 148:315-27 (wife's English origins); MJ 18:91-92, 27:35-36.

KING, THOMAS, b. 1613/4, d. Scituate, Mass., 24 September 1691. GM2 IV:171-73; NEHGR 149:401-32 (English origins of wife).

KING, THOMAS, b. ca. 1600, d. Sudbury, Mass., between 12 March 1675/6 and 20 June 1676. MJ 18:92-93.

KING, THOMAS, b. ca. 1615, d. Watertown, Mass., December 1644. GM2 IV:168-70.

KING, WILLIAM, b. ca. 1595, d. Salem, Mass., after 26 June 1649. GM2 IV:174-77.

KING, WILLIAM, of Boston, Mass. William[2] at TAG 56:246-48

KINGMAN, HENRY, b. ca. 1594, d. Weymouth, Mass., 5 June 1667. GM2 IV:178-82.

KINGSBURY, HENRY, b. ca. 1596, d. Boston, Mass., after 1636. GMB II: 1131-33.

KINGSBURY, HENRY, b. ca. 1615, d. Haverhill, Mass., 1 October 1687. Eleazer[3] Joseph[2] at WRR, pp. 54-64.

KINGSBURY, JOSEPH, b. ca. 1610, d. Dedham, Mass., between 3 May 1675 and 1 June 1676. AL, pp. 345-46.

KINGSLEY, JOHN, d. Rehoboth, Mass., 9 January 1678/9. Pond, 272.

KINNEY, HENRY, b. 1623, d. Salem, Mass., after 1692. EB, pp. 322-27; JPG I:463-91.

KINSMAN, ROBERT, b. ca. 1605, d. Ipswich, Mass., 28 January 1664/5. GM2 IV:188-91; TAG 66:111-18 (daughter Tabitha).

KIRBY, RICHARD, b. ca. 1610, of Lynn and Sandwich, Mass., d. Oyster Bay, N.Y., 1688. Johnson, pp. 225-27; JPG I:492-505; AL, pp. 346-54.

KIRTLAND, NATHANIEL, b. 1613, d. Lynn, Mass., December 1686. GM2 IV:192-98; Jessup, pp. 586-95; TAG 65:65-69 (English origins).

KIRTLAND, PHILIP, b. 1611, d. Lynn, Mass., between 22 March 1654/5 and 13 June 1657. GM2 IV:198-201; TAG 65:65-69 (English origins); TAG 67:69-73 (sons John[2] and Nathaniel[2]).

KITCHELL, ROBERT, b. 1601, d. Guilford, Conn., after 1665. Nichols, pp. 233-36.

KITCHIN, JOHN, b. ca. 1611, d. Salem, Mass., between 20 December 1675 and 30 May 1676. GM2 IV:201-7.

KNAPP, NICHOLAS, b. ca. 1606, d. Stamford, Conn., between 15 and 27 April 1670. GMB II:1135-37.

KNAPP, ROGER, of Fairfield, Conn. Wife d. there November 1653. LENE, pp. 25-26.

KNAPP, WILLIAM, b. 1580/1, d. Watertown, Mass., 30 August 1659. GMB II:1143-46; Mower, pp. 371-76; 26Imm, pp. 175-88; Morgan; son John[2] at Thompson, pp. 190-92, et al.; Sex, pp. 100-2, et al.; NEHGR 147:315-28 (English origins).

KNIGHT, ALEXANDER, fl. Ipswich, Mass., 1630s. Stevens, 47; TAG 76:1-16 (English ancestry of his wife).

KNIGHT, JOHN, b. 1595, d. Newbury, Mass., May 1670. GM2 IV:208-12; Davis II:396-401 [Phoebe Tilton], including English origins; Johnson, p. 227.

KNIGHT, JOHN, b. ca. 1595, d. Charlestown, Mass., 29 March 1674. EB, pp. 327-29; JPG I:506-10.

KNIGHT, RICHARD, b. 1602/3, d. Newbury, Mass., 4 August 1683. GM2 IV:212-14; MBT #930.

KNIGHT, ROBERT, b. ca. 1614, d. Marblehead, Mass., 28 October 1691. Ordway, pp. 357-63; NEHGR 144:138-42.

KNIGHT, WILLIAM, b. ca. 1596, d. Lynn, Mass., 5 March 1655. Stevens, 55; TEG 18:71-78.

KNOPP SEE KNAPP

KNOWER, GEORGE, b. ca. 1611, d. Malden, Mass., 13 February 1674/5. GMB II:1146-48.

KNOWER, THOMAS, b. ca. 1602, d. Mystic River, Mass., 9 November 1641. GMB II:1148-50.

KNOWLES, HENRY, d. Portsmouth, R.I., between 2 and 20 January 1670. JPG I:511-15.

KNOWLES, JOHN, of Watertown, Mass., returned to England and died there after 1655. Thompson, pp. 66-74, et al.

KNOWLES, RICHARD, d. Eastham, Mass., between 1670 and 1675. Croll, 101.

KNOWLTON, BENJAMIN, fl. Reading, Mass., 1670s. Sex, pp. 47-53, et al.

KNOWLTON, WILLIAM, b. ca. 1584, d. Hingham, Mass., ca. 1632. JPG I:516-21 with English origins; JPG II:241-46; Stevens, 56.

LADD, DANIEL, b. ca. 1615, d. Haverhill, Mass., 27 July 1693. GM2 IV: 217-21.

LAGROVES, NICHOLAS, b. ca. 1645, d. Beverly, Mass., before 11 February 1702/3. EB, pp. 249-51.

LAKE, HENRY, of Boston, Mass. His wife, Alice, d. 1650. LENE, pp. 17-18.

LAKE, JOHN, b. 1590, d. England, but wife Margaret (Reade) Lake emigrated, d. Ipswich, Mass., between 30 August and 24 September 1672. Davis II:402-11 [Bethia Harris], including English origins, and Davis III: 260-66 [Bethia Harris] (Sandell ancestry of the Lakes). Wife's Reade ancestry given at Davis III:209-15; EB, pp. 329-31.

LAKIN, JOHN, b. 1628, d. Groton, Mass., 21 March 1697/8. JPG I:522-25; TAG 70:142-48 (English origins).

LAKIN, WILLIAM, b. ca. 1623, d. Groton, Mass., 22 February 1700/1. TAG 70:142-48 (English origins).

LAMB, EDWARD, b. ca. 1608, d. Boston, Mass., between 27 June 1648 and 1650. GMB II:1151-52; EB, pp. 331-32; JPG I:526-28.

LAMB, THOMAS, b. ca. 1599, d. Roxbury, Mass., 28 March 1646. GMB II:1153-55; Pond, 245; TAG 56:99.

LAMBERT, FRANCIS, d. Rowley, Mass., September 1647. NGSQ 68:13-14 (clues to English origins).

LAMBERT, RICHARD, b. ca. 1611, d. Salem, Mass., between 29 November 1655 and 14 December 1657. GM2 IV:223-25.

LAMBERTON, GEORGE, of New Haven, Conn. TAG 80:194 (baptisms of two daughters).

LAMBSON, BARNABAS, b. ca. 1602, d. Cambridge, Mass., after 1636. GM2 IV:226-28.

LANCTON, ROGER, b. ca. 1600, d. Haverhill, Mass., before 24 January 1671/2. GM2 IV:228-30.

LANE, WILLIAM, b. ca. 1581, d. Dorchester, Mass., between 28 February 1650/1 and 5 July 1654. GM2 IV:230-33; JPG II:448-54; TAG 64:214-15 (clue to origins); TAG 65:106; MJ 19:91-92, 27:36.

Langhorn see Longhorn

Langsford, Richard, b. ca. 1690, d. Gloucester, Mass., before 21 May 1734. NEHGR 156:246-61 (four generation study).

Langstaff, Henry, b. ca. 1610, d. Dover, N.H., July 1705. GMB II:1156-60; Pond, 284.

Langton, George, d. Northampton, Mass., 29 December 1676. Lyon, pp. 429-30.

Lanphear, George, b. ca. 1638, d. Westerly, R.I., 6 October 1731. NEHGR 153:131-40, 159:333-40 (this is one article despite the six year gap, and will be continued in 2006), English origins and three generation study.

Lapham, Thomas, b. ca. 1612, d. Scituate, Mass., before 23 January 1648/9. GM2 IV:234-36; Johnson, pp. 227-28; TAG 71:134-36 (daughter Rebecca).

Larkin, Edward, b. ca. 1611, d. Charlestown, Mass., before 14 January 1651/2. Kempton3, pp. 291-97; Goodman, pp. 295-98; Nichols, p. 61; Lyon, pp. 430-31; some possible relation, Mary and Edward Larkins (*sic*) of Charlestown at Sex, pp. 137-38.

Larkin, Edward, b. ca. 1625, d. Westerly, R.I., after 26 June 1687. Elizabeth Brock Larkin, *Edward Larkin of R.I.: Freeman of Newport 1655 and of Westerly 1664: The First Six Generations* (Saline, MI: McNaughton & Gunn, 2004). Reviews: RIR 31:45-46, NYGBR 136:149, MD 54:183, TAG 79:319.

Larrabee, Greenfield, d. Saybrook, Conn., before 17 October 1661. EB, pp. 332-35.

Larrabee, Stephen, b. ca. 1630, d. North Yarmouth, Me., September 1676. TEG 19:224-29, 20:44-51, 111-15, 176-77.

Laskin, Hugh, b. ca. 1587, d. Salem, Mass., before 21 March 1658/9. GM2 IV:238-40; JPG I:529-30.

Lassell, John, d. Hingham, Mass., 21 October 1700. Davis II:412-21 [Sarah Miller].

Latham, Mary, b. ca. 1626, d. Boston, Mass., 21 March 1644. LENE, pp. 10-11.

Latham, Robert, b. ca. 1613, d. Bridgewater, Mass., before 28 February 1688/9. MF15 three generations all lines; Pond, 268.

LATTIN SEE LETTEN

LAUGHTON, THOMAS, b. ca. 1610, d. Lynn, Mass., 8 August 1697. TEG 17:45-49.

LAUGHTON, THOMAS, d. Lynn, Mass., 8 August 1697. Wife Sarah (Lenthall)'s parentage at TG 19:222-30.

LAUNDER, THOMAS, b. ca. 1613, d. Sandwich, Mass., 11 November 1675. GM2 IV:240-44.

LAW, JOHN, of Concord, Mass., Sex, pp. 135-36.

LAWES, FRANCIS, b. ca. 1595, d. Salem, Mass., between 6 November 1665 and 28 June 1666. Davis II:422-27 [Sarah Stone], including English origins.

LAWRENCE, GEORGE, b. ca. 1637, d. Watertown, Mass., 21 March 1708/9. MBT #554; Sex, p. 100, et al.

LAWRENCE, HENRY, b. ca. 1595, d. Charlestown, Mass., before 22 July 1646. GM2 IV:244-46.

LAWRENCE, JOHN, b. 1610, d. Groton, Mass., 11 July 1667. GM2 IV:246-54; EB, pp. 335-37; CN 14:525-29.

LAWRENCE, THOMAS, d. 1624/5 in England. His widow Joan (Antrobus) married John Tuttle and immigrated to New England with her Lawrence children. GM2 I:67-69; Thomas's royal line at RD600, pp. 562-64; TG 10:3-30. Children: John, Mary, Thomas, and William at GM2 IV:254-68.

LAWSON, CHRISTOPHER, b. ca. 1616, d. Boston, Mass., before 20 November 1682. RD600, pp. 399-400.

LAWTON, GEORGE, b. 1607, d. Portsmouth, R.I., 5 October 1693. AL, pp. 368-71, including English ancestry.

LAWTON, THOMAS, b. 1614, d. Portsmouth, R.I., before 29 September 1681. AL, pp. 368-71, including English ancestry; RIR 13:2.

LAY, JOHN, of Saybrook, Conn. CN 30:216-17, marriage record found; TAG 64:88-89, identification of John[2] (the younger)'s wife.

LEACH, LAWRENCE, b. ca. 1583, d. Salem, Mass., before 25 June 1662. GMB II:1161-64; Mower, pp. 379-93; Stevens, 68.

LEADBETTER, HENRY, b. ca. 1633, d. Dorchester, Mass., 20 April 1722. Goodman, pp. 301-4.

Learned, William, b. ca. 1581, d. Woburn, Mass., 1 March 1645/6. GMB II:1164-66; Kempton4, pp. 429-50; JPG I:531-38; Mower, pp. 395-403; Lyon, pp. 432-34.

Leavitt, John, b. ca. 1612, d. Hingham, Mass., 20 November 1691. GM2 IV:270-76.

Leddra, William, d. Boston, Mass., 14 March 1661. LENE, pp. 29-32.

Lee, Henry, d. Manchester, Mass., between 12 February 1674 and 21 July 1675. Stevens, 60.

Lee, John, of Boston, Mass., d. before 1691. Widow Rebecca and daughter of the same name at Sex, pp. 159-64.

Lee, Peter, b. ca. 1665, d. East Greenwich, R.I., after 1730/1. TAG 59: 239-44.

Lee, Robert, d. Plymouth, Mass., after 1662. EB, pp. 338-39.

Lee, Samuel, b. 1640, d. Malden, Mass., 1676. Marion Edwards Lee, *The Lees of New England and Some Allied Families* (Ponca City, OK: the author, 1981). Reviews: CN 15:159-60.

Lee, Thomas, b. ca. 1610, d. 1645, on board ship to America. Angell, pp. 393-413.

Lee, Walter, b. ca. 1632, d. Westfield, Mass., 9 February 1718. Johnson, pp. 228-30.

Leeds, Richard, b. ca. 1605, d. Dorchester, Mass., 18 March 1692/3. EB, pp. 339-41.

Leete, William, of Conn. RD600, pp. 538-39; TAG 69:171-73 (John[3-2]).

Legge, John, b. ca. 1608, d. Marblehead, Mass., between 16 November 1672 and 25 May 1674. GMB II:1166-68.

Leighton, Thomas, b. ca. 1604, d. Dover, N.H., 22 January 1671/2. Perley M. Leighton, *A Leighton Genealogy: Descendants of Thomas Leighton of Dover, N.H.,* (Boston, MA: New England Historic Genealogical Society, 1989), two volume multi-generational work. Reviews: NHGR 8:137-38, MG 12:51-52, CN 23:324, NYGBR 121:251, TAG 66:188-89, NGSQ 79:228-29.

Leland, Henry, b. ca. 1625, d. Sherborn, Mass., 4 April 1680. Kempton4, pp. 453-76; JPG I:539-51; Lyon, pp. 434-41.

LEONARD, JAMES, b. ca. 1616, d. Taunton, Mass., before 1691. Jessup, pp. 595-602; AL, pp. 371-75, including English ancestry.

LEONARD, SOLOMON, b. ca. 1610, d. Bridgewater, Mass., before 1 May 1671. MF15, three generations all lines; Nichols, pp. 62-63.

LESTER, ANDREW, of Gloucester, Mass., d. New London, Conn., 7 June 1669/70. Daughter Ann at Doctors, pp. 61-62.

LETHERLAND, WILLIAM, b. ca. 1608, d. Boston, Mass., after 10 June 1684. GMB II:1169-73.

LETTEN, RICHARD, b. 1608/9, of Concord, Mass., and Fairfield, Conn., d. Oyster Bay, N.Y., 1673. NYGBR 117:219-24 (English origins).

LEVENS, JOHN, b. ca. 1582, d. Roxbury, Mass., 15 November 1647. GMB II:1173-75.

LEVER, THOMAS, d. Rowley, Mass., 26 December 1683. NGSQ 68:11-12 (clues to his and his wife's English origins).

LEVERETT, THOMAS, b. ca. 1585, d. Boston, Mass., 3 April 1650. GMB II:1175-78.

LEVERICH, WILLIAM, b. ca. 1603, of Boston, Duxbury, and Sandwich, Mass., d. Newtown, Long Island, before 19 June 1677. GMB II:1178-80.

LEWIS, EDMOND, b. ca. 1610, d. Lynn, Mass., between 13 January and 12 February 1650/1. GM2 IV:278-81.

LEWIS, GEORGE, b. 1600, d. Barnstable, Mass., between 3 June 1662 and 1 March 1663/4. GM2 IV:281-84; TAG 68:24-28 (English origins); TAG 72:311-20; TAG 72:321-28 (wife's identity and English ancestry); TAG 74:258 (corrections); Jessup, pp. 604-10; Barbara Lewis Williams, *400 Years with a New England Lewes-Lewis Family* (Baltimore, MD: Gateway Press, 1990). Reviews: CN 24:135.

LEWIS, JOHN, b. 1606, d. Boston, Mass., after 23 August 1669. GM2 IV:284-87; TAG 68:24-28 (English origins).

LEWIS, JOHN, b. ca. 1613, d. Malden, Mass., September 1657. GM2 IV:287-92.

LEWIS, JOHN, b. ca. 1630, d. Westerly, R.I., ca. 1690. Johnson, pp. 230-39.

LEWIS, JOHN, b. ca. 1631, d. Lynn, Mass., 1710. TEG 2:119.

LEWIS, PETER, b. ca. 1644, d. Isle of Shoals, N.H., between 3 February 1712/3 and 4 April 1716. Jessup, pp. 611-12.

LEWIS, THOMAS, b. ca. 1590, d. Saco, Me., between 7 May 1637 and 28 April 1640. GMB II:1181-84; Davis II:428-65 [Charity Haley, Nicholas Davis], including English origins. Wife Elizabeth Marshall's ancestry given at Davis II:577-81 [Nicholas Davis] and 613-25 [Nicholas Davis]. Her royal line at RD600, pp. 330-31; PA, p. 497; MCA, p. 118. His royal line at RD600, pp. 570-71.

LEWIS, WILLIAM, b. ca. 1595, d. Farmington, Conn., 2 August 1683. GMB II:1184-86; EB, pp. 341-47.

LIBBY, JOHN, b. ca. 1602, d. Scarborough, Me., before 9 February 1682, Davis II:466-78 [Joseph Waterhouse]; TAG 73:258-71 (Sarah[3] Anthony[2]).

LILLY, GEORGE, b. ca. 1637, d. Reading, Mass., 14 February 1690/1. Cooley, pp. 159-90; CN 18:618-20.

LINCOLN, SAMUEL, b. 1622, d. Hingham, Mass., 26 May 1690. Stone, pp. 183-92, including English origins; son Mordecai[2] at NEHGR 143:131-33.

LINCOLN, THOMAS, d. Hingham, Mass., 28 September 1691. TAG 64:214-15 (clue to origins); TAG 65:106; MJ 19:92-93.

LINDALL, JAMES, b. ca. 1610, d. Duxbury, Mass., 1652. Johnson, pp. 239-40.

LINDSEY, CHRISTOPHER, b. ca. 1617, d. Lynn, Mass., 10 April 1669. TEG 7:17-26, 71-76, 123-28, 194-98.

LINDSLEY, FRANCIS, of New Haven and Branford, Conn., d. Newark, N.J., ca. 1704. Lyon, pp. 441-47.

LINNEKIN, DENNIS, of Little Compton, R.I., Westport, Mass., and Boothbay, Me., d. there after 30 July 1756. RIR 11:54-55.

LINNELL, ROBERT, b. ca. 1584, d. Barnstable, Mass., 27 February 1662/3. Croll, 146; Jessup, pp. 612-16.

LINSFORD, THOMAS, b. ca. 1630, d. Boston, Mass., between 1652 and 1655. Johnson, pp. 240-41.

LIPPITT, JOHN, b. ca. 1597, d. Warwick, R.I., after May 1669. JPG I: 552-57.

LISCOMB, JOHN, b. ca. 1633, d. Boston, Mass., between 27 August and 30 September 1680. NEHGR 156:213-21 (identity of wife and her ancestry).

LITTLE, THOMAS, b. ca. 1608, d. Marshfield, Mass., March 1671/2. MF18, four generations all lines; GMB II:1189-92; PM, pp. 305-9.

LITTLEFIELD, EDMUND, b. 1592, d. Wells, Me., between 11 and 17 December 1661. Davis II:479-86 [Annis Spear], including English origins; EB, pp. 347-51; TAG 75:16-25 (Caleb[3] Anthony[2]); MG 27:179-82 (Moses[3] Thomas[2]).

LITTLEHALE, RICHARD, b. ca. 1620, d. Haverhill, Mass., 18 February 1663/4. GM2 IV:294-96.

LITTLEJOHN, GEORGE, of Portsmouth, N.H. MJ 27:37.

LIVERMORE, JOHN, b. ca. 1606, d. Watertown, Mass., 14 April 1684. GM2 IV:297-302; NEHGR 150:433-35 (English origins).

LOBDELL, NICHOLAS, d. Hingham, Mass., ca. 1645. JPG I:558-64.

LOCKE, WILLIAM, b. 1628, d. Woburn, Mass., 16 June 1720. GM2 IV:302-8; Nichols, pp. 21-22.

LOCKWOOD, EDMUND, b. ca. 1600, d. Cambridge, Mass., between 9 May 1632 and 3 March 1634/5. GMB II:1192-94; CA 27:9-18.

LOCKWOOD, ROBERT, b. 1600/1, d. Fairfield, Conn., between 21 May 1657 and 11 September 1658. GM2 IV:308-15; Johnson, pp. 241-43; CA 27:9-18, 64-70, 141-47 (mostly Ephraim[2]'s descendants).

LOKER, HENRY, b. 1576/7, d. England, 1631. Wife Elizabeth (French) immigrated with her daughters. Nichols, pp. 64-65; 50Imm, pp. 321-28; JPG I:565-69; NEHGR 143:325-31 (English origins).

LOMBARD, THOMAS, b. 1581/2, d. Barnstable, Mass., between 10 June 1663 and 8 February 1664/5. GMB II:1194-98; TAG 67:47-53 (widow Joyce); MJ 1:43-44, 6:129-41, 18:95-96, 26:43-47.

LONG, JOSEPH, d. Dorchester, Mass., before 1651. MJ 18:96-97.

LONG, ROBERT, b. ca. 1590, d. Charlestown, Mass., 9 January 1663/4. GM2 IV:316-20; JPG I:570-75; granddaughter Hannah[3] Michael[2] at Sex, pp. 88-89, 182-85.

LONGFELLOW, WILLIAM, b. 1650, d. Newbury, Mass., 1 December 1690. TEG 15:18-30, 104-112B; Russell Clare Farnham, *A Longfellow Genealogy: Comprising the English Ancestry and Descendants of the Immigrant William Longfellow of Newbury, Massachusetts* (Inverness, FL: Walrus Publishers, 2002). Reviews: MG 24:143, TAG 77:155, CN 35:630-31, CN 36:231-32, 455-56.

LONGHORN, RICHARD, d. Rowley, Mass., 12 February 1668. NGSQ 68:12-13 (clues to English origins).

LONGHORN, THOMAS, b. ca. 1621, d. Cambridge, Mass., 6 May 1685. Sex, pp. 130-32, et al.

LOOKE, THOMAS, b. ca. 1627, d. Rowley, Mass., after July 1675. Davis II:487-91 [Amos Towne].

LOOMAN, ANN, b. ca. 1600, d. Weymouth, Mass., 13 August 1659. GM2 IV:322-24.

LOOMIS SEE ALSO LUMMUS

LOOMIS, JOSEPH, b. ca. 1590, d. Windsor, Conn., 25 November 1658. EB, pp. 351-53; Lyon, pp. 448-53.

LORD, NATHAN, b. ca. 1620, d. Kittery, Me., before February 1690/1. MG 27:179-82 (daughters Mary and Martha).

LORD, RICHARD, b. 1611/2, d. Hartford, Conn., 10 May 1662. GMB II:1198-1201.

LORD, ROBERT, b. ca. 1603, d. Ipswich, Mass., 21 August 1683. GM2 IV:325-30; EB, pp. 353-55.

LORD, THOMAS, b. ca. 1585, d. Hartford, Conn., after 29 January 1643/4. GM2 IV:331-35.

LORING, THOMAS, b. ca. 1600, d. Hull, Mass., 4 April 1661. GM2 IV:340-45; wife Jane (Newton) at Doctors, pp. 59-60; NEHGR 143:133-40; MJ 18:97-100, 26:47-49, 27:37-38.

LOTHROP, JOHN, b. 1584, d. Barnstable, Mass., 8 November 1653. GM2 IV:345-51; CN 19:518-26, 716-25; TAG 70:250-52 (English ancestry).

LOTHROP, MARK, d. Bridgewater, Mass., 25 October 1685. Pond, 266.

LOVELL, ALEXANDER, b. 1619, d. Medfield, Mass., 20 December 1709. Elisabeth Lovell Bowman, *Alexander Lovell Genealogy: The Ancestors and Descendants of Alexander Lovell of Medfield, Massachusetts 1619-1709* (Baltimore, MD: Gateway Press, 2000). Reviews: VG 6:41, NEHGR 155:423, NGSQ 89:145-46, CN 34:222.

LOVELL, ROBERT, b. ca. 1595, d. Weymouth, Mass., between 3 April 1651 and 6 November 1658. GM2 IV:352-54.

LOVELL, WILLIAM, b. ca. 1585, of Dorchester and Marblehead, Mass., d. after 4 September 1638. GMB II:1206-8.

LOVETT, DANIEL, b. ca. 1618, d. Mendon, Mass., 1691. Johnson, pp. 243-44; Lyon, pp. 457-58.

LOVETT, JOHN, b. ca. 1610, d. Beverly, Mass., 8 March 1686. Lyon, pp. 453-57.

LOW, JOHN, d. Rehoboth, Mass., 26 March 1676. Davis II:492-97 [Annis Spear].

LOW, THOMAS, d. Ipswich, Mass., 8 September 1677. Davis II:498-501 [Phoebe Tilton]; EB, pp. 355-57.

LOWELL, PERCIVAL, b. ca. 1570, d. Newbury, Mass., 8 January 1664. Stone, pp. 193-99, including English origins; Davis II:503-20 [Phoebe Tilton], including English origins. Royal line at RD600, p. 332; PA, p. 471; MCA, p. 533; NEHGR 157:309-19; MJ 19:93-96, 25:46-47.

LUDDINGTON, WILLIAM, b. ca. 1607, d. New Haven, Conn., before 1 October 1661. TAG 74:81-96, 209-24 (English origins).

LUDKIN, GEORGE, b. ca. 1591, d. Braintree, Mass., 20 or 22 February 1647/8. GM2 IV:358-59.

LUDLOW, ROGER, b. 1590, of Dorchester, Mass., and Windsor and Fairfield, Conn., d. in Ireland before 1666. GMB II:1211-13; RD600, pp. 285-86; PA, p. 477; MCA, p. 538; MJ 1:44-46, 70, 3:30-33, 6:145-50, 11:75-78, 17:42-44 (wife Mary Cogan); MJ 26:49-51.

LUFF, JOHN, b. ca. 1585, d. Salem, Mass., 1668. Johnson, p. 244.

LUFKIN, THOMAS, d. Gloucester, Mass., 3 March 1708. Stevens, 4.

LUGG, JOHN, b. 1595, of Boston, Mass., buried Gloucester, Gloucestershire, England, 10 September 1646. Kempton4, pp. 479-94. Wife Jane (Deighton) at PA, p. 263; RD600, pp. 259-62; MCA, p. 265; NEA 1:2:38-41.

LUM, JOHN, b. ca. 1615, d. Fairfield, Conn., after 1689. NYGBR 120:1-9, 98-101, 142-47, 229-36, 121:96-101, including English origins of him and his wife.

LUMBERT, BERNARD, b. ca. 1608, d. Barnstable, Mass., after 28 February 1668/9. Pond, 281.

LUMMUS, EDWARD, b. ca. 1607, d. Ipswich, Mass., 29 August 1682. GM2 IV:361-65.

LUMPKIN, WILLIAM, d. Yarmouth, Mass., ca. 1671. Croll, 138.

LUNT, HENRY, b. ca. 1610, d. Newbury, Mass., between 8 July and 30 September 1662. GM2 IV:365-68; Davis II:521-61 [Abel Lunt]; NEHGR 151:308-12 (Joseph[3] Daniel[2]).

Lurvey, Peter, d. Ipswich, Mass., after 1685. NEHGR 154:387-409, 155:69-90, 167-88 (five generation study of the descendants of Peter[2]).

Lusher, Eleazer, d. Dedham, Mass. TAG 67:54.

Luther, John, of Dorchester and Taunton, Mass., d. Chesapeake Bay area ca. 1645. Mower, pp. 405-15; AL, pp. 380-85.

Lyford, John, b. ca. 1590, of Plymouth, Nantasket, and Salem, Mass., d. in Virginia ca. 1628. GMB II:1214-17; PM, pp. 309-13.

Lyman, Richard, b. 1580, d. Hartford, Conn., between 22 April 1640 and 3 March 1640/1. GMB II:1217-20; EB, pp. 357-64; Nichols, pp. 183-85, 237-38; MJ 25:88-93 (son Richard[2]).

Lynde, Simon, b. 1624, d. Boston, Mass., 22 November 1687. RD600, pp. 463-65; PA, p. 483; MCA, p. 545.

Lynde, Thomas, b. ca. 1597, d. Charlestown, Mass., 30 December 1671. GM2 IV:369-78.

Lyndon, Augustin, fl. Boston, Mass., ca. 1673, d. in England before August 1699. WRR, pp. 208-13.

Lynn, Henry, b. ca. 1611, of Boston, Mass., and York, Me., d. Virginia before 1643. GMB II:1220-22.

Lyon, Richard, b. ca. 1590, d. Fairfield, Conn., before 17 October 1678. Johnson, pp. 245-46.

Lyon, William, b. ca. 1621, d. Roxbury, Mass., May 1692. GM2 IV:379-82; Lyon, pp. 459-66.

MacCallum see Callum

MacCarwithy, James, b. ca. 1630, d. Dedham, Mass., after 1702. Kempton4, pp. 497-500.

MacCoone, John, d. Cambridge, Mass., 8 October 1705. RIR 13:7-9; TAG 227-33.

Macomber, William, d. Marshfield, Mass. English origins at TG 2:170-71; MJ 19:96-98.

Macoone, John, d. Westerly, R.I., after 29 March 1681. TAG 76:227-33.

Macy, Thomas, d. Nantucket, Mass., 19 June 1682. Jessup, pp. 618-23.

Mahurin, Hugh, d. Taunton, Mass., May 1718. NEHGR 136:17-30, 115-32, 242-53, a multi-generational study.

Main, Ezekiel, d. Stonington, Conn., before 13 July 1714. Identity of wife at RIR 17:16-19.

Mainwaring, Oliver, b. 1633/4, d. New London, Conn., 3 November 1723. RD600, pp. 294-95; PA, p. 492; MCA, p. 564; TAG 76:46-49 (disproof of a royal line).

Makepeace, Thomas, b. 1595, d. Boston, Mass., between 30 June 1666 and 2 March 1666/7. Makepeace, pp. 3-79, including English origins; EB, pp. 365-66.

Mallett, Hosea, d. Kennebec, Me., before 2 November 1690. EB, pp. 366-67.

Manchester, Thomas, b. ca. 1620, d. Portsmouth, R.I., ca. 1691. AL, pp. 385-87.

Manley, Lazarus, b. 1668, d. Mansfield, Conn., ca. 10 March 1748/9. Colonial, pp. 119-81, with possible English origins.

Mann, Richard, d. Scituate, Mass., before 16 February 1655/6. TAG 70:220-22 (possible English origins).

Mann, William, b. ca. 1612, of R.I. MJ 18:100.

Manning, William, d. Cambridge, Mass., between 17 February 1665 and 28 April 1666. Cameos, pp. 117-21 (son Samuel[2]).

Mansfield, John, b. ca. 1601, d. Charlestown, Mass., 26 June 1674. PA, p. 298; NEHGR 155:3-35; RD600, pp. 167-68; MCA, p. 311. English origins of wife Mary (Shard) at NHGR 11:174-79, 12:96.

Mansfield, Robert, b. ca. 1594, d. Lynn, Mass., 16 December 1666. Pond, 264; Geneva A. Daland and James S. Mansfield, *Mansfield Genealogy: Descendants of Robert and Elizabeth Mansfield and Sons Andrew and Joseph Who Came to Lynn 1639-1640* (Hampton, NH: Peter Randall, 1980). Reviews: TAG 57:121-22, NYGBR 112:58, NGSQ 69:141.

Marbury see Hutchinson and Scott

March, Hugh, b. ca. 1618, d. Newbury, Mass., 12 March 1693. Davis II:562-74 [Abel Lunt].

Marret, Thomas, b. ca. 1588, d. Cambridge, Mass., 30 June 1664. Grandsons at Cameos, pp. 299-301.

Marsh, George, d. Hingham, Mass., 2 July 1647. Stevens, 24; MBT #1890.

MARSH, JOHN, b. ca. 1611, d. Salem, Mass., 16 November 1674. EB, pp. 367-70; NEHGR 157:158-65 (Jonathan[3] Zachariah[2]).

MARSH, JOHN, of Boston, Mass., fl. 1670-1698. Davis II:575 [Charity Haley].

MARSH, JOHN, d. Charlestown, Mass., 1 January 1665/6. Lyon, p. 467.

MARSH, JOHN, of Hadley, Mass. TAG 67:174-76 (Ebenezer[3] Daniel[2]'s wife's identity).

MARSHALL, JAMES, b. 1608/9, of Windsor, Conn., d. Exeter, England, January 1665/6. MJ 18:100-2.

MARSHALL, THOMAS, b. ca. 1608, d. Andover, Mass., 15 January 1708/9. TEG 16:158-68.

MARSHALL, THOMAS, b. ca. 1610, d. Boston, Mass., before 8 December 1664. JPG I:576-81; TEG 16:158-68.

MARSHALL, THOMAS, b. ca. 1614, d. Lynn, Mass., 23 December 1689. Mower, pp. 417-21; TEG 16:158-68.

MARSHFIELD, THOMAS, b. ca. 1600, d. Windsor, Conn., between 1642 and 1649. TAG 63:161-63 (English origins); TAG 67:11-14; TAG 74:127 (note); TAG 74:225 (further note).

MARSTON, WILLIAM, b. ca. 1590, d. Hampton, N.H., d. 30 June 1672. Davis II:582-87 [Sarah Stone], including English origins.

MARTIN, FRANCIS, of Casco Bay, Me., returned to England. His daughter Mary b. ca. 1625, d. Boston, Mass., 18 March 1647. LENE, pp. 12-13.

MARTIN, GEORGE, b. ca. 1618, d. Amesbury, Mass., between 15 March and 15 April 1686. Stone, pp. 201-5; TAG 56:155-59; wife Susannah, a Salem witchcraft victim, at TAG 58:193-204, 59:11-22; LENE, pp. 74-78.

MARTIN, GEORGE, b. ca. 1648, d. Ipswich, Mass., 14 April 1734. TAG 56:155-59.

MARTIN, JOHN, b. 1634/5, d. Swansea, Mass., 21 March 1713. MQ 49:170-79.

MARTIN, JOHN, of Dover, N.H., d. Piscataway, N.J., 5 July 1687. Pond, 285.

MARTIN, JOSEPH, b. ca. 1624, d. Newport, R.I., after 1657. Johnson, p. 247.

MARTIN, RICHARD, b. 1609, d. Rehoboth, Mass., 2 March 1694/5. MJ 19:98-100; MQ 49:170-79.

Martin, Richard, of Charlestown, Mass., d. 1690 at sea. Wife Elizabeth (Trumbull) at Sex, pp. 88-89, 182-85, et al.

Marvin, Matthew, b. 1600, d. Norwalk, Conn., before 13 July 1680. Johnson, pp. 247-49.

Mason, Arthur, biscuit maker, fl. Boston, Mass., 1667-1670. WRR, pp. 107-11.

Mason, Hugh, b. ca. 1605, d. Watertown, Mass., 10 October 1678. 26Imm, pp. 189-208; MBT #514; Thompson, pp. 43-50, 68-69, et al.; TAG 78:161-64 (English origins).

Mason, John, b. ca. 1605, d. Norwich, Conn., between 9 May and 6 June 1672. GMB II:1225-30.

Mason, Robert, b. ca. 1630, d. Boston, Mass., before 26 January 1679/80. NHGR 20:131-40, 21:57-64, 102-12.

Mason, Sampson, b. ca. 1620, d. Rehoboth, Mass., 15 September 1676. Mower, pp. 423-37.

Massey, Jeffrey, b. ca. 1591, d. Salem, Mass., 9 November 1676. GMB II:1230-34; TEG 3:121-25.

Masters, John, b. ca. 1581, d. Cambridge, Mass., 21 December 1639. GMB II:1234-36; Jessup, pp. 626-30; Johnson, pp. 249-50; Thompson, pp. 66-67, et al.

Masters, Nathaniel, b. ca. 1631, d. Mancester, Mass., 1708. Stevens, 63.

Masterson, Richard, b. ca. 1594, d. Plymouth, Mass., 1633. GMB II:1236-38; PM, pp. 316-18; Nichols, p. 66; NEHGR 144:23-28, 154:353-69.

Mather, Richard, b. 1596, d. Dorchester, Mass., 22 April 1669. Pond, 243; grandson Cotton[3] Increase[2] at Puritans, pp. 135-44; Cotton's daughter Abigail[4] at Doctors, pp. 109-10; CA 32:1-4 (single line of descent through Timothy[2]); NEHGR 140:3-15; NEQ 60:341-62; Kenneth Silverman, *The Life and Times of Cotton Mather* (New York, NY: Harper & Row Publishers, 1984). Reviews: NEQ 57:592-94; Michael G. Hall, *The Last American Puritan: The Life of Increase Mather* (Middletown, CT: Wesleyan University Press, 1988). Reviews: NEQ 62:116-20.

Matson, Thomas, b. ca. 1602, d. Boston, Mass., between 9 June 1676 and 26 April 1677. GMB II:1238-41; TAG 70:128-41 (Joshua[2]).

Matteson, Henry, b. 1646, d. West Greenwich, R.I., 1690. Johnson, pp. 250-53.

Matthews, Francis, d. Portsmouth, N.H., between 10 May and 19 December 1648. MJ 17:97-98.

Maverick, John, b. 1578, d. Dorchester, Mass., 3 February 1635/6. GMB II:1241-43; wife Mary (Gye) at RD600, p. 377; PA, p. 370; MCA, p. 397; Johnson, pp. 169-72, 253-56; son Moses[2] in MF17, four generations all lines; MJ 1:46-48, 71, 3:35-37, 7:1-14, 13:13, 17:98-101.

Maxham see Muxum

May, Edward, d. Plymouth, Mass., 10 August 1691. Children by second wife Dorcas (Billington) in MF5 and MF21, three generations all lines; JPG II:247-53; TAG 67:2-7.

May, John, b. ca. 1590, d. Roxbury, Mass., 28 April 1670. Chase, pp. 303-9; Ephraim[3] John[2] at TAG 57:173-75.

May, Samuel, fl. Boston, Mass., 1699. WRR, pp. 54-64.

Mayer, Walter, of Saco, Me., d. Boston, Mass., after 10 June 1698. Davis II:589 [Charity Haley].

Mayhew, Thomas, b. 1593, d. Martha's Vineyard, Mass., 25 March 1682. GMB II:1243-46; Thompson, pp. 42-43, 92-93, et al.; TAG 76:94-98 (English ancestry of wife).

Mayo, John, d. Yarmouth, Mass., May 1676. Croll, 118.

McAllister, Angus, b. ca. 1670, d. Londonderry, N.H., after 12 October 1737. NGSQ 68:163-78.

McEwen, Robert, b. 1662, d. Stratford, Conn., 4 February 1740. Ruth McEwen Coleman, *Descendants of Robert McEwen and Sarah Wilcoxson, Stratford, Connecticut* (Decorah IA: Anundsen Publishing Co., 1992). Reviews: CN 25:446.

McIntosh, Henry. RD600, pp. 112-13.

Mead, William, b. 1592, d. Stamford, Conn., after 27 March 1657. TAG 73:1-10 (English origins).

Meader, John, b. ca. 1630, d. Oyster River (Durham), N.H., after 1715. Granddaughter Elizabeth[3] John[2] (Meader) Hanson at Puritans, pp. 229-44; Jessup, pp. 636-41, including English origins.

MEAKINS, THOMAS, b. ca. 1589, d. Braintree, Mass., between 1641 and 1651. GMB II:1246-47; EB, pp. 373-76; NEHGR 157:31-33 (English origins).

MEARS, ROBERT, b. ca. 1592, d. Boston, Mass., 20 February 1666/7 and 10 September 1667. TAG 60:201-2 (English origins).

MEEKER, ROBERT, d. Fairfield, Conn., before 10 May 1684. CN 34:548-54 (daughter Mary).

MEIGS, VINCENT, b. ca. 1583, d. Killingworth, Conn., 1 December 1658. EB, pp. 376-78; MJ 16:137-38 (English origins); wife Emma (Strong)'s identity at MJ 19:101-2, 25:47-48, 102, 27:100-2.

MELLENS, RICHARD, b. ca. 1620, d. Charlestown, Mass., after 1644. Johnson, pp. 256-57.

MELLOWES, ABRAHAM, b. ca. 1570, d. Charlestown, Mass., between 23 April and 30 December 1638. GMB II:1248-50; wife Martha (Bulkeley) at PA, p. 164; RD600, pp. 442-44, MCA, p. 147.

MELVILLE, DAVID, b. ca. 1670, d. Boston, Mass., before 1 January 1729/30. NGSQ 74:257-62.

MELVIN, JOHN, b. ca. 1653, d. Concord, Mass., 21 August 1726. Stone, pp. 207-11.

MENDALL, JOHN, b. ca. 1638, d. Marshfield, Mass., between 1711 and 8 February 1720. Sidney D. Smith, *Descendants of John Mendall, Sr. ca. 1638-1720 of Marshfield, Mass., by ca. 1660* (Baltimore, MD: Gateway Press, 1984). Reviews: TAG 60:250.

MENDUM, ROBERT, b. ca. 1602, d. Kittery, Me., between 1 and 16 May 1682. GMB II:1251-55; PM, pp. 319-24.

MERO, DENNIS, b. ca. 1650, d. Norwich, Conn., after 13 July 1713. NEHGR 149:155-72 (five generation study).

MERRIAM, JOSEPH, b. ca. 1600, d. Concord, Mass., 1 January 1640/1. Mower, pp. 439-51; MBT #526.

MERRICK, WILLIAM, of Eastham, Mass., by 1641, d. there between 3 December 1687 and 6 March 1688. Son William[2], MF6, three generations all lines; Croll, 115.

MERRILL, NATHANIEL, b. 1601, d. Newbury, Mass., March 1654/5. Goodman, pp. 307-18, including English origins; EB, pp. 378-84.

MERRIMAN, NATHANIEL, b. ca. 1614, d. Wallingford, Conn., 13 February 1694. Johnson, pp. 257-59; JPG II:254-59.

MERROW, HENRY, b. ca. 1625, d. Woburn, Mass., 5 November 1685. Jessup, pp. 664-69.

MERRY, WALTER, b. ca. 1608, d. Boston Harbor, Mass., 28 August 1657. GMB II:1255-57.

MERWIN, MILES, b. 1623/4, d. Milford, Conn., 23 April 1697. First wife's identity at JIC, pp. 59-69; NEHGR 138:42-43 (note); NEHGR 149:295-311 (English origins); NEHGR 150:220-21 (correction); NEHGR 152:179-83 (third wife); MJ 25:93-96.

MESSENGER, ANDREW, b. ca. 1618, of New Haven, Conn., d. Jamaica, N.Y., before 12 April 1681. Johnson, pp. 259-60; NEHGR 152:353-72.

MESSENGER, EDWARD, b. ca. 1630, d. Windsor, Conn., after 3 February 1685/6. NEHGR 152:353-72.

MEW, ELLIS, of New Haven, Conn. TAG 76:1-16 (English origins); 78:116-19 (more English ancestry).

MIGHILL, THOMAS, d. Rowley, Mass., June 1654. NEHGR 158:255-79, 364-79, 159:360 (three generation study of the descendants of John[2]).

MILBORNE, WILLIAM, b. ca. 1643, d. Boston, Mass., August 1694. NYGBR 129:67-75, 174-82 (English origins).

MILES, JOHN, d. Swansea, Mass., 3 February 1682/3. Wife Anne (Humphrey) at RD600, pp. 154-57; PA, p. 406; MCA, p. 884.

MILES, RICHARD, b. 1598, d. New Haven, Conn., 1666/7. TAG 75:72-73 (English ancestry).

MILLARD, JOHN, d. Rehoboth, Mass., after 30 June 1684. JPG I:582-88.

MILLER, JOHN, b. ca. 1639, d. Cape Porpoise, Me., after 1685. Davis II:602-11 [Sarah Miller], including possible origins.

MILLER, ROBERT, b. ca. 1695, d. Fryeburg, N.H., after 17 February 1779. NEHGR 140:17-22.

MILLETT, THOMAS, b. 1604, d. Brookfield, Mass., between 3 June 1675 and 23 September 1676. TAG 75:81-93, 310-19 (correct English origins).

MILLINGTON, JOHN, b. ca. 1635, d. Windsor, Conn., 26 March 1720. TAG 80:38-52, 140-53, 224-35 (five generation study).

MILLS, JOHN, b. 1692, d. Hampton, N.H., 29 May 1780. NEHGR 153:97-109 (English origins).

MILLS, JOHN, b. ca. 1597, d. Braintree, Mass., 5 July 1678. GMB II:1259-62.

MILLS, JOHN, b. ca. 1610, d. Scarborough, Me., before 8 March 1664. GMB III:2082-83.

MILLS, PETER, b. ca. 1622, d. Windsor, Conn., 17 April 1710. Helen Schatvet Ullmann, *Descendants of Peter Mills of Windsor, Connecticut: Formerly Named Pieter Wouterse vander Meulen* (Camden, ME: Penobscot Press, 1998), winner of the Donald Lines Jacobus Award for 1999. Reviews: CN 31:423, NYGBR 129:295, TAG 73:317, NEHGR 152:493-94, NGSQ 87:64-65.

MILLS, RICHARD, b. ca. 1620, of Stratford and Stamford, Conn., d. Westchester, N.Y., ca. February 1664. NEHGR 154:189-210.

MILLS, ROBERT, d. York, Me., before July 1647. EB, pp. 384-85.

MILLS, SAMUEL, b. 1673, d. Greenwich, Conn., between 5 August 1751 and 19 April 1758, son of Samuel[2] George[1] of Jamaica, N.Y. NEHGR 156:112-20.

MINGAY, JEFFREY, b. 1608, d. Hampton, N.H., 4 June 1658. English origins at NHGR 8:145-56.

MINOR, THOMAS, b. 1608, d. New London, Conn., 23 October 1690. GMB II:1262-67; NEHGR 138:182-85 (note); NYGBR 115:163-65; John Augustus Miner, *Thomas Minor Descendants 1608-1981* (Trevett, ME: the author, 1981). Reviews: CN:515-16, NYGBR 115:58; MJ 17:101-2, 25:49.

MINOT, GEORGE, b. 1592, d. Dorchester, Mass., 24 December 1671. GMB II:1267-69; Kempton3, pp. 299-326, including English origins; Goodman, pp. 321-31, including English origins.

MITCHELL, CHRISTOPHER, b. ca. 1639, d. Kittery, Me., April 1688. Jessup, pp. 670-75.

MITCHELL, EXPERIENCE, b. ca. 1603, d. Bridgewater, Mass., between 2 June 1685 and 14 May 1689. MF12, four generations all lines for his first three children by first wife Jane (Cooke); GMB II:1270-73; PM, pp. 324-29; MBT #570; notes on second wife at MD 49:144-45; TAG 59:28-31 (note on which children are Mayflower descendants).

MITCHELL, MATTHEW, b. ca. 1590, d. Stratford, Conn., 1645. NYGBR 120:1-9, 98-101, 142-47, 229-36, 121:96-101, including English origins of him and his wife.

MITCHELSON, EDWARD, b. ca. 1603, d. Cambridge, Mass., 7 March 1680/1. Son Thomas[2] at Sex, pp. 73-74.

MITTON, MICHAEL, d. Falmouth, Me., between 25 August 1660 and 7 October 1661. 26Imm, pp. 209-14; MBT #538.

MIX, THOMAS, b. ca. 1628, d. New Haven, Conn., 1691. Goodman, pp. 333-35.

MIXER, ISAAC, b. 1602, d. Watertown, Mass., between 8 May and 19 June 1655. Nichols, pp. 31-32; MBT #802.

MONROE, JOHN, d. Bristol, R.I., before 10 November 1691. JPG II:455-66; Joan S. Guilford, *The Monroe Book: Being the History of the Munro Clan from Its Origins in Scotland to Settlement in New England and Migration West 1652-1850 and Beyond* (Franklin, NC: Genealogy Publishing Service, 1993). Reviews: CN 27:417, TAG 70:64.

MONROE, WILLIAM, b. ca. 1625, d. Lexington, Mass., 27 January 1717/8. Joan S. Guilford, *The Monroe Book: Being the History of the Munro Clan from Its Origins in Scotland to Settlement in New England and Migration West 1652-1850 and Beyond* (Franklin, NC: Genealogy Publishing Service, 1993). Reviews: CN 27:417.

MONTAGUE, RICHARD, b. ca. 1615, d. Hadley, Mass., 14 December 1681. Gateway #3592; NEHGR 142:149-64 (English origins); TAG 74:161-74, 299-308 (English ancestry of wife).

MOODY, CALEB, b. ca. 1672, d. Exeter, N.H., before 21 April 1729. TAG 61:221-33.

MOODY, JOHN, b. 1593, d. Hartford, Conn., between 24 July and 6 December 1655. GMB II:1273-76; TAG 64:1-11 (Chenery ancestry); TAG 66:197-204 (Norwich ancestry).

MOODY, WILLIAM, b. 1598, d. Newbury, Mass., 25 October 1673. EB, pp. 385-89.

MOORE, FRANCIS, b. 1592, d. Cambridge, Mass., 20 August 1671. Lyon, pp. 467-68.

MOORE, JOHN, b. ca. 1603, d. Windsor, Conn., 18 September 1677. GMB II:1276-78; MJ 1:48-49, 2:98, 7:15-32.

Moore, John, b. ca. 1611, d. Salem, Mass., after 4 August 1646. GMB II:1278-80.

Moore, John, b. ca. 1611, d. Sudbury, Mass., 6 January 1673/4. EB, pp. 390-92; Lyon, pp. 469-70; wife Elizabeth (Rice) at EB, pp. 476-79; English origins at TAG 66:75-77; Nichols, pp. 33-34; MBT #534; Joseph[2] at TAG 60:53-56.

Moore, John, b. ca. 1685, d. Richmond, R.I., between 1 July 1752 and 1 October 1753. TG 14:211-55.

Moore, Matthew, of Newbury, Mass., d. Woodbridge, N.J., 20 March 1691. Freeman, pp. 649-738.

Moore, Miles, d. Milford, Conn., after 1680. MJ 19:104-5.

Moore, Samuel, b. ca. 1610, d. Salem, Mass., ca. 1638. GMB II:1280-81.

Moore, Samuel, b. ca. 1630, of Newbury, Mass., d. Woodbridge, N.J., 14 July 1683. Freeman, pp. 649-738.

More, Richard, *Mayflower* passenger, b. 1614, d. Salem, Mass., before 20 April 1696. PA, p. 516; RD600, pp. 163-66; MCA, p. 586. MF15, five generations all lines; GMB II:1283-87; PM, pp. 330-35; NEA 4:1:18-21; MD 43:123-32, 44:11-20, 109-18 (English origins); TEG 16:200-1; wife Christian (Hunter) at GM2 III:472-73, TAG 78:241-44 (wife's English origins); MQ 64:41-48; MQ 65:315-21; David Lindsay, *Mayflower Bastard: A Stranger Among the Pilgrims* (New York, NY: Thomas Dunne Books/St. Martin's Press, 2002). Reviews: MD 52:89-90, TAG 77:318-19, MQ 70:157-58.

Morey, Roger, b. ca. 1608, d. Providence, R.I., 5 January 1668. Crosby II:366-85.

Morey, Walter, b. ca. 1643, d. Milton, Mass., 1727. Johnson, pp. 260-61.

Morgan, James, d. Boston, Mass., 11 March 1686. LENE, p. 56.

Morgan, James, of New London, Conn., d. Killingworth, Conn., ca. 1685. Son James[2] at TG 14:118-28.

Morgan, Richard, b. ca. 1635, d. New London, Conn., before 4 June 1698. NEHGR 154:63-77; 156:389-90 (correction); 157:338-54 (Jonathan[2]).

Morran, Patrick. NEA 5:5/6:57-58.

Morrill, Isaac, b. ca. 1588, d. Roxbury, Mass., 18 December 1662. GMB II:1289-92.

Morris(on), Edward, b. 1631/2, d. Woodstock, Conn., before 27 October 1690. NEHGR 146:261-78 (English origins); NEHGR 149:173-86 (addition to English ancestry).

Morris, Rice, b. ca. 1609, d. Charlestown, Mass., 25 April 1647. GMB II:1292-93.

Morris, Thomas, b. ca. 1608, d. New Haven, Conn., 21 July 1673. NEHGR 147:11-34 (English origins).

Morrison, Daniel, d. Rowley, Mass., between 3 November 1736 and 10 May 1737. Davis II:626-28 [Annis Spear].

Morse, Anthony, b. ca. 1606, d. Newbury, Mass., 12 October 1686. EB, pp. 392-95.

Morse, Samuel, b. 1576, d. Medfield, Mass., 5 December 1654. EB, pp. 395-97; Lyon, pp. 471-78; additions to wife's ancestry at TAG 62:235-40.

Mortimer, Edward, b. ca. 1650, d. Boston, Mass., 24 July 1704. TW, pp. 301-5.

Morton, Charles, b. ca. 1627, d. 1698. RD600, pp. 524-25.

Morton, George, b. ca. 1587, d. Plymouth, Mass., June 1624. GMB II:1296-97; PM, pp. 336-37; EB, pp. 397-99.

Morton, Thomas, b. ca. 1592, d. Plymouth, Mass., ca. 1627. GMB II:1298-99; PM, pp. 338-39; NEHGR 134:282-90.

Mosely, John, b. ca. 1638, d. East Windsor, Conn., 18 August 1690. Nichols, pp. 188-89.

Moses, John, b. ca. 1616, d. Portsmouth, N.H., after 1690. GMB II:1300-2; Davis II:629-47 [Joseph Waterhouse].

Mosher, Hugh, b. ca. 1613, d. Casco, Me., before 26 September 1666. GMB II:1302-4; MJ 19:105-8.

Mosher, Hugh, b. ca. 1633, d. Newport, R.I., before 7 December 1713. Mildred (Mosher) Chamberlain and Laura (McGaffey) Clarenbach, *Descendants of Hugh Mosher and Rebecca Maxson through Seven Generations* (Madison, WI: the authors, 1990). Reviews: TAG 66:250-51, NGSQ 69:226-27, MQ 58:185.

Mosman, James, b. 1626, d. Boston, Mass., between 20 July and 5 November 1722. Kenneth Freeman Mosman, *James Mosman: Early Eighteenth Cen-*

tury Boston Nonagenarian and His Descendants (Baltimore, MD: Gateway Press, 1989), 2 volumes. Reviews: TAG 65:253-54, 66:256.

MOTT SEE TALCOTT

MOTT, JOHN, b. ca. 1570, d. Portsmouth, R.I., after 3 July 1656. AL, pp. 405-6.

MOULTHROPP, MATTHEW, b. 1607/8, d. New Haven, Conn., 21 or 22 December 1668. TAG 74:81-96, 209-24 (English origins).

MOULTON, JAMES, b. ca. 1603, d. Wenham, Mass., between 28 February 1678 and 6 January 1679. AL, pp. 407-9, including English ancestry; NEHGR 144:245-63 (revision of English ancestry); NEHGR 147:129-45 (more on English ancestry).

MOULTON, JOHN, b. ca. 1599, d. Hampton, N.H., between 23 January 1649/50 and 1 October 1650. NEHGR 141:313-29 (English origins); NEHGR 142:260-63 (wife's Green ancestry); NEHGR 144:245-63 (revision of English ancestry); NEHGR 147:129-45 (more on English ancestry).

MOULTON, ROBERT, b. ca. 1587, d. Salem, Mass., between 20 February 1654/5 and 26 June 1655. GMB II:1304-6; EB, pp. 399-404; Stevens, 58; TAG 74:161-74, 299-308 (English ancestry of the wife of Robert[2]).

MOULTON, THOMAS, b. 1608, d. York, Me., between 1699 and 1703. NEHGR 141:313-29 (English origins); NEHGR 144:245-63 (revision of English ancestry); NEHGR 147:129-45 (more on English ancestry).

MOULTON, THOMAS, b. ca. 1609, d. Malden, Mass., between 5 October and 24 December 1657. GMB II:1306-9; EB, pp. 405-11.

MOULTON, WILLIAM, b. ca. 1615, d. Hampton, N.H., 18 April 1664. 50Imm, pp. 211-46; MBT #382; NEHGR 141:313-29 (English origins).

MOUSALL, RALPH, b. ca. 1603, d. Charlestown, Mass., 30 April 1657. GMB II:1309-12; son John[2] at Sex, pp. 175-76.

MOWER, RICHARD, b. ca. 1615, d. Lynn, Mass., 1 January 1688/9. Mower, pp. 11-47; TEG 16:195-99, 17:40-44.

MOWRY, ROGER, b. ca. 1600, d. Providence, R.I., 5 January 1666/7. GMB II:1312-15; Angell, pp. 415-34.

MULLINS, WILLIAM, *Mayflower* passenger, b. 1571, d. Plymouth, Mass., winter 1621. Daughter Priscilla married John Alden—see Alden entry for descendants; GMB II:1315-16; PM, pp. 339-40; Spooner; Jessup, pp. 699-703; MD 44:39-44; TAG 79:161-78; MQ 65:125-41.

Mumford, Thomas, b. ca. 1625, d. Kingstown, R.I., before 12 February 1692. Johnson, pp. 261-62.

Munro, John, d. Bristol, R.I., before 10 November 1691. TAG 61:180-84.

Munro, William, d. Lexington, Mass., 1719. NEA 4:1:30-32, 5:1:54-55.

Munt, Thomas, b. ca. 1616, d. Boston, Mass., 27 July 1664. GMB II: 1316-18.

Muxum, Samuel, b. ca. 1680, d. Rochester, Mass., autumn 1763. TAG 57:209-18, 58:45-49.

Nash, James, d. Weymouth, Mass., between 13 September 1679 and 9 January 1679/80. NEHGR 151:166-70 (probable English origins); Richard H. Benson, *The Nash Family of Weymouth, Massachusetts* (Boston, MA: Newbury Street Press, 1998), a multi-generational work on this family. Reviews: CN 32:240, TAG 76:75, NEHGR 152:497.

Nash, Samuel, b. ca. 1602, d. Duxbury, Mass., between 6 July 1682 and 1683/4. GMB II:1321-24; PM, pp. 341-43.

Nason, Richard, d. Kittery, Me., between 14 July 1694 and 22 December 1696. TAG 68:106-12 (Mary[3] Benjamin[2]).

Neale, John, d. Salem, Mass., 12 May 1672. Davis III:21-37 [Sarah Stone]; Jeremiah[2] at TAG 59:71-76.

Neale, John, fl. Woburn, Mass., 1660s. Sex, pp. 119-20.

Needham, Anthony, Stratford, Conn. TAG 73:23-32 (wife's English ancestry); TAG 79:309-15 (additional Fenn ancestry).

Needham, Edmund, b. ca. 1606, d. Lynn, Mass., 16 May 1677. TEG 9:25-32, 98-104, 149-54.

Needham, John, d. Boston, Mass., 14 January 1689. TEG 9:203-11; Sex, pp. 24-39 (John[2]).

Negus, Benjamin, b. ca. 1612, d. Boston, Mass., before 19 January 1693/4. TG 6:195-231.

Negus, Jonathan, b. ca. 1601, d. Boston, Mass., before 11 April 1682. TG 6:195-231; wife Jane (Deighton) at RD600, pp. 259-62; PA, p. 263; MCA, p. 265; NEA 1:2:38-41.

NELSON, JOHN, b. 1654, d. Boston, Mass., 15 November 1734. RD600, pp. 184-85; PA, p. 66; MCA, p. 611.

NELSON, PHILIP, b. 1634/5, d. Rowley, Mass., 19 August 1691, RD600, pp. 52-58; PA, p. 685; MCA, p. 778.

NELSON, THOMAS, b. 1636, d. Rowley, Mass., 5 April 1712. RD600, pp. 52-58; PA, p. 685; MCA, p. 778; NEHGR 148:130-40 (royal line of mother).

NETTLETON, SAMUEL, b. ca. 1610, d. Branford, Conn., before 10 September 1658. EB, pp. 411-14; TAG 71:181-84 (John[2]).

NEVERS, RICHARD, fl. Charlestown, Mass., 1670s, d. Woburn, Mass., after 1698. Sex, pp. 78-87.

NEWBERRY, THOMAS, b. 1594, d. Dorchester, Mass., between 12 December 1635 and 28 January 1637. NEXUS 15:105-8, 16:21-25, 195-98; Nichols, pp. 190-92; MJ 13:3-8, 17:103-10, 25:96, 26:51.

NEWCOMB, FRANCIS, b. ca. 1605, d. Braintree, Mass., 27 May 1692. Davis III:38-43 [Annis Spear]; John[2] at TAG 61:111-14.

NEWELL, ABRAHAM, d. Roxbury, Mass., 13 June 1672. JPG I:589-90; Lyon, pp. 478-80; MBT #890.

NEWELL, ANDREW, b. ca. 1581, d. Charlestown, Mass., before 1664. Goodman, pp. 343-48.

NEWELL, THOMAS, d. Farmington, Conn., 13 September 1689. Lyon, pp. 480-82.

NEWGATE, JOHN, b. ca. 1588, d. Boston, Mass., between 8 May and 8 September 1665. GMB II:1327-32.

NEWHALL, ANTHONY, d. Lynn, Mass., 21 January 1656. Chase, pp. 311-23; TAG 65:65-69 (English origins); TAG 73:119-22; TEG 17:215-19.

NEWHALL, THOMAS, b. ca. 1589, d. Lynn, Mass., 25 September 1674. Kempton4, pp. 503-30, including possible English origins; Chase, pp. 311-23; Lyon, pp. 483-85; TAG 65:65-69 (English origins); TAG 73:119-22; TAG 74:50-52; TEG 15:38-47, 93-103, 153-60, 210-19, 16:44-47.

NEWMAN, THOMAS, d. Ipswich, Mass., before November 1675. EB, pp. 414-16; Stowers, pp. 401-4.

NEWTON, ANTHONY, b. ca. 1610, d. Milton, Mass., 5 May 1704. TAG 65:13-16; MJ 19:108-10, 27:38-39.

NEWTON, RICHARD, b. ca. 1610, d. Marlborough, Mass., 24 August 1701. Stone, pp. 213-18; Nichols, pp. 41-45; NEHGR 143:325-31 (wife's Loker ancestry).

NEWTON, THOMAS, b. ca. 1600, d. Fairfield, Conn., 27 May 1650. LENE, pp. 18-19.

NICHOLS, ADAM, d. Hartford, Conn. TAG 79:208 (possible English origins).

NICHOLS, FRANCIS, b. 1575, d. Stratford, Conn., before 8 January 1650/1. AL, pp. 409-10; CA 31:102-7, single line of descent through Isaac[2]; TAG 68:113-14 (note); TAG 75:267-71 (English origins); TAG 76:38 (baptism of Isaac[2]).

NICHOLS, JAMES, b. in Ireland ca. 1660, d. Londonderry, N.H., 28 March 1726. MBT #246.

NICHOLS, RICHARD, d. Reading, Mass., 11 November 1674. Nichols, various pages.

NICHOLS, THOMAS, b. ca. 1624, d. East Greenwich, R.I., after 1708. Johnson, pp. 262-67.

NICHOLS, WILLIAM, b. ca. 1599, d. Topsfield, Mass., between 26 April 1693 and 17 February 1695. TEG 8:128-31.

NICKERSON, WILLIAM, b. ca. 1603, d. Yarmouth, Mass., 27 February 1684. Crosby, pp. I:59-64, including English origins; TW, pp. 307-14, including English ancestry.

NILES, JOHN, b. ca. 1601, d. Braintree, Mass., 8 February 1693/4. TAG 75:16-25 (Nathaniel[3] Joseph[2]); TAG 75:149-50 (Joseph[2]); NEHGR 153: 339-43.

NIMS, GODFREY, d. Deerfield, Mass., before 12 March 1704/5. Elizabeth C. Suddaby, editor, *The Nims Family: Seven Generations of Descendants from Godfrey Nims* (Greenville, SC: Southern Historical Press, 1990). Reviews: CN 24:131-32.

NORCROSS, JOHN, of Cambridge, Mass., d. in England after 1642. JPG II:288-93.

NORMAN, RICHARD, b. ca. 1580, d. Marblehead, Mass., between 22 April 1653 and 27 June 1664. GMB II:1334-36; Davis III:44-53 [Sarah Stone]; Johnson, pp. 267-68; TAG 77:102-3 (English origins); MJ 18:102-3.

NORRIS, OLIVER, b. ca. 1655, d. Plymouth, Mass., between 25 June and 7 December 1715. EB, pp. 416-18.

NORTH, JOHN, b. ca. 1615, d. Farmington, Conn., 1691/2. Lyon, pp. 485-90.

NORTH, RICHARD, d. Salisbury, Mass., 1 March 1667. Daughter Susannah, a Salem witchcraft victim, at TAG 58:193-204, 59:11-22; LENE, pp. 74-78; TAG 68:65-70 (English origins).

NORTHEY, JOHN, b. 1604/5, d. Marblehead, Mass., 30 June 1694. TEG 19:81-85, 169-72.

NORTHROP, JOSEPH, of Milford, Conn. Clues to English origins at TG 16:182; CN 37:182-201 (Gamaliel[3] Daniel[2]).

NORTHRUP, STEPHEN, b. ca. 1630, d. North Kingstown, R.I., after 1687. Johnson, pp. 269-70.

NORTHWAY, JOHN, b. 1647, d. Portsmouth, R.I., before 1697. RIR 12:2-6.

NORTON, GEORGE, b. ca. 1610, d. Salem, Mass., between June and November 1659. GMB II:1336-39; NEHGR 148:181-82 (wife of Freegrace[3] George[2]).

NORTON, HENRY, b. 1618, d. ca. 1659, of York, Me. NEHGR 150:327-28 (royal line disproved).

NORTON, NICHOLAS, b. ca. 1610, d. Martha's Vineyard, Mass., ca. 17 April 1690. MJ 19:112-14, 26:51-52.

NORTON, THOMAS, b. 1609, d. Guilford, Conn., ca. 1648. Jessup, pp. 705-11, including English origins; TAG 56:170-72 (ancestry of wife Grace Wells).

NORTON, WALTER, b. ca. 1580, d. in Connecticut summer 1633. GMB II:1339-41; NEHGR 150:327-28 (royal line disproved).

NORTON, WILLIAM, b. ca. 1608, d. Ipswich, Mass., 30 April 1694. Chase, pp. 325-33, including English origins.

NORWOOD, FRANCIS, b. ca. 1636, d. Gloucester, Mass., 4 March 1709. TEG 18:198-207, 208-18 (Thomas[2]).

NOWELL, INCREASE, b. ca. 1603, d. Charlestown, Mass., 1 November 1655. GMB II:1342-64; RD600, pp. 416-21.

NOYES, JAMES, b. ca. 1608, d. Newbury, Mass., 22 October 1656. NEHGR 149:105-21 (English origins).

NOYES, NICHOLAS, b. ca. 1614, d. Newbury, Mass., 23 November 1701. Davis III:54-61 [Abel Lunt], including English origins; NEHGR 149:105-21 (English origins).

NOYES, PETER, b. 1590, d. Sudbury, Mass., 23 September 1657. EB, pp. 418-22; Johnson, pp. 270-71; JPG II:467-70; Mower, pp. 453-58; NEHGR 152:259-85, 492 (English origins).

NUDD, THOMAS, b. 1629/30, d. Hampton, N.H., 31 January 1712/3. NEHGR 142:263-66 (English origins).

NURSE, FRANCIS, b. ca. 1619, d. Salem, Mass., 22 November 1695. Davis III:62-78 [Sarah Johnson]; MBT #414; wife Rebecca, a Salem witchcraft victim, LENE, pp. 70-74; TAG 69:81-85 (Francis[2]).

NUTT, MICHAEL, b. 1598, d. Malden, Mass., 2 July 1671. 50Imm, pp. 247-55; MBT #1788; NEHGR 141:56 (note on English ancestry).

NUTTER, HATEVIL, b. ca. 1603, d. Dover, N.H., between 28 December 1674 and 28 June 1675. TAG 72:263-84 (English origins); Frederick R. Boyle, *Hatevil Nutter of Dover, N.H., and His Descendants* (Portsmouth, NH: Peter E. Randall Publisher, 1997). Reviews: MG20:140-41, NHGR 14:185-86, TAG 74:76, NEHGR 152:499-500.

NUTTING, JOHN, b. ca. 1620, d. Groton, Mass., 13 March 1676. MBT #358.

NYE, BENJAMIN, d. Sandwich, Mass., between 9 June 1704 and 17 May 1707. NEHGR 158:345-60, 159:69-80, 364 (clues to English origins); TAG 80:53-55.

O'BARRY SEE BERRY

O'KILLEA, DAVID, b. ca. 1636, d. Yarmouth, Mass., between 10 February and 27 July 1697. NEHGR 151:131-52, 313-28 (three generation study); TAG 80:304-7 (note on Amos[3] Jeremiah[2]).

ODLIN, JOHN, b. ca. 1602, d. Boston, Mass., 18 December 1685. GMB II:1347-50; RIR 15:85-90; TAG 65:148.

OLDHAM, THOMAS, b. 1624, d. Scituate, Mass., 7 March 1711/2. 26Imm, pp. 215-22; JPG II:471-75; MJ 19:114-17.

OLIVER, DAVID, b. ca. 1640, d. Casco Bay, Me., before 1676. MG 27:147-68 (a line through David[3-2]).

OLIVER, THOMAS, b. ca. 1580, d. Boston, Mass., 1 January 1657/8. GMB II:1354-57; NEHGR 157:34-36 (English origins).

OLIVER, THOMAS, b. ca. 1610, d. Salem, Mass., before 25 February 1679/80. Second wife Bridget, a Salem witchcraft victim. See TAG 57:129-38, 58:163; LENE, pp. 64-69; TAG 64:207 (her origins).

OLMSTEAD, JAMES, b. 1580, d. Hartford, Conn., before 28 September 1640. GMB II:1357-60.

OLNEY, THOMAS, b. before 1605, d. Providence, R.I., between 16 June and 9 October 1682. Angell, pp. 437-65. Wife Marie Ashton's English origins given at Angell, pp. 185-93; RIR 13:22; William[4] John[3] Epenetus[2] at RIR 23:59-68, 105.

ONGE, FRANCES, b. ca. 1583, d. Watertown, Mass., November 1638. GMB II:1360-63; Cameos, pp. 199-204.

ORDWAY, JAMES, b. 1621, of Dover, N.H., by 1633, d. Newbury, Mass., between 1712 and 1714. Ordway, pp. 1-117, including English ancestry.

OSBORN, JOHN, of Windsor, Conn. NEHGR 156:333-36 (wife of John[2]).

OSBORN, WILLIAM, b. ca. 1642, d. Salem, Mass., before 5 February 1729/30. TEG 17:195-201.

OSGOOD, JOHN, b. 1595, d. Andover, Mass., 24 October 1651. MBT #860.

OSGOOD, WILLIAM, b. ca. 1609, d. Salisbury, Mass., 1700. MBT #898.

OTIS, JOHN, b. ca. 1581, d. Hingham, Mass., 31 May 1657. Lyon, pp. 495-97.

OTIS, RICHARD, b. ca. 1625, d. Dover, N.H., 28 June 1689. First wife Rose (Stoughton) at RD600, p. 376; MCA, p. 783.

OXENBRIDGE, JOHN, b. 1608/9, d. Boston, Mass., 28 December 1674. PA, p. 563; RD600, pp. 160-62; MCA, p. 640; JIC, pp. 133-36. Wife Frances (Woodward) at RD600, pp. 385-86; daughter Bathshua and son-in-law Richard Scott at Cameos, pp. 167-72.

PABODIE, WILLIAM, b. ca. 1620, d. Little Compton, R.I., 13 December 1707. MF16, four generations all lines; Jessup, pp. 711-18.

PACKARD, SAMUEL, b. 1605, d. Bridgewater, Mass., between 29 October 1684 and March 1684/5. Pond, 265.

PADDOCK, ROBERT, d. Plymouth, Mass., 25 July 1650. Spooner; MJ 19:117-18, 25:49-50.

PAGE, JOHN, b. 1586, d. Watertown, Mass., 18 December 1676. GMB III:1365-69; Thompson, pp. 192-95, et al.; Sex, pp. 176-77, et al.

PAGE, JOHN, b. ca. 1614, d. Haverhill, Mass., 23 November 1687. Stevens, 23; MBT #944, 952.

Page, Robert, b. ca. 1604, d. Hampton, N.H., 22 September 1679. MBT #766; NEHGR 141:114-27 (wife's identity and ancestry).

Page, Thomas, b. ca. 1606, d. Saco, Me., before 21 October 1645. TAG 71:216-19 (wife's English origins).

Paine, Anthony, b. ca. 1585, d. Portsmouth, R.I., ca. 1650. Johnson, pp. 272-73; AL, pp. 454-55.

Paine, Moses, d. Braintree, Mass., 21 June 1643. Son Stephen[2] and wife Elizabeth at Sex, pp. 132-33, 185-86, et al.

Paine, Stephen, b. ca. 1602, d. Rehoboth, Mass., August 1679. AL, pp. 455-58, including English ancestry; John[3] Stephen[2] and Nathaniel[3-2] both at RIR 13:49-53; wife's identity at TAG 62:107; NEHGR 143:291-302 (English origins).

Paine, Thomas, of Yarmouth, Mass., by 1639. Son Thomas[2] (who died at Eastham, Mass., 16 August 1706) at MF6, three generations all lines.

Paine, William, b. ca. 1598, d. Boston, Mass., between 2 October and 14 November 1660. NEHGR 146:377-82 (Hannah[3] John[2]).

Palfrey, Peter, b. ca. 1605, d. Reading, Mass., 15 September 1663. GMB III:1369-72.

Palgrave, Richard, b. ca. 1585, d. Charlestown, Mass., between 8 June and 8 August 1651. GMB III:1373-76; RD600, pp. 333-34; PA, p. 564; MCA, p. 642; daughter Sarah at Doctors, pp. 1-4.

Palmer, Henry, b.c 1618, d. Newport, R.I., after 1685. TG 17:175-85; TG 18:97-98; MQ 58:216-22.

Palmer, Walter, b. ca. 1589, d. Stonington, Conn., 10 November 1661. GMB III:1379-83; Doris Palmer Buys, *Walter Palmer of Charlestown and Rehoboth, Massachusetts and Stonington, Connecticut: A 400-Year (1585-1985) Family History* (Orem, UT: Historical Publications, 1986). Reviews: CN 19:707, NYGBR 118:250, NGSQ 75:235-36.

Palmer, William, b. ca. 1581, d. Duxbury, Mass., between 7 and 13 November 1637. GMB III:1383-86; PM, pp. 349-52; MQ 58:216-22, 59:192-93; MQ 66:152-54.

Palmer, William, b. ca. 1585, d. Hampton, N.H., between 29 September 1646 and 21 March 1647. John Calvin Palmer, *A Genealogical Record of the Descendants of William Palmer of Hampton, N.H., 1638* (Decorah,

IA: Anundsen Publishing Co., 1998, 2 volumes). Reviews: NEHGR 153:300-1.

PALMES, EDWARD, b. ca. 1637, d. New London, Conn., 21 March 1714/5. RD600, pp. 312-13.

PANTRY, WILLIAM, b. 1597, d. Hartford, Conn., November 1649. Goodman, pp. 351-56, including English origins.

PARDEE, GEORGE, b. 1623/4, d. New Haven, Conn., April 1700. MJ 18:104-6, 27:39-42.

PARISH, ROBERT, b. ca. 1635, d. Groton, Mass., before 5 September 1709. Davis III:79-83 [Sarah Hildreth].

PARKE, ROBERT, b. 1580, d. Stonington, Conn., 4 February 1664/5. TG 4:173-86. Wife Alice (Freeman) at RD600, pp. 540-43; Pond, 247-48; EB, pp. 423-27; Stowers, pp. 417-28.

PARKE, WILLIAM, b. 1607, d. Roxbury, Mass., 11 May 1685. GMB III: 1386-91.

PARKER, ABRAHAM, b. 1619, d. Chelmsford, Mass., 12 August 1685. NEHGR 153:81-96 (English origins), NEHGR 159:360; TEG 25:33-46, 83-94, 137-46.

PARKER, GEORGE, of Jamestown, R.I. Son Peter[2] at TAG 57:15-23.

PARKER, JACOB, b. 1626, d. Billerica, Mass., 7 January 1688/9. Nichols, p. 102; NEHGR 153:81-96 (English origins), NEHGR 159:360; TEG 24:153-63, 205-16.

PARKER, JAMES, b. ca. 1605, of Dorchester and Weymouth, Mass., and Portsmouth, N.H., d. in Barbados between 21 August 1648 and 26 August 1652. GMB III:1391-93.

PARKER, JAMES, b. ca. 1617, d. Groton, Mass., 1 August 1701. JPG I:591-601; Morgan; NEHGR 153:81-96 (English origins), NEHGR 159:360; TEG 13:146-51, 210-17, 14:28-38, 97-105, 165-71, 16:225-28.

PARKER, JOHN, b. 1603/4, d. Boston, Mass., before 15 July 1646. TAG 76:185-89 (English origins); TAG 80:27-37 (John[2]).

PARKER, JOHN, b. 1615, d. Billerica, Mass., 14 June 1667. NEHGR 153:81-96 (English origins), NEHGR 159:360.

PARKER, JOHN, d. Boston, Mass., ca. 1685. EB, pp. 427-29.

PARKER, JOHN, of Salem, Mass. LENE, p. 97 (wife Alice).

PARKER, JOSEPH, b. 1622, d. Groton, Mass., 1690. NEHGR 153:81-96 (English origins), NEHGR 159:360; TEG 17:78-86.

PARKER, JOSEPH, b. ca. 1614, d. Andover, Mass., 5 November 1678. TEG 18:154-63, 235-38.

PARKER, NATHAN, b. ca. 1619, d. Andover, Mass., 25 June 1685. TEG 19:30-35, 87-97.

PARKER, NICHOLAS, b. ca. 1606, of Roxbury and Boston, Mass., d. Plymouth, England, after 4 April 1659. GMB III:1394-96.

PARKER, ROBERT, b. ca. 1603, d. Cambridge, Mass., between 21 March 1684/5 and 7 April 1685. GMB III:1396-99; niece Rachel Smith at Cameos, pp. 61-65; JPG II:476-77; TEG 24:46-53.

PARKER, THOMAS, b. ca. 1609, d. Wakefield, Mass., 12 August 1683. Mower, pp. 461-82; TEG 15:48-54, 75-83, 145-52, 205-9, 16:8-43.

PARKER, WILLIAM, b. ca. 1600, d. Saybrook, Conn., 28 December 1686. Johnson, pp. 273-75.

PARKHURST, GEORGE, b. ca. 1588, of Watertown, Mass., d. in England June 1675. 50Imm, pp. 256-88; Johnson, pp. 275-76; MBT #704.

PARKMAN, ELIAS, b. ca. 1611, of Windsor and Saybrook, Conn., and Boston, Mass., d. at sea before 20 July 1662. GMB III:1399-1403; MJ 26:52-53.

PARMENTER, JOHN, b. ca. 1588, d. Roxbury, Mass., 1 May 1671. EB, pp. 429-30; NEHGR 147:377-82 (English origins).

PARRIS, SAMUEL, b. 1653, d. Sudbury, Mass., 27 February 1720. James F. Cooper, Jr. and Kenneth P. Minkema, eds., *The Sermon Notebook of Samuel Parris, 1689-1694*, Volume 66 of the Publications of the Colonial Society of Massachusetts (Boston, MA: Colonial Society of Massachusetts, 1993). Reviews: NEQ 67:660-62.

PARSONS, BENJAMIN, b. 1625, d. Springfield, Mass., 24 August 1689. NEHGR 143:101-19 (probable English origins); NEHGR 146:297-98; NEHGR 148:215-38, 345-59, 149:53-72; MJ 18:106-9.

PARSONS, HUGH, d. Portsmouth, R.I., between 11 January and 14 March 1684. AL, pp. 459-60.

PARSONS, HUGH, of Springfield, Mass., d. Boston, Mass., after 1654. His wife Mary d. 29 May 1651. LENE, pp. 20-24; Johnson, pp. 276-77; NEHGR 148:215-38, 345-59, 149:53-72.

PARSONS, HUGH, of Watertown, Mass. Thompson, pp. 109-10, 186-87, et al.

PARSONS, JEFFREY, b. 1630, d. Gloucester, Mass., 16 August 1689. NEHGR 142:245-49 (English origins); Mary H. Sibbalds, *Descendants of Jeffery Parsons of Gloucester, Massachusetts, Volume One: Generations 1-5* (Salem, MA: Higginson Book Co., 2003).

PARSONS, JOHN, b. ca. 1650, d. York, Me., 25 January 1691/2. Brewer, pp. 458-59.

PARSONS, JOSEPH, b. 1620, d. Springfield, Mass., 9 October 1683. NEHGR 143:101-19 (probable English origins); NEHGR 146:297-98; NEHGR 148:215-38, 345-39, 149:53-72; MJ 18:106-9; Gerald James Parsons, *The Parsons Family, Volume One: The English Ancestry and Descendants to the Sixth Generation of Cornet Joseph Parsons (1620-1683)* (Baltimore, MD: Gateway Press, 2002). Reviews: TAG 59:247 (1984 edition), NYGBR 134:67, TAG 78:75-76, NGSQ 92:71, CN 35:453 (2002 edition), CN 36:226.

PARSONS, JOSEPH, b. ca. 1635, d. Simsbury, Conn., 15 April 1687. NEHGR 148:215-38, 345-59, 149:53-72.

PARSONS, PHILIP, b. ca. 1675, d. Enfield, Conn., after 1 February 1753. TAG 66:193-96.

PARSONS, THOMAS, b. 1608/9, d. Windsor, Conn., 23 September 1661. NEHGR 143:101-19 (probable English origins); NEHGR 148:215-38, 345-59, 149:53-72; MJ 18:106-9.

PARSONS, THOMAS, b. ca. 1635, d. Suffield, Conn., 10 April 1701. NEHGR 148:215-38, 345-59, 149:53-72.

PARSONS, WILLIAM, b. ca. 1630, d. Simsbury, Conn., 1702. NEHGR 148:215-38, 345-59, 149:53-72.

PARTRIDGE, JOHN, b. ca. 1620, d. Medfield, Mass., 28 May 1706. Goodman, pp. 359-61.

PARTRIDGE, NATHANIEL, of Boston, Mass., by 1643. Sex, pp. 176-77.

PARTRIDGE, RALPH, b. 1579, d. Duxbury, Mass., May 1658. JPG II:294-301.

PARTRIDGE, WILLIAM, d. Salisbury, Mass., 9 July 1654. TAG 65:65-69 (English origins); further clues to English origins at NHGR 9:180-81; Stevens, 34.

PASCO, HUGH, b. ca. 1640, d. Enfield, Conn., 29 August 1706. TAG 70:205-8 (identity of wife); NEHGR 150:131-40.

PATCH, EDMUND, b. 1601, d. Salem, Mass., 10 November 1680. MJ 18:109-11.

PATCH, NICHOLAS, b. 1597, d. Beverly, Mass., before 26 November 1673. Lyon, pp. 497-500; MJ 18:109-11.

PATRICK, DANIEL, b. ca. 1605, d. Stamford, Conn., late 1643. GMB III: 1403-8; Thompson, pp. 187-88, et al.; NEHGR 153:466-84.

PATTEE, PETER, b. ca. 1644, d. Haverhill, Mass., 19 October 1724. NEHGR 146:315-36, 147:73-86, 174-87 (five generation study).

PATTEN, HECTOR, b. ca. 1695, d. Surry, Me., ca. 1780. Davis III:97-125 [James Patten].

PATTEN, MATTHEW, b. ca. 1691, d. Biddeford, Me., 25 September 1773. Davis III:84-96 [James Patten].

PATTEN, NATHANIEL, d. Dorchester, Mass., 31 January 1671/2. MJ 18:111-13, 27:43.

PATTEN, ROBERT, d. Arundel, Me., between 15 March and 10 April 1775. Davis III:129-55 [James Patten].

PATTEN, WILLIAM, d. Boston, Mass., between 28 August and 14 September 1770. Davis III:126-28 [James Patten].

PATTEN, WILLIAM, d. Cambridge, Mass., 10 December 1668. Son Nathaniel[2] at Cameos, pp. 249-55.

PATTEN, WILLIAM, d. Wells, Me., between 17 January and 6 April 1752. Davis III:156-62 [James Patten].

PATTISON, JAMES, fl. Billerica, Mass., 1660s, d. there ca. 1701. Sex, pp. 117-18.

PAULE, WILLIAM, d. Taunton, Mass., 1704. TAG 73:312-15.

PAYSON, GILES, b. 1609, d. Roxbury, Mass., 28 January 1688/9. NEHGR 148:45-60 (English origins of his wife and his possible origins).

PEABODY, JOHN, b. ca. 1611, d. Newport, R.I., 12 April 1687. Kempton, pp. 365-72; AL, pp. 462-63.

PEABODY, JOHN, d. Bridgewater, Mass., between 16 July 1649 and 27 April 1667. MBT #840.

PEACH, ARTHUR, d. Plymouth, Mass., 4 September 1638. LENE, p 7.

PEACH, JOHN, b. ca. 1613, d. Marblehead, Mass., between 10 Janaury 1687/8 and 21 May 1694. MJ 19:118-21, 26:53-54.

PEAKE, CHRISTOPHER, b. ca. 1612, d. Roxbury, Mass., 23 May 1666. GMB III:1413-14.

PEARCE, JOHN, d. York, Me., ca. 1692. Davis III:163-64 [Sarah Stone].

PEARSON, JOHN, b. ca. 1616, d. Lynn, Mass., before 25 June 1679. TEG 13:200-9, 14:39-44, 115.

PEASE, HENRY, b. ca. 1591, d. Boston, Mass., 7 August 1648. GMB III: 1415-17.

PEASE, JOHN, d. Martha's Vineyard, Mass., between 1677 and 1689. TAG 70:205-8.

PEASE, ROBERT, d. Salem, Mass., 1644. TAG 70:205-8.

PEASLEY, JOSEPH, b. ca. 1605, d. Amesbury, Mass., 3 December 1660. Croll, 202; EB, pp. 430-32.

PECK, JOSEPH, b. 1587, d. Rehoboth, Mass., 23 December 1663. 50Imm, pp. 289-98.

PECK, WILLIAM, b. ca. 1604, d. New Haven, Conn., 14 October 1694. Johnson, pp. 277-79.

PECKHAM, JOHN, b. 1595, d. Little Compton, R.I., after 1681. Jessup, pp. 724-27; TAG 71:151-54 (daughter Phebe).

PEDRICK, JOHN, b. ca. 1624, d. Marblehead, Mass., between 2 August and 7 October 1686. TEG 14:143-49, 211-19.

PEDRICK, JOHN, b. ca. 1650, d. Marblehead, Mass., between 22 November 1699 and 28 November 1706. TEG 14:219-21.

PELHAM, HERBERT, b. ca. 1600, of Cambridge, Mass., d. Bures, Suffolk, England, in 1674. RD600, pp. 154-57; PA, pp. 573-74; MCA, p. 650. Second wife Elizabeth (Bosvile) at RD600, pp. 178-79; PA, p. 133; MCA, p. 114. First wife Jemima (Waldegrave) at RD600, pp. 397-98; PA, p. 166; MCA, pp. 149-50; MJ 18:113-16.

PEMBERTON, JAMES, b. ca. 1608, d. Malden, Mass., 5 February 1661/2. GMB III:1419-21; TEG 19:206-10.

PEMBERTON, JAMES, b. ca. 1622, d. Boston, Mass., 1696. TEG 19:206-10.

PENDLETON, BRIAN, b. ca. 1599, d. Portsmouth, N.H., between 30 June 1680 and 5 April 1681. Thompson, pp. 42-43, et al.

PENHALLOW, SAMUEL, b. 1665, d. Boston, Mass., 2 December 1726. RD600, pp. 524-25.

PENLEY, SAMPSON, d. Falmouth, Me., between April 1687 and December 1688. TAG 73:223-27 (clues to English origins).

PENNEY, THOMAS, d. Gloucester, Mass., ca. 1692. Stevens, 3.

PENNEY, WILLIAM, b. ca. 1690, of Harwich, Mass., d. Oblong, N.Y., after 1747. NYGBR 133:83-98, 201-16.

PENNIMAN, JAMES, b. 1599, d. Braintree, Mass., 26 December 1664. GMB III:1426-30; Goodman, pp. 363-67; TAG 71:12-18 (English origins).

PENTICOST, JOHN, b. ca. 1597, d. Charlestown, Mass., 19 October 1687. TAG 62:118-20 (English origins).

PERCIVAL, JAMES, d. Falmouth, Mass., between 19 January and 23 March 1691/2. CN 21:310-17; NEHGR 141:251-54.

PERHAM, JOHN, b. ca. 1632, d. Chelmsford, Mass., 23 January 1720/1. Kempton4, pp. 533-45.

PERKINS, ABRAHAM, b. ca. 1613, d. Hampton, N.H., 31 August 1682. Carolyn C. Perkins, *Descendants of Abraham Perkins of Hampton, N.H., to the Eighth Generation* (Portsmouth, NH: Peter E. Randall Publisher, 1993). Reviews: CA 44:101, CN 27:60.

PERKINS, JOHN, b. 1583, d. Ipswich, Mass., between 28 March and 27 September 1654. GMB III:1431-33; Davis III:165-82 [Dudley Wildes], including English origins; EB, pp. 437-39; Stowers, pp. 431-36; Stevens, 46; MBT #1882; full ancestry at John Brooks Threlfall, *The Ancestry of Thomas Bradbury (1611-1695) and His Wife Mary (Perkins) Bradbury (1615-1700) of Salisbury, Massachusetts* (Madison, WI: the author, 1995, 2nd edition). Reviews: TAG 64:58-59, NEHGR 144:268-69.

PERKINS, WILLIAM, b. 1607, d. Topsfield, Mass., 21 May 1682. GMB III:1433-38; MBT #646; TEG 3:65-76.

PERLEY, ALLAN, b. 1608, d. Ipswich, Mass., 28 December 1675. MBT #856.

PERRY, ANTHONY, d. Rehoboth, Mass., Feb./Mar. 1682/3. JPG I:602-6.

PERRY, EDWARD, b. ca. 1630, d. Sandwich, Mass., between 29 December 1694 and 9 April 1695. Jessup, pp. 734-39; AL, pp. 466-67.

PERRY, FRANCIS, b. ca. 1608, of Salem and Lynn, Mass., d. in Barbados between 5 and 11 November 1659. GMB III:1438-41.

PERRY, JOHN, b. ca. 1612, d. Roxbury, Mass., September 1642. GMB III:1442-43; Lyon, pp. 500-6.

PERRY, WILLIAM, b. ca. 1606, d. Watertown, Mass., 9 September 1683. EB, pp. 439-44.

PERRY, WILLIAM, d. Marshfield, Mass., before 16 January 1692/3. TAG 70:42-48, 84; NEHGR 146:230-34 (wife identified).

PETERSON, JOHN, b. ca. 1636, d. Duxbury, Mass., between 29 April 1718 and 16 March 1719/20. Soule, four generations all lines.

PETTEE, WILLIAM, b. ca. 1595, d. Weymouth, Mass., between 14 April and 24 June 1679. Stone, pp. 219-21.

PETTINGILL, RICHARD, b. ca. 1620, d. Newbury, Mass., after 1695. Davis III:183-92 [Abel Lunt].

PHELPS, GEORGE, d. 8 May 1687. Descendant Nathaniel's wife Grace Martin at TAG 58:223-28; Nathaniel[2] at TAG 64:157-59; TAG 68:239-41 (Isaac[2]); NGSQ 77:249-55; MJ 1:49-50, 72, 7:33-61, 12:45-53; MJ 19:121-22.

PHELPS, HENRY, d. Salem, Mass., between 1645 and 1648. MBT #1644; NGSQ 75:289-302 (Henry[2] and Nicholas[2]'s wife Hannah).

PHELPS, WILLIAM, b. ca. 1593, d. Windsor, Conn., 14 July 1672. GMB III:1444-46; TAG 58:243-44 (comments on English origins); son Joseph[2]'s wife identified at TAG 65:13-16; TAG 65:161-66 (English origins), TAG 75:26 (correction); MJ 1:50-51, 72, 2:94, 98, 7:63-100, 12:45-53, 15:52, 19:123-24, 25:50-51, 26:54-55.

PHILBRICK, THOMAS, b. 1584, d. Hampton, N.H., before 8 October 1667. 26Imm, pp. 223-26; NEHGR 147:327 (wife's English origins).

PHILLIPS, GEORGE, b. ca. 1593, d. Watertown, Mass., 1 July 1644. GMB III:1446-50; Thompson, pp. 64-74, et al.; son Jonathan[2] at Thompson, pp. 191-92, et al.; Jonathan also at Sex, pp. 77-81, et al.

PHILLIPS, JOHN, b. ca. 1605, d. Boston, Mass., 16 December 1682. GMB III:1452-56.

PHILLIPS, JOHN, of Marshfield, Mass. Son John[2] at NEA 5:1:21.

PHILLIPS, MICHAEL, of R.I. Son William[2] at NEHGR 143:221-33.

PHILLIPS, NICHOLAS, b. ca. 1610, d. Weymouth, Mass., between 2 June 1671 and 7 September 1672. EB, pp. 446-48.

PHILLIPS, WALTER, b. ca. 1619, d. Lynn, Mass., before 2 December 1704. TEG 16:153-57, 221-24.

PHILLIPS, WILLIAM, b. 1614, d. Boston, Mass., November 1683. RF2, four generations all lines through third wife Bridget (Hutchinson).

PHINNEY, WIDOW OF ROBERT, b. ca. 1570, d. Plymouth, Mass., 22 April 1650. Croll, 173; AK, p. 439; JPG II:180-84; NEHGR 148:315-27 (English origins of Robert).

PHIPPEN, DAVID, d. Boston, Mass., before 31 October 1650. MJ 17:110-12.

PHIPPS, SOLOMON, d. Charlestown, Mass., between 24 May 1670 and 14 December 1671. Family at Sex, pp. 137-38.

PICKERAM, JOHN, b. ca. 1580, d. Watertown, Mass., December 1630. GMB III:1457-58.

PICKERING, JOHN, b. ca. 1609, d. Portsmouth, N.H., between 11 and 29 January 1668/9. GMB III:1458-61.

PICKETT, JOHN, d. at sea, 16 August 1667. Brewster, two generations all lines; Brewster3, three generations all lines.

PICKWORTH, JOHN, b. ca. 1606, d. Manchester, Mass., between 27 June and 25 August 1663. GMB III:1462-64; PM, pp. 353-56; Stevens, 64.

PIDGE, THOMAS, b. ca. 1594, d. Roxbury, Mass., 30 December 1643. GMB III:1464-66; JPG II:478-81.

PIERCE, ABRAHAM, b. ca. 1605, d. Duxbury, Mass., before 3 June 1673. GMB III:1466-69; PM, pp. 356-59; EB, pp. 432-37; MQ 49:57-67.

PIERCE, JOHN, b. ca. 1606, d. Boston, Mass., 17 September 1661. GMB III:1469-72.

PIERCE, MICHAEL, b. ca. 1615, d. Rehoboth, Mass., 26 March 1676. EB, pp. 448-50; Lyon, pp. 507-13.

PIERCE, RICHARD, b. ca. 1620, d. Portsmouth, R.I., between 22 August 1677 and 28 October 1678. AL, pp. 463-65.

PIERCE, THOMAS, b. ca. 1583, d. Charlestown, Mass., 7 October 1666. JPG I:607-22.

PIERCE, WILLIAM, b. ca. 1591, d. Providence Island 13 July 1641. GMB III:1472-78.

Pike, James, d. Reading, Mass., 6 December 1699. Nichols, pp. 67-68; appears with daughter Mary at Sex, pp. 47-53, et al.

Pike, John, b. ca. 1573, d. Salisbury, Mass., 26 May 1654. Freeman, pp. 739-84; TAG 73:256-57 (baptisms of two children); NEHGR 153:319-22 (wife's English origins); Allen Raymond Pike, *The Family of John Pike of Newbury, Massachusetts (Some Descendants), 1635-1995* (Camden, ME: Penobscot Press, 1995). Reviews: MG 20:93-94.

Pike, Robert, of Providence, R.I. MJ 18:118-19.

Pinder, Henry, b. ca. 1580, d. Ipswich, Mass., February 1661. 50Imm, pp. 301-2; Stevens, 30; MBT #1806.

Pinion see Briggs

Pinkham, Richard, b. ca. 1613, d. Dover, N.H., between 1671 and 5 May 1688. NHGR 22:1-7, 63-67, 115-25, 164-71, to be continued in 2006 (multi-generational work concentrating on descendants of John[2]).

Pinney, Humphrey, b. 1605, d. Windsor, Conn., 20 August 1683. GMB III:1478-81; CN 26:542-46; MJ 1:51-52, 2:89, 98, 3:38-40, 7:101-10, 12:43-44, 54-56, 17:112-18, 27:43.

Pitcher, Andrew, d. Dorchester, Mass., 19 February 1660. John[2] at TAG 59:201-10; MJ 19:127-28.

Pitts, William, d. Hingham, Mass., before 1655. EB, pp. 450-51; AL, pp. 467-68.

Place, Enoch, d. Kingstown, R.I., ca. May 1695. TAG 79:76-81 (Thomas[2]).

Place, John, b. ca. 1643, d. Portsmouth, N.H., after 1678. NHGR 15:13-21, 17:22-28, 90, 18:88-91, 19:11-14, 72-76, 117-18, 20:16-21, 64-69.

Place, Peter, b.c. 1615, d. Boston, Mass., before 22 April 1675. TAG 78:256-64 (daughter Hannah).

Plaine, William, d. New Haven, Conn., June 1646. LENE, p. 12.

Platt, Richard, b. 1604, d. Milford, Conn., before 13 February 1684/5. JIC, pp. 109-33 (English origins); JPG I:623-28.

Platts, Jonathan, b. ca. 1630, d. Rowley, Mass., 1680. EB, pp. 451-53.

Plumb, John, b. 1594, d. Branford, Conn., July 1648. EB, pp. 453-54; Nichols, pp. 193-94; Lyon, pp. 518-21; TAG 70:65-74, 149-55 (additions to English ancestry).

PLUMMER, FRANCIS, b. ca. 1594, d. Newbury, Mass., 17 January 1672/3. GMB III:1482-86; NGSQ 83:112-23.

POLLY, JOHN, b. ca. 1618, d. Roxbury, Mass., 2 April 1689. Mower, pp. 485-91; Lyon, pp. 522-24.

POMEROY, ELTWEED, b. 1585, d. Northampton, Mass., March 1673. GMB III:1486-90; MJ 13:40-41, 17:119-21, 25:51.

POND, ROBERT, d. Dorchester, Mass., before 27 December 1637. Pond, 208; 31Imm, pp. 164-68.

PONTUS, WILLIAM, b. ca. 1585, d. Plymouth, Mass., 9 February 1652/3. GMB III:1491-93; PM, pp. 360-62; EB, pp. 454-56.

POOLE, EDWARD, b. ca. 1609, d. Weymouth, Mass., between 22 August and 16 September 1664. MJ 19:141.

POOLE, JOHN, b. ca. 1609, d. Reading Mass., 1 April 1667. GMB III:1493-96; Nichols, pp. 9-11; son Jonathan[2] at Sex, pp. 176-77; TEG 21:209-21.

POOLE, WILLIAM, b. 1593, d. Dorchester, Mass., 24/5 February 1674. PA, p. 82; RD600, pp. 171-72; MCA, p. 788; MJ 19:136-40, 26:55-56.

POPE, JOHN, d. Dorchester, Mass., 12 February 1646/7. EB, pp. 456-60.

POPE, THOMAS, b. ca. 1612, d. Darmouth, Mass., between 9 July and 4 August 1683. GMB III:1496-99; PM, pp. 362-65.

POPE, THOMAS, mariner of Boston and Charlestown, Mass., fl. 1680s. Sex, pp. 151-52.

POPE, WALTER, b. ca. 1609, d. Charlestown, Mass., before 1640. GMB III:1499-1500.

PORTER, EDWARD, b. 1608/9, d. Boston, Mass., between 28 July and 3 August 1677. NEHGR 148:45-60 (English origins).

PORTER, JOHN, b. 1594, d. Windsor, Conn., 21 April 1648. EB, pp. 460-61; Johnson, pp. 279-80.

PORTER, JOHN, b. ca. 1595, d. Salem, Mass., 6 September 1676. Davis III:193-202 [Dudley Wildes]; Mower, pp. 495-506.

PORTER, JOHN, b. ca. 1608, d. Pettaquamscutt, R.I., after 25 April 1674. GMB III:1501-4.

PORTER, RALPH, b. ca. 1583, d. Watertown, Mass., 3 April 1654. Wife Grace (Ravens)'s origins at TAG 62:65-77, 161-70.

Post, Stephen, d. Saybrook, Conn., 16 August 1659. Spooner; NEGHR 146:211-29, 356-76, 147:49-63, 383-84 (three generation study of Abraham[2]).

Post, Thomas, d. Cambridge, Mass., 1691. Cameos, pp. 195-98.

Pote, William, b. 1638, d. Marblehead, Mass., ca. 1695. MG 25:11-20.

Potter, Luke, b. 1615, d. Concord, Mass., 13 October 1697. 26Imm, pp. 227-40; MBT #258.

Potter, Nathaniel, b. ca. 1615, d. Portsmouth, R.I., 1643. Johnson, pp. 280-82; AL, pp. 475-77.

Potter, Nicholas, b. 1604, d. Salem, Mass., 18 August 1677. TEG 19: 142-53.

Potter, William, d. New Haven, Conn., 6 June 1662. LENE, pp. 32-33.

Potwine, John, d. Windsor, Conn., 1706. Nichols, pp. 171-72.

Poulter, John, b. ca. 1635, d. Medford, Mass., 20 May 1676. NEHGR 141:215-27 (English origins).

Powers, Walter, b. ca. 1639, d. Concord, Mass., 22 February 1707/8. Kempton4, pp. 1-58.

Pratt, John, b. 1607, d. Hartford, Conn., 8 July 1655. GMB III:1507-10; NEHGR 149:374-78 (English origins proved); NEHGR 150:215 (correction).

Pratt, Joshua, b. ca. 1605, d. Plymouth, Mass., between 29 June 1652 and 5 October 1656. GMB III:1510-13; PM, pp. 365-69; Jessup, pp. 744-53; TAG 71:76 (John[3] Benajah[2]'s wife identified).

Pratt, Macuth, b. ca. 1595, d. Weymouth, Mass., 29 October 1672. TAG 65:33-43, 89-96 (English origins); TAG 68:29-31 (daughter Mary).

Pratt, Phineas, b. ca. 1593, d. Charlestown, Mass., 19 April 1680. MF8, four generations all lines; GMB III:1514-18; PM, pp. 369-74.

Pratt, William, b. 1609, d. Saybrook, Conn., 1678. Jessup, pp. 753-59; Morgan; NEHGR 149:374-78 (English origins proved); NEHGR 150:215 (correction).

Pray, Quentin, b. ca. 1595, d. Braintree, Mass., on 17 April or June 1667. EB, pp. 462-66.

PRENCE, THOMAS, b. ca. 1600, d. Plymouth, Mass., 29 March 1673. Brewster, three generations all lines; Brewster2, four generations all lines; GMB III:1518-24; PM, pp. 374-81; Croll, 105.

PRENTICE, HENRY, b. ca. 1605, d. Cambridge, Mass., 9 June 1654. 26Imm, pp. 241-46; MBT #544; NEHGR 143:24 (English origins).

PRENTICE, THOMAS, b. ca. 1620, d. Cambridge, Mass., 7 July 1709. Cameos, pp. 139-44.

PRENTICE, VALENTINE, b. ca. 1601, d. Roxbury, Mass., before 3 April 1634. GMB III:1525; TAG 77:173-75 (English origins).

PRESCOTT, JOHN, b. ca. 1604, d. Lancaster, Mass., 1 December 1681. JPG I:629-48; Lyon, pp. 524-27.

PRESTON, WILLIAM, b. 1590/1, d. New Haven, Conn., 1647. Jessup, pp. 759-62.

PRICE, HUGH, d. Plymouth or Plympton, Mass., before 8 June 1691. MF12, three generations all lines.

PRIEST, DEGORY, *Mayflower* passenger, b. ca. 1579, d. Plymouth, Mass., 1 January 1620/1. MF8, five generations all lines; GMB III:1526; PM, pp. 382-83; TAG 80:241-60 (a review of his possible English origins).

PRIME, JAMES, d. Milford, Conn., 1685. Nichols, p. 103-4.

PRINCE, JOHN, b. ca. 1610, d. Hull, Mass., 16 August 1676. NEHGR 143:247-54.

PRINCE, MARY, d. Salem, Mass., before 1647. EB, pp. 466-67.

PROCTOR, GEORGE, b. ca. 1602, d. Dorchester, Mass., 29 November 1661. MJ 25:51-55, 26:56.

PROCTOR, JOHN, b.1595, d. Ipswich, Mass., between 28 August and 28 November 1672. Johnson, pp. 283-86; JPG II:484-86; Lyon, pp. 528-30; Stevens, 44; son John[2] at LENE, pp. 83-84; TAG 79:274-77 (Joseph[2]); Leland H. Procter, *John Proctor of Ipswich and Some of His Descendants* (Springfield, MA: Research Associates, 1985). Reviews: CN 19:326-27, NYGBR 118:177.

PROCTOR, ROBERT, b. 1624, d. Chelmsford, Mass., 28 April 1697. Nichols, pp. 105-7; JPG II:482-83.

PROUT, TIMOTHY, b. 1620, d. Boston, Mass., 13 November 1702. Chase, pp. 335-40, including English origins; MJ 18:120-21; Dale Ellison Prout,

Ancestry and Descendants of Captain Timothy Prout of Boston (Baltimore, MD: Gateway Press, 2002). Reviews: CN 35:629.

PRUDDEN, PETER, b. ca. 1601, d. Milford, Conn., 1656. Horton R. Prudden, *Rev. Peter Prudden and His Descendants in America* (Madison, CT: the author, 1983). Reviews: CN 16:516-18.

PUDDINGTON SEE PURRINGTON

PUDEATOR, JACOB, d. Salem, Mass., 1685. LENE, pp. 99-100 (wife Ann).

PULLEN, EDWARD, fl. Boston and Hingham, Mass., 1650s-1660s. JPG I: 649-53.

PURCHASE, AQUILA, b. ca. 1589, of Dorchester, Mass., d. at sea 1633. GMB III:1527-28; MJ 17:121-25, 25:55.

PURCHASE, THOMAS, b. ca. 1577, d. Lynn, Mass., 11 May 1678. GMB III:1529-34; MJ 17:121-25.

PURRIER, WILLIAM, of Ipswich and Salisbury, Mass., d. Southold, N.Y., before 1675. TAG 65:65-69 (English origins).

PURRINGTON, GEORGE, b. ca. 1597, d. York, Me., between 3 July 1647 and 5 June 1649. MJ 18:121-26.

PUTNAM, JOHN, b. 1579/80, d. Salem, Mass., 30 December 1662. Chase, pp. 341-56; EB, pp. 467-71; AK, pp. 432-36; Mower, pp. 509-19; TAG 68:77-83, 69:212-18 (Edward[3] Thomas[2]'s wife).

PYNCHON, WILLIAM, b. 1590, of Roxbury and Springfield, Mass., d. in England 29 October 1662. GMB III:1536-38; CN 23:388-98, 626-35; TAG 76:211-16 (mother's English ancestry); son John[2]'s wife Amy (Wyllys) at RD600, pp. 314-15; PA, p. 761; MCA, p. 886; NEA 1:2:38-41; Carl Bridenbaugh, ed., *The Pynchon Papers, Volume 1: Letter of John Pynchon 1654-1700*, Volume 60 of the Publications of the Colonial Society of Massachusetts (Boston, MA: Colonial Society of Massachusetts, 1982). Reviews: NEQ 56:290-93; Carl Bridenbaugh, ed., *The Pynchon Papers, Volume 2: Selections from the Account Books of John Pynchon 1651-1697* (Boston, MA: Colonial Society of Massachusetts, 1985). Reviews: NEQ 60:296-99.

QUINCY, EDMUND, b. 1602, d. Boston, Mass., ca. 1639. GMB III:1539-42; NEHGR 157:31-33 (English origins).

RAINSFORD, EDWARD, b. 1609, d. Boston, Mass., 16 August 1680. GMB III:1543-48; RD600, pp. 374-75; PA, p. 605; MCA, p. 692; Edward[3]

David[2] at TAG 56:174-78; NEHGR 139:225-38, 296-315 (English origins and three generation study); NEHGR 154:219-26 (royal line).

RALPH, THOMAS, d. Warwick, R.I., before 15 June 1682. JPG I:654-59.

RAMSDELL, JOHN, b. ca. 1602, d. Lynn, Mass., 27 October 1688. 50Imm, pp. 303-6; MBT #644; TEG 10:25-32, 79-84, 213-16, 11:44-46, 81, 133, 14:116.

RAMSDEN, JOSEPH, d. Plymouth, Mass., 25 May 1674. MF9, four generations all lines; JPG II:489-96.

RAND, ROBERT, b. ca. 1595, d. Charlestown, Mass., ca. 1639/40. Goodman, pp. 369-84, including English origins; Lyon, pp. 530-32; TEG 21: 28-35.

RANDALL, JOHN, d. Westerly, R.I., before May 1684. CN 16:41-44; clues to English origins at RIR 29:57-69.

RANDALL, NATHANIEL, of New London, Conn. CN 16:41-44.

RANDALL, PHILIP, b. ca. 1590, d. Windsor, Conn., 6 May 1662. GMB III:1548-50; MJ 19:141-43.

RANDALL, WILLIAM, d. Scituate, Mass. NEHGR 146:230-34 (wife identified).

RANKIN, HUGH, b. ca. 1673, d. Londonderry, N.H., 6 January 1755. MBT #242.

RANSOM, ROBERT, b. ca. 1636, d. Lakenham [a village in Plympton, now Carver], Mass., ca. 1697. EB, pp. 471-74; JPG I:660-70.

RAWLIN(G)S, JAMES, b. ca. 1613, d. Dover, N.H., between 16 December 1685 and 13 August 1687. GMB III:1552-55.

RAWLIN(G)S, JASPER, b. ca. 1575, d. Boston, Mass., between 17 January 1665/6 and 13 June 1667. GMB III:1555-57.

RAWLIN(G)S, THOMAS, b. between 1583 and 1595, d. Boston, Mass., 15 March 1659/60. Kempton, pp. 375-85; GMB III:1557-60.

RAWLIN(G)S, THOMAS, b. ca. 1618, d. Boston, Mass., before 29 April 1692. MJ 19:143.

RAWSON, EDWARD, b. 1615, d. Boston, Mass., 27 August 1693. Daughter Rebecca[2] at WRR, pp. 46-53; MJ 17:125-27, 26:97-101.

RAY, DANIEL, b. ca. 1597, d. Salem, Mass., 24 June 1662. GMB III:1560-62; PM, pp. 385-88; Lyon, pp. 532-35; Uzziel[4] Daniel[3] Joshua[2]'s wife identified at TAG 65:143-47.

RAY, SIMON, d. Braintree, Mass., 30 September 1641. TAG 56:94-96 (connections to cousins Hester [Wells] Mason and Martha [Ray] Brackett).

RAYMENT, JOHN, b. ca. 1616, d. Beverly, Mass., 18 January 1703. Davis III:203-6 [Bethia Harris], including English origins.

RAYMENT, RICHARD, b. ca. 1602, d. Saybrook, Conn., 1692. GMB III:1563-65. Mercy (Sands) wife of Joshua[3-2] at Doctors, pp. 69-72; Johnson, pp. 286-87.

RAYNSFORD SEE RAINSFORD

REA SEE RAY

READ, ESDRAS, b. ca. 1598, d. Boston, Mass., 27 July 1680. 50Imm, pp. 307-10; MBT #706; NEHGR 140:180 (note); MJ 18:126-27.

READ, JOHN, b. ca. 1645, d. Freetown, Mass., 3 January 1721/2. AL, pp. 482-83.

READ, PHILIP, d. Concord, Mass., 10 May 1696. Cameos, pp. 135-38.

READ, THOMAS, b. 1612, of Salem, Mass., d. England, between 25 July and 6 November 1662. GMB III:1565-67; Davis III:209-15 [Bethia Harris].

READ, THOMAS, d. Salem, Mass., before 5 April 1667. Richard H. Benson, *The Read Family of Salem, Massachusetts* (Boston, MA: Newbury Street Press, 2005), a multi-generation genealogy on this family. Reviews: MD 54:182-83, TAG 80:239.

READ, WILLIAM, b. ca. 1587, of Dorchester, Scituate, Brookline and Woburn, Mass., d. Newcastle-Upon-Tyne, England, 1656. 26Imm, pp. 247-50; Johnson, pp. 288-89; MBT #814.

READ, WILLIAM, b. ca. 1605, d. Weymouth, Mass., between January 1657/8 and 6 April 1658. AL, pp. 483-90; MJ 25:55.

READ, WILLIAM, b. ca. 1607, d. Boston, Mass., before 28 November 1667. Second wife Ruth (Crooke) at WRR, pp. 208-13.

READE SEE READ

REDD SEE ALSO REED

REDDING, JOSEPH, b. ca. 1613, d. Ipswich, Mass., 19 February 1674/5. GMB III:1567-69.

REDDING, THOMAS, b. ca. 1607, d. Casco, Me., before 10 March 1673/4. TG 3:161-71; Billie Redding Lewis, *The Redding Family and Its Relatives* (Lake Wales, FL: the author, 1982). Reviews: CN 16:156-57.

REDDINGTON, JOHN, d. Topsfield, Mass., 15 November 1690. Second wife Sarah at NEHGR 141:19-21.

REDMAN, JOHN, b. ca. 1615, d. Hampton, N.H., 16 February 1700, NHGR 18:7.

REDWAY, JAMES, b. ca. 1618, d. Rehoboth, Mass., March 1684. Johnson, pp. 289-90; NEGHR 146:337-42 (James[3] John[2]'s wife correctly identified).

REED, JOHN, of Norwalk, Conn. TAG 67:246-48 (grandson John[3]).

REED, SAMUEL, d. Marblehead, Mass., March 1716. LENE, pp. 98-99 (wife Wilmot).

REED, WILLIAM, of Weymouth, Mass. Son James[2] at MD 40:123-32.

REEVE, ROBERT, of Hartford, Conn. TAG 74:97-100 (wife identified).

REEVES, JOHN, b. ca. 1609, d. Salem, Mass., between 22 June and 29 November 1681. Kempton, pp. 387-97, with possible English origins.

REMINGTON, JOHN, d. Roxbury, Mass., after 1658. AL, pp. 490-98; son Jonathan[2] at Cameos, pp. 129-34.

REYNOLDS, ELECTIUS, b. ca. 1653, d. Middleboro, Mass., 19 June 1738. EB, pp. 474-76; TAG 70:205-8 (identity of wife).

REYNOLDS, JAMES, b. ca. 1625, d. Kingstown, R.I., ca. September 1700. AL, pp. 498-502.

REYNOLDS, SAMUEL, fl. Watertown, Mass., 1660s, Sex, pp. 120-23.

REYNOR, HUMPHREY, d. Rowley, Mass., September 1660. NEHGR 156:309-21 (wife's ancestry); NEHGR 156:322-26 (note).

REYNOR, JOHN, d. Dover, N.H., 21 April 1669. NEHGR 156:322-26 (note).

RHODES, HENRY, b. ca. 1608, d. Lynn, Mass., 1703. TEG 4:74-78, 14:156-64, 222-29, 15:31-37, 84-92.

RHODES, WALTER, b. ca. 1577, d. Providence, R.I., 1653. TEG 22:201-14, 23:37-50.

RICE, EDMUND, b. ca. 1594, d. Sudbury, Mass., 3 May 1663. NEA 3:4:50-51 (DNA Study); NEA 6:4:48-50 (DNA Study); Nichols, pp. 69-70; Lyon, pp. 136-50; MBT #532; wife Thomasine Frost's Strutt ancestry at TAG 61:161-66; Thomasine's paternal ancestry at TAG 63:129-37; TAG 65:241-47 (more on Strutt ancestry).

RICE, JOHN, b. ca. 1646, d. Warwick, R.I., 6 January 1731. RIR 24:153-68; John[2] at RIR 25:81-118, 26:57-84, 27:1-26.

RICHARDS, EDWARD, b. ca. 1610, d. Lynn, Mass., 26 January 1689/90. TEG 12:142-56, 205-10, 13:29-39, 105-11.

RICHARDS, THOMAS, b. 1596, d. Weymouth, Mass., between 17 December 1650 and 18 January 1650/1. GMB III:1575-79; MJ 13:82-85, 17:127-30, 25:55-56, 26:57.

RICHARDSON, EZEKIEL, b. 1604, d. Woburn, Mass., 21 October 1647. GMB III:1580-83; Davis III:216-28 [Sarah Hildreth], including English origins; Nichols, pp. 108-11; NEHGR 139:147-49 (Duxford ancestry).

RICHARDSON, SAMUEL, b. 1604, d. Woburn, Mass., 23 March 1657/8. Wife Joanna (Thake)'s ancestry at 50Imm, pp. 467-70; NEHGR 139:147-49 (Duxford ancestry); NEHGR 158:228-30 (Mary[3] Stephen[2]).

RICHARDSON, THOMAS, b. 1608, d. Woburn, Mass., 28 August 1651. Stone, pp. 223-27, including English origins; Davis III:216-18 [Sarah Hildreth], including English origins; NEHGR 139:147-49 (Duxford ancestry).

RICHMOND, JOHN, b. ca. 1594, d. Taunton, Mass., 20 March 1664. Chase, pp. 357-66; JPG I:671-86.

RICKARD, GILES, of Plymouth, Mass., by 1641, d. there between 8 January and 5 March 1684/5. Son Samuel[2], MF7, three generations all lines; sons Josiah[2] and Eleazer[2], MF9, three generations all lines; Brewer, p. 460; MJ 18:127-28, 25:56-57, 27:44-45; MQ 49:122-29 (John[3] Giles[2] and John[3-2]).

RIDDAN, THADDEUS, b. ca. 1624, d. Marblehead, Mass., 6 January 1690/1. TEG 11:76-81, 134-39.

RIDDLESDALE SEE LOKER

RIDDLESDALE, EDWARD, b. ca. 1592, d. England February 1630/1. His wife Mary remarried to John Wyatt and emigrated to New England with her children. 50Imm, pp. 311-20.

RIDER, SAMUEL, b. 1601, d. Yarmouth, Mass., 2 December 1679. Croll, 152; son Samuel[2] in MF18, three generations all lines for children from first wife Sarah (Bartlett); Bartlett; TAG 80:128-39.

RIDLEY, MARK, d. after1674. MG 21:3-12.

RIDLEY, THOMAS, b. ca. 1685, d. Truro, Mass., 28 August 1767. MG 21: 3-12.

RIGGS, EDWARD, b. ca. 1593, d. Roxbury, Mass., 5 March 1671/2. GMB III:1583-85; NEA 6:3:46-48 (DNA Study).

RING, MARY, WIDOW, b. ca. 1589, d. Plymouth, Mass., 15 or 19 July 1631. GMB III:1586-88; PM, pp. 389-91; son Andrew[2], MF6, four generations all lines. Her possible identification at TAG 42:193-205, hence her now universal identification as the wife of William.

RISHWORTH, EDWARD, b. ca. 1618, d. York, Me., 1689. EB, pp. 479-82.

RISLEY, RICHARD, d. East Hartford, Conn., ca. 1648. TAG 70:162-70 (daughter Sarah).

ROBBINS, GEORGE, b. ca. 1640, d. Chelmsford, Mass., 1689. NEHGR 151:387-407, 152:83-114, 243-44.

ROBBINS, ROBERT, b. ca. 1645, d. Groton, Mass., ca. 1719. JPG I:687-93; NEHGR 151:387-407, 152:83-114, 243-44.

ROBERTS, GILES, d. Scarborough, Me., between 25 January 1666/7 and 20 June 1667. Joann H. Nichols, *Descendants of Giles Roberts of Scarborough, Me.* (Baltimore, MD: Gateway Press, 1994), a multi-generation study of this family. Reviews: NHGR 12:47-48, CN 28:249, TAG 70:63.

ROBERTS, THOMAS, b. ca. 1600, d. Dover, N.H., between 27 September 1673 and 30 June 1674. Pond, 286.

ROBERTS, WILLIAM, d. Durham, N.H., before 29 March 1676. Davis III:229-33 [Lydia Harmon].

ROBINSON, ANDREW, b. ca. 1652 of Charlestown and Malden, Mass. Sex, pp. 45-53, 75-81, et al.

ROBINSON, ISAAC, b. ca. 1610, d. Barnstable, Mass., 1704. GMB III:1590-94; PM, pp. 391-95; mother's White ancestry at MD 43:183-86; possible son Thomas at CN 30:542-44; TAG 56:147 (second wife Mary).

ROBINSON, JOHN, b. 1611/2, d. near Hampton, N.H., 10 November 1675. NEHGR 143:141-51 (English origins).

Robinson, Joseph, d. Salem, Mass., before 4 February 1647/8. 50Imm, pp. 329-30; MBT #848.

Robinson, Thomas, b. ca. 1610, d. Boston, Mass., 23 March 1665/6. EB, pp. 482-84.

Robinson, Walter, d. New Haven, Conn., 4 March 1655. LENE, p. 28.

Robinson, William, b. ca. 1640, d. Newton, Mass., March 1693. Mower, pp. 521-36.

Robinson, William, d. Boston, Mass., 22 October 1659. LENE. pp. 29-32.

Rockwell, John, b. 1621, of Stamford, Conn., d. Westchester, N.Y., before 18 May 1677. NEA 4:2:51-53 (DNA Study); TAG 77:104-9, 79: 299-308.

Rockwell, John, d. Windsor, Conn., 1662. NEA 4:2:51-53 (DNA Study).

Rockwell, Josiah, d. Norwich, Conn., 1676. NEA 4:2:51-53 (DNA Study).

Rockwell, William, b. 1590/1, d. Windsor, Conn., May 1640. GMB III:1594-97; NEA 4:2:51-53 (DNA Study); MJ 1:52-53, 72, 2:90-91, 98, 3:41-42, 7:111-36, 17:131-33.

Rodick, George, b. ca. 1700, d. York, Me., after 1749. Brewer, pp. 461-78.

Rodman, Thomas, b. 1640, d. Newport, R.I., 11 January 1727/8. RF2, four generations all lines through his third wife Hannah (Clarke).

Rogers, John, b. ca. 1610, d. Weymouth, Mass., 11 February 1660/1. Kempton, pp. 399-404.

Rogers, John, d. Billerica, Mass., 25 January 1686/7. TEG 21:169-70.

Rogers, John, d. Marshfield, Mass., 1661. Davis III:234-38 [Joseph Neal].

Rogers, Robert, b. ca. 1617, d. Newbury, Mass., 23 December 1663. NEHGR 140:203-10; son John[2] at NEXUS 3:288-90.

Rogers, Thomas, b. ca. 1588, d. Watertown, Mass., 12 November 1638. Wife Grace (Ravens)'s origins at TAG 62:65-77, 161-70.

Rogers, Thomas, *Mayflower passenger*, b. ca. 1571, d. Plymouth, Mass., winter 1620/1. English origins of him and his wife at TG 9:138-49; MF19, five generations all lines; GMB III:1597-99; PM, pp. 396-97; Croll, 140; EB, pp. 484-92; Brewer, pp. 479-80; JPG I:694-701.

ROGERS, WILLIAM, b. ca. 1680, d. Voluntown, Conn., between 25 December 1727 and 8 July 1729. NEHGR 147:107-28, 261-77, 360-70 (five generation study).

ROGERS, WILLIAM, of Reading, Mass. by 1678, d. Charlestown, Mass., 15 November 1683. Stone, pp. 229-32.

ROICE, ROBERT, b. ca. 1613, d. Boston, Mass., before 27 October 1668. GMB III:1599-1600.

ROLFE, HENRY, d. Newbury, Mass., 1 March 1642/3. His grandson Samuel[3] John[2] at Cameos, pp. 295-97.

ROLLINS SEE RAWLINGS

ROOD, THOMAS, d. Hartford, Conn., 18 October 1672. LENE, p. 46; Johnson, pp. 291-93.

ROOT, JOHN, b. 1608, d. Farmington, Conn., 17 July 1684. Nichols, pp. 195-96.

ROOT, THOMAS, b. 1605, d. Hartford, Conn., 17 July 1694. JPG I:702-12, including English origins.

ROPER, JOHN, b. ca. 1588, d. Dedham, Mass., after 1664. Mower, pp. 539-43.

ROPER, WALTER, b. ca. 1611, d. Ipswich, Mass., July 1680. Davis III:239-41 [Phoebe Tilton].

ROSE, JOSEPH, d. Marshfield, Mass., after 1700/1. TAG 67:155.

ROSE, ROBERT, b. ca. 1594, d. Branford, Conn., between 25 August 1664 and 4 April 1665. Christine Rose, *Descendants of Robert Rose of Wethersfield and Branford, Connecticut: Who Came on the Ship "Francis" in 1634 from Ipswich, England* (San Jose, CA: Rose Family Association, 1983), winner of the Donald Lines Jacobus Award for 1987. Reviews: CN 16:705, TAG 59:60, NYGBR 115:121, NGSQ 76:73-74.

ROSE, THOMAS, b. ca. 1653, d. Preston, Conn., 19 April 1744. JPG II:497-501.

ROSE, THOMAS, d. Scituate, Mass., 2 May 1710. TAG 63:96-101.

ROSEMORGIE SEE MORGAN

ROSS, FENNEL, b. ca. 1621, d. Ipswich, Mass., before 12 February 1683/4. NEHGR 157:229-36, 395-97.

Ross, James, d. Sudbury, Mass., 18 September 1690. Daughter Mary at Sex, pp. 27-28, et al.

Ross, John, b. ca. 1645, d. Ipswich, Mass., after 8 February 1707/8. NEHGR 157:37-52, 395-97.

Ross, Killicress, d. Ipswich, Mass., between 11 June 1683 and 20 February 1683/4. NEHGR 157:166-75, 395-97.

Rossiter, Edward, b. ca. 1575, d. Dorchester, Mass., 23 October 1630. GMB III:1600-1; NEHGR 138:4-16 (English origins); MJ 1:53-54, 72-73, 3:43-44, 7:137-46, 17:133-36, 25:21-31; Doctors, pp. 27-30 (Joanna[3] Bray[2]); MJ 17:12-16, 25:7-8 (wife Elizabeth Alsop of Bray[2]).

Round, John, b. ca. 1645, d. Swansea, Mass., 7 October 1716. H.L. Peter Rounds, *The John Round Family of Swansea and Rehoboth, Massachusetts: The First Six/Seven Generations* (Baltimore, MD: Gateway Press, 1983), winner of the Donald Lines Jacobus Award for 1984. Reviews: RIR 10:3, TAG 59:56, NEHGR 138:51-54, NYGBR 114:248, NGSQ 73:61, MQ 49:144-45.

Rouse, Emmanuel, b. ca. 1673, d. Smithfield, R.I., after 15 June 1739. RIR 19:70-82.

Row, Elias, mariner of Charlestown, Mass., fl. 1670s and 1680s. Son John at Sex, pp. 61-69

Rowell, Thomas, b. 1594/5, d. Andover, Mass., 8 May 1662. Stevens, 29; MBT #1804; 50Imm, pp. 331-42; NEHGR 138:128-29 (note).

Rowlandson, Thomas, d. Lancaster, Mass., 17 November 1657. Daughter-in-law Mary (White) Rowlandson at Puritans, pp. 31-75.

Rowley, Henry, b. ca. 1605, d. Barnstable, Mass., between 29 May 1670 and July 1673. GMB III:1602-4; PM, pp. 398-400.

Royce, Robert, d. New London, Conn., 1676. NEA 5:1:44-47, 51 (DNA Study).

Ruddock, John, b. ca. 1609, d. Marlborough, Mass., between 28 January and 14 March 1692/3. Wife's identity at TAG 59:5-10.

Ruggles, George, b. ca. 1608, d. Boston, Mass., before 18 June 1669. GMB III:1604-7.

Ruggles, Thomas, b. 1584, d. Roxbury, Mass., 15 November 1644. Lyon, pp. 536-37.

RULE, MARGARET, fl. Boston, Mass., ca. 1692-3. WRR, pp. 27-31.

RUNDLETT, CHARLES, b. ca. 1652, d. Exeter, N.H., 1 April 1709. Chase, pp. 367-71.

RUSCOE SEE SEYMOUR

RUSCOE, WILLIAM, b. ca. 1593, of Norwalk, Conn., d. Jamaica, N.Y., between 5 August 1680 and 13 December 1682. CN 36:2-22 (John²).

RUSSELL, JOHN, b. ca. 1608, d. Dartmouth, Mass., 13 April 1694/5. AL, pp. 504-7.

RUSSELL, JOHN, d. Woburn, Mass., 1 June (4 mo.) 1676. NEXUS 4:19-20 (possible English origins and marriage record).

RUSSELL, WILLIAM, b. ca. 1647, d. Salem, Mass., between 11 January 1731/2 and 22 December 1733. George Ely Russell, *Descendants of William Russell of Salem, Mass., 1674* (Middletown, MD: Catoctin Press, 1989). Reviews: TAG 65:253, NEGHR144:170-71, NGSQ 79:67.

RUSSELL, WILLIAM, b. ca. 1690, d. Hampton Falls, N.H., before 6 November 1761. TAG 79:135-53.

RYALL, WILLIAM, b. ca. 1608, d. Dorchester, Mass., 15 June 1676. GMB III:1610-13.

SABIN, WILLIAM, b. 1609, d. Rehoboth, Mass., February 1686/7. Gordon Alan Morris and Thomas J. & Dixie Prittie, *The Descendants of William Sabin of Rehoboth, Massachusetts* (Camden, ME: Penobscot Press, 1994). Reviews: CN 28:411, NYGBR 126:284, MQ 61:233.

SACKETT, SIMON, b. ca. 1602, d. Cambridge, Mass., between 5 and 10 October 1635. GMB III:1615-16; TAG 63:179 (death date).

SAFFORD, THOMAS, d. Ipswich, Mass., between 20 February 1666 and 26 March 1667. Davis III:242-59 [Phoebe Tilton]; EB, pp. 493-97.

SALE, EDWARD, b. 1609, d. Weymouth, Mass., 1693. AL, pp. 508-10, including English ancestry.

SALES, JOHN, b. ca. 1600, of Charlestown and Boston, Mass., d. New Netherland between 17 April and 9 August 1645. GMB III:1616-18; NYGBR 123:65-73; Johnson, pp. 293-95; John² at Dorothy Higson White, *Descendants of Roger Williams Book III: The Sayles Line Through His Daughter Mary Williams* (East Greenwich, RI: Roger Williams Family Association, 2002). Reviews: RIR 29:207. Judith A. Hurst, *Sayles Country: A Social History 1660-1986 and Some Descendants of John and Mary (Williams)*

Sayles of Providence, R.I. (Baltimore, MD: Gateway Press, 1986). Reviews: TAG 62:190-91, RIR 12:42, NYGBR 118:177, 122:180.

SALLOWS, MICHAEL, d. Salem, Mass., between 19 November and 31 December 1646. EB, pp. 497-98; TAG 72:1-14, 115-34 (a five generation study).

SALTER, FRANCIS, fl. Marblehead, Mass., 1700s. Brewer, pp. 481-82.

SALTER, HENRY, fl. Charlestown, Mass., 1660s. Appears with wife Hannah in Sex, pp. 146-48, 184-85, et al.

SALTONSTALL, RICHARD, b. 1610, of Ipswich, Mass., d. Hulme, Lancashire, England, 29 April 1694. PA, p. 636; RD600, p. 198; MCA, p. 721. Wife Muriel (Gurdon) at RD600, p. 182-83; PA, p. 369; MCA, p. 396; father's sketch at GMB III:1618-21; NEHGR 142:24 (daughter Muriel's baptism); TAG 76:173 (note); NEQ 53:483-507 (Gurdon[4] Nathaniel[3] Richard[2]).

SAMPSON, HENRY, *Mayflower* passenger, b. 1603/4, d. Duxbury, Mass., 24 December 1684. MF20, five generations all lines; English ancestry at TG 6:166-86; GMB III:1621-24; PM, pp. 401-4; 31Imm, pp. 169-79; TAG 56:141-43 (paternal grandfather); MQ 71:125-28.

SAMSON, ABRAHAM. Sons Isaac[2] and Abraham[2] in MF14, three generations all lines; TAG 63:207-10.

SANBORN, JOHN, b. ca. 1620, d. Hampton, N.H., 20 October 1692. Son Nathaniel[2]'s wife Sarah (Waters)'s identity and English origins at NHGR 13:145-51. Elizabeth[3] Jonathan[2] at NHGR 14:80-83.

SANDERS, EDWARD, of Watertown, Mass., d. after 1671. Thompson, pp. 110-14, 186-87, et al.

SANDERS, JAMES, b. ca. 1643, d. Haverhill, Mass., 9 December 1721. Stevens, 22.

SANDERS, JOHN, b. 1627/8, d. Braintree, Mass., ca. 1689. Goodman, pp. 391-96, including English origins.

SANDERS, JOHN, b. ca. 1613, d. Newbury, Mass., 8 February 1664. TEG 23:229-35.

SANDERS, JOHN, b. ca. 1685, d. Needham, Mass., 24 April 1743. Kempton4, pp. 557-60.

SANDERS, JOHN, d. Cape Porpoise, Me., between 13 June and 3 August 1670. TEG 23:229-35.

SANDERS, JOHN, d. Salem, Mass., before 28 December 1643. TEG 23:229-35.

SANDERS, TOBIAS, b. ca. 1620, d. Westerly, R.I., 1695. CN 29:583-88 (English origins).

SANFORD, JOHN, b. 1608, d. Portsmouth, R.I., between 22 June and 15 November 1653. GMB III:1626-29; RF2, four generations all lines; AK, pp. 144-45; RIR 10:50.

SANFORD, MARY, d. Hartford, Conn., 25 June 1662. LENE, pp. 33-41.

SARGENT, WILLIAM, b. ca. 1611, d. Amesbury, Mass., between 24 February 1673/4 and 8 April 1675. GMB III:1630-33; MBT #940.

SARGENT, WILLIAM, b. ca. 1624, d. Gloucester, Mass., 9 February 1715/6. NEHGR 148:67-78 (English origins).

SARGENT, WILLIAM, d. Gloucester, Mass., before 4 May 1711. Chase, pp. 373-80.

SARGENT, WILLIAM, d. Barnstable, Mass., ca. 9 March 1679/80. RD600, pp. 540-43.

SAUNDERS SEE SANDERS

SAVAGE, THOMAS, b. 1607, d. Boston, Mass., 16 February 1681/2. RF2, four generations all lines; MBT #558; son Thomas[2] at NEXUS 9:25-29, 57-60.

SAVORY, THOMAS, b. ca. 1617, d. Plymouth, Mass., between 6 April 1674 and 28 January 1675/6. GMB III:1634-38; PM, pp. 405-9.

SAWDY, JOHN, b. ca. 1619, d. Boston, Mass., or at sea, before 21 March 1670. NEHGR 148:141-60, 268-90, 361-62 (six generation study).

SAWTELL, RICHARD, b. 1611, d. Watertown, Mass., 21 August 1694. 50Imm, pp. 343-52; MBT #552; MJ 18:129-31, 25:57-61.

SAWYER, JAMES, d. Gloucester, Mass., 31 May 1703. TEG 8:76-85.

SAWYER, JOHN, d. Marshfield, Mass., after 8 March 1704/5. MF18, three generations for children of his first wife Mercy (Little).

SAWYER, THOMAS, d. Lancaster, Mass., 12 September 1706. TAG 75:51-54 (Nathaniel[2]).

SAXTON, THOMAS, d. Boston, Mass., before 2 December 1686. Morgan.

SAYLES SEE SALES

SAYWARD, HENRY, b. ca. 1617, d. York, Me., before 22 April 1679. EB, pp. 498-506.

SCADLOCK, WILLIAM, d. Cape Porpoise, Me., between 7 January 1661/2 and 3 July 1662. 31Imm, pp. 180-86.

SCAMMON, RICHARD, b. ca. 1600, d. Dover, N.H., ca. 1660. EB, pp. 506-7.

SCHOOLER, WILLIAM, d. Boston, Mass., 28 September 1637. LENE, p. 6.

SCOFIELD, DANIEL, b. ca. 1616, d. Stamford, Conn., before March 1669/70. CA 41:43-54, 63-94, 144, 176-77, 42:11-45, 81-100, 123-55, 159-68, 43:23-47, 78-106, 117-41, 147-62, 44:22-51, 74-100, 125-34; NEHGR 152:179-83 (wife).

SCOFIELD, RICHARD, b. ca. 1613, d. Stamford, Conn., before 6 March 1671. CA 39:123-30, 157-73, 40:16-47, 64-94, 117-34, 153-71.

SCOTT, BENJAMIN, d. Rowley, Mass., between 6 June and 26 September 1671. LENE, pp. 97-98 (wife Margaret Stevenson).

SCOTT, RICHARD, d. Providence, R.I., 1679/80. Wife Katherine (Marbury) at TG 13:189-98; RD600, pp. 278-81; PA, p. 493; MCA, p. 565. RF2, five generations in all lines; notable descendants at NEXUS 11:140-45; RIR 14:97-98; NEHGR 138:317-20 (notes on Chamberlain ancestry); TAG 67:201-10 (Marbury ancestry); NEHGR 153:164-72 (more on English ancestry).

SCOTT, ROBERT, b. ca. 1613, d. Boston, Mass., before 21 February 1653/4. GMB III:1638-41.

SCOTT, THOMAS, b. 1594/5, d. Ipswich, Mass., between 8 and 28 March 1653/4. Davis III:267-70 [Phoebe Tilton], including English origins; MBT #838; NEHGR 141:34-37 (wife's Strutt ancestry).

SCOTTOW SEE ALSO HARWOOD

SCOTTOW, JOSHUA, b. ca. 1615, d. Boston, Mass., 1698. NEXUS 9:25-29, 57-60.

SCRUGGS, THOMAS, b. ca. 1590, d. Salem, Mass., 1654. Davis III:271-77 [Bethia Harris], including English origins.

SCUDDER, THOMAS, b. ca. 1586, d. Salem, Mass., 1657. TAG 72:285-300 (English origins).

SCULLARD, SAMUEL, b. ca. 1616, d. Newbury, Mass., before 7 April 1647. TAG 75:181-86 (English origins); TEG 25:95-105 (daughter Mary[2]).

SEABURY, JOHN, of Boston, Mass., d. Barbados ca. 1649. JPG II:302-9.

SEARLE, WILLIAM, d. Ipswich, Mass., 16 August 1667. Davis III:278-81 [Bethia Harris].

SEARS, RICHARD, b. ca. 1595, d. Yarmouth, Mass., 5 September 1676. GMB III:1642-44; PM, pp. 409-12; Spooner; wife's origins at TAG 58: 244-46.

SEAVER, ROBERT, b. ca. 1608, d. Roxbury, Mass., 5 June 1683. GMB III:1644-46; Chase, pp. 381-86; Johnson, pp. 295-96.

SEAVEY, WILLIAM, b. ca. 1601, d. Portsmouth, N.H., after September 1676. MJ 18:131-32.

SEDGWICK, ROBERT, ca. 1613, d. Jamaica, West Indies, 24 May 1656. Goodman, pp. 399-409, including English origins. Wife's Blake ancestry given at Goodman, pp. 77-79.

SEELEY, OBADIAH, d. Stamford, Conn., 1657. NEA 6:2:46-47, 51 (DNA Study).

SEELEY, ROBERT, b. 1602, d. Huntington, Conn., before 17 October 1668. GMB III:1647-50; NEA 6:2:46-47, 51 (DNA Study).

SEGAR, RICHARD, b. ca. 1595, d. Newport, R.I., 1682. AL, pp. 510-13.

SELBY, THOMAS, b. ca. 1670, d. Boston, Mass., before August 1727. NGSQ 76:17-24.

SELLECK, DAVID, b.1613/4, of Dorchester and Boston, Mass., d. Virginia between 1 June and 7 September 1654. TG 19:3-40.

SENSION, MATTHEW, d. Norwalk, Conn., ca. January 1669/70. NEHGR 149:401-32 (English origins of his wife).

SEWALL, HENRY, b. 1576, d. Rowley, Mass., March 1657. EB, pp. 507-12; NEHGR 159:35-39 (note on Henry[A]); Samuel[2] at NEQ 55:354-67, 58:598-601, 70:355-67; Judith S. Graham, *Puritan Family Life: The Diary of Samuel Sewall* (Boston, MA: Northeastern University Press, 2000). Reviews: NEQ 74:343-45.

SEWARD, WILLIAM, b. ca. 1627, d. Guilford, Conn., 29 March 1689. Jessup, pp. 783-85.

SEYMOUR, RICHARD, b. 1604/5, d. Norwalk, Conn., between 29 July and 10 October 1655. Goodman, pp. 411-25, including English origins; wife's

Ruscoe ancestry given at Goodman, pp. 387-88; Cooley, pp. 127-56; CN 22:24 (father's will).

SHAPLEIGH, JOHN, b. ca. 1642, d. Kittery, Me., April 1706. MJ 17:136-38; 27:47-52; Brian J.L. Berry, *The Shapleigh, Shapley and Shappley Families: A Comprehensive Genealogy 1635-1993* (Baltimore, MD: Gateway Press, 1993). Reviews: CN 27:415, NEHGR 149:317-18.

SHAPLEY, DAVID, b. ca. 1650, d. Marblehead, Mass., before 30 December 1720. Johnson, pp. 296-99. Brian J.L. Berry, *The Shapleigh, Shapley and Shappley Families: A Comprehensive Genealogy 1635-1993* (Baltimore, MD: Gateway Press, 1993). Reviews: CN 27:415, NEHGR 149:317-18.

SHAPLEY, NICHOLAS, d. Charlestown, Mass., 15 February 1662/3. Brian J.L. Berry, *The Shapleigh, Shapley and Shappley Families: A Comprehensive Genealogy 1635-1993* (Baltimore, MD: Gateway Press, 1993). Reviews: CN 27:415, NEHGR 149:317-18.

SHARP, SAMUEL, b. ca. 1593, d. Salem, Mass., ca. 1656. GMB III:1652-55.

SHATSWELL, JOHN, b. ca. 1600, d. Ipswich, Mass., between 2 February 1646/7 and 30 March 1647. GMB III:1656-58; Davis III:282-87 [Annis Spear]; Jessup, pp. 785-87; NEHGR 150:180-89.

SHATSWELL, THEOPHILUS, b. ca. 1617, d. Haverhill, Mass., 17 August 1663. EB, pp. 512-13; Jessup, pp. 785-87; NEHGR 150:180-89.

SHATTUCK, WILLIAM, b. ca. 1622, d. Watertown, Mass., 14 August 1672. Son John[2] at Sex, pp. 77-78.

SHAW, ABRAHAM, b. 1589/90, d. Dedham, Mass., ca. November/ December 1638. EB, pp. 513-18; English origins at TG 9:86-97; 50Imm, pp. 353-64; son Joseph[2] at TG 9:98-133; MBT #1150; TAG 57:85-87; Fearnot[3] Joseph[2] at NEHGR 134:48-58; John[2]'s wife at TAG 68:23.

SHAW, ANTHONY, d. Little Compton, R.I., 21 August 1705. Chase, pp. 387-89.

SHAW, JOHN, b. ca. 1597, d. Plymouth, Mass., after 30 January 1663/4. GMB III:1659-62; PM, pp. 413-16; NEHGR 151:259-85, 417-37, 152:492 (three generation study).

SHAW, JOHN, d. Boston, Mass., before 23 July 1691. TG 9:98-133.

SHAW, ROGER, b. ca. 1600, d. Hampton, N.H., 29 May 1661. NEHGR 158:309-18, 159:360 (English origins of him and his wife).

SHAW, THOMAS, b. ca. 1625, d. Stonington, Conn., 7 January 1700/1. TG 9:98-133.

SHEAFE, SAMPSON, b.1646, d. Newcastle, N.H., after 6 December 1725. 26Imm, pp. 251-74.

SHED, DANIEL, d. Billerica, Mass., 27 July 1708. Sex, pp. 134-40.

SHEFFIELD, ICHABOD, of Newport, R.I. TAG 80:10 (note on Nathaniel[2]).

SHELDON, ISAAC, b. 1629, d. Northampton, Mass., 29 July 1708. EB, pp. 518-21; Nichols, pp. 197-98; JPG I:713-20.

SHELDON, JOHN, b. ca. 1628, d. Pawtuxet, R.I., 27 September 1708. Johnson, pp. 300-2; AL, pp. 516-19; Keith M. Sheldon, *John Sheldon of Providence (and Records of His Descendants)* (Evansville, IN: Whippoorwill Publications, 1984). Reviews: NEHGR 139:326-29.

SHELLEY, ROBERT, b. ca. 1587, d. Boston or Roxbury, Mass., before 1637. GMB III:1662-63; son Robert[2] at Croll, 156; JPG I:721-26; wife of Robert[2], Judith (Garnett), at GM2 III:26-27.

SHEPARD, EDWARD, b. 1596, d. Cambridge, Mass., before 20 June 1680. Pond, 209, including English origins; servant Robert Shepard at Cameos, pp. 61-65.

SHEPARD, JOHN, b. ca. 1599, d. Braintree, Mass., before 22 September 1650. TAG 68:145 (marriage record); MJ 25:61.

SHEPARD, RALPH, b. ca. 1606, d. Charlestown, Mass., 20 August 1693. 26Imm, pp. 275-82; JPG I:727-31; MBT #736, TAG 67:29 (marriage).

SHEPARD, THOMAS, b. 1605, d. Cambridge, Mass., 28 August 1649. Appears with son Thomas at Sex, pp. 72-73, et al.

SHEPARD, WILLIAM, b. ca. 1624, d. New Haven, Conn., between 11 March and 7 December 1664. Ordway, pp. 365-91; NEHGR 155:215-16 (note).

SHEPARD, WILLIAM, d. Westfield, Conn., after 1677. TAG 70:82-83.

SHEPARDSON, DANIEL, b. ca. 1612, d. Charlestown, Mass., 26 July 1644. GMB III:1663-66.

SHEPLEY, JOHN, b. ca. 1587, d. Chelmsford, Mass., 10 September 1678. Kempton4, pp. 563-66.

SHERBURNE, HENRY, b. 1611, d. Portsmouth, N.H., before June 1681. GMB III:1666-69; Davis III:288-300 [Joseph Waterhouse], including English origins. His daughter Mary's family record at Davis III:305-14.

SHERIFF, THOMAS, b. ca. 1620, d. Providence, R.I., 29 May 1675. Croll, 88.

SHERMAN, JOHN, b. 1612, d. Watertown, Mass., 25 January 1690/1. Thompson, pp. 43-50, 60-62, et al.; TAG 61:79-82; mother Grace (Ravens)'s origins at TAG 62:65-77, 161-70.

SHERMAN, JOHN, b. 1613, d. Watertown, Mass., 8 August 1685. Wife Mary (Launce) at RD600, p. 217, PA, p. 443; MCA, p. 504; Nichols, pp. 71-72; Thompson, pp. 73-80, et al.

SHERMAN, PHILIP, b. 1610/1, d. Portsmouth, R.I., before 19 March 1686/7. GMB III:1670-73; Johnson, pp. 302-3; wife at Johnson, pp. 271-72; AL, pp. 520-27, including English ancestry; RIR 10:2; TAG 73:176-80 (wife's ancestry).

SHERMAN, RICHARD, b. ca. 1577, d. Boston, Mass., 30 May 1660. Mower, pp. 545-51.

SHERMAN, WILLIAM, b. ca. 1613, d. Marshfield, Mass., October 1679. GMB III:1673-75; PM, pp. 416-19.

SHERWOOD, THOMAS, b. ca. 1586, d. Fairfield, Conn., between 21 July and 7 September 1665. TAG 80:278-82 (English origins).

SHORE, SAMPSON, b. ca. 1614, d. Plymouth, Mass., 3 February 1678. B.E. Shorey, *Sampson Shore and his Shorey Descendants* (Camden, ME: Penobscot Press, 1993). Reviews: MG 22:47; Samuel[3] Jonathan[2] at MG 26:99-109.

SHORT, CLEMENT, d. Kittery, Me., 18 March 1689. Daughter Mercy[2] at WRR, pp. 27-31.

SHOVE, GEORGE, b. 1634, d. Taunton, Mass., 21 April 1687. NEHGR 157:338-54 (Seth[2]).

SHURT, ABRAHAM, b. ca. 1584, d. Pemaquid, Me., ca. 1669. MJ 18:132-33.

SHURTLEFF, WILLIAM, b. 1624, d. Marshfield, Mass., 23 June 1666. NEA 5:1:21-22.

SHUTE, RICHARD, b. ca. 1631, d. Boston, Mass., 2 October 1703. Alan H. Shute and Clark H. Flint, *Richard Shute of Boston, Massachusetts 1631-1703 & Selected Progeny* (Bowie, MD: Heritage Books, 1995). Reviews: TAG 71:189-90.

SIBLEY, JOHN, d. Salem, Mass., ca. 1661. 31Imm, pp. 187-93.

Sikes, Richard, b. ca. 1619, d. Springfield, Mass., 16 March 1675/6. Arthur M. Sikes, Jr., *Richard Sikes: And His Descendants, the First Seven Generations* (n.p., Sikes Family Association, 2000). Reviews: CN 26:412-13, 34: 48-49.

Silsbee, Henry, b. ca. 1620, d. Lynn, Mass., between 17 March 1698/9 and 16 December 1700. TEG 8:99-105.

Silver, Thomas, b. ca. 1624, d. Newbury, Mass., 6 September 1682. Davis III:301-4 [Phoebe Tilton]; Stevens, 41; TEG 22:86-99.

Silvester, Richard, b. ca. 1608, d. Marshfield, Mass., between 15 June and 27 September 1663. GMB III: 1677-81; Stone, pp. 233-38; MJ 1:54-55, 7:147-62.

Simmons, Moses, b. ca. 1605, d. Duxbury, Mass., between 17 June 1689 and 10 September 1691. GMB III:1681-83; PM, pp. 419-22; NEA 5:3:54-55; Lyon, pp. 538-41.

Singletary, Richard, b. ca. 1599, d. Haverhill, Mass., 25 October 1687. 26Imm, pp. 283-88; MBT #948; NEA 6:5/6:50-51 (Jonathan[2]).

Sisson, Richard, b. ca. 1608, d. Dartmouth, Mass., between 18 December 1683 and 26 April 1684. Jessup, pp. 802-5; Johnson, pp. 304-5.

Skelton, Samuel, b. 1592/3. d. Salem, Mass., 2 August 1634. GMB III:1684-87; EB, pp. 522-23.

Skepper, William, b. 1597, d. Boston, Mass., before 1646. RD600, pp. 149-53; PA, p. 657; MCA, p. 752; TAG 69:129-39 (royal line).

Skerry, Henry, b. ca. 1606, d. Salem, Mass., 1691. NEHGR 147:146-47 (wife identified).

Skidmore, Thomas, b. ca. 1605, d. Fairfield, Conn., ca. 31 October 1684. Warren Skidmore, *Thomas Skidmore (Scudamore), 1605-1684, of Westerleigh, Gloucestershire, and Fairfield, Connecticut; His Ancestors and His Descendants to the Ninth Generation* (n.p., the author, 1980). Reviews: TAG 57:121, NYGBR 112:55, 117:178, NGSQ 69:142.

Skinner, John, d. Windsor, Conn., before 23 October 1651. TAG 74:97-100.

Skinner, Thomas, b. ca. 1644, d. Boston, Mass., 28 December 1690. His children by his second wife Elizabeth (Maverick) at MF17, three generations all lines.

Skipper see Skepper

SLADE, WILLIAM, b. ca. 1638, d. R.I., after 12 October 1682. AL, pp. 527-92.

SLATER, JOHN, fl. Concord, Mass., 1650s. Sex, pp. 180-82, et al.

SLOCUM, ANTHONY, b. ca. 1590, of Taunton, Mass., d. North Carolina between 26 November 1688 and 7 January 1689/90. NEA 4:4:49-50 (DNA Study).

SLOCUM, GILES, of Portsmouth, R.I., d. there between 10 October 1681 and 12 March 1683. NEA 4:4:49-50 (DNA Study); Giles[2] at RIR 19:13-24; Giles[3] Ebenezer[2]'s wife Mary (Manchester)'s parentage identified at RIR 17:7-8, 23:50; MJ 18:133-35.

SLOPER, RICHARD, d. 16 October 1716, Portsmouth, N.H. His wife Mary (Sherburne)'s family record at Davis III:305-14 [Joseph Waterhouse].

SMALL SEE SMALLEY

SMALLEY, EDWARD, d. Saco, Me., after June 1655. TAG 71:137-44 (Daniel[3] Francis[2]'s wife identified); MJ 19:147-48.

SMALLEY, JOHN, b. ca. 1613, of Plymouth and Eastham, Mass., d. Piscataway, N.J., 30 July 1692. GMB III:1687-89; PM, pp. 422-24.

SMEDLEY, BAPTISTE, b. 1609, d. Concord, Mass., between 7 August and 27 October 1675. 50Imm, pp. 365-70; MBT #738; clues to origins at TAG 56:97-98; NEHGR 139:61-62 (English origins).

SMITH SEE ALSO BLAND

SMITH, CHRISTOPHER, b. ca. 1600, d. Providence, R.I., June 1676. Angell, pp. 467-79.

SMITH, CHRISTOPHER, d. Dedham, Mass., 7 November 1676. CN 36:559-75 (John[2]).

SMITH, GILES, b. ca. 1603, d. Fairfield, Conn., 1 December 1669. Johnson, pp. 305-6.

SMITH, HENRY, b. ca. 1610, of Dorchester and Springfield, Mass., d. in England between 1 August 1681 and 24 October 1682. GMB III:1691-92.

SMITH, HENRY, b. ca. 1619, d. Stamford ca. 5 July 1687. CA 45:3-20, 62-84, 128-46, 155-76.

SMITH, HENRY, d. Rehoboth, Mass., 1649. Lyon, pp. 541-42; AL, p. 596.

SMITH, JAMES, b. ca. 1590, d. Marblehead, Mass., between 9 October 1660 and 27 June 1661. TEG 17:209-14.

SMITH, JAMES, d. Durham, N.H., 6 July 1690. Croll, 200.

SMITH, JOHN, b. ca. 1600, d. Lancaster, Mass., 16 July 1669. Angell, pp. 481-500; TAG 57:232-42; TAG 61:18-31.

SMITH, JOHN, b. ca. 1609, d. New London, Conn., ca. 1680. Wife Joanna at Doctors, pp. 83.

SMITH, JOHN, b. ca. 1618, d. Dorchester, Mass., 29 April 1678. Mower, pp. 553-57; Lyon, pp. 542-45.

SMITH, JOHN, b. ca. 1618, d. Dartmouth, Mass., 15 January 1691/2. AL, pp. 595-96.

SMITH, JOHN, b. ca. 1670, d. Worcester, Mass., after 19 April 1737. TAG 57:242-46.

SMITH, JOHN, d. Boston, Mass., before 13 June 1674. EB, pp. 523-24.

SMITH, JOHN, d. Martha's Vineyard, Mass., after 14 February 1670. TAG 61:18-31.

SMITH, JOHN, d. Middleborough, Mass., before 3 July 1727. TAG 61:7-10.

SMITH, JOHN, d. Salem, Mass., 1680. Davis III:315-22 [Sarah Johnson]. His wife Margaret (Thompson)'s ancestry at Davis III:405 [Sarah Johnson]; her Ward ancestry given at Davis III:405-8 [Sarah Johnson]; RD600, pp. 450-51.

SMITH, JOHN, d. Sandwich, Mass., ca. 1710. TAG 61:2-6.

SMITH, JOHN, d. Watertown, Mass., after 28 February 1636. Mower, pp. 559-68.

SMITH, JOSEPH, b. ca. 1630, d. Hartford, Conn., 17 January 1690. JPG I:732-36; CN 22:43, 217.

SMITH, NEHEMIAH, b. ca. 1605, d. Norwich, Conn., ca. 1686. Spooner; Johnson, pp. 306-8.

SMITH, RALPH, b. ca. 1616, d. Eastham, Mass., 14 September 1685. GMB III:1697-99; son Samuel[2], MF6, three generations all lines.

SMITH, RICHARD, b. ca. 1583, d. after 1669, prob. at Wethersfield, Conn. Cooley, pp. 193-209; Pond, 254; TAG 64:226-32; NEHGR 143:240-46 (English origins); NEHGR 158:33-39 (English origins of his wife).

SMITH, RICHARD, b. ca. 1596, d. Wickford, R.I., 1666. Johnson, pp. 308-10.

SMITH, ROBERT, b. ca. 1611, d. Hampton, N.H., 30 August 1706. Stevens, 37; TAG 73:258-71 (Israel[3] John[2]).

SMITH, ROBERT, d. Rowley, Mass., between 7 August and 26 September 1693. Davis III:323-40 [Amos Towne]; 50Imm, pp. 371-76; MBT #320.

SMITH, SAMUEL, b. ca. 1575, d. Salem, Mass., between 5 October and 27 December 1642. 50Imm, pp. 377-84.

SMITH, SAMUEL, b. ca. 1602, d. Hadley, Mass., between 23 June 1680 and 17 January 1681. Johnson, pp. 311-13; son Philip[2] at NEA 4:5/6:35-37.

SMITH, SAMUEL, d. Taunton, Mass., after July 1675. EB, pp. 524-25.

SMITH, SIMON, b. ca. 1628, d. Haddam, Conn., 1668. Johnson, p. 313.

SMITH, THOMAS, b. ca. 1601, d. Watertown, Mass., 10 March 1692/3. Kempton, pp. 425-42.

SMITH, THOMAS, b. ca. 1638, d. Charlestown, Mass., 14 February 1689/90. Goodman, 427-32.

SMITH, THOMAS, d. Bradford, Mass., winter 1681/2. 50Imm, pp. 385-90; MBT #834; NEHGR 142:41-55; TAG 79:274-77.

SMITH, WILLIAM, b. ca. 1632, d. Topsfield, Mass., before 1 March 1691/2. 50Imm, pp. 391-96; MBT #326.

SMITON, WILLIAM, d. Portsmouth, R.I., between 13 June and 6 July 1671. AL, pp. 596-97.

SNELL, GEORGE, d. Portsmouth, N.H., between 9 May 1706 and March 1707/8. EB, pp. 525-27.

SNELLING, JOHN, b. 1624/5, d. Boston, Mass., November 1672. RD600, p. 335.

SNOW, ANTHONY, d. Marshfield, Mass., between 8 and 31 August 1692. MF18, four generations all lines.

SNOW, NICHOLAS, b. ca. 1599, d. Eastham, Mass., 15 November 1676. MF6, four generations all lines; GMB III:1701-4; PM, pp. 428-32; EB, pp. 527-30; Brewer, pp. 487-88.

SNOW, RICHARD, b. ca. 1597, d. Woburn, Mass., 5 May 1677. Kempton3, pp. 329-38.

SNOW, THOMAS, d. Boston, Mass., ca. 1668/9. Pond, 222.

SNOW, WILLIAM, b. ca. 1617, d. Bridgewater, Mass., 31 January 1708. MF7, four generations, all lines.

SOLART, JOHN, d. Wenham, Mass., 29 June 1672. Lyon, pp. 545-48; LENE, pp. 69-70 (Sarah[2]).

SOMERBY, HENRY, b. ca. 1612, d. Newbury, Mass., 2 October 1652. Mower, pp. 571-75.

SOMES, MORRIS, b. ca. 1603, d. Gloucester, Mass., 13 January 1688/9. MBT #936.

SOULE, GEORGE, *Mayflower* passenger, b. ca. 1600, d. Duxbury, Mass., before 22 January 1678/9. Soule, five to six generations all lines; GMB III:1704-8; PM, pp. 432-36; Nathaniel[2] at TAG 57:193-203.

SOUTHWICK, LAWRENCE, of Salem, Mass. Son John[2] at TG 12:223-31 and TG 16:40-41; TAG 71:193-97 (English origins of him and his wife).

SOUTHWORTH, CONSTANT, b. ca. 1612, d. Duxbury, Mass., 11 March 1678/9. GMB III:1709-12; PM, pp 437-40; RD600, pp. 308-9; NEA 5:1:22; sons William[2] and Edward[2] in MF16 for three generations all lines; Spooner.

SOUTHWORTH, THOMAS, b. ca. 1617, d. Plymouth, Mass., 8 December 1669. GMB III:1712-15; PM, pp. 440-43; RD600, pp. 308-9.

SPALDING, EDWARD, d. Chelmsford, Mass., 26 February 1669/70. MBT #752.

SPARROW, RICHARD, b. ca. 1605, d. Eastham, Mass., 8 January 1660/1. GMB III:1715-18; PM, pp. 443-47; Croll, 171.

SPEAR, GEORGE, b. ca. 1613, of Braintree, Mass., d. Pemaquid, Me., after 1680. Davis, III:341-67 [Annis Spear]; EB, pp. 530-35; Verne Raymond Spear, *The Descendants of George Spear Who Settled at Braintree, Massachusetts 1642-1988* (West Springfield, MA: The Trade Press, 1988), a multigenerational study of this family. Reviews: CN 21:706.

SPENCER, GEORGE, d. New Haven, Conn., 8 April 1642. LENE, p. 9.

SPENCER, GERARD, b. 1614, d. Haddam, Conn., between 17 September 1683 and 29 June 1685. CN 29:592-615.

SPENCER, THOMAS, b. 1607, d. Hartford, Conn., 11 September 1687. GMB III:1718-21; CN 29:14-27.

SPENCER, WILLIAM, b. 1601, d. Hartford, Conn., ca. May 1640. GMB III:1721-25; Lyon, pp. 548-50; CN 27:32-37; wife Agnes (Harris) at RD600, pp. 548-50; MCA, p. 416; her origins at TAG 63:33-45; MJ 17:78-81 (wife Agnes).

SPERRY, RICHARD, b. ca. 1606, d. New Haven, Conn., 1698. Spooner; Johnson, pp. 314-18.

SPINK, ROBERT, b. ca. 1615, d. Kingstown, R.I., between 2 December 1685 and 27 March 1695. Johnson, pp. 318-22; JPG II:310-15; TAG 78:214-21 (Nicholas[2]).

SPOFFORD, JOHN, b. 1611, d. Rowley, Mass., between 7 October and 6 November 1678. 50Imm, pp. 397-424; MBT #418; two descendants of Mary (Spofford) Wood distinguished at TAG 57:149-50.

SPOONER, WILLIAM, b. ca. 1630, d. Plymouth or Dartmouth, Mass., 1684. Spooner (descendant Judah Paddock[5] Thomas[4] John[3-2] treated extensively with descendants). Also single line descent from William to Judah; Jessup, pp. 811-17.

SPRAGUE, FRANCIS, b. ca. 1590, d. Duxbury, Mass., between 1670 and 2 March 1679/80. GMB III:1725-28; PM, pp. 447-50.

SPRAGUE, RALPH, b. ca. 1595, d. Malden, Mass., November 1650. GMB III:1728-31; Goodman, pp. 435-45, including English origins; son Samuel[2] married Rebecca Crawford, for whom see GM2 II:230-31; Mower, pp. 577-92; MJ 17:141-43.

SPRAGUE, WILLIAM, b. ca. 1611, d. Hingham, Mass., 26 October 1675. GMB III:1735-39; JPG II:502-16; AL, pp. 598-600, including English ancestry.

SPRING, JOHN, b. ca. 1589, d. Watertown, Mass., after 21 March 1656/7. Son Henry[2] at Thompson, pp. 196-97, et al.; family at Sex, pp. 77-78, et al.

SPROUT, ROBERT, d. Middleborough, Mass., between 23 November and 11 December 1712. MF20, four generations all lines; TAG 61:200-6; NEHGR 141:203-14 (Ebenezer[2]).

STAINWOOD, PHILIP, d. Gloucester, Mass., 7 August 1672. MBT #938.

STANCLIFT, JAMES, b. ca. 1639, d. East Middletown, Conn., 2 or 3 October 1712. Sherry Smith and Robert C. Stancliff, *The Descendants of James Stanclift of Middletown, Connecticut and Allied Families* (Cincinnati, OH: S.S. Research, 1995). Reviews: CN 29:233, NEHGR 152:497-98.

STANDISH, MYLES, *Mayflower* passenger, b. ca. 1584, d. Duxbury, Mass., 3 October 1656. MF14, five generations all lines; GMB III:1741-47; PM, pp. 451-57; MQ 50:179, MQ 52:109-14; MQ 66:207-9.

STANDISH, THOMAS, b. ca. 1612, d. Wethersfield, Conn., 5 December 1692. Lyon, pp. 550-52.

STANFORD, THOMAS, d. Falmouth, Me., before January 1683/4. TAG 73:223-27 (clues to English origins).

STANHOUSE, JAMES, mariner, fl. Charlestown 1680s. Sex, pp. 151-52.

STANLEY, JOHN, b. 1598, d. at sea shortly before 3 March 1634/5. TAG 80:217-23 (correct English origins); TAG 80:223 (note on John[2]'s second marriage).

STANLEY, THOMAS, b. 1601, d. Hadley, Mass., January 1663/4. TAG 80:217-23 (correct English origins).

STANLEY, TIMOTHY, b. 1604, d. Hartford, Conn., before 16 October 1648. TAG 80:217-23 (correct English origins).

STANYAN, ANTHONY, b. ca. 1611, d. Hampton, N.H., before 21 February 1688/9. 50Imm, pp. 425-32; MBT #920.

STAPLES, JEFFREY, b. ca. 1594, d. Weymouth, Mass., March 1647. Jessup, pp. 820-29.

STARR, COMFORT, d. Boston, Mass., 2 January 1659/60. Lyon, pp. 553-58.

STEARNS, ISAAC, b. ca. 1600, d. Watertown, Mass., 19 June 1671. GMB III:1747-50; son Samuel[2] at Cameos, pp. 117-21; 50Imm, pp. 433-50; JPG I:737-48; Mower, pp. 595-601; Lyon, pp. 558-62; MBT #800.

STEBBINS, EDWARD, b. 1594/5, d. Hartford, Conn., between 8 October 1663 and 19 August 1668. GMB III:1750-53.

STEBBINS, ROWLAND, b. 1592, d. Northampton, Mass., 14 December 1671. Samuel[3] John[2] at TAG 80:265-77.

STEDMAN, ISAAC, b. 1605, d. Boston, Mass., 3 October 1678. TAG 69:155-59 (English origins); TAG 71:856 (Nathaniel[2]); TAG 80:24-25 (marriage).

STEELE, GEORGE, b. ca. 1583, d. Hartford, Conn., between 24 May 1663 and 21 December 1664. GMB III:1754-56; Goodman, pp. 447-53, including English origins.

STEELE, JOHN, b. 1591, d. Farmington, Conn., 27 February 1664/5. GMB III:1756-59; Edward Eugene Steele, *A Steele Family History: Planters of Old England, New England, and the American West* (St. Louis, MO: Creative Imaging, 2001). Reviews: TAG 77:80, CN 35:228-29.

STEEVENS, JOHN, b. ca. 1600, d. Guilford, Conn., between 27 August and 2 September 1670. EB, pp. 539-44.

STEPHENS, THOMAS, b. ca. 1621, of Taunton, Mass., Jessup, pp. 829-30.

STEPHENSON, JOHN, b. ca. 1690, d. Cohasset, Mass., 9 April 1773. Stone, pp. 239-43.

STETSON, ROBERT, b. 1615, d. Duxbury, Mass., 1 February 1702/3. EB, pp. 535-39; NEHGR 151:438-41; MJ 17:143-44, 26:57-58.

STEVENS SEE ALSO STEEVENS AND STEPHENS

STEVENS, HENRY, b. ca. 1644, d. Stonington, Conn., ca. 1726. EB, pp. 544-53.

STEVENS, JOHN, b. ca. 1605, d. Andover, Mass., 11 April 1662. TEG 24:35-44, 54, 83-103.

STEVENS, JOHN, b. ca. 1611, d. Salisbury, Mass., February 1688/9. Stone, pp. 245-46.

STEVENS, WILLIAM, d. Gloucester, Mass., after 1667. Stevens, 70.

STEVENSON SEE ALSO SCOTT

STEVENSON, ANDREW, b. ca. 1612, d. Cambridge, Mass., ca. 1681. Son Andrew[2] at Cameos, pp. 129-34.

STEVENSON, MARMADUKE, d. Boston, Mass., 22 October 1659. LENE. pp. 29-32.

STEWART, JOHN, b. ca. 1690, d. Blandford, Mass., July 1747. Ronald L. Stewart, *John Stewart of Blandford, Massachusetts and His Descendants* (Albuquerque, NM: the author, 2004). Reviews: NYGBR 136:226 (1993 edition).

STICKNEY, WILLIAM, d. Rowley, Mass., January 1664. NEHGR 139:319-21 (English origins).

STILEMAN, ELIAS, b. 1587, d. Salem, Mass., before 30 September 1662. GMB III:1759-62.

STILES, FRANCIS, of Windsor, Conn., d. Stratford, Conn., before 1665. CN 13:380-83 (English origins).

STINNINGS, RICHARD, d. Plymouth, Mass., 4 September 1638, LENE, p. 7.

STOCKBRIDGE, JOHN, b. ca. 1607, d. Boston, Mass., 13 October 1657. JPG II:517-25; Stowers, pp. 445-48; NEHGR 133:93-101, 187-93, 286-93, 134:70-73, 135-47, 228-36, 291-98, 135:36-44, 121-32, 139:316-18 (five generation study); NGSQ 74:111-18 (English origins).

STOCKER, THOMAS, b. ca. 1620, d. Chelsea, Mass., after 28 May 1698. TEG 10:155-60, 208-12, 11:35-43.

STOCKMAN, JOHN, b. 1645, d. Salisbury, Mass., 10 December 1686. RD600, pp. 282-84; PA, p. 687; MCA, p. 782; Katharine Dickson, *The Stockman Story: The English Ancestry of Mr. John Stockman of Salisbury, Massachusetts* (Henniker, NH: Katharine Brown, 1992). Reviews: CN 25:604-5.

STOCKWELL, QUENTIN, b. ca. 1640, d. Suffield, Conn., 22 January 1713/4. Puritans, pp. 79-89; Irene Dixon Stockwell, *The Stockwell Family: Adventures into the Past 1626-1982* (Janesville, WI: Janesville Printing Co., 1982). Reviews: CN16:151-52.

STODDARD SEE ALSO DOWNING

STODDARD, ANTHONY, d. Boston, Mass., 16 March 1687. JPG I:749-61; Ralph J. Coffman, *Solomon Stoddard* (Boston, MA: Twayne Publishers, 1978). Reviews: NEQ 53:424-26 (Solomon^2).

STODDARD, JOHN, d. Hartford, Conn., 9 October 1678. LENE, p. 53-54.

STODDARD, JOHN, d. Hingham, Mass., 19 December 1661. Stone, pp. 247-51.

STONE SEE ALSO CUTTING

STONE, GREGORY, b. 1592, d. Cambridge, Mass., 30 November 1672. Stone, pp. 1-36, including English ancestry; TAG 71:86. For the relationship of the Stone, Cutting, Kimball, and Lovering families of Watertown, see Kempton, p. 449; 50Imm, pp. 451-62; MBT #1084.

STONE, HUGH, d. Boston, Mass., 2 January 1690. LENE, p. 60.

STONE, JOHN, d. Salem, Mass., between 1667 and 1677. Davis III:377-98 [Sarah Stone].

STONE, SAMUEL, b. 1602, d. Hartford, Conn., 20 July 1663. GMB III:1768-73; Goodman, pp. 455-62, including English origins; Nichols, pp. 149-52.

STONE, SIMON, b. 1585/6, d. Watertown, Mass., 22 September 1665. Lyon, pp. 562-66.

STONE, WILLIAM, b. ca. 1608, d. Guilford, Conn., 16 November 1683. Edward Perry Stone, Sr., *The Family of William Stone, One of the First Settlers of Guilford, Connecticut* (Baltimore, MD: Gateway Press, 1980). Reviews: CN 13:522, TAG 57:184-85, NYGBR 111:244.

STORY, WILLIAM, b. ca. 1614, d. Ipswich, Mass., January 1702/3. Robert L. Pratt, *The Descendants of William Story Who Came to Ipswich, Massachusetts in 1637: The First Eight Generations* (Baltimore, MD: Gateway Press, 2000). Reviews: VG 5:184, NEHGR 154:502-3.

STOUGHTON, ISRAEL, b. 1602/3, of Dorchester, Mass., d. in England 1644. GMB III:1773-77; Foundations 1:1:46-50 (correction to English ancestry).

STOUGHTON, THOMAS, b. 1592/3, d. Windsor, Mass., 25 March 1661. GMB III:1777-79; Nichols, including English ancestry, various pages; Foundations 1:1:46-50 (correction to English ancestry); MJ 1:55-56, 73-74, 3:45-46, 7:163-72, 11:94-97, 26:101-4.

STOVER, GEORGE, b. ca. 1670, d. York, Me., before 2 April 1753. Brewer, pp. 491-92.

STOW, JOHN, b. 1582/3, d. Roxbury, Mass., 26 October 1648. Kempton3, pp. 341-67, including English origins; JPG I:762-75; MBT #1080.

STOWELL, SAMUEL, d. Hingham, Mass., 9 November 1683. Stone, pp. 253-55.

STOWERS, NICHOLAS, b. ca. 1585, d. Charlestown, Mass., 17 May 1646. GMB III:1779-82; Stowers, pp. 19-52; son John[2] at Thompson, pp. 69-70, et al.; son Richard[2] and wife Hannah at Sex, pp. 132-33: MJ 18:135-36, 27:52-63.

STRANGE, JOHN, b. 1619, d. Portsmouth, R.I., after 15 October 1687. AL, pp. 600-1, including English origins; TAG 56:148-50 (English origins).

STRATTON, JOHN, b. ca. 1585, d. England, 1627. His widow Anne (Derehaugh) immigrated to Salem, Mass. Her royal line at RD600, pp. 397-98; PA, pp. 266-67; MCA, p. 275. His royal line at RD600, pp. 528-29; son John[2] at GMB III:1782-85; NEHGR 155:367-90, 156:39-61, 156:390, 157:394 (Anne Derehaugh's English ancestry).

STRATTON, SAMUEL, b. ca. 1592, d. Watertown, Mass., 25 December 1672. TAG 65:200-2 (English origins); TAG 68:84-86 (English ancestry).

STRAW, WILLIAM, d. Amesbury, Mass., between 23 May 1709 and 2 October 1712. 50Imm, pp. 463-64; MBT #452.

STREET, NICHOLAS, b. 1603, d. New Haven, Conn., 22 April 1674. MJ 17:145, 25:61-64, 26:58-59.

STRICKLAND, JOHN, b. ca. 1595, of Charlestown, Mass., then Wethersfield and Fairfield, Conn., d. Jamaica, N.Y., between 5 September and 13 December 1672. GMB III:1785-87.

STRICKLAND, PETER, b. ca. 1646, d. New London, Conn., between 23 February 1718/9 and 7 April 1723. Angell, pp. 503-13.

STRONG, JOHN, d. Northampton, Mass., 14 April 1699. MJ 1:56-59, 74-75, 2:98-99, 3:47-48, 8:1-138, 11:80-82, 12:32-33, 15:36-47, 17:146-50, 25:64-65, 26:59-60, 27:63, 102-16.

STROUT, CHRISTOPHER, b. ca. 1655, d. Truro, Mass., between October 1712 and 9 July 1714. Brewer, pp. 493-512.

STUART, DUNCAN, b. ca. 1623, d. Rowley, Mass., 30 August 1717. 50Imm, pp. 465-66; Johnson, pp. 322-24.

STUBBS, RICHARD, b. ca. 1619, d. Hull, Mass., between 22 May and 2 June 1677. NEHGR 143:332-37; Marjorie Anne Stubbs Heaney, *The Descendants of Richard Stubbs, 1619-1677 of Hull, Mass.* (Deleon Springs, FL: E.O. Painter Printing, 1984). Reviews: TAG 60:187.

STURGIS, EDWARD, d. Yarmouth, Mass., before 12 October 1695. Son Edward[2] in Howland1, four generations all lines.

STURTEVANT, SAMUEL, b. ca. 1622, d. Plymouth, Mass., before 29 October 1669. EB, pp. 553-55; Robert Hunter Sturtevant, *Descendants of Samuel Sturtevant* (Waco, TX: the author, 1986). Reviews: MG 12:50.

SUMMERS, JOHN, d. Rochester, Mass., between 10 October 1721 and 25 April 1722. Jessup, pp. 833-36.

SUMNER, WILLIAM, b. 1604/5, d. Dorchester, Mass., 9 December 1688. Chase, pp. 391-99, including English origins; EB, pp. 555-64.

SUNDERLAND, JOHN, b. ca. 1618, d. Eastham, Mass., 26 Dec 1703. TAG 78:256-64 (daughter Hannah).

SUTTON, JOHN, b. ca. 1605, d. Rehoboth, Mass., 1 June 1672. 31Imm, pp. 194-200.

SWAINE, RICHARD, b. 1595, d. Nantucket, Mass., 14 April 1682. TAG 74:241-49 (English origins).

SWAN, JOHN, b. ca. 1620, d. Cambridge, Mass., 5 June 1708. MF8, three generations all lines.

SWARTON, JOHN, d. North Yarmouth, Me., 1689. Wife Hannah/Joanna at Puritans, pp. 147-57.

SWAYN, DICK, fl. Boston, Mass., 1699. WRR, pp. 54-64.

SWEET, JOHN, b. ca. 1603, d. Salem, Mass., between 6 June and 25 December 1637. GMB III:1789-90; Johnson, pp. 324-27; TAG 67:177-83 (James[3] John[2]).

SWIFT, WILLIAM, b. ca. 1596, d. Sandwich, Mass., before 29 January 1642/3. Makepeace, pp. 219-35; Crosby II:386-93; TAG 77:161-72 (English origins).

SYMMES, ZECHARIAH, b. 1599, d. Charlestown, Mass., 4 February 1670/1. 26Imm, pp. 289-306; MBT #1118.

SYMONDS, JOHN, d. Salem, Mass., between 16 August and 19 September 1671. Davis III:399-401 [Dudley Wildes].

SYMONDS, MARK, b. ca. 1584, d. Ipswich, Mass., April 1659. Johnson, pp. 327-28; TAG 74:114-16 (probable English origins).

SYMONDS, SAMUEL, b. 1595, d. Boston, Mass., between 2 and 7 October 1678. TAG 70:65-74, 149-55 (additions to English ancestry).

SYMONDS, WILLIAM, b. ca. 1611, d. Woburn, Mass., 7 June 1672. MBT #442; NEHGR 148:239 (Benjamin[2]'s wife).

TABOR, PHILIP, b. ca. 1605, d. Providence, R.I., between 24 February 1671/2 and 27 April 1682. GMB III:1791-94; Jessup, pp. 836-62; Johnson, pp. 328-29; TAG 72:329-32 (Joseph[2]).

TAFT, ROBERT, d. Mendon, Mass., 8 February 1725. JPG I:776-82; son Benjamin[2] at NEXUS 13:196-99.

TAINTOR, JOSEPH, b. ca. 1613, d. Watertown, Mass., 20 February 1689/90. Thompson, pp. 44-46, et al.

TALBOT, JARED, b. ca. 1640, d. Dighton, Mass., 17 September 1686. NECL, pp. 121-73; AL, pp. 603-8.

TALBOT, PETER, of Dorchester, Mass. RD600, pp. 544-45.

TALBY, JOHN, d. Salem, Mass., before 1644. TAG 78:1-8; wife Dorothy d. 10 December 1638. LENE, pp. 7-8; TAG 78:256-64 (Stephen[2]).

TALCOTT, JOHN, b. ca. 1594, d. Hartford, Conn., March 1660. GMB III:1794-97; Goodman, pp. 465-80, including English origins. Wife's Mott ancestry given at Goodman, pp. 337-40; NEHGR 148:240-58 (second wife Mary's ancestry).

TALLMAN, PETER, b. 1623, d. R.I., ca. 1708. AL, pp. 608-13, with English ancestry.

TALMAGE, THOMAS, b. ca. 1580, of Lynn, Mass., d. Easthampton, N.Y., before 9 December 1653. GMB III:1798-1800.

TAPP, EDMUND, b. ca. 1592, d. New Haven, Conn., before 1 April 1653. Nichols, p. 112; TAG 72:65-80, 73:65-73 (English origins).

TAPPAN, ABRAHAM, b. ca. 1606, d. Newbury, Mass., 5 November 1672. TW, pp. 329-36.

TAPPIN, JAMES, d. Middletown, Conn., 6 August 1712. Jessup, pp. 868-70.

TAPRILL, ROBERT, d. Portsmouth, N.H., November 1678. Davis III:402-4 [Lydia Harmon].

TARBELL, THOMAS, d. Charlestown, Mass., 11 June 1678. MBT #412.

TARBOX, JOHN, b. ca. 1618, d. Lynn, Mass., 26 May 1674. TEG 20:132-43.

TARR, RICHARD, of Rockport, Mass. Son Samuel[2] at TG 16:131-50.

TATMAN, JOHN, b. ca. 1615, d. Roxbury, Mass., 28 October 1670. GMB III:1800-2.

TAY, WILLIAM, b. ca. 1608, d. Boston, Mass., before 12 April 1683. JPG I:783-87; MBT #444.

TAYLOR, EDWARD, b. ca. 1640, d. Yarmouth, Mass., 1705. NGSQ 74:175-88 (descendants of Jacob[2]).

TAYLOR, EDWARD, b. ca. 1642, d. Westfield, Mass., 24 June 1729. Thomas M. and Virginia L. Davis, eds., *The Unpublished Writings of Edward Taylor* (3 vols., Boston, MA: Twayne Publishers, 1981). Reviews: NEQ 55:120-23; Karen E. Rowe, *Saint and Singer: Edward Taylor's Typology and the Poetics of Meditation* (Cambridge, England: Cambridge University Press, 1986). Reviews: NEQ 61:139-44.

TAYLOR, JAMES, b. 1647, d. Lynn, Mass., 30 July 1716. RD600, pp. 403-4; PA, p. 708; MCA, pp. 813-14.

TAYLOR, JASPER, of Barnstable, Mass. TAG 75:94-98 (Seth[2]).

TAYLOR, ROBERT, b. ca. 1620, d. Newport, R.I., 13 January 1688. Earl P. Crandall, *Five Families of Charlestown, R.I.* (Salem, MA: Higginson Book Co., 1993). Reviews: RIR 19:100-1.

TAYLOR, WILLIAM, b. ca. 1618, d. Concord, Mass., 6 December 1696. Makepeace, pp. 237-47.

TAYLOR, WILLIAM, b. ca. 1620, d. Wethersfield, Conn., after February 1686/7. TAG 76:174-84.

TEFFT SEE TIFT

TENNEY, THOMAS, b. 1615, d. Bradford, Mass., 20 February 1699/1700. Johnson, pp. 329-30; NEHGR 151:329-41 (English origins).

TENNEY, WILLIAM, b. 1616, d. Rowley, Mass., 5 August 1685. NEHGR 151:329-41 (English origins).

TERRY, STEPHEN, b. 1608, d. Hadley, Mass., September 1668. GMB III:1804-7; Goodman, pp. 483-91, including English origins; Lyon, pp. 567-68; MJ 1:59, 75, 2:99, 3:49-51, 9:1-24, 17:150-56.

TEWELLS SEE TUELLS

THACHER, ANTHONY, d. Yarmouth, Mass., before 30 October 1667. Son John[2] in Howland1, four generations all lines; wife's origins at TAG 58:244-46.

THATCHER, SAMUEL, d. Watertown, Mass., 30 November 1669. Thompson, pp. 187-89, et al.

THAXTER, THOMAS, d. Hingham, Mass., 14 February 1654. Pond, 256.

THAYER, RICHARD, b. 1601, d. Barbados between 6 and 12 October 1664. Stone, pp. 257-69, including English origins; TAG 73:81-90, 209-19.

THAYER, THOMAS, b. 1596, d. Braintree, Mass., 4 April 1665. Kempton3, pp. 369-93, including English origins; 31Imm, pp. 201-8; Pond, 213; JPG II:526-36; TAG 73:81-90, 209-19.

THOMAS, JOHN, b. ca. 1640, d. North Kingstown, R.I., 1728. Johnson, p. 331.

THOMAS, WILLIAM, d. Newport, R.I., 9 June 1671. LENE, p. 45.

THOMPSON SEE ALSO TOMSON

THOMPSON, ALEXANDER, b. ca. 1627, d. Ipswich, Mass., 17 December 1695. 50Imm, pp. 471-76.

THOMPSON, DAVID, b. 1592, d. Thomson's Island, Boston, Mass., ca. 1628. NHGR 9:110-16; GMB III:1807-9; Pond, 217; MJ 19:149-51.

THOMPSON, JAMES, b. ca. 1593, d. Woburn, Mass., between 28 February 1681/2 and 22 September 1682. GMB III:1809-11; Brewer, pp. 513-15; TAG 74:101-4 (English origins).

THOMPSON, JOHN, b. ca. 1610, d. East Haven, Conn., 1655. Johnson, pp. 331-32.

THOMPSON, WILLIAM, b. ca. 1597, d. Braintree, Mass., 10 December 1666. NEHGR 140:3-15.

THORLEY, RICHARD, d. Rowley, Mass., 10 November 1685. 50Imm, pp. 477-78; MBT #1710.

THORNDIKE, JOHN, b. 1611, of Ipswich and Salem, Mass., d. London, England, November 1668. GMB III:1811-14; Lyon, pp. 568-75; NEHGR 154:459-76 (English origins); Scott C. Steward and John Bradley Arthaud, *A Thorndike Family History: Descendants of John and Elizabeth (Stratton) Thorndike* (Boston, MA: Newbury Street Press, 2000). Reviews: TAG 79:158-59, NGSQ 91:151-52.

THORNTON, THOMAS, b. ca. 1608, d. Boston, Mass., 15 February 1699/1700. GMB III:1814-17; NEHGR 149:401-32 (English origins of wife).

THROCKMORTON, JOHN, b. 1601, of Providence, R.I., d. Middletown, N.J., 1687. RD600, pp. 296-97, PA, p. 712; MCA, p. 821; notable descendants at NEXUS 11:140-45; AK, pp. 81-85; TAG 77:110-24, 229-34, 290-97 (English ancestry of his wife).

THROOP, WILLIAM, b. ca. 1637, d. Bristol, R.I., 4 December 1704. 31Imm, pp. 209-19; TAG 57:110-12; TAG 62:53-54 (proposed English origins); TAG 62:55-56 (William[2]).

THURSTON, EDWARD, b. ca. 1618, d. Newport, R.I., 1 March 1707. AL, pp. 619-20.

THURSTON, JOHN, b. 1610/11, d. Medfield, Mass., 1 November 1685. Kempton3, pp. 395-423, including English origins; JPG I:788-91.

TIBBETTS, HENRY, b. ca. 1596, d. Dover, N.H., 1676. Jessup, pp. 877-86.

TICHENOR, MARTIN, of New Haven, Conn., d. Newark, N.J., ca. 1672. Harold A. Tichenor, *Tichenor Families in America* (Napton, MO: the author, 1988). Reviews: CN 21:705; NYGBR 120:54.

TIDD, JOHN, b. ca. 1595, d. Woburn, Mass., before 24 April 1656. Nichols, pp. 23-24; Johnson, pp. 332-33; Mower, pp. 603-9.

TIFFANY, HUMPHREY, b. 1630, d. Swansea/Boston, Mass., 15 July 1685. NEA 5:1:22; NEHGR 153:453-65.

TIFT, JOHN, b. ca. 1620, d. Kingstown, R.I., before 26 January 1676. AL, pp. 616-19; son Joshua[2] at LENE, p. 49-50; NEA 6:2:25-29; RIR 18:76-80.

TILDEN, NATHANIEL, b. 1583, d. Scituate, Mass., 1641. Davis III:409-37 [Joseph Neal], including English origins; Johnson, pp. 334-36; Lyon, pp. 575-81.

TILESTON, THOMAS, b. ca. 1611, d. Dorchester, Mass., 24 June 1694. Johnson, pp. 336-37.

TILLEY, HUGH, b. ca. 1613, d. Yarmouth, Mass., 28 January 1647/8. GMB III:1820-22.

TILLEY, JOHN, d. Saybrook, Conn., 1636. CN 28:387-89.

TILLEY, JOHN, *Mayflower* passenger. Daughter Elizabeth married John Howland—see Howland entry for descendants; GMB III:1822; PM, pp. 462-63; AL, pp. 620-23, including English ancestry; TAG 60:171-73; MQ 49:16-17 (John²); MQ 56:118-21; MQ 62:56-58 (wife); MQ 65:322-25 (Robert²).

TILLEY, WILLIAM, of Barnstable, Mass. TAG 71:113 (wife Alice's identity).

TILLINGHAST, PARDON, b. ca. 1622, d. Providence, R.I., 29 January 1718. Johnson, pp. 337-44; John³ Pardon² at RIR 19:36-41.

TILLOTSON, JOHN, b. 1618, d. Lyme, Conn., before 7 June 1670. Margaret Tillotson Ragsdale, *Tillotson, Tillison and Tillitson: Descendants of John Tillotson, Immigrant to the American Colonies from the West Riding, Yorkshire, England* (Decorah, IA: Anundsen Publishing, Co., 1998, 2 volumes). Reviews: TAG 75:166-67.

TILSON, EDMUND, d. Plymouth, Mass., before 5 March 1660/1. TAG 69:37-44.

TILTON, WILLIAM, b. ca. 1589, d. Lynn, Mass., 1653. Davis III:438-79 [Phoebe Tilton]; TEG 7:129-39, 9:18-24, 93-97, 142-48, 199-202, 10:91-99, 11:47-51, 12:24-29, 94-99, 199-204 (five generations of son Daniel²).

TIMBERLAKE, HENRY, d. Newport, R.I., before 30 January 1671. AL, p. 623.

TINKER, JOHN, b. 1613, d. Hartford, Conn., October 1662. NEHGR 149:401-32 (English origins).

TINKHAM, EPHRAIM, b. ca. 1626, d. Plymouth, Mass., between 17 January 1683/4 and 20 May 1685. MF7, four generations all lines; MJ 25:97-98; MQ 60:222-24 (probable English origins).

TISDALE, JOHN, b. ca. 1614, d. Taunton, Mass., 27 June 1675. Lyon, pp. 581-84; AL, pp. 633-35; Robert L. Tisdale, *The Descendants of John Tisdale (1614-1675) Colonial Massachusetts* (n.p., the author, 1981). Reviews: NHGR 9:144, NYGBR 117:183.

TITUS, ROBERT, b. ca. 1600, of Brookline, Weymouth, and Rehoboth, Mass., d. Long Island, N.Y., ca. 1654. AL, pp. 635-37.

TOLLES, HENRY, b. ca. 1640, d. New Haven, Conn. Nichols, pp. 81-83.

TOLMAN, THOMAS, b. 1608, d. Dorchester, Mass., 18 June 1690. Goodman, pp. 493-97; Mower, pp. 611-25; MJ 1:60, 9:25-40.

TOMKINS, RALPH, b. ca. 1585, d. Salem, Mass., before 12 November 1666. TAG 68:14-22 (note on wife's English origins).

TOMLINS, TIMOTHY, b. 1606/7, d. Lynn, Mass., before 17 March 1645/6. GMB III:1828-30; CN 27:570-82.

TOMPSON, JOHN, b. ca. 1616/7, d. Middleborough, Mass., 16 June 1696. MF12, four generations all lines; Jessup, pp. 898-904.

TOOGOOD, NATHANIEL, b. ca. 1645, d. Swansea, Mass., 11 March 1702/3. AL, pp. 637-38.

TOOTHAKER, ROGER, b. ca. 1612, d. Plymouth, Mass., before 5 February 1638. TAG 69:1-8, 98-108.

TOPPING, RICHARD, b. ca. 1598, of Boston, Mass., d. England, between 20 August 1657 and 9 April 1658. GMB III:1830-32.

TORREY, JAMES, b. ca. 1612, d. Scituate, Mass., 6 July 1665. MJ 13:35-39, 76-78, 17:156-59.

TORREY, JOSEPH, b. ca. 1621, d. Newport, R.I., ca. 1675-6. MJ 13:35-39, 76-78, 17:156-59.

TORREY, PHILIP, b. ca. 1614, d. Roxbury, Mass., 12 May 1686. MJ 13:35-39, 76-78, 17:156-59.

TORREY, WILLIAM, b. 1608, d. Weymouth, Mass., 10 June 1690. MJ 13:35-39, 72-75, 17:156-59, 19:77-82 (wife Jane); MJ 25:65-67; wife Jane (Haviland) at RD600, pp. 180-81; PA, p. 390; MCA, p. 422-23.

TOWER, JOHN, b. 1609, d. Hingham, Mass., 13 February 1701/2. Davis III:480-83 [Annis Spear], including English origins; Stone, pp. 271-78, including English origins.

TOWNE, WILLIAM, b. 1598/9, d. Topsfield, Mass., before 1673. Davis III:485-507 [Amos Towne, Dudley Wildes, Sarah Johnson], including English origins; wife's Blessing ancestry at Davis I:193-99 [Dudley Wildes, Sarah Johnson]; MBT #830. Three daughters were Salem witchcraft victims in 1692: Rebecca Nurse (LENE, pp. 70-74); Mary Easty (LENE, pp. 101-2); and Sarah Cloyes, who escaped execution. See NEXUS 9:108-11 for their notable descendants.

TOWNER, RICHARD, b. ca. 1650, d. Branford, Conn., 22 August 1727. CN 31:397-401.

TOWNSEND, ROBERT, b. ca. 1695, d. Charleston, Me., after 1766. Stone, pp. 279-82.

TOWNSEND, THOMAS, b. 1594/5, d. Lynn, Mass., 22 December 1677. TEG 13:152-65, 218-28, 14:45-52.

TRACY, STEPHEN, b. 1596, of Plymouth and Duxbury, Mass., d. in England after 20 March 1654/5. GMB III:1832-34; PM, pp. 463-65; Croll, 116.

TRASK, OSMUND, d. Beverly, Mass., ca.1676. TEG 15:55-56 (Joseph[2]).

TRASK, WILLIAM, b. 1585, d. Salem, Mass., between 15 and 18 May 1666. GMB III:1834-37; MJ 18:138-41; TEG 21:24-27.

TREADWAY, NATHANIEL, b. ca. 1615, d. Watertown, Mass., 20 July 1689. Kempton, pp. 451-61, including English origins. His mother's Howe ancestry given at Kempton, pp. 337-42; Thompson, pp. 44-50, et al.; TAG 70:171-80 (English origins); TAG 71:86.

TREAT, MATTHIAS, d. Wethersfield, Conn., 8 July 1662. Pond, 253.

TREAT, RICHARD, b. 1584, d. Wethersfield, Conn., between October 1669 and January 1669/70. Pond, 229 and 230, including English ancestry; MJ 27:63-82.

TREAT, ROBERT, b. 1584, d. Wethersfield, Conn., between 13 February 1668/9 and 3 March 1669/70. Goodman, pp. 499-506, including English origins. Wife's Gaylord ancestry given at Goodman, pp. 199-201; MJ 27:63-82.

TRERISE, NICHOLAS, b. ca. 1598, of Woburn, Mass., d. at sea ca. 1652-53. NEHGR 143:25-29; NEHGR 159:235 (marriage).

TRESCOTT, WILLIAM, b. ca. 1615, d. Dorchester, Mass., 11 September 1699. EB, pp. 566-68.

TREVITT, HENRY, b. ca. 1624, d. Marblehead, Mass., after 1684. TEG 17: 96-101.

TREWORGIE, JAMES, d. Kittery, Me., before 2 July 1650. Daughter Elizabeth at Doctors, pp. 51-52; MJ 19:154, 26:59-60, 27:82-84.

TRIPP, JOHN, b. ca. 1610, d. Portsmouth, R.I., between 6 December 1677 and 28 October 1678. TG 4:59-128, 5:257-62; English origins at TG 9:195-99; Johnson, pp. 344-47; AL, pp. 638-43.

TROTT, THOMAS, b. ca. 1613, d. Dorchester, Mass., 28 July 1696. Goodman, pp. 509-13.

TROWBRIDGE, JOHN, of Marshfield, Mass. TAG 67:155 (marriage).

TROWBRIDGE, THOMAS, b. ca.1600, of New Haven, Conn., d. Taunton, Somerset, England, 7 February 1672/3. RD600, pp. 551-52; TG 9:3-39; TAG 57:31 (ancestor table for Thomas[2]); MJ 18:141-44.

TRUANT, MORRIS, b. ca. 1606, d. Marshfield, Mass., 21 April 1685. GMB III:1838-40; JPG II:323-27.

TRUMBULL, JOHN, d. Rowley, Mass., July 1657. Stevens, 21.

TUCKER SEE ALSO HARWOOD

TUCKER, RICHARD, b. 1594, d. Portsmouth, N.H., before 19 September 1679. GMB III:1841-42.

TUELLS, RICHARD, of Boston, Mass. TAG 78:309-13 (Benjamin[2]).

TUFTS, PETER, b. ca. 1617, d. Malden, Mass., 13 May 1700. Family at Sex, pp. 45-53, et al.

TURNER, GEORGE. Son John[2] at TAG 61:129-32.

TURNER, HUMPHREY, b. ca. 1595, d. Scituate, Mass., between 1 November 1672 and 29 May 1673. GMB III:1843-46; PM, pp. 466-70; NEHGR 151:286-90 (wife identified with English origins).

TURNER, JOHN, b. ca. 1590, d. Hammersmith (Lynn), Mass., after 1654. Johnson, pp. 347-48.

TURNER, JOHN, *Mayflower* passenger, b. ca. 1590, d. Plymouth, Mass., 1620/1. GMB III:1846-47; PM, pp. 470-71.

TURNER, MICHAEL, of Sandwich, Mass., d. after 23 April 1675. MQ 53:248-54, 54:44-46.

TURNER, NATHANIEL, b. ca. 1601, of Lynn, Mass., then New Haven, Conn., died at sea January 1646/7. GMB III:1847-50; Goodman, pp. 515-17.

TURNER, ROBERT, b. ca. 1613, d. Boston, Mass., between 9 July and 24 August 1664. GMB III:1851-55.

TURNER, ROBERT, d. Boston, Mass., between 14 August and 3 December 1651. Chase, pp. 401-6.

TUTTLE, BENJAMIN, d. Hartford, Conn., 13 June 1677. LENE, p. 53.

TUTTLE, JOHN, b. 1596, d. in Ireland 30 December 1656. Jessup, pp. 906-14, including English origins; TAG 59:211-15.

TUTTLE, RICHARD, b. ca. 1593, d. Boston, Mass., 8 May 1640. Goodman, pp. 519-25, including English origins; TAG 56:143 (baptisms of children).

TWINING, WILLIAM, d. Eastham, Mass., 15 April 1659. EB, pp. 568-69.

TWISDEN, JOHN, b. 1592, d. York, Me., before November 1660. Davis III:508-11 [Joseph Neal], including English origins.

TWISS, PETER, b. ca. 1654, d. Peabody, Mass., ca. 1743. TEG 10:192-97, 11:27-34.

TWITCHELL, JOSEPH, b. 1582, d. Dorchester, Mass., 13 September 1657. GMB III:1855-56; Kempton3, pp. 425-37, including English origins.

TYLER, JOB, b. ca. 1619, d. Mendon, Mass., ca. 1700. Lyon, pp. 584-86.

TYNG, WILLIAM, d. Braintree, Mass., 18 January 1652/3. Wife Elizabeth (Cotymore) at RD600, pp. 199-200; PA, pp. 244-45; MCA, p. 243; JIC, pp. 136-49; NEGHR 138:39-41 (note); NGSQ 69:115.

UFFORD, THOMAS, b. ca. 1596, d. Milford, Conn., before 6 December 1660. GMB III:1857-58.

UMFREVILLE, JOHN, d. New Haven, Conn., after 20 September 1720. RD600, pp. 530-31; TAG 72:15-19 (English origins).

UNDERHILL, JOHN, b. ca. 1609, of Boston, Mass., Exeter, N.H., and Stamford, Conn., d. Oyster Bay, N.Y., 21 September 1672. GMB III:1859-65; NYGBR 127:22-23.

UNDERWOOD, WILLIAM, b. ca. 1615, d. Chelmsford, Mass., 12 August 1697. Davis III:512-14 [Sarah Hildreth]; Nichols, p. 113.

UPHAM, JOHN, b. ca. 1600, d. Malden, Mass., 25 February 1680/1. Morgan; son Phineas[2] at Sex, pp. 84-85; William[4] Phineas[3-2] at TAG 63:216-22; MJ 19:155-58.

UPSALL, NICHOLAS, b. ca. 1596, d. Boston, Mass., 20 August 1666. GMB III:1865-69; MJ 1:60-61, 9:41-44, 19:158-61.

UPSON, STEPHEN, b. ca. 1612, d. Sudbury, Mass., ca. 1637. Johnson, pp. 352-53; JPG I:792-93.

VANE, HENRY, b. 1613, d. 1662. RD600, pp. 158-59.

VARNEY, THOMAS, d. Boston, Mass., 1707. NEHGR 149:3-27, 141-54, 244-64 (six generation study).

VARNUM, GEORGE, d. Ipswich, Mass., between 21 April and 12 October 1649. Son Samuel[2] and family at Sex, pp. 48-53.

VASSALL, WILLIAM, b. 1592, of Boston and Scituate, Mass., d. Barbados between 31 July 1655 and 12 June 1657. GMB III:1871-75.

VAUGHAN, JOHN, b. ca. 1615, d. Newport, R.I., after 23 July 1687. Johnson, pp. 353-55.

VENNER, THOMAS, b. ca. 1615, of Salem, Mass., d. London, England, 19 January 1661. MJ 18:145.

VENNEY, WILLIAM, b. ca. 1670, d. Wells, Me., between 1702 and 1705. TAG 80:304-7 (note).

VERMAYES, WIDOW ALICE, of Salem, Mass., d. Boston, Mass., 9 February 1655/6. Her Blessing ancestry and Vermayes descendants at Davis I:186-99 [Dudley Wildes, Sarah Johnson].

VERRY, WIDOW BRIDGET, of Salem, Mass. TAG 60:174-84; 72:285-300 (English origins).

VICKERY, GEORGE, b. ca. 1615, d. Hull, Mass., 13 July 1679. NEHGR 143:338-46.

VINAL, WIDOW ANN, d. Scituate, Mass., 6 October 1664. Lyon, pp. 586-95.

VINCENT, JOHN, of Duxbury by 1637, Sandwich in 1639, d. Yarmouth, Mass., between 1662 and 1667. Cooley, pp. 213-29; Spooner.

VINCENT, WILLIAM, b. ca. 1610, d. Gloucester, Mass., 17 September 1690. Davis III:515-22 [Charity Haley, Nicholas Davis]; MJ 18:146.

VINES, RICHARD, b. ca. 1600, d. Barbados April 1651. GMB III:1877-81.

VORE, RICHARD, b. ca. 1600, d. Windsor, Conn., 22 August 1683. MJ 18:146-48.

WADE, JONATHAN, b. 1612, d. Salem, Mass., 13 June 1683. GMB III:1883-88; son Jonathan[2] in RF1, four generations all lines. Son Nathaniel[2] in RF1, three generations all lines.

WADE, NICHOLAS, b. ca. 1616, d. Scituate, Mass., 7 February 1683. JPG I:794-819; Lyon, pp. 595-614.

WADSWORTH, CHRISTOPHER, b. ca. 1609, d. Duxbury, Mass., between 31 July 1677 and 27 October 1680. GMB III:1888-91; PM, pp. 473-76; Johnson, pp. 355-60.

WADSWORTH, WILLIAM, b. 1594/5, d. Hartford, Conn., between 16 June and 18 October 1675. GMB III:1892-96; Goodman, pp. 527-40, including English origins; Nichols, pp. 138-40; CN 30:197-207.

WAINWRIGHT, FRANCIS, d. Salem, Mass., 19 May 1692. Stowers, pp. 469-72; Stevens, 45; son Francis at Cameos, pp. 289-94.

WAIT, GAMALIEL, b. 1605/6, d. Boston, Mass., 9 December 1685. GMB III:1896-99; TAG 67:193-200 (English origins).

WAIT, RICHARD, b. 1604, d. Boston, Mass., 17 September 1680. TAG 67:193-200 (English origins).

WAIT, THOMAS, b. 1612, d. Portsmouth, R.I., before 13 September 1665. TAG 67:193-200 (English origins).

WAKEMAN, JOHN, b. 1601, d. Hartford, Conn., 1661. Goodman, pp. 543-47, including English origins; Nichols, pp. 252-53.

WAKEMAN, SAMUEL, b. 1603, d. Providence Island 1641. GMB III:1899-1901; daughter Hannah at NYGBR 127:65-75.

WALDEN, EDWARD, b. ca. 1625, d. Wenham, Mass., June 1679. Johnson, p. 360.

WALDO, CORNELIUS, b. ca. 1624, d. Chelmsford, Mass., 3 January 1700/1. EB, pp. 570-73; NEHGR 157:199-208 (Elizabeth[2]).

WALES, NATHANIEL, b. 1586, d. Boston, Mass., 4 December 1661. CN 33:37-40.

WALFORD, THOMAS, b. ca. 1599, d. Portsmouth, N.H., between 15 and 21 November 1666. GMB III:1902-6.

WALKER, FRANCIS, b. ca. 1640, d. Middleboro, Mass., ca. 1701. Soule, four generations all lines.

WALKER, JOHN, b. ca. 1603, d. Portsmouth, R.I., after 18 March 1647/8. GMB III:1906-8; daughter Sarah at Doctors, pp. 75-81; Jessup, pp. 921-22; RIR 11:21-22.

WALKER, JOHN, b. ca. 1640, fl. Charlestown, Mass., 1690s. Sex, pp. 137-39.

WALKER, RICHARD, b. ca. 1611, d. Lynn, Mass., May 1687. GMB III:1908-12.

WALKER, ROBERT, b. 1607/8, d. Boston, Mass., 29 May 1687. GMB III: 1912-15.

WALKER, SAMUEL, b. ca. 1615, d. Woburn, Mass., 6 November 1684. 26Imm, pp. 307-10.

WALKER, SAMUEL, of Boston, Mass., d. East Jersey before 16 July 1708. NEXUS 9:25-29, 57-60.

WALKER, THE WIDOW, d. Rehoboth, Mass., after 18 February 1646/7. AL, pp. 672-73.

WALKER, WILLIAM, b. ca. 1620, d. Eastham, Mass., between 8 March 1697 and 25 October 1703. MF6, three generations all lines.

WALL, JAMES, b. ca. 1600, d. Hampton, N.H., 3 October 1659. TAG 80:102-16, 201-16 (English origins).

WALLBRIDGE, HENRY, d. Norwich, Conn., 25 July 1729. EB, pp. 569-70.

WALLEN, RALPH, b. ca. 1595, d. Plymouth, Mass., before 1644. GMB III:1915-16; PM, pp. 476-77; TAG 67:47-53 (widow Joyce); TAG 73:91-100 (Thomas[2]).

WALLER, WILLIAM, b. ca. 1610s, d. Lyme, Conn., between 4 May and 17 July 1674. Angell, pp. 515-29, including English origins of both parents. Mother Sarah (Wolterton) Waller's ancestry at Angell, pp. 569-77; TAG 68:160-75 (Wolterton ancestry).

WALLEY, FRANCIS, of Boston, Mass. Son John[2] at TAG 64:133-38.

WALLIS, JOHN, b. ca. 1627, d. Gloucester, Mass., 13 September 1690. NEHGR 152:286-310, 391-414, 153:29-51, 183-206, 293-318, 489-98 (six generation study); NEHGR 153:291-92 (wife's identity).

WALTON, GEORGE, b. ca. 1615, d. Great Island, N.H., March 1685/6. Davis III:523-47 [Lydia Harmon].

WALTON, WILLIAM, b. ca. 1598, d. Marblehead, Mass., 9 November 1668. Pond, 262-63; NEHGR 142:361-68 (wife's Cooke ancestry); MJ 17:163-64.

WARD, ANDREW, b. ca. 1603, d. Fairfield, Conn., between 8 June and 18 October 1659. GMB III:1918-21.

WARD, GEORGE, d. Branford, Conn., before October 1665. Nichols, pp. 221-28.

WARD, SAMUEL, d. Charlestown, Mass., 30 August 1682. JPG I:820-23; NEHGR 143:346-49.

WARD, THOMAS, b. ca. 1620, d. Hampton, N.H., 1680. NEHGR 141:114-21 (possible English ancestry).

WARD, WILLIAM, d. Marlborough, Mass., 10 August 1687. Nichols, pp. 27-29.

WARDWELL, THOMAS, b. 1603/4, d. Exeter, N.H., 10 December 1646. MG 18:147-52, including English origins; LENE, pp. 100-1 (Samuel[2]); TEG 21:85-88 (Samuel[2]).

WARDWELL, WILLIAM, b. 1606/7, d. Boston, Mass., between 18 and 25 April 1670. GMB III:1922-24; Davis III:548-52 [Annis Spear]; son Uzell[2] at RIR 16:69-73, 104-11, 17:28-30; RIR 17:85-90.

WARFIELD, JOHN, b. ca. 1631, d. Mendon, Mass., between 12 January 1714/5 and 19 March 1718/9. TAG 73:11-21.

WARHAM, JOHN, b. 1595, d. Windsor, Conn., 1 April 1670. GMB III:1925-28; NEXUS 15:105-8, 16:21-25, 195-98; JPG I:824-31; CN 27:182-86; MJ 1:61-62, 2:99, 9:45-61, 11:98-101B, 12:1-26, 17:164-74, 25:68-69, 26:60, 27:84-85, 116-26.

WARNER, ANDREW, b. ca. 1599, d. Hadley, Mass., 18 December 1684. GMB III:1928-32; EB, pp. 573-77.

WARNER, JOHN, b. ca. 1615, d. Farmington, Conn., 1679. Davis P. Warner, *Descendants of John Warner of Farmington* (Camden, ME: Penobscot Press, 1997). Reviews: CN 31:423-24.

WARNER, WILLIAM, b. ca. 1585, d. Ipswich, Mass., before 1648. CN 35:587-98.

WARREN, JOHN, b. 1585, d. Watertown, Mass., 13 December 1667. GMB III:1932-34; Kempton, pp. 463-90, including English origins; 50Imm, pp. 479-94; Mower, pp. 627-31; MBT #806.

WARREN, RICHARD, *Mayflower* passenger, d. Plymouth, Mass., 1628. MF18, five generations all lines; GMB III:1935-37; PM, pp. 477-80; Pond, 258; Spooner; Crosby II:394-400; Lyon, pp. 615-16; AL, pp. 673-74; TAG 78:81-86, 274-75 (marriage record); MQ 51:109-12; MQ 69:214-19 (wife Elizabeth).

WASHBURN, JOHN, b. 1597, d. Duxbury, Mass., early 1671. GMB III:1937-39; PM, pp. 480-83; son John[2] at MF12, three generations all lines; TAG 75:215-24 (Joseph[3] John[2]).

WATERBURY, WILLIAM, of Boston, Mass. GMB III:1939-40.

WATERHOUSE, JACOB, b. ca. 1618, d. New London, Conn., before 21 September 1676. EB, pp. 580-84; Morgan.

WATERHOUSE, RICHARD, d. Portsmouth, N.H., between 14 March 1717/8 and 23 June 1718. Davis III:557-87 [Joseph Waterhouse].

WATERMAN, RICHARD, b. ca. 1605, d. Providence, R.I., 26 October 1673. GMB III:1941-43; RIR 13:47; son Resolved[2] at *Descendants of Roger Williams, Book I: The Waterman and Winsor Lines Through His Daughter Mercy Williams* (Baltimore, MD: Gateway Press, 1991).

WATERMAN, ROBERT, d. Marshfield, Mass., 10 December 1652. EB, pp. 577-80.

WATERS, LAWRENCE, d. Charlestown, Mass., 9 December 1687. NEHGR 146:57-58 (Josiah[3] Samuel[2]'s wives).

WATERS, RICHARD, b. 1604, d. Salem, Mass., between 16 July 1676 and 29 November 1677. Lyon, pp. 616-19.

WATERS, THOMAS, fl. Woburn and Boston, Mass., 1680s. Sex, pp. 79-81.

WATHEN SEE WORTHEN

WATSON, GEORGE, b. ca. 1602, d. Plymouth, Mass., 31 January 1688/9. GMB III:1944-47; PM, pp. 483-87; AL, pp. 677-78.

WATSON, JOHN, b. 1605, d. Roxbury, Mass., 5 January 1671/2. GMB III:1947-49.

WATSON, JOHN, b. ca. 1610, d. Hartford, Conn., 1650. Goodman, pp. 549-52; NEHGR 144:48-50 (Cyprian[2]'s wife).

WATSON, JOHN, b. ca. 1618/9, d. Cambridge, Mass., 20 May 1711. Makepeace, pp. 249-59; Cameos, pp. 161-65; 205-11, 309-11.

WATSON, JOHN, d. North Kingstown, R.I., 11 March 1729. George C. Davis, compiler, Jean Adams Bradley, editor, *The American Family of John Watson of the Narragansett Country, R.I.* (Kingston, RI: The Pettaquamscutt Historical Society, 1983). Reviews: CN 18:148, TAG 61:60-61, NEHGR 139:326-29, NYGBR 116:184.

Watson, Jonathan, b. ca. 1650, d. Dover, N.H., 1714. David Watson Kruger, *Jonathan Watson (1650?-1714) of Dover, New Hampshire: Who Settled There by 1672* (Boston, MA: Newbury Street Press, 1998), winner of the Donald Lines Jacobus Award for 2000. Multi-generational study of the males lines of this family. Reviews: NHGR 16:92-93, TAG 74:314, NGSQ 88:69-70.

Watson, Matthew, b. ca. 1670, d. Leicester, Mass., 1720. AL, pp. 674-77.

Watson-Challis, see Challis.

Watts see Allanson

Way, George, b. ca. 1614-19, d. Providence, R.I., ca. 1684. Angell, pp. 531-59; daughter Agnes at Doctors, pp. 65-66; Harry Abel Way II, *The Connecticut Way Family: Being the Descendants of Sgt. George Way of Maine, and Providence* (Decorah, IA: Anundsen Publishing Co., 1989). Reviews: NEHGR 144:171.

Way, Henry, b. ca. 1573, d. Dorchester, Mass., 24 May 1667. GMB III:1951-53; TAG 61:241-56 (English origins); MJ 1:62-63, 2:92, 99, 9:63-75, 12:41-42, 18:148-50, 27:85.

Weare, Peter, b. ca. 1618, d. York, Me., February 1691/2. Lyon, pp. 619-22; MBT #530.

Weaver, Clement, b. ca. 1590, d. Newport, R.I., after 20 October 1683. Jessup, pp. 923-25; Johnson, pp. 361-63; MJ 19:164-65, 25:69-70.

Webb, John, d. Richmond, R.I., between 20 June 1752 and 31 August 1757. AL, pp. 678-80.

Webb, Jonathan, b. ca. 1617, d. Charlestown, Mass., before 1667. Sex, pp. 132-33, 177-80.

Webb, Jonathan, b. ca. 1690, d. Salem, Mass., before 9 September 1765. Chase, pp. 407-8.

Webster, James, b. ca. 1630, d. Boston, Mass., between 19 October 1688 and 15 October 1689. TAG 60:41-48, 157; TAG 77:220-28 (Abigail[3] James[2]).

Webster, John, b. 1590, d. Hadley, Mass., 15 April 1661. Goodman, pp. 555-67, including English origins.

Webster, Thomas, b. 1631, d. Hampton, N.H., 5 January 1714/5. NEHGR 142:266-68 (English origins).

WEED, JOHN, b. ca. 1627, d. Amesbury, Mass., 15 March 1688/9. Stevens, 12.

WEED, JONAS, b. ca. 1610, d. Stamford, Conn., between 26 November 1672 and 5 June 1676. GMB III:1956-59; Johnson, pp. 363-65.

WEED, SAMUEL, b. ca. 1675, d. Wilton, Conn., 11 November 1755. CA 33:1-3.

WEEDEN, EDWARD, b. ca. 1613, d. Boston, Mass., 1679. Johnson, pp. 365-66.

WEEKS, GEORGE, b. ca. 1596, d. Dorchester, Mass., 1650. MJ 17:174.

WEEKS, JOSEPH, b. ca. 1670, d. Kittery, Me., between 19 November and 14 December 1741. Brewer, p. 516.

WEEKS, LEONARD, b. 1633, d. Greenland, N.H., between 15 May 1706 and 7 July 1707. Wife Mary's identity at NHGR 15:145-51; NHGR 19:41-49, 101-13.

WELCH, JAMES, d. Plainfield, Conn., before 22 November 1726. MF21, two generations all lines.

WELD, JOSEPH, b. ca. 1599, d. Roxbury, Mass., October 1646. EB, pp. 584-86.

WELD, THOMAS, b. 1595, of Roxbury, Mass., d. London, England, 23 March 1660/1. GMB III:1961-63.

WELLER, RICHARD, d. Westfield, Mass., early 1690. Lyon, pp. 623-24.

WELLES, THOMAS, b. ca. 1590, d. Wethersfield, Conn., 14 January 1659/60. TAG 56:228-29 (dispute over wife Alice Tomes's maternity); Donna Holt Siemiatkoski, *The Descendants of Governor Thomas Welles of Connecticut 1590-1658 and his wife Alice Tomes* (Baltimore, MD: Gateway Press, 1990). Reviews: CN 23:718, NYGBR 122:182.

WELLINGTON, ROGER, b. ca. 1609, d. Watertown, Mass., 11 March 1697/8. Thompson, pp. 123-24, 156-57, et al.

WELLS, ELIZABETH, fl. Charlestown and Malden, Mass., 1660s. Sex, pp. 45-57, et al.

WELLS, FRANCES (ALBRIGHT), b. ca. 1600, d. Hadley, Mass., before 26 March 1678. TAG 72:81-88 (Jonathan[3]); NEHGR 146:28-34, 298 (English origins).

WELLS, JOHN, b. ca. 1635, d. Hatfield, Mass., 18 October 1692. Son of widow Frances above, see NEHGR 146:28-34, 298.

WELLS, THOMAS, b. ca. 1629, d. Hadley, Mass., between 30 September and 14 December 1676. Johnson, pp. 366-69; NEGHR 146:28-34, 298 (mother's ancestry [see widow Frances above]).

WENTWORTH, WILLIAM, b. 1615/6, d. Dover, N.H., 15 March 1696/7. RD600, pp. 399-400; TG 7/8:127-31; NEXUS 11:104-8 (notable descendants); Johnson, pp. 369-75.

WEST, FRANCIS, b. ca. 1635, d. Kingstown, R.I., after 6 September 1687. Soule, four generations, all lines.

WEST, JOHN, b. ca. 1588, d. Saco, Me., between 29 September and 5 October 1663. Davis III:601-3 [Charity Haley].

WESTCOTT, STUKELY, b. ca. 1592, d. Portsmouth, R.I., 12 January 1677. RIR 14:6-7; MJ 19:165-66, 25:70, 103, 26:60-61.

WESTON, EDMUND, b. ca. 1605, d. Duxbury, Mass., between 18 April and 3 June 1686. NGSQ 71:41-63 (three generation study).

WESTON, JOHN, b. ca. 1630, d. Reading, Mass., 29 August 1719. Stone, pp. 283-85.

WESTON, THOMAS, b. 1584, of Weymouth, Mass., d. Bristol, England, between 1 May 1646 and 23 November 1647. GMB III:1967-70; PM, pp. 490-93.

WESTOVER, JONAS, b. 1628, d. Simsbury, Conn., 15 January 1708/9. Lyon, pp. 625-28.

WESTWOOD, WILLIAM, b. ca. 1607, d. Hadley, Mass., 9 April 1669. Goodman, pp. 569-72.

WETHERELL SEE WITHERELL

WHALE, PHILEMON, b. 1599, d. Sudbury, Mass., 22/4 February 1675/6. English origins at TG 6:131-41.

WHALLEY, EDWARD, d. Hadley, Mass., ca. 1675. RD600, pp. 463-65; NEQ 60:515-48.

WHARFE, NATHANIEL, d. Casco, Me., ca. 1673. TEG 14:150-55, 205-10 (Nathaniel[2]).

WHEATON, ROBERT, b. ca. 1606, d. Rehoboth, Mass., 1696. TAG 76:263-78; TAG 80:68-78 (Obadiah[2]).

WHEELER, GEORGE, b. 1605/6, d. Concord, Mass., between 28 January 1684/5 and 2 June 1687. Kempton3, pp. 439-69, including English origins; 50Imm, pp. 495-500; MBT #522; son William[2] at Sex, pp. 142-43, et al.

WHEELER, JOHN, b. 1611, d. Newbury, Mass., between 28 March 1668 and 11 October 1670. Davis III:604-6 [Annis Spear], including English origins; EB, pp. 586-90; Stevens, 6.

WHEELER, OBADIAH, of Concord, Mass., by 1641, d. there 27 October 1671. Son Obadiah[2], MF13, three generations all lines.

WHEELER, RICHARD, b. ca. 1611, d. Lancaster, Mass., 9 February 1675/6. Lyon, pp. 628-31.

WHEELER, THOMAS, b. 1604, d. Concord, Mass., 30 July 1687. Goodman, pp. 575-83, including English origins; 50Imm, pp. 501-8; MBT #524.

WHEELOCK, RALPH, b. ca. 1600, d. Medfield, Mass., after 3 March 1681. Nichols, pp. 35-36; NEHGR 152:311-12; NGSQ 74:3-6 (marriage).

WHEELWRIGHT, JOHN, b. ca. 1599, d. Salisbury, Mass., 15 November 1679. EB, pp. 590-92; NEQ 64:22-45.

WHELDEN, GABRIEL, d. Yarmouth, Mass., between 11 February 1653/4 and 4 April 1654. Croll, 145.

WHIPPLE, JOHN, b. 1596, d. Ipswich, Mass., 30 June 1669. Lyon, pp. 631-33; Blaine Whipple, *History and Genealogy of "Elder" John Whipple of Ipswich, Massachusetts: His English Ancestors and American Descendants* (Victoria, BC: Whipple Development Corp., 2003). Reviews: NGSQ 93:66-67.

WHIPPLE, JOHN, b. ca. 1617, d. Providence, R.I., 16 May 1685. GMB III:1970-74; Benjamin[3-2] in Scott Campbell Steward and Newbold Le Roy, 3rd, *The Le Roy Family in America 1753-2003* (Boston, MA, and Laconia, NH: the authors, 2003), p. 7.

WHIPPLE, MATTHEW, b. ca. 1590, d. Ipswich, Mass., 28 September 1647. Jessup, pp. 926-32; Johnson, pp. 376-77.

WHISTON, JOHN, b. ca. 1616, d. Scituate, Mass., before 4 October 1664. GMB III:1974-76; PM, pp. 493-95.

WHITAKER, JOHN, b. 1636, d. Billerica, Mass., after 1679. TG 18:232-55; Thompson, pp. 178-83, et al.; Sex, pp. 59-60, 68-69, et al.

WHITCOMB, JOHN, b. ca. 1588, d. Lancaster, Mass., 24 September 1662. MJ 18:150-52, 26:61-73.

WHITE, ANTHONY, d. Watertown, Mass., March 1686. Thompson, pp. 184-85, et al.

WHITE, GAWEN, b. 1607, d. Scituate, Mass., before 3 March 1664/5. Davis III:607-12 [Joseph Neal], including English origins; MJ 18:152-53.

WHITE, JOHN, b. ca. 1597, d. Hartford, Conn., 23 January 1683/4. GMB III:1976-79; Colonial, pp. 183-97; Nichols, pp. 163-65; Johnson, pp. 377-79.

WHITE, JOHN, b. ca. 1601/2, d. Salem, Mass., between 10 March 1672/3 and 28 May 1673. MJ 18:153-56.

WHITE, JOHN, d. Brookline, Mass., 15 April 1691. Chase, pp. 409-12.

WHITE, NICHOLAS, b. ca. 1611, d. prob. Taunton, Mass., before July 1697. Kempton4, pp. 569-74; Jessup, pp. 933-36.

WHITE, THOMAS, b. ca. 1599, d. Weymouth, Mass., between 5 July and 28 August 1679. Kempton, pp. 493-521; Thomas[2] at TAG 68:29-31; NEHGR 152:184-85 (John[3] Joseph[2]).

WHITE, WILLIAM, b. ca. 1666, d. Salisbury, Conn., 5 January 1750/1. NYGBR 123:1-9, 103-9, 163-67, 214-19, 124:36-40, 95-101, 161-68, 214-16 (three generation study).

WHITE, WILLIAM, *Mayflower* Passenger, d. Plymouth, Mass., 21 February 1620/1. MF13, five generations all lines; GMB III:1980-81; PM, pp. 495-96; AL, pp. 681-84; TAG 61:207-12; MD 53:67-69 (review of wife's identity); NEHGR 154:109-18 (wife's identity); MQ 70:61-63.

WHITEHAND, GEORGE, b. ca. 1608, d. Charlestown, Mass., after 25 June 1646. GMB III:1981-82.

WHITEHORNE, GEORGE, b. 1661/2, d. Boston, Mass., 7 May 1722. NEHGR 146:3-27, 161-77 (five generation study).

WHITFIELD, HENRY, b. ca. 1590, of Guilford, Conn., d. in England September 1657. 50Imm, pp. 509-18; MBT #1114; TAG 56:236-45 (initial article on his ancestry); NEHGR 137:291-305 (Sheafe ancestry); John Brooks Threlfall, *The Ancestry of Reverend John Whitfield (1590-1657) and His Wife Dorothy Sheafe (159?-1669) of Guilford, Connecticut* (Madison, WI: the author, 1989).

WHITING, JOSEPH, b. Long Island ca. 1692, d. Stamford, Conn., 6 August 1757. Son of Rev. Joseph and Rebecca (Bishop) Whiting of Southampton, N.Y. CA 45:51-61, 111-20.

WHITING, SAMUEL, b. 1597, d. Lynn, Mass., 11 December 1679. Wife Elizabeth (St. John) at PA, p. 629; RD600, pp. 442-44; MCA, p. 716; TEG 23:218-28.

WHITMAN, ROBERT, b. ca. 1615, d. Ipswich, Mass., after 1647. TAG 76:1-16 (wife's English ancestry).

WHITMARSH, JOHN, b. ca. 1596, d. Weymouth, Mass., before 1644. EB, pp. 592-94; MJ 25:70-71.

WHITMORE, JOHN, b. ca. 1592, d. Stamford, Conn., 1648. Johnson, pp. 379-82; Francis$^{3-2}$ at CN 21:699-702.

WHITNEY, JOHN, b. 1592, d. Watertown, Mass., 1 June 1673. Kempton, pp. 523-51; Lyon, pp. 633-36; Eleazer^3 Thomas^2 at Sex, pp. 27-28; TAG 69:9-14 (notes on English origins); TAG 74:197-208 (Joshua^3 Benjamin^2).

WHITRIDGE, WILLIAM, b. ca. 1599, d. Ipswich, Mass., 9 December 1668. TEG 22:151-61.

WHITTEMORE, THOMAS, b. 1593, d. Malden, Mass., 26 May 1661. Johnson, pp. 382-87.

WHITTIER, THOMAS, b. ca. 1620, d. Haverhill, Mass., 28 November 1696. Stevens, 25; MBT #954.

WHITTINGHAM, RICHARD, d. in England after 6 March 1615/16. Wife Elizabeth (Bulkeley) at PA, p. 165; RD600, pp. 442-44; MCA, p. 147.

WICKHAM, THOMAS, b. 1624, d. Wethersfield, Conn., 11 January 1688. NEHGR 150:260-76 (English origins).

WIGGIN, THOMAS, b. ca. 1592, d. Squamscott, Mass., between 29 March and 31 December 1666. GMB III:1982-85.

WIGGLESWORTH, EDWARD, b. 1603, d. New Haven, Conn., 1 October 1653. Chase, pp. 37-47; son Michael^2 at Sex, pp. 165-67, 185-88, et al.; NEHGR 156:309-21 (wife's English origins and ancestry and ancestry of Michael^2's wife); NEHGR 156:322-26 (note).

WIGHTMAN, JOHN, b. 1599, d. Warwick, R.I., 1669. Johnson, pp. 388-91.

WILBOR, WILLIAM, d. Portsmouth, R.I., between 1 March and 15 August 1710. Chase, pp. 413-24, including English origins; AL, pp. 684-87, including English ancestry.

Wilbore, Samuel, b. ca. 1595, d. Boston, Mass., 29 September 1656. GMB III:1986-88; JPG I:832-44; RIR 10:26; son Shadrach[2] at TAG 59: 224-30.

Wilcox, Edward, b. 1603/4, d. R.I., after May 1638, but before 1660. Johnson, pp. 391-95; Stephen[4-3-2] at RIR 21:99-114; NEGHR 147:188-91 (English origins).

Wilcoxson, William, b. ca. 1601, d. Stratford, Conn., ca. 1652. Pond, 250; TAG 59:33-46 (four generation study).

Wild, John, d. Braintree, Mass., October 1732. Makepeace, pp. 261-68.

Wildes, John, b. ca. 1618, d. Topsfield, Mass., 14 May 1705. Davis III:613-48 [Dudley Wildes].

Wiley, John, b. ca. 1610, d. Reading, Mass., 5 September 1672. Goodman, pp. 585-86.

Wilford, Gilbert, b. ca. 1640, d. Haverhill, Mass., before 28 July 1676. Johnson, pp. 395-96; Lyon, pp. 636-37.

Wilkins, Bray, b. ca. 1611, d. Salem, Mass., 12 January 1701/2. GMB III:1991-94; TAG 60:1-18, 101-13 (three generation study).

Wilkins, John, b. ca. 1633, d. Mt. Hope, R.I., between 3 and 15 January 1703/4. RIR 7:53.

Wilkinson, Prudence, b. ca. 1595, d. Malden, Mass., between 9 January 1654/5 and 26 July 1655. GMB III:1995-97; possible family member Thomas at Sex, pp. 133-153, et al.

Willard, John, b. ca. 1662, d. Salem, Mass., 19 August 1692. LENE, pp. 84-85.

Willard, Simon, b. 1605, d. Charlestown, Mass., 24 April 1676. Nichols, pp. 114-15; TAG 80:25 (marriage).

Willet, Thomas, b. ca. 1610, d. Swansea, Mass., 3 August 1674. GMB III:1997-2002; PM, pp. 497-503.

Willex, Balthasar, b. 1595, d. Salisbury, Mass., 23 January 1650/1. Brewer, pp. 517-19.

Williams, Charles, b.1652, of Hadley, Mass., d. Colchester, Conn., 12 April 1740. CA 41:33-42.

Williams, George, b. ca. 1605, d. Salem, Mass., between 23 September and 18 October 1654. GMB III:2002-5.

WILLIAMS, JOHN, b. ca. 1600, d. Haverhill, Mass., 10 February 1674. Stevens, 36.

WILLIAMS, JOHN, d. Boston, Mass., 28 September 1637. LENE, pp. 6-7.

WILLIAMS, MATTHEW, b. ca. 1623, d. Wethersfield, Conn., between 13 November 1654 and 8 July 1659. Fred Russell Williams, Jr., *Williams Genealogy: Matthew, Thomas, Miles and Swain 1623-2003* (Baltimore, MD: Gateway Press, 2003). Reviews: MD 53:86-87; Lyle Keith Williams, *Matthew Williams (ca. 1612 – ca. 1666) of Wethersfield, Connecticut and Descendants* (Fort Worth, TX: the author, 1994). Reviews: CN 28:51, TAG 71:59-60.

WILLIAMS, MOYLES, b. ca. 1605, of Ipswich, Mass., and Newport, R.I., d. Hempstead, N.Y., ca. 1645. NYGBR 119:80-84, 133-42; NYGBR 120:211-13 (notes on wife's English origins).

WILLIAMS, NATHANIEL, d. Boston, Mass., 23 April 1661. EB, pp. 594-95.

WILLIAMS, RICHARD, b. 1607/8, d. Taunton, Mass., August 1693. Wife Frances (Deighton) at RD600, pp. 259-62; PA, p. 263; MCA, p. 265; NEA 1:2:38-41.

WILLIAMS, ROBERT, b. 1607, d. Roxbury, Mass., 1 September 1693. Mower, pp. 633-37; Lyon, pp. 637-39; son John[2] (Harvard Class of 1683) at Puritans, pp. 167-226.

WILLIAMS, ROGER, b. ca. 1606, d. Providence, R.I., between 27 January and 15 March 1682/3. GMB III:2007-10; PM, pp. 503-6; Johnson, pp. 396-99; RIR 7:2; NEQ 57:323-46, 63:624-48, 66:199-225; *Descendants of Roger Williams, Book I: The Waterman and Winsor Lines Through His Daughter Mercy Williams* (Baltimore, MD: Gateway Press, 1991). Reviews: TAG 68:124-25; *Book II: The Hart Line Through His Daughter Freeborn Williams* (1998), *Book III: The Sayles Line Through His Daughter Mary Williams* (2002). Reviews: RIR 29:207; W. Clark Gilpin, *The Millenarian Piety of Roger Williams* (Chicago, IL: University of Chicago Press, 1979). Reviews: NEQ 53:551-54; Glenn W. LaFantasie, ed., *The Correspondence of Roger Williams, Volume 1, 1629-1653, Volume 2, 1654-1682* (Hanover, NH: Brown University Press, 1988). Reviews: NEQ 62:436-40.

WILLIAMS, ROGER, b. ca. 1610, d. Boston, Mass., after 1650. GMB III:2006-7; MJ 1:63, 9:77.

WILLIAMS, THOMAS, b. ca. 1630, d. Wethersfield, Conn., 5 February 1692/3. TAG 79:38-56 (three generation study); Fred Russell Williams, Jr., *Williams Genealogy: Matthew, Thomas, Miles and Swain 1623-2003* (Baltimore, MD: Gateway Press, 2003). Reviews: MD 53:86-87.

WILLIAMS, THOMAS, b. ca. 1644, d. New London, Conn., 24 September 1705. Angell, pp. 561-66.

WILLIAMS, THOMAS, fl. Boston, Mass., 1660s. JPG II:541-45.

WILLIAMS, WILLIAM, b. 1588, d. Watertown, Mass., after 1644. George E. Williams, *A Genealogy of Some of the Descendants of William Williams of Salem, Mass.,* (Bonita, CA: the author, 1987). Reviews: CN 20:323.

WILLIAMS, WILLIAM, b. ca. 1623, d. Hartford, Conn., December 1689. TAG 69:87-94, 174-83; TAG 71:49-50 (daughter Ruth).

WILLIS, GEORGE, of Cambridge, Mass., d. Medford, Mass., 16 September 1690. JPG I:845-48.

WILLIS, JOHN, b. ca. 1610, d. Bridgewater, Mass., ca. 1692-3. Pond, 260.

WILLIS, RICHARD, d. Plymouth, Mass., before 1645. EB, pp. 596-97.

WILLOUGHBY, FRANCIS, b. 1615, d. Charlestown, Mass., between 4 June 1670 and 10 April 1671. TAG 56:12-13 (baptism, marriage records in England).

WILMARTH, THOMAS, b. ca. 1610, d. Rehoboth, Mass., May 1694. AL, pp. 687-88.

WILMOT, BENJAMIN, of New Haven, Conn. NEHGR 151:329-41 (wife of Benjamin[2]'s English origins).

WILSON, GOWEN, b. ca. 1618, d. Kittery, Me., before 6 August 1686. Brewer, pp. 520-21.

WILSON, HENRY, d. Dedham, Mass., 8 February 1689. Ken Stevens, *Wilsons from New England: Volume P: Descendants of Henry Wilson of Dedham, Massachusetts* (Walpole, NH: the author, 1996). Reviews: VG 2:136-37.

WILSON, JACOB b. ca. 1618, d. Braintree, Mass., between 2 June 1641 and 18 May 1653. Ken Stevens, *Wilsons from New England: Volume V: Descendants of Jacob Wilson of Braintree, Massachusetts* (Walpole, NH: the author, 1988). Reviews: NYGBR 121:113, NEHGR 144:270.

WILSON, JAMES, b. ca. 1692, d. Colrain, Mass., 2 June 1781. Ken Stevens, *Wilsons from New England: Volume L: Scotch Wilsons from Western Massachusetts* (Walpole, NH: the author, 1993).

WILSON, JOHN, b. ca. 1591, d. Boston, Mass., 7 August 1667. GMB III:2012-15; 31Imm, pp. 221-33; wife Elizabeth (Mansfield) at PA, p. 298; NEHGR 155:3-35; RD600, pp. 167-68; MCA, p. 311.

WILSON, JOHN, d. Woburn, Mass., between December 1677 and 3 August 1687. Ken Stevens, *Wilsons from New England: Volume J: Descendants of John Wilson of Woburn, Massachusetts* (Walpole, NH: the author, 1991). Reviews: NEHGR 147:280-81.

WILSON, PAUL, b. ca. 1639, fl. Malden, Mass., 1650s. Sex, pp. 84-90, et al.

WILSON, PHINEAS, d. Hartford, Conn., 22 May 1692. Ken Stevens, *Wilsons from New England: Volume R: Five Families from Hartford County, Connecticut* (Walpole, NH: the author, 1989). Reviews: CN 22:705-6.

WILSON, ROBERT, b. ca. 1689, d. Blandford, Mass., 21 March 1768. Ken Stevens, *Wilsons from New England: Volume L: Scotch Wilsons from Western Massachusetts* (Walpole, NH: the author, 1993).

WILSON, ROBERT, d. Farmington, Conn., 21 July 1655. Ken Stevens, *Wilsons from New England: Volume R: Five Families from Hartford County, Connecticut* (Walpole, NH: the author, 1989). Reviews: CN 22:705-6.

WILSON, SAMUEL, b. ca. 1622, d. Kingstown, R.I., ca. 1682. NEHGR 144:291-317 (a six generation study).

WILSON, THOMAS, b. ca. 1595, d. Exeter, N.H., between 9 January and 18 February 1642/3. GMB III:2016-19.

WILSON, THOMAS, d. Wells, Me., ca. October 1702. NEHGR 154:135-58.

WILSON, WILLIAM, d. Boston, Mass., 1646. NEHGR 155:217-24 (children Mary[2] and John[2]).

WILTON, DAVID, b. 1608, d. Windsor, Conn., 5 February 1677/8. GMB III:2019-21; JPG I:849-54; NEHGR 143:101-19 (probable English origins); MJ 13:42-44, 18:156-57.

WINCH, SAMUEL, d. Framingham, Mass., August 1718. Nichols, pp. 75-76.

WINCHESTER, ALEXANDER, b. ca. 1610, d. Rehoboth, Mass., 16 July 1647. Johnson, pp. 399-400.

WINCOLL, THOMAS, b. ca. 1587, d. Watertown, Mass., 10 June 1657. GMB III:2021-23.

WING, ROBERT, fl. Worcester, Mass., 1689-90, Sex, pp. 148-49, et al.

WINKLEY, SAMUEL, b. ca. 1666, d. Portsmouth, N.H., 1736. NHGR 12: 49-65, 107-15, 164-76.

WINN, EDWARD, d. Woburn, Mass. Josiah[3] Joseph[2] at MG 26:116-30, 175-82, 27:33-46, 78-94.

WINSLEY, SAMUEL, d. Salisbury, Mass., 2 June 1663. Stevens, 13.

WINSLOW, EDWARD, *Mayflower* passenger, b. 1595, d. West Indies 8 May 1655. MF5, five generations all lines. GMB III:2023-26; PM, pp. 507-10; clues to English ancestry at NEHGR 154:78-108; NEA 4:5/6:56-59; NEA 5:4:15-20; NEHGR 154:109-18 (wife's identity); MD 53:67-69 (review of wife's identity); MQ 65:49-51 (Winslow house built for Isaac[3] Josiah[2]); MQ 69:306-9; Jeremy Dupertuis Bangs, *Pilgrim Edward Winslow: New England's First International Diplomat* (Boston, MA: New England Historic Genealogical Society, 2004). Reviews: MD 54:84-85, TAG 79:323, MQ 70:124-25, 71:293.

WINSLOW, JOHN, b. 1597, d. Boston, Mass., between 12 March 1673/4 and 21 May 1674. MF15, four generations all lines; GMB III:2027-30; PM, pp. 511-15; clues to English ancestry at NEHGR 154:78-108; Pond, 269.

WINSLOW, JOSIAH, b. 1605/6, d. Marshfield, Mass., November/December 1674. GMB III:2031-33; PM, pp. 515-17; clues to English ancestry at NEHGR 154:78-108.

WINSLOW, KENELM, b. 1599, d. Salem, Mass., September 1672. GMB III:2033-36; PM, pp. 518-21; clues to English ancestry at NEHGR 154:78-108.

WINSOR, JOSEPH, d. Sandwich, Mass., after July 1678. MQ 53:248-54, 54:44-46.

WINSOR, JOSHUA, d. Providence, R.I., 1679. Son Samuel[2] at *Descendants of Roger Williams, Book I: The Waterman and Winsor Lines Through His Daughter Mercy Williams* (Baltimore, MD: Gateway Press, 1991).

WINSTON, JOHN, b. ca. 1620, d. New Haven, Conn., 21 February 1696/7. TAG 79:250-52 (English origins).

WINTER, CHRISTOPHER, b. ca. 1610, d. Marshfield, Mass., 22 December 1683. MJ 25:71-76.

WINTER, JOHN, b. ca. 1585, d. Richmond Island between 20 May 1645 and 10 October 1648. GMB III:2036-38; Lyon, pp. 639-41; NEQ 57:184-204.

WINTHROP, JOHN, b. 1587/8, d. Boston, Mass., 26 March 1649. GMB III:2038-42; Thompson, pp. 78-79, et al.; Sex, pp. 111-13, et al.; Brewer, pp. 523-25; wife Margaret (Tyndal) at RD600, pp. 424-25; MCA, p. 843-44; TAG 79:283-91 (English ancestry of wife Margaret Tyndal); Francis J. Bremer, *John Winthrop: America's Forgotten Founding Father* (New York, NY: Oxford University Press, 2003). Reviews: MG 25:143, NEHGR

158:394, NEQ 77:320-22; Richard S. Dunn, James Savage, and Laetitia Yeardle, *The Journal of John Winthrop 1630-1649* (Cambridge, MA: Belknap Press, 1996). Reviews: NEQ 70:477-80.

WISE, HUMPHREY, d. Ipswich, Mass., 1638. EB, pp. 597-98; Stevens, 7; TAG 68:216-24 (English ancestry of him and his wife).

WISE, JOSEPH, b. ca. 1615, d. Roxbury, Mass., 12 September 1684. Pond, 246; TAG 56:80-82.

WISWALL, THOMAS, b. 1601, d. Cambridge, Mass., 6 December 1683. Son Ichabod[2] at MF16, three generations all lines; Cameos, pp. 267-70; 50Imm, pp. 519-28; MBT #810; TAG 58:110-15 (English origins).

WITHERELL, WILLIAM, b. ca. 1604, d. Scituate, Mass., 9 April 1684. TG 14:118-28; JPG II:537-40; wife Mary (Fisher)'s ancestry at 26Imm, pp. 311-38; son Daniel[2] at Brewster, two generations all lines; Brewster3, three generations all lines.

WITHERS, THOMAS, b. ca. 1606, d. Kittery, Me., between 22 December 1684 and 30 March 1685. GMB III:2044-49.

WITT, JOHN, b. ca. 1617, d. Lancaster, Mass., before 27 June 1673. NEHGR 141:19-21 (Sarah[2]); TEG 18:164-73.

WITTER, WILLIAM, b. ca. 1584, d. Swampscott, Mass., before 15 November 1659. EB, pp. 598-601.

WODELL, WILLIAM, b. ca. 1615, d. Portsmouth, R.I., ca. 1693. Jessup, pp. 939-42; AL, pp. 692-94.

WOLCOTT, HENRY, b. 1578, d. Windsor, Conn., 30 May 1655. GMB III:2049-52; MJ 1:64-65, 76-78, 2:99, 3:52-55, 9:79-110, 11:62-66, 92-93, 102-8, 17:174-77, 26:73-83, 27:86; John Benjamin Wolcott and Charles V. Waid, *Wolcott Immigrants and Their Early Descendants (the first six generations)* (2 vols., Rochester, WA: Gorham Printers, 2002), pp. 1-420. Reviews: CN 35:453-54, 36:233.

WOLCOTT, JOHN, b. 1599, d. Watertown, Mass., July 1638. MJ 25:76-78; John Benjamin Wolcott and Charles V. Waid, *Wolcott Immigrants and Their Early Descendants (the first six generations)* (2 vols., Rochester, WA: Gorham Printers, 2002), pp. 421-76. Reviews: CN 35:453-54, 36:233.

WOLCOTT, WILLIAM, b. ca. 1620, d. Salem, Mass., after 1652. John Benjamin Wolcott and Charles V. Waid, *Wolcott Immigrants and Their Early Descendants (the first six generations)* (2 vols., Rochester, WA: Gorham Printers, 2002), pp. 477-584. Reviews: CN 35:453-54, 36:233.

WOLTERTON SEE WALLER

WOOD SEE ALSO ATWOOD

WOOD, DANIEL, d. Ipswich, Mass., before 27 March 1649. Davis III:649-50 [Dudley Wildes].

WOOD, EDMUND, b. ca. 1585, of Springfield, Mass., and Wethersfield and Stamford, Conn., d. Southampton, N.Y., after 1661. NYGBR 120:1-9, 98-101, 142-47, 229-36, 121:96-101, including English origins of him and his wife; NYGBR 132:37-45, 119-28, 186-94, 281-84 (descendants of Timothy[2]).

WOOD, EDWARD, b. 1598, d. Charlestown, Mass., 27 November 1642. Kempton3, pp. 471-98, including English origins; TG 9:90-159, a four generation study.

WOOD, GEORGE, b. ca. 1690, d. Fairfield, Conn., after 1722. NYGBR 124:207-13, 125:30-33.

WOOD, ISAIAH, b. ca. 1627, d. Concord, Mass., after 7 December 1710. NEHGR 148:307-14.

WOOD, JOHN, d. Portsmouth, R.I., before 7 May 1655. Chase, pp. 425-30; AL, pp. 694-700; MD 54:27-28 (identities of daughters Elizabeth and Susannah).

WOOD, NICHOLAS, d. Medfield, Mass., 7 February 1670. JPG II:546-50.

WOOD, WILLIAM, b. ca. 1610, d. Sandwich, Mass., after 3 June 1650. GMB III:2052-54.

WOODBRIDGE, JOHN, b. 1612/3, d. Newbury, Mass., 17 March 1694/5. RF1, four generations all lines.

WOODBURY, JOHN, b. ca. 1579, d. Beverly, Mass., before 8 February 1642/3. GMB III:2054-57; Chase, pp. 431-39; son Humphrey[2]'s wife Elizabeth (Hunter) at GM2 III:473-74; Brewer, pp. 527-28; Lyon, pp. 641-43; MJ 18:157-59, 25:78-79, 26:83.

WOODBURY, WILLIAM, b. ca. 1588, d. Salem, Mass., between 5 June 1663 and 16 June 1677. JPG I:855-65; Lyon, pp. 643-45; MJ 18:157-59, 25:78-79, 26:83.

WOODCOCK, JOHN, b. ca. 1614, d. Weymouth, Mass., 1700. MJ 19:166-67, 26:83-84.

WOODFORD, THOMAS, b. ca. 1614, d. Northampton, Mass., 6 March 1666/7. GMB III:2057-60; EB, pp. 602-4; Nichols, pp. 199-200; JPG I:866-70.

WOODHOUSE, RICHARD, b. ca. 1610, d. Boston, Mass., 1676. TW, pp. 380-86.

WOODIN, JOHN, b. ca. 1620, d. Beverly, Mass., between 1694 and 1721. EB, pp. 605-8; TAG 64:65-74, 150-56, 238-45 (a three generation study), TAG 65:166.

WOODMAN, EDWARD, of Salem, Mass., d. Boston, Mass., between 22 September 1693 and 25 October 1698. MF17, three generations all lines.

WOODMAN, JOHN, b. 1637, d. Little Compton, R.I., 24 April 1713. Helen Denny Woodman, *The Woodmans of R.I.: Descendants of John Woodman of Little Compton, R.I.* (St. Petersburg, FL: Genealogy Publishing Service, 1989). Reviews: RIR 17:68, NYGBR 127:118.

WOODMANSEE, GABRIEL, b. ca. 1640, d. New London, Conn., 1688. EB, pp. 608-9; NEGHR 147:35-48.

WOODMANSEE, ROBERT, b. ca. 1595, d. Boston, Mass., 13 August 1667. JPG I:871-76; NEHGR 147:35-48.

WOODS, JOHN, b. ca. 1610, d. Marlborough, Mass., 10 July 1678. EB, pp. 601-2.

WOODSUM, JOSEPH, b. 1680/1, d. Berwick, Me., between 31 October 1759 and 1770. Joseph C. Anderson II, *The Woodsum (Woodsome/Woodsom) Family in America: The Descendants of Joseph Woodsum of Berwick, Me.* (Baltimore, MD: Gateway Press, 1990). Reviews: MG 12:80-81, CN 28:250; TAG 66:56-57, NEHGR 144:361.

WOODWARD, HENRY, b. 1607, d. Northampton, Mass., 7 April 1683. Johnson, pp. 400-2.

WOODWARD, NATHANIEL, b. ca. 1580, d. Boston, Mass., before 11 December 1675. MG 20:147-68 (English origins); EB, pp. 609-13; 26Imm, pp. 339-50; NEHGR 158:213-27 (English origins of Mary, wife of Nathaniel[2]).

WOODWARD, NATHANIEL, b. ca. 1615, d. Taunton, Mass., between 14 September 1686 and 1 February 1694/5. GMB III:2061-64.

WOODWARD, RICHARD, b. ca. 1590, d. Watertown, Mass., 16 February 1666. Son George[2] and granddaughter Susannah at Thompson, pp. 189-90, et al.; Lindsay S. Reeks, *Woodward/Woodard Ancestors of New England* (Baltimore, MD: Gateway Press, 1995). Reviews: CA 44:102, NYGBR 127:117, TAG 72:63-64.

WOODWORTH, WALTER, b. ca. 1612, d. Scituate, Mass., between 26 November 1685 and 25 February 1685/6. GMB III:2064-67; PM, pp. 521-24; Lyon, pp. 645-48; Stowers, pp. 475-82; Jeanette Woodworth Behan, *The Woodworth Family in America: Descendants of Walter Woodworth of 1630 Through Six Generations* (Torrington, CT: Rainbow Press, 1988). Reviews: CN 21:706.

WOOLCOTT, JOHN, d. Watertown, Mass., before 17 July 1638. MBT #1708.

WOOLFE, PETER, b. ca. 1610, d. Beverly, Mass., 6 December 1675. GMB III:2067-69; EB, pp. 613-14; TEG 14:109-10.

WOOLLEY, EMMANUEL, d. Newport, R.I., after 1667. RD600, p. 346.

WORCESTER, WILLIAM, d. Salisbury, Mass., 28 October 1662. TAG 65:65-69 (clues to English origins); TAG 71:50-51 (more clues to English origins); TAG 73:119-22.

WORDEN, PETER, b. ca.1576, d. Lynn, Mass., February 1639. RD600, pp 416-21; MCA, p. 901.

WORMALL, JOSEPH, b. ca. 1620, d. Scituate, Mass., before 24 June 1662. MD 43:153-62.

WORMSTALL, ARTHUR, b. 1617, d. Saco, Me., after 1686. 31Imm, pp. 234-40, including English origins.

WORMWOOD, WILLIAM, d. York, Me., after 1651. Davis III:651-55 [Annis Spear].

WORTH, WILLIAM, b. 1642, d. Nantucket, Mass., March 1724/5. Jessup, pp. 947-54.

WORTHEN, GEORGE, b. ca. 1597, d. Salem, Mass., between 29 June 1641 and 27 December 1642. NEHGR 148:67-78 (English origins); NEHGR 154:325-52 (three generation study).

WRIGHT, DOROTHY, WIDOW, b. ca. 1605, d. Marlborough, Mass., 1 March 1703. Johnson, pp. 402-6; JPG I:876-79.

WRIGHT, RICHARD, b. ca. 1596, d. Podunk, Conn., after 15 March 1667/8. GMB III:2072-74; Davis III:656-60 [Joseph Neal]; TAG 67:32-46.

WRIGHT, RICHARD, b. ca. 1608, d. Plymouth, Mass., 9 June 1691. MF12, four generations all lines; Johnson, pp. 406-8; TAG 59:165-70.

WRIGHT, THOMAS, b. 1610, d. Wethersfield, Conn., after 21 April 1670. JPG I:880-93, including English origins.

WRIGHT, THOMAS, d. Scituate, Mass., before 22 December 1710. JPG II: 328-34.

WYATT, JOHN, b. ca. 1590, d. Ipswich, Mass., December 1665. MBT #650; NEHGR 143:213-20 (English ancestry of his Riddlesdale wife).

WYATT, JOHN, d. Haddam, Conn., before 7 September 1668. Pond, 275.

WYETH SEE WISE

WYMAN, FRANCIS, b. ca. 1595, d. in England September 1658. Two sons Francis and John emigrated to New England. 50Imm, pp. 529-38; MBT #446; NEHGR 139:147-49 (Duxford ancestry).

YALE, THOMAS, d. England, 1620. His widow (Anne Lloyd) married Theophilus Eaton and moved to New Haven, Conn., as did Yale's children. RD600, pp. 393-94; PA, pp. 788-89; MCA, p. 910. Anne's royal line at RD600, p. 408; daughter Anne (Yale) Hopkins at WRR, pp. 194-97; TAG 56:1-11, 101-5 (descent from Braiose and Clare families).

YEATON, RICHARD, b. ca. 1658, d. Isle of Shoals, N.H., ca. August 1732. Son Samuel[2]'s wife Catherine's identity at MG 23:113-15; family study for four generations at NHGR 21:27-40, 65-76, 113-21, 170-81, 22:67.

YORK, RICHARD, d. Dover, N.H., 23 March 1672. Stone, pp. 287-89.

YOUNG, JOHN, b. ca. 1624, d. Eastham, Mass., 28 January 1690/1. Croll, 124; MD 54:97-113, to be continued in 2006; Joseph[3-2] at MG 9:99-107, 127-31, 10:10-13, 42-45, 11:95.

YOUNG, ROBERT, b. before 1690, d. Providence, R.I., 2 June 1727. Angell, pp. 579-607.

YOUNGLOVE, SAMUEL, b. ca. 1605, d. Ipswich, Mass., before 24 October 1689. EB, pp. 614-18.

YOUNGS, ALICE, d. Hartford, Conn., 26 May 1647. LENE, pp. 13-14.

Supplemental Index

ABBOTT
Thomas, 1
family, 27

ADAMS
Hannah, 2
Joanna, 2
John, 2
Joseph, 2

ALCOCK
John, 3
Sarah, 3

ALDEN
John, 3, 148
Priscilla (Mullins), 148

ALLEN
Elizabeth (Bacon), 4
George, 4
Jane, 34
Katherine (Deighton), 4
Margaret (Wyatt), 4
Martha, 3
Samuel, 4
Thomas, 4
William, 4

ALLERTON
Bartholomew, 4

ALSOP
Elizabeth, 11, 176

AMSDEN
Isaac, 5

ANDREW
Samuel, 5
William, 5

ANGELL
Alice (Ashton), 6

ANTROBUS
Joan, 130

APPLETON
Judith (Everard), 7

APSLEY
Alice, 74

ARNOLD
Joan, 6
Samuel, 7, 110
Sarah (Holmes), 7, 110

ASHTON
Alice, 6
Marie, 154

ATWOOD
Nathaniel, 8

AVERILL
Sarah, 9

BABSON
Thomas, 9

BACON
Elizabeth, 4

BAKER
Joseph, 11
Ruth, 11

Martha, 142

BULL
Elisha, 35
John, 35

BULLARD
Jacob, 35

BULLOCK
Elizabeth, 48
Elizabeth (Billington), 35
Henry, 35
John, 35

BUMPAS
Elizabeth, 35
Philip, 35

BUMSTEAD
Jeremiah, 35

BURNAP
Thomas, 36

BURNHAM
Job, 36
Mary (Lawrence), 36
Rebecca, 36
Thomas, 36

BURROUGHS
George, 37
Hannah (Fisher), 37
Sarah (Church), 37

BURT
John, 37

BUSHNELL
Francis, 38

BUTLER
Samuel, 38

BUTTERWORTH
John, 38

CANE
Jonathan, 40

CAPEN
Hannah, 40
John, 40

CARD
John, 40

CARDER
John, 40
Richard, 40

CARGILL
Janet, 91

CARLETON
Ellen (Newton), 40

CARPENTER
Abiah, 41
Agnes, 41
Alice, 41
Benjamin, 41
John, 41
Joseph, 41
Juliana, 41
Mary, 41
Oliver, 41
Priscilla, 41
William, 41

CARR
Caleb, 41
Peleg, 41

CARTER
Joseph, 41

CARY
Francis, 42
John, 42

CATLIN
Elizabeth, 42

CHADBOURNE
Humphrey, 42
William, 42

CHAMBERLAIN
Sarah, 43